THE COUNTER-REVOLUTION OF 1776

The Counter-Revolution of 1776

Slave Resistance and the Origins of the
United States of America

Gerald Horne

NEW YORK UNIVERSITY PRESS
New York and London

NEW YORK UNIVERSITY PRESS
New York and London
www.nyupress.org

References to Internet websites (URLs) were accurate at the time of writing.
Neither the author nor New York University Press is responsible for URLs that
may have expired or changed since the manuscript was prepared.

Library of Congress Cataloging-in-Publication Data
Horne, Gerald.
The counter-revolution of 1776 : slave resistance and the origins of the United States of
America / Gerald Horne.
pages cm
Includes bibliographical references and index.
ISBN 978-1-4798-9340-9 (hardback)
ISBN 978-1-4798-0689-8 (paperback)
1. Antislavery movements—United States—History—18th century. 2. United States—
History—Revolution, 1775-1783—Social aspects. 3. Slavery—United States—History—
18th century. 4. African Americans—History—To 1863. I. Title.
E446.H83   2014
973.3'1—dc23   2013043412

New York University Press books are printed on acid-free paper,
and their binding materials are chosen for strength and durability.
We strive to use environmentally responsible suppliers and materials
to the greatest extent possible in publishing our books.

Manufactured in the United States of America

10 9 8 7 6 5

Also available as an ebook

CONTENTS

It was January 2012 and I was ecstatic—and with good reason.

I had been working on the book at hand for some time and had traveled extensively. However, building renovations had prevented my access to the New York Historical Society in Manhattan until my tardy arrival in early 2012. However, as it turns out, my wait was rewarded amply when I encountered the richly informative Daniel Parish, Jr. Slavery Transcripts, which cover extensively colonial slavery in North America—and beyond.[1] Unfortunately, this treasure trove is not organized adroitly, which may account for its relative absence in the footnotes of scholars—and also sheds light on the nature of my references to it. Still, my research peregrination has convinced me that this collection should be better known to scholars seeking to unravel the complexities of the 1776 revolt against British rule.[2]

For it is the argument of this book that slavery permeated colonial North America, underpinning the pre-1776 economy, in terms of not only agriculture but insurance, banking, shipbuilding, and the like. Yet the enslaved resisted fiercely, as we will see, and did so quite often, at times with the aid of competing colonial powers, notably Spain and, to an extent, France. Their resistance helped to drive settlers from the Caribbean to the mainland, particularly in the years leading up to 1776. The sprawling land mass of the mainland—versus the limited land mass of the Caribbean—allowed European empires to more easily bump into one another, for example, on the Georgia-Florida border, causing sparks to fly.[3]

The crucial turning point for North America—and arguably, the British Empire as a whole—emerged in 1688 with the so-called Glorious Revolution, which, inter alia, caused the monarchy to retreat and led to the ascendancy of a rising class of merchants. This, in turn, empowered the "private" or "separate" merchants—entrepreneurs—who wished to enter into the lushly lucrative market in enslaved Africans,[4] to the detriment of the Royal African Company. These entrepreneurs descended maniacally upon Africa, igniting a quantum leap in the slave trade which at once developed immensely the economy of the Americas—and, likewise, engendered ever more angry resistance from the enslaved, causing ever more anxious settlers to migrate to the mainland. The year 1688, with its simultaneous launching of vast economic transformation—particularly in North America—and a riotous instability driven by enslavement, is the hinge moment in the creation of what is now routinely referred to today as modernity.

As the economy developed on the mainland, thoughts of "independency" grew accordingly—along with slave resistance. The latter was manifested most dramatically in Manhattan in 1712 and 1741 and South Carolina in 1739. It is an error to view the history of colonial British North America as simply "pre-U.S. history" in a teleological manner. It is likewise useful to integrate events in the Caribbean into our contemplation of the mainland. Though London's provinces in the Americas may not have been wholly unitary, it remains true that North Americans had been trained to regard the southern mainland colonies as part of an extended Caribbean region that was a primary source of wealth.[5] Put simply, London realized that massive slave uprisings in Jamaica and Antigua, most particularly, could portend the collapse of the Caribbean colonial project as a whole, as Africans strained to assert themselves forcefully, if not rule altogether: such rebelliousness made London more susceptible to sweet reason—and, ultimately, abolition—as it considered the further expenditure of blood and treasure that could have gone to bolster British India or territories elsewhere. At the same time, slave rebelliousness caused settlers—particularly on the mainland—to dig in their heels, hastening the split between province and metropolis.

This slave resistance was aided immeasurably not only by the indigenous but also, as noted, by competing colonial powers. As London jousted with Madrid in the Americas, both came to rely upon armed Africans, and this crucial factor, along with the substantial resources that had to be expended in order to maintain a slave system, inexorably helped to spur a nascent abolitionist movement. Increasingly, the development of the economy on the mainland—including the ability to engage in mutually profitable trade arrangements with French settlers in Hispaniola—along with apprehension about the presumed anti-slavery tendencies of the British Crown, evidenced by the notorious edict of Lord Dunmore in November 1775 in Virginia, helped to push the colonists into open revolt by 4 July 1776.

Though it may be hard to imagine at this late date, my conclusion in this book is that many Africans had different plans for the destiny of colonial North America that decidedly did not include a starring role by the now famed Founding Fathers and their predecessors but, instead, contemplated a polity led by themselves in league with the indigenous and, perhaps, a compliant European power. As such, the ongoing persecution of descendants of mainland enslaved Africans is—in part—a continuing expression of what tends to befall those who are defeated in bloody warfare: often they are subjected to a heinous collective punishment.

In essence, simply because Euro-American colonists prevailed in their establishing of the U.S., it should not be assumed that this result was inevitable. History points to other possibilities, and contemplating them may shed light on—at least—why Africans suffered so grievously in the aftermath of the founding of the republic: strikingly, as London was moving toward abolition, the republic was supplanting the British isles as the kingpin of the global slave trade.[6]

Hence, this book diverges sharply from the consensus view of the origins of the post-1776 republic—a view which has united a stunningly diverse array of scholars.[7] In short, unlike previous analysts, I do not view the creation of the republic as a great leap forward for humanity—though I concede readily that it improved the lives of a countless number of Europeans. More than this, I believe that—perhaps understandably—there has been a desire to create an uplifting anti-colonial narrative to explain and undergird the fruits of 1776. The problem is that—irrespective of the diverse ideological persuasions of the creators—this narrative serves to obscure the point that as 4 July 1776 approached, Africans had been involved steadily in the poisoning and murdering and immolating of settlers, creating (at least) a yawning deficit of trust between Africans and Europeans. Portraying the Africans as bit players supporting a revolt in 1776 dominated by Europeans—as the uplifting narrative tends to do—not only distorts and caricatures the historical record but also obscures a trust deficit that may still be of relevance today.

* * *

Hence, 1688 gave rise to a "cousins' war"[8] but also a continuing civil war that was evidenced not only in 1776[9] (when Africans largely sided with the Crown) but also in 1836 (when Texas split from Mexico, with the abolitionism of the latter being a signal factor) and then 1861–1865, when—finally—the Africans were able to escape bondage. In sum, 1688 delivered a promise of modernity or bourgeois society or what has been called of late "the end of history" in the form of capitalism dripping in the blood of Africans who involuntarily provided the impetus for the takeoff[10] and the republicanism which helped to unite Europeans in this enterprise[11] in the Americas in the face of perpetual sedition and liquidation plots from this rambunctious labor force. However, this was an exceedingly elongated process that took decades to lurch toward a sort of justice in 1865 (or, perhaps, 1888—a precise two centuries after the tumult in London—with abolition in Brazil).

To the extent that 1776 led to the resultant U.S., which came to captain the African Slave Trade—as London moved in an opposing direction toward a revolutionary abolition of this form of property—the much-celebrated revolt of the North American settlers can fairly be said to have eventuated as a counter-revolution of slavery.[12] To the extent that the tumultuous events leading to 1776 tracked the accelerated decline of the Royal African Company of the sceptered isle and the rise of newly empowered slave traders in the new republic, 1776 can fairly be said to have eventuated as a counter-revolution of slavery. Defenders of the so-called Confederate States of America were far from bonkers when they argued passionately that their revolt was consistent with the animating and driving spirit of 1776.[13] Slavery fueled a rising capitalism. However, ironically, breaking the bonds of slavery was necessary if capitalism was to realize its full potential, not least since enslaved Africans were fiercely determined to destroy the wealth they were creating, along with the lords of the lash. Contradictorily, slavery was both a boost for nascent capitalism and ultimately a fetter on its productive force. More than this, chattel slavery grounded in racist chauvinism—of a uniquely republican and toxic type—was one of the more profound human rights violations of the previous millennium. To the extent that 1776 gave such slavery a renewed lease on life, it was truly a lineal ancestor of 1861 and, thus, a counter-revolution of slavery.[14]

It is evident that this book sits on the shoulders of the work of previous scholars.[15] Nevertheless, my own opinion is that it is more instructive to place this work in the context of a long line of writings by people of African descent which have called into sharp question the events that constructed today's Americas[16] and the steep price paid by Africans as a result.[17]

Certainly, much has been written about the "revolutionary" era and the role of Africans and the indigenous, though beginning the story in the 1770s—as this book is intended to show—evades the pre-existing dynamics that crucially shaped this critical decade. An armed revolt, particularly in its incipient stages, creates a dynamic of its own, causing rebels to engage in actions—for example, positive overtures to Africans and indigenes—inconsistent with their previous (and to a degree subsequent) behaviors.

Moreover, I feel compelled to stress that when officials of colonial Cuba and Spanish Florida lent aid to Africans in the Carolinas, they were motivated more by self-interest than abolition—otherwise, slavery in Havana would have ended well before the late 19th century. The same holds true for London's abolitionism, which too was self-interested and hardly inevitable. It emerged in part from a unique set of circumstances, shaped indelibly by the Crown's growing reliance on armed Africans, just as the rise of China in the 21st century was hardly inevitable but shaped indelibly by the late 20th-century circumstance of apprehension of the Soviet Union.[18] Similarly, when Washington allied with Moscow from 1941 to 1945, this alliance was driven by realpolitik, as opposed to the cosigning of the entire Soviet agenda. "The enemy of my enemy is my friend" continues to be the engine of international diplomacy and was certainly operative in pre-1776 North America. And to echo a current phrase, during a good deal of the colonial era, as far as Africans in the British colonies were concerned, Spain simply had the "cleanest dirty shirt."

Nevertheless, there was faint recognition on the mainland of a reality recognized by a latter-day scholar: "in contrast to Spanish and French slaves, who were considered an inferior subject," wrote Thomas James Little in 1989, "English slaves were considered to be a unique type of property."[19] Quite able to tease out meaningful distinctions, rebellious Africans, when they were not engaged in hell-raising, tended to flee from Carolina to Florida, from New York to Quebec, and from Jamaica to Cuba—not vice versa—all to London's detriment, creating a crisis for London that was hard to resolve without severe rupture. Then when the rapturous rebels revolted in 1776, their previous concern about the supposed ubiquitous hand of Madrid stirring up Africans was transferred smoothly to hysterical concern about the supposed hand of London doing the same thing. This meant that their triumph forged a conflation of anti-monarchism, and republicanism—and Africans standing in the way of the two—in a manner that virtually guaranteed that the path ahead would be exceedingly rocky for those who became U.S. Negroes, then African Americans.

Nonetheless, as one of the few who has investigated systematically the dilemma of Africans enslaved and "free" from the 17th century to the present, across continents and far-flung seas alike, I am tempted to conclude that the older radical slogan—"black and white, unite and fight"—as a prescription for transformative change in this republic[20] needs to be supplemented (or supplanted altogether) in favor of a less poetic and catchy "Africans here and abroad unite and fight in league with a powerful foreign ally." Such a conclusion inferentially suggests a design flaw at the heart of the republic—Africans being excluded and persecuted not by accident but purposively—that compels this sizeable class of citizens to disregard republican sovereignty in pursuit of justice.

This aforementioned slogan is not the only aspect of this book that continues to resonate. The *deregulation* of the slave trade led to the mass entry into this dirty business of "separate" and "private" traders, which coincided with *free trade* in Africans and *capital flight* of this same valuable commodity: all of these italicized terms are part of today's jargon and should remind us of their less-than-glorious antecedents and their role as recurring building blocks of today's capitalist society. More than this, those who reside in a nation constructed by slavery need to think longer and harder about contemporary manifestations of this peculiar institution, not least in terms of the kind of capitalism and republicanism that now obtains in North America but, as well, the degradation of labor[21] in this nation and how the racist stigmatizing of a formidable segment of the working class can reinforce a reactionary conservatism that bedevils the nation.[22]

* * *

My Manhattan ecstasy in January 2012 proved to be short-lived, as I sought futilely to hail a taxi from the sidewalk abutting the New York Historical Society on Central Park West after gathering my glittering research nuggets on colonial slavery. Yet I recall thinking at the time that these taxi drivers—some of whom had a dark skin tone similar to my own—were rudimentarily reenacting the drama I had just researched moments earlier: that is, I was seemingly enduring what is now a reigning Manhattan cliché: being bypassed by taxis because of the color of my skin, the outward manifestation of African ancestry. That is to say, as a putative descendant of mainland Africans who had fought the formation of a slaveholding republic, then a Jim Crow regime, I was continuing to incur a penalty as a result, this time in the form of having to walk part of the way to my next destination. As had happened previously in Gotham when I was subjected to such a slight, I recalled my experience earlier in the century teaching at Hong Kong University, when this former colony had just reverted to Beijing's rule. There taxis would zip past Chinese to pick me up on the presumed premise—perhaps—that I was not an indigene but, possibly, a tourist or diplomat capable of a nice tip or, at least, a foreigner bearing no felonious intent. On the face of things, Chinese cabbies perceived me to be less of a threat than those in my ostensible homeland. Even then I was wondering if China's rise would have a positive impact on the dire plight of my ebony compatriots in North America, just as Spain had centuries earlier. As I ambled along in the wintry clime of Manhattan,

I smiled to myself, thinking that—dialectically—the added exercise I was receiving might allow me to live to fight another day, confirming the continuing viability of jujitsu-like maneuvers which had allowed us Africans to survive for centuries in an ocean of hostility, a heartening thought to ponder roughly 240 years since abolitionism had begun to assert itself dramatically in London.

Introduction

It was just past ten in the morning on 22 June 1772 in a London court-room. And the presiding magistrate, Lord Mansfield, had just made a ruling that suggested that slavery, the blight that had ensnared so many, would no longer obtain, at least not in England. A few nights later, a boisterous group of Africans, numbering in the hundreds, gathered for a festive celebration; strikingly, none defined as "white" were allowed—though they toasted Lord Mansfield, the first Scot to become a powerful lawyer, legislator, politician, and judge, with unbounded enthusiasm.[1]

Others were not so elated, particularly in Virginia, where the former "property" in question in this case had been residing. "Is it in the Power of Parliament to make such a Law? Can any human law abrogate the divine? The Law[s] of Nature are the Laws of God," wrote one querulously questioning writer.[2] Indicating that this was not a sectional response, a correspondent in Manhattan near the same time assured that this ostensibly anti-slavery ruling "will occasion a greater ferment in America (particularly in the islands) than the Stamp Act itself," a reference to another London edict that was then stirring controversy in the colonies.[3] The radical South Carolinian William Drayton—whose colony barely contained an unruly African majority—was apoplectic about this London decision, asserting that it would "complete the ruin of many American provinces."[4]

This apocalyptic prediction was shaped inexorably by the inflammatory statements emanating from the London courtroom. The lawyer for the enslaved man at issue sketched a devastating indictment of slavery, an institution that undergirded immense fortunes in the colonies. He observed that slavery was dangerous to the state, perhaps a veiled reference to the forced retreat of colonists in Jamaica a few decades earlier in the face of fierce resistance by African warriors designated as "Maroons": their militancy seemed to augur at one point the collapse of the colonial regime.[5]

Caribbean revolts were so frequent that—according to one analyst—this unrest "underscored colonists' pathological fear of Africans as their natural enemy"[6]—a situation that was inherently unsustainable but, simultaneously, indicated why this London case had fomented such raw emotion.

This lawyer's reproach of slavery was not only part of enlightened conversation in London, for as far afield as Madrid and Paris, serious reconsideration of this institution had arisen. In the late 1750s in Hispaniola, dozens of Europeans and thousands of livestock had succumbed to poisons administered by African herbalists. Unsurprisingly, French "physiocrats" had begun to raise searching questions about the future viability of slavery.[7]

Slavery inevitably bred angry disaffection that could be quite destabilizing—particularly when combined with intervention by other European powers. Consequently, this attorney railed against the "unlawfulness of introducing a new slavery into England from our American colonies or any other country." Yes, he conceded, "by an unhappy occurrence of circumstances, the slavery of Negroes is thought to have become necessity in America"[8]—but why should this pestilence be extended?

Hanging ominously in the air was the implication that if slavery were to be deemed null and void in London, then why not in Charleston? Even before these foreboding words were uttered in London, the **Virginia Gazette**—whose audience had few qualms about enslavement of Africans—had noticed that since this case had commenced, "the spirit of Liberty had diffused itself so far amongst the species of people"— namely Negroes—"that they have established a club near Charing Cross where they meet every Monday night for the more effectual recovery of their freedom."[9]

The New Yorker was prescient, as we know, while the man from Carolina summarized neatly what was to befall the British holdings south of the Canadian border. The eminent 20th-century historian Benjamin Quarles has argued that this London case "hastened" slavery's "downfall in New England."[10] Moreover, what came to be known as "Somerset's case" emerged in the wake of a number of decisions emanating from London that unnerved the powerful slaveholders of North America— and was followed by others—all of which aided in lighting a fuse of revolt that detonated on 4 July 1776.

*   *   *

This is a book about the role of slavery and the slave trade in the events leading up to 4 July 1776 in igniting the rebellion that led to the founding of the United States of America[11]—notably as the seditiousness of rebellious Africans intersected with the machinations of European powers, Spain and France most particularly. It is a story that does not see the founding of the U.S.A. as inevitable—or even a positive development: for Africans (or indigenes) most particularly.[12] I argue that a number of contingent trends led to 1776. As we know, the now leading metropolis that is New York was once controlled by the Dutch; the area around Philadelphia once was colonized by the Swedes; New Orleans had French, then Spanish, then French rule once more; Jamaica went from Spain to Britain in the mid-17th century. The colonizing of the Americas was a chaotic process for which teleology is particularly inappropriate: it was not foreordained that the Stars and Stripes would flutter at all, least of all over so much of North America. The colonizing of the Americas was a wild and woolly process. Guy Fawkes and Oliver Cromwell were surging to prominence as London's creation of colonies in the Americas was accelerating: these two men represented plotting and attempting to overturn an already unstable status quo that was hard to hide from Africans. Moreover, the colonial project unfolded alongside a kind of Cold War between Catholics and Protestants[13] (studded with the periodic equivalent of a kind of "Sino-Soviet" split that from time to time disunited Madrid and Paris). The chaos of colonialism combined with this defining religious rift ironically created leverage for Africans as they could tip the balance against one European power by aligning with another—or with the indigenous. Then there was the developing notion of "whiteness," smoothing tensions between and among people hailing from the "old" continent, which was propelled by the need for European unity to confront raging Africans and indigenes: this, inter alia, served to unite settlers in North America with what otherwise might have been their French and Spanish antagonists, laying the basis for a kind of democratic advance, as represented in the freedom of religion in the emergent U.S. Constitution. Surely, the uniting of Europeans from varying ethnicities under the umbrella of "whiteness" broadened immeasurably the anti-London project, with a handsome payoff delivered to many of the anti-colonial participants in the form of land that once was controlled by the indigenous, often stocked with enslaved Africans—not to mention a modicum of civil rights denied to those who were not defined as "white." Ironically, the founders of the republic have been hailed and lionized by left, right, and center for—in effect—creating the first apartheid state.

Assuredly, as with any epochal event, the ouster of London from a number of its North American colonies was driven by many forces—not just slavery and the slavery trade—a point I well recognize.[14] As ever, there were numerous economic reasons for a unilateral declaration of independence. When British forces in 1741 were in the midst of attacking Cuba and Cartagena, an officer of the Crown mused—in case of victory—about settling North American colonists in the "East End of Cuba" since if they "could be settled there, it would be much better than their returning home to a Country over-peopled already, which runs them on setting up manufactures, to the prejudice of their Mother Country."[15] Nine years earlier, another Londoner fretted that while once "almost all the sugar made" in the West Indies "was brought to England in British built ships[,] now it is as notorious that one ship in three, which bring that commodity are New England built and navigated by New England sailors. From whence it follows that New England has supplanted Britain in its Navigation to those colonies one part in three." These North American colonies were surpassing Britain in making hats, so useful in frequently inclement weather; thus, it was concluded portentously, "independency" of these colonies "must [be] the consequence: a fatal consequence to this Kingdom!" This "independency" was "highly probable."[16] By 1761, yet another Briton was arguing that these North America colonies were "far from being beneficial to Great Britain, that it would have been much better if no such Continent or no such colonies had ever existed" since "from their very establishment [they] have been a growing evil to Great Britain, which [has] thereby *laid* the *Foundation of an* EMPIRE *that may hereafter make her a* COLONY" (emphasis original).[17]

These economic conflicts were all very real and deeply felt by settlers and Londoners alike. Yet, even when one posits this economic conflict as overriding all others in sparking revolt, the larger point was that it was slavery that was driving these fortunes, particularly in the North American colonies. For example, in Rhode Island—epicenter of the slave trade during a good deal of the 18th century[18]—these merchants of odiousness moved rapidly to plow their vast fortunes into sectors

that competed aggressively with the "Mother Country," notably manufacturing, insurance, and banking, indicating that slavery remained at
the root of the conflict.[19] "Negroes were considered essential to New
England's prosperity," argues historian Lorenzo Greene, speaking of the
colonial era.[20] In South Carolina, always on edge because of the presence of a restive African majority often in league with Spanish Florida,
care was taken to build roads and establish ferries in order to more
effectively gain access to lands rocked by slave revolt—but this infra-
structure spending also spurred economic development generally.[21]

In sum, the argument between these colonies and London was—in a
sense—a chapter in a larger story whose first lines were written in 1688 during the "Glorious Revolution" when the Crown was forced to take a step
back as a rising merchant class stepped forward,[22] not least in corroding
the monarch's hegemony in the slave trade. Arguably, it was then that the
groundwork was laid for the takeoff of capitalism—a trend in which slavery and the slave trade played an indispensable role.[23] The growing influence of merchants in the aftermath of 1688 turbocharged the African Slave
Trade, which allowed for spectacular profits growing from investments in
the Americas and the forging of a wealthy class there which chafed under
London's rule. It was in 1696 that the House of Commons received a petition objecting to the monopoly on this hateful trade in humans then held
by the Royal African Company (RAC). The petition was signed by individuals referring to themselves as "merchants and traders of Virginia and
Maryland," who argued that their "plantations" were "capable" of much
greater profit and production and if they were "sufficiently supplied with
Negroes, they would produce twice the quantity they do now"—indeed,
"the shortage of slaves was hindering the development of the tobacco colonies." After wrangling, their prayers were answered, leading to spectacular
increases in the number of Africans in chains crossing the Atlantic.[24]

This business benefited handsomely some entrepreneurs in New
England—notably in Massachusetts and Rhode Island—where the trade
flourished. This region contained the "greatest slave-trading communities in America," according to Lorenzo J. Greene: "the profits from the
slave trade were almost incredible. Seldom has there been a more lucrative commerce than the traffic in Negroes," since "gross profits [were]
sometimes as high as sixteen hundred percent," as "the slave trade
easily became the most lucrative commerce of the seventeenth and

eighteenth centuries."[25] The "Puritan colonies," says Greene, "were the greatest slave-trading communities in America. From Boston, Salem and Charlestowne in Massachusetts; from Newport, Providence and Bristol in Rhode Island; and from New London and Hartford" emerged these vessels of opprobrium —and profit. And "of the American ships involved in [shipboard] insurrections, those from New England suf-fered the most," with Massachusetts leading the pack.[26] Simultaneously, this phenomenon bonded colonies—north and south—on the altar of slavery and nervousness about African intentions.

To be sure, for the longest period it was the sugar colonies of the Caribbean that were the cash cow for London. In 1700, the average English person consumed five pounds of sugar per year. In 1850, the fig-ure was thirty-five pounds. By value, sugar had become Britain's num-ber-two import, after cotton. Poor people in England spent about 5% of their wages on sugar. Sugar planters, as a result, became fabulously wealthy and influential in London itself, as William Beckford—whose fortune was centered in Jamaica—became Lord Mayor of this sprawling metropolis, only to be mocked as "Negro whipping Beckford."[27]

Yet, because the gain was so potentially stupefying, this dirty busi-ness bred conflict among the European powers almost effortlessly, igniting piracy and privateering—all of which, as we shall see, allowed Africans to tip the balance against one of these powers, which in most cases meant disfavoring London and its colonies. In a like fashion, the gargantuan wealth generated by trade in human commodities fed con-flict between London and the colonies over taxes and who should pay—importers or exporters—not to mention clashes between insurers and merchants over losses at sea or the much-dreaded shipboard insurrec-tions. At a certain point, some colonists may have wondered if delug-ing the mainland with Africans was part of a ploy by the metropolis to place in their backyard a force that could discipline—if not eliminate—them. Africans were victimized by this trade, but the clash of interests opened the door for their engaging in political arbitrage.

This influx of Africans also bailed out the colonial enterprise in another sense, for as the historian Colin G. Calloway has observed, "up until the end of the seventeenth century the British had feared for the sur-vival of their infant American colonies."[28] By 1698, the RAC was obliged to yield and rescued the colonial enterprise when so-called separate traders and private traders filled the breach with slave-trade profits—and filled their pockets with filthy lucre, many of them enabled to climb the class ladder to esteemed merchant status. Thus, in the fifteen years prior to 1698, slavers transported close to fifty-five hundred enslaved Africans to the North American mainland, and in the fifteen years after, the figure increased dramatically to more than fifteen thousand. The heralded reforms flowing in the aftermath of 1688 were as important to slave-trade escalation as the reforms of 1832 were to slave emancipation.[29] Finally, in 1750, London declared the trade to Africa to be even more free and open, which sent a cascade of Africans across the Atlantic to the mainland, with wide consequences hardly envisioned at the time.[30]

This enormous influx of Africans laid the foundation for the concomitant growth of capitalism. The advent of this system has been seen widely and schematically as a leap forward from the strictures of feudalism and, therefore, a great leap forward for humanity as a whole.[31] Nonetheless, this trade did not signal progress for Africans, as their continent was besieged by "separate traders" with the demented energy of crazed bees. It was an early example of the immense profit and productivity (and devastation) that accompanied "free trade"—but this time in Africans. In fact, to the extent that 1776 led to the ossification of slavery and an increase in the illegal slave trade captained by U.S. nationals—particularly after 1808, when it was thought to have gone into desuetude—1776 marks a counter-revolution.[32] The de facto repudiation of "Somerset's Case" on the mainland was an affirmation of the necessity of slavery, and this—at least for the Africans—meant a counter-revolution. This affirmation in turn made the explosion in 1861—a deepening of the "counter-revolution of slavery" and the continuously heightened denunciation of the import of "Somerset's Case"—virtually inevitable. Such was the onrushing momentum, the electrifying intensity, of this powerful counter-revolution that—arguably—it continues today, albeit in a different form.[33]

Inexorably, the process of brutal and hurried enslavement generated an opposing and fierce resistance. Reports of various plots and conspiracies by the enslaved were rising sharply in the years preceding 1776.[34] What was at play was a crisis of rapid change: when the pace, force, and pressure of events increase sharply in a frenzied manner, making pervasive ruptures veritably unavoidable. The enormous influx of Africans—and the settlers' intoxication with the wealth they produced—meant that more "whites" had to be attracted to the continent to countervail the ferocity of the fettered labor force, and ultimately, an expanded set of rights for these European migrants, along with land seized from the indigenous, was critical in enticing them.

The unforgiving racial ratios in the Caribbean basically determined that slave rebellions would be more concentrated and riotous there; yet this placed London in a vise, for—as noted—there were growing reservations about focusing investment in North America given that region's growing competitiveness, while militant Africans were driving settlers away from the Caribbean, precisely to North America. Yet this brought London no surcease since the arrivals of these enterprising individuals in North America brought as well those who had experienced the fright of riotous Africans. It was in early 1736 that a conspiracy was exposed in Antigua for the enslaved to liquidate the European settlers—according to the authorities, "all the white inhabitants of this island were to be murdered and a new form of government to be established by the slaves among themselves," as they were determined to "possess the island . . . entirely."[35] This was preceded by yet another "horrid" plot that was exposed in early 1729, in which the enslaved were determined to "cutt off every white inhabitant" of Antigua.[36]

Eliza Lucas, the daughter of the lieutenant governor of Antigua, promptly migrated to South Carolina, where she became the spouse of Charles Pinckney, a leader of this colony, and their sons became leaders of the revolt against London. Unsurprisingly, she found "Carolina greatly preferable to the West Indies"—though by March 1741 she was anxiety ridden once more as Charleston, she thought, was to be "destroyed by fire and sword to be executed by the Negroes before the first day of next month."[37] Then, as some of these colonists fled northward, they brought with them enslaved Africans well aware that their oppressors were vulnerable, which was not the kind of insight conducive to stability in the mainland colonies. Among these was the influential Isaac Royall, who by 1737, it was said, had arrived in Massachusetts with "a Parcel of Negroes designed for his own Use" and a willingness to "pay the Duty of Impost" in a province where—as elsewhere—nervousness about the growing presence of enslaved Africans was growing.[38] Then there was Josiah Martin, the final colonial governor in North Carolina, who outraged fellow settlers in the immediate prelude to 1776 by allegedly threatening to free and unleash Africans against rebels: he too had roots in Antigua and, thus, had reason to possess a healthy regard for the fighting spirit of Africans and their own desire for domination—a point that may have occurred to residents of what became the Tarheel State.[39]

As settlers fled from the Caribbean to the mainland of North America, they brought with them nerve-jangling experiences with Africans that hardened their support of slavery—just as abolitionism was arising in London. But the point was that rebellious Africans were causing Europeans to flee the Caribbean for the mainland, as the productive forces in the latter were already burgeoning: the following pages will reveal that slave resistance in the Caribbean too merits consideration when contemplating the origins of the U.S.

Thus, in 1750, fifty thousand more Africans lived in the islands than on the mainland, but as 1776 approached, thirty thousand more Africans lived on the mainland than on the islands. Likewise, in 1680, almost nine out of ten Africans under London's jurisdiction in the Americas lived in the Caribbean, and half resided on the small island of Barbados, while the Negro population on the mainland was relatively small.[40] This rapid transition to the mainland by 1750 reflected many forces—particularly investors betting on the mainland more than the islands, as Africans had inflamed these small territories. But this transition occurred as restiveness was growing on the mainland about the nature of colonial rule.

The mainland and the metropolis were approaching confrontation for another reason: abolitionism was rising in London not least because Britain was becoming increasingly dependent on African soldiers and sailors: it was not easy to enslave those of this important category of workers, particularly when they carried weapons. One observer detected "twelve 'black moore' sailors serving in one of the King's ships at Bristol in 1645, nor was it unknown that black body-servants to rise into battle alongside their Roundhead or Cavalier masters"; some of these men "whose presence was recorded on Civil War battlefields may well have been born in these islands."[41] The Civil War in which these Africans participated and the fractiousness of English, then British, politics virtually preordained that various island factions would seek the support of Africans—notably as their numbers escalated in the 18th century.

Moreover, a number of Irishmen, quite dissatisfied with London, often sought succor with the Crown's most obstinate foes, providing further impetus for reliance on Africans. Strikingly, in early 1748 in

South Carolina, a plot of the enslaved was uncovered to liquidate European settlement, which was said to be assisted by an Irishman, Lawrence Kelley.[42] In the run-up to 1776, there were numerous Irish soldiers of fortune who had thrown in their lot with His Catholic Majesty in Spain, including Alejandro O'Reilly, Spain's chief representative in New Orleans, and General Richard Wall, who served in the post of "Spanish Secretary of State." The powerful O'Reilly was deemed to be the most respected figure in the military of Spain.[43]

Many Scots were similarly unhappy—a discontent that has yet to disappear.[44] The Act of Union, formally consolidating Scotland's role in the United Kingdom, came only in 1707. There were two massive uprisings—1715 and 1745—that had a particular resonance in the Highlands, where resistance was the strongest, which happened to be a point of departure for numerous migrants to North America. Some of these migrations were involuntary, as prisoners of war were shipped en masse to the colonies, many of whom arrived in no mood to compromise with London and eager for revenge.[45] Satisfying the needs of these migrants often meant massive land grants to them in the colonies,[46] necessitating either enslaved Africans to work the land or armed Africans offshore to protect them from attack, goals at cross-purposes leading to strains in the colonial project.

Thus, in early 1776, Arthur Lee of Virginia was gleeful, as he reported from London. The "Irish troops go with infinite resistance" to North America, he averred, and "strong guards are obliged to be kept upon the transports to keep them from deserting wholesale. The Germans too, I am well informed, are almost mutinous." London, he said, "found it impossible to recruit in England, Ireland or Scotland, though the leading people of the last are [to] a man almost violently against America."[47] The presumed unreliability of the Irish and Scots facilitated London's increased reliance on African soldiers and sailors.

Yet the sight of armed Africans was quite unsettling to the settlers. It was in 1768 that Bostonians were treated to the sight of Afro-Caribbean drummers of the 29th Regiment actually punishing their fellow "white" soldiers. In the heart of Boston Commons, these Negroes whipped about ten alleged miscreants for various misdeeds. One can only imagine how such a sight would have been received in Carolina, though such displays gave resonance to the growing perception that London would move to free the enslaved, arm them, and then squash colonies already perceived as a growing rival. It was also in Boston in 1768 that John Hancock and other eminent petitioners accused the redcoats of encouraging slaves to "cut their masters' throats and to beat, insult and otherwise ill treat said masters"; it was felt that with the arrival of more redcoats, the Africans surmised they would soon "be free [and] the Liberty Boys slaves."[48]

It was not only the British who felt compelled to place weapons in the arms of Africans. It was in 1766 that Louisiana's governor, Etienne Boucher Perier de Salvert, asserted that since "soldiers fled at the first flash of the Indian gun," it "would be much better to trust Negroes on the battle-field and use them as soldiers . . . because they, at least, were brave men."[49] Actually, the governor was an inadequate sociologist, for what drove the indomitable courage of Africans was the perception that, if captured, they could easily wind up in slavery, while their European counterparts—alternatively—had numerous options available, including becoming property owners stocked precisely with the enslaved.

London felt compelled to rely upon Negro soldiers and sailors, as the colonists came to rely upon Negro slaves: this was becoming an unbridgeable chasm. The Crown—the sovereign in both London and the colonies—had created a highly combustible political volcano. This instability was also propelled by another contradiction that the Crown helped to create: the model in the "Mother Country" was based upon a certain privilege for the English, as against the Irish and Scots. In contrast, the colonies—desperate for men and women defined as "white" to counter the fearsome presence of Africans in the prelude to 1776—could empower the Irish and Scots and provide them with more opportunity. All this was occurring as economic conflicts brewed in the trans-Atlantic relationship. Ultimately, the mainland model based on "racial" privilege overwhelmed the London model based on "ethnic" privilege. London's "ethnic" approach implicitly—at times explicitly—sacrificed the interests of Irish and Scots and Welsh (and even the English of certain class backgrounds) and made up for the shortfall by seeking to attract Africans to the banner, a policy propelled not least by competition with Madrid. But such a policy could only alienate mainland settlers, driving them toward a unilateral declaration of independence on 4 July 1776.

One espies part of this trend unfolding in the Chesapeake during this tumultuous era. Beginning in the 1680s and stretching until at least 1720, there was a decided shift from the use of servants to the use of slaves; as the population of the latter increased at twice the rate of the European-derived population, instability increased. But for present purposes, note that the term "white"—the vector of a potently rising identity politics still operative centuries later—only began to supplant "Christian" and "free" as favored designations in the 1690s, as the monopoly of the Royal African Company eroded and "separate" and "private" traders began descending in droves on Africa, providing the human capital for economic expansion.[50] In short, the privilege of "whiteness" was based heavily upon the increased presence of Africans, but since mainlanders were coming to suspect that London would deploy the Negroes against them—or, at least, had a more expansive view of their deployment than settlers—this meant that independence in 1776 was tied up with complicated, even fearful, sentiments about humans designated as slaves. This expansion in the colonies fueled by enslavement of Africans then undergirded the conflict with London that erupted in 1776.

Unfortunately for London and its energetic North American colonies, there were other forces that had a vote on their future. In retrospect, it seems appropriate that the Spanish term for "Blacks"—that is, "Negros"—invaded the English language almost as effortlessly as the bronze troops of His Catholic Majesty invaded the territory ostensibly controlled by London. For as early as 1555, Madrid was deploying in the Americas attacking forces heavily composed of Africans, and by 1574 in Havana the darkest of us all had their own militias under African command.[51] Thus, as Africans began flooding into North America, forced to endure the most heinous of circumstances, this prepared a delicate recipe for the exquisite taste of Spain, which wished to reverse London's gains. It was in mid-1742, as London and Spain were at war once more, that Madrid's man in Havana barked out blunt orders: "after taking possession of Port Royal [South Carolina], it will be proper to send out Negroes of all languages (some of which [should] accompany the militia of this place for this very purpose) to convoke the slaves of the English in the plantations round about, and offer . . . in the name of our King, liberty, if they will deliver themselves up of their own accord and to say that the lands will be assigned them in the territories of Florida, which they may cultivate and use themselves as owners, under the direction and laws of the Kingdom of Spain."[52] In the long run, enslaved Africans in the British colonies—and then the early U.S. itself—may have absorbed

Iberian notions about the relation between slavery and freedom, notably the seditious notion that freedom was a permissible goal for a slave.[53]

The threat from Spanish Florida led directly to the creation of London's colony in Georgia. A motive force for the founding in 1733 was to forge a "white" buffer—where African slavery was to be barred—between South Carolina, which labored anxiously with a Negro majority, and Spanish Florida, from whence armed Africans continually probed. Establishing Georgia evidently did not hamper unduly Madrid's plans, particularly when a few years after the founding, South Carolina endured the Stono revolt, the bloodiest in the history of colonial North America, in which—it appears—Spain played a starring role. Thus, it was also in mid-1742 that the founding father of Georgia, James Oglethorpe, confessed disconsolately that the devilish "Spaniards" had "fomented" a "mutinous temper at Savannah," and, as a result, the "destruction of that place was but part of their scheme for raising a general disturbance through all North America. Their correspondence [with] the Negroes too fatally manifested itself in the fire at New York & Cha Town [Charleston] & the insurrection of the Negroes in Carolina."[54]

These were not Oglethorpe's views alone. The idea was growing that the South Carolina, then Georgia, border separating British from Spanish soil was the soft underbelly, the Achilles' heel of London's mainland colonial project that could push the Union Jack back to the Canadian border. It was in mid-1741 that an official investigation poking through the debris of the September 1739 Stono uprising by the enslaved, which led to buckets of blood being shed by Carolina colonists (more than two dozen were slaughtered), observed that these Africans "would not have made this insurrection had they not depended" on Florida "as a place of reception afterwards"—this was "very certain and that the *Spaniards* had a hand in prompting them to this particular action, there was but little room to doubt" (emphasis original); for the previous July, a Spanish official in Florida arrived in Charleston with about 30 aides, "one of which was a *Negro* that spoke *English* very well." This arrival was "under the pretence of delivering a letter" to Oglethorpe, though it must have been known that he did not reside there. It was feared that this Negro was tasked to incite Carolina Africans.[55]

Oglethorpe thought he knew why Madrid relied so heavily on armed Africans, and inexorably, given the intensity of religiosity, the reason was to be found in Catholicism. Madrid and Paris, he stressed, contained "one hundred thousand *Cloyster'd Females*, not permitted to *propagate* their Species and the Number of Males in a State of *Celibacy* is still abundantly greater"—besides, "a considerable part of their great Armies" tended to "resolve against Marriage," meaning a birth dearth that could only be resolved by a more dedicated inclusion of Africans that Protestant London abjured.[56] If Oglethorpe had paid closer attention to Iberian politics, he might have noticed that—like Scotland—Catalonia, which included Barcelona, was not wholly reconciled to being administered by Madrid. It was on 11 September 2012 that an estimated 1.5 million Catalonians called for more autonomy for this region, which contained a population of about 7.5 million: it was on that date in 1714 at the end of the War of Spanish Succession that the Bourbon monarchy suppressed regional institutions.[57] Madrid's reliance upon Africans in the Americas may have seemed less risky than reliance upon men with roots in Catalonia.

Ultimately the clash between London and Madrid at the South Carolina–Georgia–Florida border in the 1740s proved decisive for the future of what was to become the U.S., on the same level as the better-known conclusion of the Seven Years' War in 1763; yet this former struggle (even more than what befell Quebec) had the enslavement of Africans at its throbbing heart.[58] Moreover, after the 1740s, Georgia's role as a "white" equivalent of the Berlin Wall rapidly crumbled, bringing more Africans to the mainland and, thus, increasing the anxieties of mainland settlers.

There was a kind of "arms race" that ensnared London and Madrid involving competition for the often angry affections of Negroes. London, with a developing empire and a relatively small population, could hardly ignore Africans. London's negotiations in the 1730s with Jamaican Maroons suggested that the Crown recognized early on the value of an entente with Africans. In this contest, London was at a blunt disadvantage, not least since its blustering mainland colonies had opted for a development model based on the mass enslavement of Africans and the reluctance to build an "escape hatch" for free Africans. The very name St. Augustine, Florida, sent a frisson of apprehension coursing down the spines of the British, particularly after it became a citadel where armed Africans were known to reside. By the late 1720s, British subjects returning to Carolina battered and bruised from captivity in Florida told spine-shaking tales of Africans (and the indigenous) selling British scalps for thirty Spanish pieces-of-eight.[59] Unfortunately for the settlers, it was not only Carolina that was terrified by the dual prospects of internal revolt and external invasion, particularly from Spanish Florida, for this dual nightmare was a frequent topic of discussion in Virginia at the highest level.[60]

Moreover, London was administering an over-stretched empire, which too necessitated the employment of more Africans. By 1757, after a battle with Bengal's Muslim viceroy, the East India Company found itself in possession of a territory three times larger than England. Less than a decade later, the company had successfully undermined the ruler of Awadh, the largest of the Mughal Empire's provinces.[61] Yes, the "distraction" of India benefited the North American rebels—but it also underscored the importance of Africans as a military force in the Americas.

London probably undermined its cause with the mainland colonists during the all-important siege of Havana in 1762. There was conscription in North America for this campaign, which admittedly was designed in no small part to ease Spanish pressure on the Carolinas and Georgia—though these settlers thought their time could have been better spent subduing the indigenous and the land they controlled. But then London's commanders were instructed that the "corps of Negroes to be raised in Jamaica" for this battle "should have an equal share in all booty gained from the enemy in common with his regular troops": this only served to add heft to the gnawing feeling on the mainland that settlers were being treated like Africans—which, in their argot, meant being treated like slaves.[62]

Britain finally ousted the Spanish from rule in St. Augustine in 1763—though the future Sunshine State continued to be the dog that didn't bark, since it was the "fourteenth" colony that did not revolt in 1776, perhaps because Africans continued to play a martial role there and like most Africans were not enthusiastic about a settlers' revolt that augured an ossification of slavery; strikingly, Africans also fled en masse as London took the reins of power.[63] Interestingly, in 1776, Governor Patrick Tonyn, in what was then British East Florida, created four black militia companies to join in defense of the province—mostly with success—designed to foil attacks from Georgia, which these companies then proceeded to attack.[64]

In summary, the post-1688 tumult brought London mixed blessings. Surely, the enhanced slave trade it augured lined the pockets of numerous merchants in Bristol and Liverpool—but in Rhode Island too, which instigated dreams of independence. This tumult delivered more Africans to the hemisphere who were not immune to the seductive appeals of Madrid. This tumult also brought more Negro insurrection-ists who helped to spur an abolitionist movement that served to create a gulf between London and its increasingly obstreperous colonies.

These Africans played a pivotal role in spurring once proud British subjects to revolt against the Crown, thanks to the final colonial gover-nor in Virginia, Lord Dunmore: he was viewed as a villain by the reb-els, particularly after his notorious November 1775 decree to free and arm enslaved Africans in order to squash the anti-colonial revolt. Dis-patched to bolster his deteriorating rule were 160 men from the 14th Regiment at St. Augustine.[65]

But often forgotten when Dunmore is invoked is the run-up to Novem-ber 1775, when rebellious Africans had sought to eliminate settlements, leading some colonists to feel that the world could be upended and they could assume a status below that of vassals. Thus, the threat of Negro revolt was magnified in the desperation driven by the Yamasee War, featuring the indigenous rampaging against settlers, which led to the arming of Africans in South Carolina in 1715. In other words, in addition to competing Euro-pean powers—for example, Spain—allying with Africans, settlers also had to worry about slaves bolstering revolts of the indigenous. Engaged typi-cally in dickering and arbitrage, simultaneously Africans were also negoti-ating with and cooperating with raiding parties by the indigenous. In some instances, they even entered into formal alliances with the indigenous and commenced their own unilateral wars against the colony. "There must be great caution," several planters warned, "lest our slaves when arm'd might become our masters." This was the profoundly significant fear that hov-ered like a dark cloud over the colonial project, a fear London unwittingly ignited into raging fever as 1776 approached with its tentative steps toward abolition while arming and deploying African soldiers in the colonies.[66]

Besieged by Africans, the indigenous, and European powers alike, mainland settlers found their options narrowing. Creating a buffer class of "free" Africans was a potential alternative to what appeared to be impending disaster. Indelicately, Governor William Gooch of Virginia had to explain in 1736 why such policies were inappropriate for his prov-ince. Why pass a law, he was asked, "depriving free Negroes & Mulattos of the privilege of voting at any Election of Burgesses . . . or at any other elections"? Well, he huffed, recently there was a "conspiracy discovered among the Negroes to Cutt off the English, wherein the free Negroes and

Mulattos were much suspected to have been concerned (which will for-ever be the case)." Indeed, he continued, "such was the insolence of the Free Negroes at that time, that the next assembly thought it necessary ... to fix a perpetual Brand upon Free Negroes & Mulattos by excluding them from that great privilege of a Freeman, well knowing they always did and, every will, adhere to and favour the Slaves."[67]

Mainland settlers railed against overtures to Africans while they made overtures to London's staunchest foes. In early 1751, London was informed that mainland settlers were involved in a "clandestine trade" "with the French, Dutch and Danes" that was such a "success" that now these devious merchants were seeking to "introduce foreign sugar into Great Britain" itself, along with "great quantities of foreign rum into Ireland . . . as well as into Halifax." In turn, mainlanders were bringing to North America "all kinds of French and Dutch merchandise directly interfering with those of Great Britain." This was causing "irreparable injury to the commerce and manufactures of the Mother Country and to the great increase and strength and riches of [Britain's] most danger-ous rivals," leading inexorably to "impending ruin . . . falling upon Great Britain."[68] In 1756, London railed against "an illegal trade" that had "been carried out between [British] plantations and the French settlements."[69]

Indeed, mainland trade with Hispaniola was so sizeable, particularly with regard to trade implicating slavery and the slave trade, that it may have contributed to the demographic racial imbalance leading directly to the vaunted Haitian Revolution, 1791–1804, meaning these mainland settlers were active agents in two of the major developments of the past few centuries. In 1762, British officer Jeffrey Amherst complained that "some of the merchants on this Continent, particularly those of Penn-sylvania and New York, were entering into Schemes for supplying the Havannah [Cuba] with provisions." In August 1776, the British seafarer James Stokes, who had just arrived on the French-controlled Hispan-iola, noticed armed North American vessels loading arms and ammu-nition, presumably for the anti-colonial revolt.[70]

Thus, even before 1756—or 1763—these settlers, apparently unable to resist the stupendous profits emerging from an ascending slave-driven cap-italism, were busily cutting various deals with their erstwhile opponents, particularly the French, even though London repeatedly warned that this was jeopardizing British interests. The settlers had good reason to believe that if they cut a deal with Madrid and Paris against British interests, they would emerge as the eventual winners. In other words, from 1756 to 1763, London fought an expensive and largely successful war against Paris and Madrid to oust the latter two from a good deal of North America to the benefit of the colonists, then sought to raise taxes to pay for this gigantic venture—only to have the settlers go behind the back of London and conspire with Spain and France against Britain. Yet even this gloss on the founding should not be allowed to downplay the role of Africans, for it was their conspiring with the Spaniards in Florida—in particular—which was a driving force behind the Seven Years' War that contributed to London's loss.

London had created an inherently unstable colonial project, based on mass enslavement of Africans—who could then be appealed to by Spanish neighbors and wreak havoc—and an inability to hedge against the fiasco that such a policy promised by building a buffer class of free Negroes and mulattoes. This conspicuous weakness drew London into a seemingly endless cycle of conflicts with Spain—and its frequent ally France—culminating in the so-called Seven Years' War, 1756–1763. This proved to be a catastrophic victory for London, as in eroding these external threats to the colonies, it allowed the settlers to concentrate more of their ire on London itself, leading to the 1776 unilateral declaration of independence. That is to say, before 1763, mainland settlers were huddling in fear of Negro insurrection combined with foreign invasion, particularly from Spanish Florida or, possibly, French Canada; afterward, it appeared to a number of colonists—particularly as abolitionist sentiment grew in London—that Negro insurrection would be coupled with a throttling of the colonies by redcoats, many of them bearing an ebony hue. Minimally, a mainland settler deal with Madrid in particular could forestall the eventuality of another Stono, no small matter as reports of slave conspiracies rose in the years immediately preceding 1776. The threats to London's interests were multiplying as some mainland settlers were busily conspiring with the Crown's enemies.

London did not seem to realize that when the RAC monopoly eroded, set in motion were virtually unstoppable economic forces that would place stressing strain on mainland provinces, ultimately setting them adrift toward independence. The traditional narrative of the republic's founding has emphasized insufficiently the amorality and trans-border ethos that came to define capitalism—which often was at odds with traditional notions of patriotism and even sovereignty. This trend was reflected in the earliest stages of the mainland revolt. Quite naturally, this dearth of patriotism also came to characterize Africans—the human capital which propelled this system—who had little interest in identifying their interest with that of their so-called masters.

Moreover, the settlers thought that London's special relationship with Africans had gone too far, to the point where they thought they had reason to fear that the Crown's sable arm would come down with a crash upon their heads. "Every slave might be reckoned a domestic enemy," according to Benjamin Franklin speaking almost two decades before 1776.[71] Just before 4 July 1776, a fellow Philadelphian denounced London for "not only urging savages to invade the country, but instigating Negroes to murder their masters."[72] The embodiment of colonial secession, George Washington, may have spent more time overseeing "his" enslaved Africans than he did supervising soldiers or government officials,[73] suggesting the importance of this troublesome property; by 1764, he owed one of his London creditors a still hefty eighteen hundred pounds sterling[74] and certainly had an incentive to both preserve his slave property and escape from the Crown which seemed to be calling it into question. John Adams, who earned handsome fees as legal counsel for slaveholders in cases against the enslaved, had little reason to disagree.[75] Ditto for John Hancock, whose large signature on the nascent republic's founding document was somehow appropriate since he was one of Boston's largest slave owners.[76] James Madison speculated in late 1774, "if America & Britain should come to an hostile rupture, I am afraid an Insurrection among Negroes may & will be promoted. In one of our Counties lately a few of those unhappy wretches met together & chose a leader who was to conduct them when the English Troops should arrive—which they foolishly thought would be very soon & that by revolting to them they should be rewarded with their freedom."[77]

Prominent slaveholder—and anti-London rebel—Henry Laurens of South Carolina was told that just before the April 1775 confrontation at Lexington between the republicans and the Crown, the latter planned to instigate the enslaved to revolt to blunt the settlers' initiative. By 1774, he was reportedly convinced that if London had its way, "none but Slaves & his Officers and their Task Masters shall reside in America." He may have heard of the British subject of African descent David Margrett, who was in South Carolina in 1775 preaching about abolition.[78]

As the tempting of fate by Margrett in Carolina suggested, there were strong hints from Britain that sensitive settlers may have found—in every sense—unsettling. As June 1772 approached, beating slaves was much less common in London than in the colonies. Increasingly, Londoners were beginning to see slavery and slaveholders as an American phenomenon that sophisticated metropolitans disdained as uncivilized—partly because that was the view propounded by the growing number of Africans (perhaps fifteen thousand) in British streets in the 1770s; that the colonists were prating about liberty while enforcing a draconian enslavement tended to induce an adamantly defensive response among Londoners, who began to castigate the settlers as tyrants themselves.[79]

Wittingly or not, reform proposals by London only served to incite the settlers even more, particularly those who were bent on imposing a model of development based on mass enslavement of Africans. In 1775, a leading British official proposed that London was willing to return to the status quo ante of 1763 with regard to taxes and the like if the settlers would concur with the notion that slavery was a "vice" that was "contrary to the law of God" and, thus, "every slave in North America should be entitled to his trial by jury in all criminal cases . . . as a foundation to extirpate slavery from the face of earth"; with a flourish, it was added, "let the only contention hence forward between Great Britain and America be, which shall exceed the other in zeal for establishing the fundamental rights of liberty to all mankind." Settlers may have thought that this official was either daft or engaged in a dangerous provocation, but in any case, this was not the kind of proposal designed to attract the sincere attention of rebels, many of whom had invested fortunes in slavery and the slave trade.[80] London appeared to present a clear and present danger to the lives and fortunes of settlers. The decision to rebel, though festooned in the finery of freedom, wound up depriving a countless number of Africans of the liberty that the 1776 revolt has been thought to have provided.

*   *   *

As the 21st century proceeds, one point is evident: the heroic creation myth of the founding of the U.S. is desperately in need of revisiting. In November 1965, in remarks that escaped attention for the most part, Ian Smith—the leader of the newly founded racist republic that was Rhodesia (which became Zimbabwe in 1980)—argued that his Unilateral Declaration of Independence was a replay of 1776: he and his comrades were seeking to escape the logic of decolonization, just as 1776 sought to escape the logic of slavery's abolition.[81] Smith had a coarse disregard for the aspirations of Africans, as did his counterparts in 1776. Contemporary observers should note that Smith had as much success in "integrating" Africans successfully into his ill-fated republic as did his North American counterparts in the aftermath of 1776. Smith was defeated and, justifiably, has passed into the ignominy of history. The rebels of 1776 were victorious and have been hailed widely ever since, suggesting that there is something to be said for winning in the shaping of history's judgment of a rebellion.

A few years before Smith's telling remarks, Blas Roca, a leader of what became the Communist Party in Cuba, then in a desperate confrontation with Washington, asked a question not often posed in Washington: why, he asked, was the plight of Negroes in the U.S. probably worse than that of any other group of Africans in the hemisphere?[82]

Roca's plaint reflected the point that unlike in Cuba, where the anti-colonial and anti-slavery struggles merged, in the person of Antonio Maceo,[83] or in Mexico, where an early leader was of African descent, Vicente Guerrero,[84] in what became the U.S., there was a divergence between the struggle against London and the struggle for abolition—in fact, arguably these goals were at loggerheads. With Africans on the mainland standing largely at the side of London—and even more so after independence—it was inevitable that the path ahead for U.S. Negroes would be exceedingly rocky. Indeed, one of the more striking aspects of the anti-London struggle on the mainland was how often it merged with a "Black Scare" in the form of the imprecations tossed at Lord Dunmore and Governor Martin of North Carolina.

Well after 1776, it remained striking that white supremacists were quite clear and precise as to the identity of their bête noire. For example, it has become veritable folklore that in order to escape successfully the pincers of Jim Crow, Africans with deep roots in the U.S. often began speaking in French or Spanish so as to escape the damning accusation that they were descendants of mainland slaves,[85] a group not notorious in its celebration of 1776 and quite willing to align with the republic's foes in London thereafter.[86]

Though historians have pointed in various directions in seeking to explicate what has befallen Africans on the mainland,[87] it is difficult to ignore the point that one central reason for this awful persecution has been the simple fact that this besieged group had their own ideas about the configuration of North America and that their conceptions often involved collaboration with the antagonists of Euro-American elites (be they indigenes, Madrid, or ultimately London). The Negro dalliance with London was then followed by various relationships with Mexico City,[88] Tokyo,[89] New Delhi,[90] and Moscow,[91] in a repetitive pattern of seeking leverage abroad to overcome rapacity at home. However, it was not until the 1950s that Washington came to realize that, perhaps, easing racist oppression at home might serve to foil such dangerous diplomatic alliances—until then, such relations served partially to provide further grist for the oppressive mill. Nevertheless, today the continuing invidious discrimination that undermines the descendants of enslaved Africans on the mainland[92] stems in no small part from their historically consistent and staunch opposition to the capacious plans of slaveholding rebel—then republican—elites, which too often targeted these very same Africans.

This chapter began with a remarkable instance of opposition to a sacred principle of mainland settlers—slavery—which in June 1772 helped to ignite a new departure in our complex history. Part of the background suggesting how these Africans came to be in a London courtroom and how their audacity helped to ignite a republican revolt will unwind in the following pages.

1

Rebellious Africans

How Caribbean Slavery Came to the Mainland

The news from Barbados was frightening.

In 1676, a Londoner reported breathlessly about the "bloody tragedy intended against His Majesty's subjects" there at the hands of "the Heathen, the Negroes"; fortunately, it was said, the conspiracy was "miraculously discovered eight days before the intended murder" was planned.[1] An orgy of beheadings and immolations of Africans—particularly those designated as "Coromantee or Gold Coast Negro"—ensued, but this bloodshed was insufficient to wash away fearful apprehension about what could befall this small island. For the Africans not only sought to eliminate the European settlement and establish their own polity in its stead; they also "intended," said one contemporaneous writer, "to spare the lives of the fairest and handsomest women (their mistresses and their daughters) to be converted to their own use."[2]

The authorities sought to quarantine the contagion by ordering that "no Negroes concerned in the late rebellion or convicted of other crime in Barbadoes be permitted to be bought or sold" (there was fear of what would occur if these Africans wound up in neighboring Jamaica)[3]— but this was a difficult mandate to observe when African labor was so needed beyond this island's borders. By importing Africans in such ratios to the point where they grossly outnumbered settlers, the Crown was riding a tiger: it was hard to dismount and harder still not to do so.

The colonial governor, Sir Jonathan Atkins, was convinced that foul play was planned by the Africans. Their "damnable designs," he asserted was "to destroy them all," meaning those like himself. A "more thorough inquiry" found this conspiracy "far more dangerous than was at first thought for it had spread over most of the plantations, especially amongst the [Coromantee] Negroes, who are much the greater number from any one country and are a warlike and robust people"[4]—perhaps

Africans should be dragooned from elsewhere: but that could mean enhanced conflict in Africa with the French, Spanish, and other competitors. Just a few years earlier, the Dutch had burnt to the ground an English encampment in West Africa with considerable loss. Perhaps inspired, the Africans on an island near Gambia rebelled against the European invaders in their midst, and in the resultant unrest, almost three dozen of the English were slain and about the same number of Africans. At this juncture, even the densest and least observant Londoner might have wondered about the costs of colonialism.[5]

However, as things turned out, rebellious Africans in the Caribbean did not cause London to abandon colonialism but, instead, to move more assets northward to the mainland, as a host of settlers from Barbados simply moved to South Carolina. London feared that small islands—more so than the more spacious mainland—could more easily fall victim to internal revolt by the enslaved, coupled with external attack by competing European powers. This was a reasonable assumption, though London was to find that South Carolina too was not altogether exempt from attack by Africans aided by Madrid, underscoring the difficult dilemma faced by settlers. Increasingly, settlers were referring to their principal labor force as "intestine" enemies, a deadly threat that could not be easily expelled or digested.

Moreover, as the number and importance of enslaved Africans grew on the mainland, as Caribbean colonists and their valued property made the great trek to Carolina and points northward,[6] predictably there was a concomitant nervousness about the ultimate rebellious intentions of these manacled workers. In any case, London should not have been surprised by a murderous turn of events. In 1649, a plot by the enslaved was discovered that called for the planter class in Barbados to be eliminated and—as it was reported—"their wives to be kept for the Chief of the Conspirators, their children and white servants to be their slaves."[7]

A full century before the famed lurch for independence in 1776, it seemed that other dreams of independence were brewing. The subjugation and settling of the Caribbean in particular and also the mainland was a riotous and chaotic process accompanied by frequent plots and conspiracies, involving not just the usual suspects—the indigenous and Africans—but, as well, Irish and Scots. This chaos provided opportunities for arbitrage and leverage for all concerned, the Africans not least. Ultimately, conflagrations in the Caribbean were to drive London to focus more on the mainland—but this did not provide a long-term remedy.

It was almost as if the settlers were deeply equivocal when it came to Africans, for a few decades earlier the Bahamian elite had complained that there were "too many Negroes" in their midst and sought to transport quite a number to Bermuda (and Virginia), both of which had Negro problems all their own.[8] A similar plot by the enslaved had been uncovered in Bermuda in 1673—near Christmas Day, a familiar day of revolt for Africans in the Americas. A result? The colony's free Negro population was effectively expelled, which narrowed the base of support for the colonial project, necessitating the importation of—perhaps—more unsteady Scots and Irish. A decade earlier, the authorities in recently claimed Jamaica already were hedging against the possibility of an African "mutiny."[9]

Undaunted, in 1682, recently imported enslaved Africans from Jamaica, brought to Bermuda, devised a far-reaching plan to organize brigades and murder leading planters during Sunday religious services—then flee via the highway that was the vast sea. Settlers were in a quandary since the well-founded fear of external attack meant incorporating Africans in the militia—but this decision could well give succor to the idea that the oppressed should deploy their martial skills against the local elite.[10] This fear of Africans using their weight in colonialism and numerical superiority to turn the tables on the Europeans was a lurking fear during this era, signaled, for example, in 1682 when leading English official William Blathwayt warned darkly about the rise of "piratical Negroes."[11]

Runaways were known to hide in the woods, waiting to rob—or murder—Europeans.[12] By late 1675, the authorities in Jamaica—which only had been seized from the Spanish two decades earlier—were fretting about "several insurrections and rebellions" of late by the enslaved; the planters were instructed to "take care to provide themselves with one white servant for every ten Negroes on their plantations"—but left unsaid was where these "whites" would be found who would be sufficiently intrepid to reside among angry insurrectionists.[13] Almost through absence of mind but actually driven by the desperation of mere survival, the base of support for colonialism was expanded to include groups often disfavored in London itself—for example, those who were Jewish and the Irish—now admitted into the hallowed halls of a form of colonial "whiteness."[14] In other words, the "ethnic" discrimination of the British isles had difficulty in withstanding murderous uprisings of the Africans and indigenous, and the ineluctable adaptation in the colonies was a grouping together of Europeans in the evolving "racial" category that was "whiteness": this process facilitated the degradation and subjugation of a recalcitrant African labor force. Yet, ultimately, racial formation was not a long-term solution to London's thorny problems in the Caribbean, not least since it was hard to override by fiat or otherwise the Protestant-Catholic divide.

Thus, the undeterred authorities in Barbados quickly moved to increase the "supply of servants from Scotland to strengthen the island against the outrages of the Negroes"—but casting increasingly restive Scots into this turmoil was not necessarily a formula for calm repose. A further suggestion was loosening barriers on trade between the island and New England—but far-sighted Londoners might have seen that this could only bolster independence sentiments on the mainland.[15]

In 1683, on the island of St. Helena in the South Atlantic, the governor was murdered, and the enslaved were enmeshed in seemingly perpetual plots involving poisoning.[16] That same year, yet another plot was uncovered in Barbados, and between 1685 and 1688, dozens of enslaved Africans were executed for various acts of sedition. Then in 1692 yet another major plot was revealed, as the Africans were planning to revolt on the plantations of Barbados, then move toward the urban node that was Bridgetown, where they intended to capture the fortifications, assume control, and dispense an uncertain fate to the settlers: hundreds were arrested, while dozens were executed.[17] An army of enslaved Africans intended to take advantage of the chaos of war to stage a rebellion and form their own polity, which would depend on the assistance of Irish servants as well as the French.[18]

Adding fuel to the fire was the seeming reality that as the crisis in London mounted, leading to the Glorious Revolution of 1688, tensions in the colonies proceeded accordingly. In the late 17th century, Barbados was gripped with nervousness over reports of rebellions by Africans, of which the preceding examples were merely the tip of a larger iceberg. After all, by this point many of the enslaved could understand quite well the language of the enslaver and the reports that filtered in from various vessels and overheard at dinner tables.

Ultimately, however, the mutually intelligible language best understood by the Africans and the colonizers alike was the language of force: the colonizers were encountering violent resistance at the source of their labor supply: Africa. Near Whydah in 1686, the would-be enslaved engaged in a shipboard insurrection that, it was reported with sadness, led them to "kill all the white men."[19] Near Accra in 1695, the would-be enslaved rose again and massacred their captors—though the Africans too absorbed major casualties.[20]

*   *   *

Of course, tension in London was nothing new either, as various Catholic plots had become a staple of the 17th century; that a significant Catholic population resided in Barbados contributed to the combustibility, as many of these servants were convicted political rebels banished from Ireland. There was reason to believe that this group were involved in plots to massacre island elites in 1634 and 1647; regional unrest in the 1650s was followed by regional revolts in the mid-1660s, connected to warfare in the Leeward Islands. There was a depressing suspicion in London that these servant revolts in the Caribbean were coordinated with foreign invasions—devised by, for example, France and Spain—which could only accelerate the growing fear that such a fate could befall England itself. Such was the conclusion during this tumultuous era after the French invaded Antigua and Montserrat, when a combination of Irish insurgents and invaders plundered and burned both colonies.[21]

Protestant English planters with sizeable holdings ruled Montserrat, while the Irish were small tobacco farmers, as the hierarchy of Europe was replicated in the Caribbean—which proved to be unstable in both sites. The Irish presence complicated the attempt to construct a smoothly synthetic "white" solidarity, which made more complex the overriding objective of exploiting African labor. That the Irish

could—and did—defect to "Catholic" invaders did little to dissuade the
developing notion that, perhaps, the mainland, with a more diverse and
substantial European population, was a preferable site for investment.[22]

Yet in 1689 in Maryland, there was frantic discussion "concerning
a confederacy with ye papists and Indians to destroy Protestants" that
mirrored Montserrat.[23] A decade later, a "general insurrection by the
Indians" was feared in this and "neighboring provinces," and though
Catholic—or "papist"—influence was not noted, surely they and their
external allies could have taken advantage easily of this situation.[24]

During this same era, Nevis and St. Christopher in the Caribbean
were under constant threat from the French, a threat that was magnified not only by the presence of alienated Africans but by problems in
supplying these distant outposts, leading to what Sir William Stapleton referred to as a "sad condition" featuring the "want of armies and
ammunition, the soldiers for want of pay and recruits"—generally, "destitute of everything."[25]

In the overriding context of Catholic-Protestant conflict, seizing
more Africans for enslavement, while trying to incorporate Irish and
other dissidents in the superseding category of "whiteness," made
sense—except for the Africans for which this trend was disastrous.
Incorporating the Irish was not easy either, not least because of religious rifts. After all, it was in the late 17th century that one Londoner
proclaimed haughtily that a "Papist hates a Protestant worse than he
doth" all others, just as a "Jew hates a Christian far worse than he doth
a Pagan [or] a Turk."[26] Actually, this writer—Thomas Gage—might have
written that those who were Jewish had reason to resent His Catholic
Majesty in Madrid, not least because of the Spanish Inquisition, which
led to their mass persecution and their fleeing en masse to the Americas, among other sites. Many of them were residing in Jamaica, then
Spanish soil—until the arrival of the English in 1655, in which case they
defected in huge numbers to the side of the invaders, emulating and
providing a template for Africans subsequently. Thus, London encouraged migration of Sephardim to Jamaica, and just as the Spanish had
co-opted countless Africans on English soil, the English returned the
favor with the Iberian Jews. No synagogues were built in Jamaica—until
after the Spanish were ousted. Thus, just as London was forced to try to
protect Africans under its jurisdiction from often harsh measures by

settlers, English elites in the metropolis had to act similarly in Jamaica in overriding special taxes against Jews pursued by local elites.[27]

Oliver Cromwell had been scheming against Madrid virtually from the moment he seized office—that is, when he was not squabbling with Scots and Irish and other Englishmen. When he favored a compact with France over Dunkirk in 1651 and when in 1653 he attempted to draw the Dutch into a pact for the common conquest of Spanish America, it was Madrid that was on his mind. But the ongoing religious war intervened, especially with Paris when he sought assurances about the position of the Huguenots. As things turned out, his plotting was not for naught when Jamaica was taken from the Spanish in 1655.[28]

It was well that the Jewish population rallied to London's side in Jamaica for the Africans took the opportunity to become "Maroons": that is, fleeing the Crown's jurisdiction and establishing independent communities on the island, raising the possibility of ousting European settlers altogether. London was obliged to negotiate seriously with these rebels—and grant grudging concessions—by the 1730s. "Few slave societies," argues social historian Orlando Patterson, "present a more impressive record of slave revolts than Jamaica," pointing to the 1673 rebellion (two hundred Africans kill their master and thirteen other Europeans, then plunder) and the 1678 uprising, which was similarly "serious," then the 1690 conflagration, which may have been larger than those.[29] The Maroons were implicated in the latter disturbance, and, as one subsequent report put it, "poor white men were . . . miserably butchered" as hundreds revolted: mayhem and murder ensued, Europeans were slaughtered indiscriminately, and arms were seized by Africans promising future unrest.[30]

The authorities in Jamaica were besieged. William Blathwayt, who had oversight of the Caribbean and North American colonies, in the 1680s began to receive a steady stream of ever more disturbing reports about "rebellious Negroes" in Jamaica.[31] The militancy among Africans in Jamaica eventually made that of Barbados seem mild by comparison; thus, by 1684, legislators in the former island were reminding settlers that slaveholders should search their property's houses "diligently . . . every fortnight for clubs, wooden swords and mischievous weapons." Other laws guarded against the enslaved seeking to "commit murder, rise in rebellion or make any preparation of arms . . . or conspire for that end," while any slave who sought to "do any good service against the Enemy, the French . . . shall forthwith be freed."[32]

But killing French—who fit snugly into the evolving potent category that was "whiteness"—might not have been the best incentive to dangle before Africans.[33] For as was to be the case virtually until the end of colonialism in 1962,[34] it was Jamaica that provided the most severe angst and angina for settlers. As one British writer put it in 1740, by 1690 "the Negroes began to make Disturbance; the Runaways and those descended by the Spanish slaves, who were never conquered, began to make [e]ruptions" in the midst of "unheard of barbarities," which caused other "slaves to rebel." On one plantation, hundreds revolted, entered the big house, and murdered the master, "and every white man that belonged to the plantation, seized [about] fifty muskets, blunderbusses and other arms, together with a great quantity of powder and shot." Then the Africans "marched to the next plantation where they repeated their murders and killed every White man they could find." This gave impetus to what came to be called "Maroon Wars" that surged for decades until the 1730s settlement: "what vast expense of Blood and Treasure the island" expended "to suppress the rebellious Negroes," it was said with dismay. "Despair" reigned among the colonists during this turbulent era. Neither the 1694 attack on Jamaica by the French nor the concomitant 1695 attack by London on neighboring Hispaniola settled things and, in fact, may have given impetus to the idea among Africans that the fate of these islands could only be settled by force of arms.[35] Unsurprisingly, revolts by Africans in Jamaica occurred in 1694, 1702, and 1704 as tensions with competing European powers accelerated.[36]

Punishment was articulated for the enslaved who were so bold as to become involved in "laying violent hands on their owners." A few years earlier, there was legislation promulgated concerning keeping "the number of white men . . . in proportion to the working slaves," and to ensure that "white men" were sufficient, "encouraging the . . . importation of white servants" was devised ("a ship having fifty white male servants on board shall be free from port charges"). Africans were barred from certain occupations in order to facilitate this European migration.[37] Yet this latter population failed to grow in Jamaica between 1680 and 1756 and by 1774 were only 6.1% of the isle's population, and by 1760 Jamaica endured "Tackey's Rebellion," probably the most serious and long-lasting slave uprising in London's possessions, leading to a 1761 law designed to curtail the power of peoples of color generally, anticipating legislation in the region, as well as in Bengal. However, the dilemma faced by London was exposed when the point is bruited about that bringing "white" or Irish settlers who might conspire with His Catholic Majesty or Scots, many of whom were not reconciled to being yoked in union with England, was hardly ideal.[38]

But London had few viable options. By the 1660s, the idea of enslaving Europeans (even Irish and Scots) in the Caribbean was disappearing. Simultaneously—if not sooner—the terms "Negro" and "slave" were becoming synonymous on the mainland, and this equivalence may have emerged even earlier on Providence Island, the Puritan colony in the southwestern Caribbean. One contemporary scholar has found "the first use of the generic noun *white*" in January 1661. It is easy to infer that the colonizers came to recognize that simultaneous enslavement of Europeans and Africans was too formidable a task and that narrowing bondage to the latter was more practicable.[39] Certainly this narrowing made more sense on the mainland, where competing European powers were quite close and indigenes seemed more fearsome. Moreover—and as will be detailed later—the construction of "whiteness" or the forging of bonds between and among European settlers across class, gender, ethnic, and religious lines was a concrete response to the real dangers faced by all of these migrants in the face of often violent rebellions from enslaved Africans and their indigenous comrades.

Still, enslaving Africans was hardly a consolation prize, as evidenced by the London writer who acknowledged that in the 1680s, when English ships headed for the El Dorado that was Lima, Peru, the Spanish, hearing of their impending arrival, "killed most of their . . . slaves, fearing they should revolt from them" to the English; indeed, one English seaman related, "there came a Negro to us, running away from the Spaniards. He informed us . . . if the Spaniards had not sent all the Negroes belonging to this city farther up into the country, out of our reach and communication, . . . they would all undoubtedly have revolted to us."[40] Such was the dilemma of the beset colonizing power in desperate search of a reliable labor force to exploit mercilessly. What poison should be picked: bellicose Africans or disgruntled Irish and Scots?

It was during this time that legislators in Jamaica were formulating a law with a lamenting preamble: "whereas the runaway and rebellious Negroes in this island have of late murdered several of the inhabitants . . . and have plundered and destroyed many of the small and out-settlements; and do still in great numbers continue doing what robberies and other mischiefs they are able; and daily increase their numbers, by other Negroes running away and joining with them, which may be of fatal consequence"—the latter point was blunt understatement. As before, rewards were offered to Africans who participated in fighting the French, with little regard as to how this clashed with the goal of compelling slaves to fear humans defined as "white." By 1703, caution was cast aside as a bill was devised to "encourage the importation of white men" in order to provide "Security." Little regard was accorded to the difficult reality that both Spanish and French foes could insinuate themselves into the colony since—after all—they could pass as "white men" too.[41] Frankly, who was to say that a preferred French Huguenot was not actually a despised Catholic?

Sadly for London, Jamaica was a bellwether for the region. Shipping networks carried news and updates about plots and schemes and wars from one island to another and to the North American mainland, along with printed books, pamphlets, and newspapers that substantiated oral reports.[42] Things were so bad in Jamaica that by 1696 there was such fear that one official concluded morosely that even fleeing Europeans "must of necessity fall in a short time into the hands of the Enemy from abroad or the Negroes from within"—neatly encapsulating the internal and external dilemmas faced by the colonizer.[43]

Before 1692, colonizers in Jamaica "only" had to worry about Negro insurrection combined with foreign invasion, but then in that fateful year, this anxiety was compounded with the arrival of a major earthquake. It was one of the worst in recorded history.[44] A self-described "truest and largest account" of this epochal event exuded anxiety with "fear" of "the forcible invasion of Barbarous French or Insurrection of Domestic Slaves" as the ground rumbled below. Of course, said a contemporaneous account, the "first fears were concerning our Slaves, those irreconcilable and yet intestine Enemies of ours, who are not otherwise our Subjects than as the Whip makes them; who seeing our strongest houses demolished, our arms broken and hearing of the destruction of our greatest dependency, the town of Port Royal, might in hopes of Liberty be stirred up to rise in Rebellion against us"—that is, "kill and slay all the whites, men, women and children"—combined with the "forcible invasion of our Enemies," who see "our hearts are low, our arms broken, our forts lacerated and useless." This analyst worried if the earthquake meant that God's Will had spoken—surely the nightmare he conjured was reason for reconsideration of what was going on in Jamaica.[45]

* * *

Part of the problem was that after taking Jamaica in 1655, an intoxicated London thought it could use this island as a base to take Cuba, Hispaniola, and other glittering sources of wealth.[46] London quickly found that to compete in this region it made sense to bow to best practices of colonialism, for example, those of Spain and France, which often deployed armed Africans[47]—but as Britain came to see, this would only complicate relations with the settler class, which feared this trend as much as it feared foreign invasion. In the late 17th century, in one of the many examples of clashes between the colonial powers, France sought to oust the Spanish from Cartagena with a large fleet that included dozens of Africans from Hispaniola: these were the first to be ordered to embark ashore in South America and were crucial to the attack on this growing town of twenty thousand that had a heavy concentration of Africans.[48]

At this juncture, colonial territories were up for grabs, and enlisting Africans on one's side made sense. In 1678, the Frenchman Robert Cavelier de la Salle was confident that "Mulattoes, Indians and Negroes" once promised their liberty would assist Paris in driving the Spanish from Mexico.[49] But how could this overture to "Mulattoes, Indians and Negroes" occur as colonial momentum was pointing toward the intensification of the degradation of these groups?

London was hoisted on its own petard: by the late 17th century, the colonizing project presupposed enslavement of Africans, but, simultaneously, to gain an advantage against a European competitor could involve arming Africans, which could lead gradually away from the degradation that enslavement dictated—and, ultimately, toward abolition. Seeking to fortify colonialism by trying to deploy Irish Catholics invited their defection to the "Catholic powers" of Madrid and Paris, just as France had difficulty in deploying Protestant Huguenots for fear they might defect to Protestant London; yet France's slave code was not necessarily helpful in winning the hearts and minds of Africans.[50] Paris was emulating London, which decades earlier had acquiesced to the ousting of the governor of Virginia in part because he was seen as insufficiently harsh toward Catholics (and indigenes).[51]

Late 17th-century realities were seemingly contradictory: arming Africans and enslaving Africans; incorporating religious dissidents and ousting religious dissidents. By 1684, realization of the racial stakes at play was slowly dawning on at least one Londoner, who wondered pensively, should a "man be made a slave forever merely because his beard is Red or his Eyebrows Black?" Included in this premature abolitionism was an enlightening "discourse in way of dialogue between an Ethiopian or Negro-Slave and a Christian that was his master in America."[52]

By 1693—coincidentally as demonstrated rage was rising in Jamaica and Barbados—a sober colonist in Philadelphia was arguing that Africans were a "real part of mankind" and reminding that "in some places in Europe Negroes cannot be bought and sold for money or detained to be slaves." Therefore, he continued, "in true Christian Love we earnestly recommend it to all our friends and Brethren, not to buy any Negroes."[53] By 1702, the famed Daniel Defoe was raising searching questions about the slave trade, though he later backtracked—but his initial skepticism was a reflection of the heavy price in lives and money brought by building slave-labor camps.[54]

Yet another Londoner crowed about the "growing greatness" of "distant colonies"—and the wealth and prestige these lands delivered, in contrast to the unrefined opinion of the famed novelist. However, the writer Richard Blome also complained about maltreatment of Africans in Barbados, not least since if this brutality were not eased, it would lead to crises that could ultimately throttle the goose that was laying these golden eggs, in the form of mass rebellions of the enslaved.[55] The point-counterpoint between enthusiasm for the wealth that slavery generated and apprehension about the bloodiness it engendered was reflected in a legal zigzag. Thus, as early as 1569, it had been decided that English law would not recognize the status of a slave—this was reversed in 1677, then reversed again before entering a kind of limbo that was clarified in June 1772.[56]

*　*　*

It may have been demanding too much to expect London to move toward abolition in the late 17th century, in the face of debilitating unrest in the Caribbean. Expanding operations on the mainland as a hedge against further painful losses in the Caribbean (for example, that absorbed by Spain in Jamaica in 1655) had the added advantage of countering and blocking the Spanish in Florida and the French in the north and west on the mainland.[57] London knew that—unlike diamonds—colonies were not forever, and, thus, opportunism was a necessity. This may have dawned on the famed diarist Samuel Pepys when he landed in Tangiers in September 1683 and confronted Moors far from delighted to see him. Tangiers was a possession of the Crown beginning in 1661—and ending in 1684, shortly after he had arrived.[58]

The kind of anger Pepys witnessed in North Africa was mirrored—in spades—in the Caribbean, casting doubt on the future of the colonial enterprise there. Thus, as African rebelliousness surged, the besieged planter class of Barbados began a great trek to the mainland. By the late 17th century, Caribbean settlers and their enslaved Africans from this sugar island were trickling into Newport. By the 18th century, the Rhode Islanders had learned their lessons so well that this Atlantic town became a principal hemispheric slave market: there were twenty-five distillers making rum in Newport, and their busyness meant that a healthy African male could be bought for 115 gallons of rum, with "only" 95 gallons purchasing a female—who by rough means could be induced to produce even more chattel.[59]

Yet as important as Rhode Island was to slavery and as a refuge for retreating Caribbean colonists, it was far from being singular. By the summer of 1671, about half the Europeans and more than that of the Africans who were in South Carolina—in some ways the prismatic and paradigmatic province, which illuminated the mainland as a whole[60]—hailed from Barbados. This trend continued for about two decades, at which point a continuing influx from Africa began to assert itself.

During this earlier era, what became the Palmetto State was effectively an extension of this small island. There was also little doubt that tales of bloody resistance of the enslaved in the Caribbean indelibly marked Carolina, particularly since there was a high proportion of men from the Caribbean in the legislature that came to preside there. These men were still quite active in the 1690s, as they represented some of the wealthiest and most influential colonists on the mainland. Ultimately Jamaica was to surpass Barbados—and much of the mainland—as a source of wealth for London, but before 1700, it was Barbados, though twenty-five times smaller than Jamaica, which far surpassed it in sugar production, a major source of riches. Carolina as an extension of this small island, thus, gained in importance but did so while carrying fresh Caribbean memories of rebellious Africans more than willing to upset the status quo. Surely, news of African unrest in the Caribbean received a wide audience in Carolina.[61]

Certainly the racial ratios on the mainland were more forgiving—and less dangerous—for the settlers. Nonetheless, the colonists there discovered that what had beset them in the Caribbean—Negro insurrection and foreign invasion—had not been eluded by simple arrival on the mainland. The city that became Charleston, South Carolina, was the only real defensible port between Spanish Florida and the valuable real estate that Virginia had become—and with a chain being only as strong as its weakest link, subjugating the Palmetto province with the aid of disaffected Africans could jeopardize the entire colonial project on the mainland.[62]

By 1686, the Spanish from Florida had landed with a force of Africans and indigenes to launch a surprise attack on the Carolina settlers. This occurred fifty miles south of the population node that became Charleston; it was the typical warfare of the time—plunder, along with taking prisoners and murder, along with seizing about a dozen enslaved Africans.[63] Obviously incentivized, the Spaniards attacked again in 1687, with the usual multi-racial crew and the usual result: burning and pillaging.[64] A hurricane had compelled their retreat to their base in St. Augustine—known to house an encampment of the settlers' disturbing nightmare: armed Africans. The English pillaged St. Augustine in 1702, but in the long term that only served to further enrage Africans, who scattered, recovered, and lived to fight another day.[65]

Juan Marquez Cabrera, who was part of the earlier attacking forces, reported that the enslaved he encountered asked him if he had "some canoes in which to be able to flee with them and come to St. Augustine." It was not reassuring to Carolina settlers that Africans considered to be troublemakers in Havana were routinely dispatched to St. Augustine; apparently, Carolina Africans were taken by these Spanish plunderers to Havana and in turn were capable of returning to their "home" eager to settle scores. That Carolina was facing an ongoing conflict with the indigenous that created a flood of African refugees heading southward to Florida only served to underline the fragility of this extension of Barbados on the mainland.[66]

For in 1693, His Catholic Majesty offered a kind of freedom to any enslaved African who escaped from British soil—who would accept Christian conversion[67]—which increased instability in Carolina. In turn, the Carolina elite tended to favor the arrival of French Huguenots, rather than Catholics of any type. This influx of Europeans also contributed to the increased arrival of manacled Africans, given the herculean task at hand in this vast land and since some of these new settlers arrived from Hispaniola without their most valued property.[68] Moreover, the proximity of a competing colonial power on Carolina's border provided opportunity to flee—and not just for Africans. As early as 1674, John Radcliffe—a "yeoman servant"—sought to run to Florida with—as colonial elites put it—"two of his fellow servants along with him to the Spanish habitations, . . . there to conspire and procure the ruin of this hopeful settlement and all His Majesties subjects therein."[69]

As South Carolina developed a Negro majority early on, there was little incentive to impose quality control on the type of Europeans who arrived, which came to include criminals of various types and political dissidents with little disincentive to conspire against London. The "greatest desperadoes of the western world" landed there, according to one analyst, and that pirates were strung up at the entrance to the main port apparently did little to discourage their arrival. This frail reality was overlaid by antipathy toward the Spanish to the south—who returned the disfavor by an order of magnitude.[70] For the Spaniards were able to do what the Carolinians were reluctant to pursue—form a regiment of Africans (in some cases composed of those escaping to Florida), arming them, and then unleashing them on a colony where they had scores to settle.[71]

Yet boldly, perhaps foolishly, the Carolina elite continued to import enslaved Africans, their population increasing nearly sixfold between 1685 and 1700.[72] Moreover, Carolina's importance was underscored when it became the major point of entry for arriving Africans, who were then distributed throughout the mainland colonies. The estimate is that almost half of this group brought to the mainland from 1701 to 1775 were imported via Charleston, with a preference for Angolans—no strangers to warfare to this very day—and those with roots in today's Gambia and Senegal.[73]

Suggestive of the breadth and depth of the developing slave trade was that as early as the 1690s, mainland settlers and their suppliers had rounded the Cape and had begun kidnapping Africans from Madagascar for forced labor in English possessions.[74] That this was an unwise source of supply became clear when it emerged that those from Madagascar had become leaders of the Maroon wars.[75]

But the profits were simply too handsome to ignore: Slave-labor camps on the mainland stocked with workers from Madagascar were part of a profitable trade that deposited tobacco into some of the most elegant pipes in London.[76] Others from the east of Africa may also have made it across the Atlantic at this time, not least because the mainlanders early on proved themselves to be masters of smuggling, thereby defeating the keenest statistician.[77] The profits from the slave trade and the profits wrung from slave labor created an indecent circle of riches that fed upon itself, while infuriating Africans and making them even more susceptible to seditious appeals.

This was occurring even though there was constant nervousness about what legislators referred to as the designs of the Spaniards—and the French too.[78] Not only were Africans being referred to in English by the Spanish word for "black," some mainlanders had begun to view this seditious labor supply as being—almost inherently—agents of Catholicism, no small point as religious conflict raged.[79] Despite this fright, the colonists persisted in selling what were described as "rebellious" and "runaway" Africans to the "Spanish West Indies," which required "seasoned Negroes for mines"—though these disgruntled workers could just as soon return arms in hand and eager to inflict pain on their former captors.[80] This was also occurring as Europeans themselves had to worry about their own compatriots being swept into slave markets in northern Africa and further to the east of Europe—which, at least, was suggestive of what a terrible destiny and what a frightening counter-reaction enslavement could engender, if one's cards were not played properly.[81] Ultimately, it is estimated that thousands of individuals with roots in the sceptered isle alone suffered through this plight.[82]

Mainlanders may have understood this from firsthand experience when in 1654 the Dutch from New Amsterdam conquered Delaware and reputedly sold the defeated Swedes into slavery in Virginia.[83] The point was that when subsequently mainland settlers came to fear that London was plotting with Africans against them, there was reason to suspect that they were not simply hallucinating, for back then, numerous Europeans were suffering an even more horrible fate difficult to envision today.

Delaware was an emblem of the riotous instability on the mainland that could allow Africans and indigenes alike to seize advantage. For beginning in the mid-17th century until the beginning of the 18th, Europeans of various sorts were at each other's throats. The Dutch ousted the Swedes, who were in turn ousted by the English, just as in what is now New York, the English surged to power in 1664, then were ousted by the Dutch in 1673, before returning to power shortly thereafter. It was not easy for Africans to believe in the mystique of the power of "whiteness," as propounded by the English, when Londoners were being repeatedly ousted.[84] At the same time, the unstable and unsettled nature of colonialism provided more leverage and arbitrage opportunities for Africans.

Furthermore, because of the threat from the indigenous and European powers, the colonists were forced into the ultimate indignity—arming Africans, a textbook example of tempting fate.[85] The militia system in South Carolina, designed to repel invaders and the seditious alike, was probably more comprehensive in scope than that of any of the other original thirteen colonies, not least because of proximity to Spanish soil and the presence of a large African population. Naturally, it was modeled after that of Barbados, which faced similar challenges. A 1708 Carolina census revealed the presence of a population of 9,580, including 1,800 enslaved African men, 1,100 enslaved African women, and 1,200 enslaved African children. Of this population, only 950 white men were available for military duty, a laughably small number given the threats faced, as the greater majority of the Europeans consisted of women and children deemed hardly suitable for martial duty.[86]

Carolina was the firewall that protected Virginia—the mainland's trophy colony—from Spanish depredations. This protection facilitated the rise of such grandees as William Byrd, who over a span of thirty years in the late 17th century amassed almost thirty thousand acres of land; by the 1680s, per the mainland pattern, he had switched almost wholly to the exploitation of enslaved Africans (as opposed to European servants).[87] Naturally, this trend produced unease, with cries about the growing presence of Africans emerging as early as 1677.[88] This was understandable since plots by servants had become prevalent by the early 1660s.

The famed "Bacon's Rebellion" has been described as a civil war as much as an insurrection spearheaded by servants—there were about two thousand slaves and six thousand servants in the colony's forty-thousand-strong population, as tabulated: the indigenous population also has to be accounted for when assessing the balance of class and racial forces. The growth in the population of enslaved Africans—their numbers reputedly tripled between 1680 and 1690—happened to occur as the more encompassing category of "whiteness" ascended[89] and, perhaps, as a result of this abortive revolt. This rebellion—according to a recent study—illustrates the illiberality of the settlers, making it difficult to swallow wholly the progressiveness of their revolt against London a scant century later: for, it is reported, driving this rebellion was a settler desire to enforce a quicker extermination of the indigenous, which was thought to be resisted by London's delegates. After this revolt, religion and "race"—which pointedly excluded Africans—helped to bond the colonial elite and European servants.[90]

The discernible trend on the mainland in the late 17th century was the growth and importance of the enslaved African population as the economy grew, particularly vis-à-vis the population of European servants. At a time when there were servants of European descent, indigenous and African slaves, and free Africans, the latter could belong to the militia and were expected to arm (though masters were not required to provide arms for slaves after 1640 but presumably could do so if they wished). Even Nathaniel Bacon, whose revolt took aim at the indigenous, enrolled in his ranks European servants and enslaved Africans:[91] this was also suggestive of the reality that a flood of Africans, with a resultant fear of their presence, had yet to descend on the colony. By one estimate, there were five hundred Africans in Virginia in 1645 and two thousand in 1660.[92]

This situation was to change dramatically in coming years, which did not tend to reduce the danger of exploiting slaves. The continuing arrival of embittered Africans had predictable consequences. By June 1680, there was legislation for "preventing Negroes' insurrection."[93] That this bill had little evident effect on subsequent events did not seem to deter the authorities.[94]

Reliance on the labor of enslaved Africans brought real danger, a reality that emerged when in 1687 a conspiracy of the enslaved was uncovered in the Northern Neck region of Virginia, with the aim including—according to an official report—"destroying and killing"; the "Negro Conspirators" were "in custody," but it was not self-evident that this, as was suggested, would "deter other Negroes from plotting,"[95] particularly since the "design" of the plotters was "carrying it through the whole colony of Virginia."[96] That this was taken seriously was implied when in 1688 the authorities discussed a "stricter law to be made for prevent[ing] Insurrections of Negroes," which was supplemented in 1693.[97]

Thus, by 1691, there were rampant complaints about "problems of runaways committing depredations," and the conclusion emerged that "such Negroes, mulattoes or slaves resisting, running away, or refusing to surrender may be killed and destroyed," with "compensation to master for slave killed" as a powerful incentive. (A European "bond or free intermarrying with a Negro, mulatto or Indian" was to be "banished forever," thus hastening the consolidation of "whiteness.")[98]

However, by 1700, there were an estimated twenty thousand Africans in Virginia, and according to T.H. Breen, as a direct result, "whites had achieved a sense of race solidarity at the expense of blacks," a landmark in the evolution of mainland colonies.[99] This pan-European bonding came with a steep price. By 1710, the Byrd family was facing a report of a conspiracy of the enslaved to rise against their captors. "We directed the Negroes to be arraigned for high treason," it was said, though a mere legal arrangement could not reduce the unsteadiness delivered by bonded labor.[100]

* * *

In spite of the dangers in the mainland colonies, it did appear at first glance that a master stroke had been executed by colonists by escaping from the Caribbean to the mainland. Assuredly, the racial ratios were more appealing than those of, for example, Barbados and

Jamaica—though the problem for the settlers was that a continent required many more enslaved Africans than an island, thus multiplying the danger for London. For as Carolina and Virginia suggested, escaping the wrath of rebellious Africans and their allies would require more than a simple boat ride northward.

Yet, with all the problems provided by the mainland, it seemed a tonic compared to small islands seemingly more subject to internal subversion and external attack. This may have occurred to the governor of Antigua in 1709 when he was the target of a murderous attack led by an angry African. "Sandy," the African, was accused of acting on behalf of the executive's opponents, yet another example of the opportunities for arbitrage created by enslavement. This assassination attempt came on the heels of a murder of a slaveholder a few years earlier when he refused his enslaved labor force a Christmas holiday: it was "dreadful," said one analysis, as they "actually hacked him to death."[101] His Excellency, however, escaped with mere "fractured bones" and a shriveled arm that had lost mobility and, it was said, a "great deal of torture" after a "large musket ball" hit his exposed limb. The assailant, London was told, was a "very noted fellow" who was "very remarkable for his courage" and his skill as a "good marksman," "being a native of the place and employed to shoot wild pigeons." An evil parson was blamed for this mess, but the colonizers and London too came to recognize that the difficult geography and demography of small islands had to be obviated in the long run.[102]

Unlike the mainland, small islands such as Antigua provided little room for an orderly retreat by terrorized settlers. Evacuating to the mainland would also mean a need for a larger encampment of slave labor to subdue a vast continent. Plus, another demerit for the Caribbean—from London's viewpoint—was that it was easier for the enslaved to flee a small island (albeit via swimming and/or a hijacked vessel) than a sprawling continent, and war between and among the powers only lubricated this path, a policy encouraged by competitors.[103] That the enslaved would do so at crop time wounded the colonizer more deeply.[104] Serendipitously—for the settlers—the erosion in influence of the Royal African Company meant "free trade in Africans," facilitating the spectacular growth of the enslaved population. But this jolt of adrenalin to the mainland economy also delivered terror in the form of rebellious Africans.

2

Free Trade in Africans?

Did the Glorious Revolution Unleash the Slave Trade?

The "Glorious Revolution" of 1688 was not so glorious for Africa and the Africans. The year 1688 was also a setback for Catholic rule in London, though the Bill of Rights that emerged makes understandable why this conflict has been seen widely as a step forward generally for Europeans. As for Africans, there is little need to hedge about its deadliness (though the blow absorbed by Catholics suggested that London would have to rely more heavily on armed Africans). The compelled retreat of monarchy and the strengthening of the rising class of merchants—already buoyed by the wealth generated in slave-labor encampments in the Caribbean and North America—led to a weakening of the monopoly of the Royal African Company, backed by the Crown and chartered in an earlier iteration in 1660. This weakening meant the entrance into the frenziedly lucrative business of slave trading by "separate" or "private" traders: that is, freelance merchants, ugly traffickers in humans. In a rudely choreographed pas de deux, as the monarchy took a step back in control of the slave trade, the merchants took a step forward. This deregulation of the trade in human flesh fomented a kind of "free trade" in Africans. This aided immeasurably in providing the forced labor needed to "develop" the mainland, which in turn brought this local elite into increasing conflict with London, particularly when it sought to trade with neighbors who happened to be foes of the Crown—for example, the French in Hispaniola. This strain eventually burst the garment of colonial rule, leading to 1776. Yet this increase in the slave trade also delivered deadly perils in the form of enraged Africans who could reverse the theretofore delightful fortunes of colonizers and murder them all or—as mainland settlers came to fear—ally with a European power, then murder them all.

Though this acceleration of the slave trade propelled the productive forces of nascent capitalism, "free trade" in the most unfree of commerce was a cataclysm for Africa and Africans, as kidnappings of free Negroes, the degrading of their status generally, and the like became more common, notably after the monopoly was eroded in the 1690s. Accounts of shipboard insurrections also became more common in colonial and English newspapers, which did raise doubts about the entire American enterprise, adding to the momentum of abolitionism that culminated in June 1772—which in turn unsettled the mainland, contributing to the Unilateral Declaration of Independence.

Colonial planters desired a steady supply of Africans at moderate prices, and, it was felt, the RAC was inadequate to the task, which complicated relations between London and the provinces.[1] The RAC hardly coddled African captives, but the routine maltreatment of this unit of labor may have seemed that way after a wave of gluttonous merchants entered this dirty business.[2]

Thus, the flood of Africans across the Atlantic provided the European elite in Virginia with the possibility of downplaying European labor—servants—who, as the Caribbean suggested, could more easily ally with foreign powers. When 1688 eroded the RAC monopoly in the context of a Protestant victory over Catholics in London, both epochal trends made it easier to rely more on enslaved Africans and less on often cruel exploitation of Irish and Scottish servants. Besides, after 1688, London theorists were more inclined to see the poor as a necessary resource for ensuring the prosperity of the metropolis itself, notably as a reservoir of labor that should not be squandered in colonial projects. These developments coincided with the push for the Act of Union culminating in 1707, bringing Scotland more firmly under London's hegemony, which meant that—at least technically—Glasgow was on equal footing with the rising slave-trading cities of Bristol and Liverpool: that is, increased use of forced African labor allowed for a kind of (white) racial unity in the colonies and (ethnic) unity at home.[3]

An auspicious moment for Africa and Africans arrived when Parliament mandated that on 24 June 1698 and continuing in force at least until 24 June 1712 the trade in Africans would be open "to all His Majesty's subjects"—this latter date being about sixty years to the day before the arrival of Somerset's case. This augured the further influx of "private" or "separate" traders into this unscrupulous business. By 1730, it was acknowledged by one informed source that the price of Africans had risen—but that only served to benefit merchants and their economic interests, which tended to be more diverse and entrepreneurial than that of planters. Indeed, the increased supply tended to drive up demand, as more and more need could be easily found for more and more Africans, creating a vicious circle.

The influx of these businessmen into the slave trade brought roiling complications. There was the potent point of maintaining forts in Africa, so necessary for the subduing and holding of those who were to be enslaved, and who would subsidize same—with private traders arguing for the most part that the Exchequer should bear the cost. Why? Said one propagandist, "the value of lands in Britain" itself depended on colonial products, and thus "there is not a man in this Kingdom from the highest to the lowest who does not more or less partake of the Benefits and advantages of the Royal African Company's forts and castles in Africa"—thus, there was good reason to demand that "the Publick," that is, "the whole body of the People of this Realm," pick up the tab.[4] Unfortunately for Africans, this logic tended to implicate the entire realm of His Majesty in their subjugation.

The "reforms" of the slave trade following mid-1698 marked a great leap in the number of Africans enslaved, which contributed mightily to the development of the colonial economy, while it was a world historic defeat for Africa and Africans. The battle between the "private" or "separate" traders on the one hand and the RAC on the other was to stretch throughout the next decades following 1698—but the trend line was clear early on: the ascending merchants would prevail. Jamaica and the Chesapeake colonies were prime beneficiaries when the RAC monopoly eroded, which was appropriate since merchants and planters there had been persistent and energetic opponents of the RAC.[5] Thus, in 1690, Africans and their progeny were 7% of the population on the mainland, but, emphasizes historian Robin Einhorn, "from 1750 to 1780 they were *forty* percent of the population." In South Carolina, says this scholar, "from 1720 through the Revolution, slaves were over 60 percent of the population."[6] The reluctance of Africans to be subdued mandated an increase in the settler population, which meant ushering previously disfavored Europeans into the warm embrace of "whiteness," and these migrants were enticed by heady dreams of prosperity driven by a slave society and a complement of rights—doled out via apartheid.

In 1686, when the RAC monopoly came closest to being enforceable, slavers from the isles embarked upon thirty-nine voyages. By 1729, as "free trade" in Africans ascended, there were eighty-one voyages. During this era, the company's market share of the legal trade fell from 100% to 4%, as the hoggish titans of mainland colonies in particular benefited handsomely.[7]

Of course, the path to "reform" was not smooth, with "private" traders repeatedly risking punishment by violating the RAC monopoly even before the late 1690s.[8] As early as 1689, there were loud and public complaints about the administration of the slave trade—to the disadvantage of planters and merchants. "One of the great burdens of our lives," said one, "is . . . going to buy Negroes. But we must have them; we cannot be without them and the best men" were involved in this process, and they were losing out to "the Dutch, French, Danes, Swedes and others," and the "English planters in America" were the big losers (not "the People of Africa," he added pointedly). What about the fortifications in Africa subsidized by the RAC? If a head tax were to be imposed on each captive African, "the plantations would have cheerfully submitted," eliminating that subsidy problem. Instead the RAC and its minions were treating these traders as "downright . . . Enemies," dragging them "into the Admiralty Courts," which was quite burdensome. "Of all the things" needed for development and profit, it was proclaimed, "Negroes are the most necessary and the most valuable. And therefore to have them under a Company, and under a Monopoly, whereby their prices are more than doubled, nay almost trebled, cannot but be most grievous" to the planters.[9]

Meanwhile, back in Jamaica—despite the real fear of slave uprisings—discontent rose among planters in mid-1683 at the perceived dearth of Africans.[10] Demanded were combat ships to be dispatched to Africa in order to facilitate the slave trade: such a proposal veritably guaranteed London would come into conflict with Africans, European competitors, and pirates alike.[11] Sighs of relief may have been emitted when in April 1684 a ship filled to the brim with 216 Africans arrived from Gambia.[12]

As so often happens, the "reform" only ratified what was already occurring, with "private traders"—particularly from Newport, Rhode Island, the developing epicenter of the slave trade—repeatedly violating the RAC monopoly in the prelude to 1698.[13] The RAC fought back, blaming its competition for disrupting the market for this strategically important commodity, but the tides of history did not accommodate the company's sentiment.[14] Meticulously, colonial officials kept records on numbers and prices of Africans to the colonies by the RAC and private traders, respectively, suggesting the monopoly was unraveling even as it was challenged.[15]

The merchants proved themselves to be skilled in-fighters, producing a steady stream of literature assailing the RAC and its "absurdities" and "abuses" and its monopoly, which meant "imposing what prices they please"; untold wealth was promised by these merchants, if only they and their animal spirits were unleashed on Africa, igniting the magic of the marketplace: "if the planters were furnished with Negroes from Africa, answerable to their industry, [then] four times the sugar, indigo, cottons" would be "imported every year," it was said boastfully in 1690. "Let every Rational Man judge," it was averred with a sniff, "if this would not be infinitely more advantageous to the Kingdom in general." Plus there were larger strategic concerns in the ongoing religious war, since many of the Africans were Muslims and the French had "their Priests" in Africa too— yet, said William Wilkinson, in "the space of twelve or fourteen years" on this besieged continent, "I never saw an English Minister there," and was not the RAC to blame for this nonfeasance? "Undoubtedly the Royal African Company cannot be ignorant of this defect," he charged hotly. "What opportunities and advantages they give the French and other nations, to our own ruin," was incalculable. Playing the religious card, private traders asserted vigorously that the established faith in London was losing ground in Africa, not only to the Catholics but also to Islam.[16]

Other analysts argued that the slave trade was of such magnitude and importance, requiring as it did "force and forts on the land" on another continent, that "joint stocks" corporations were mandated. There was a need for "constant coercive power" to enforce this business, which required more revenue too.[17] Surely, the state was involved in this new departure, but as capitalism was taking off, what was striking was how the rising merchant class so often complained that the state—or at least the RAC monopoly—was a hindrance, while hypocritically this class relied on the coercive power of official London for protection. To the extent that one of the most significant fruits of 1688 was a quantum leap in the slave trade, it can be affirmed that the "Glorious Revolution" was

a necessary precursor and instigator of 1776, the first stage of a transformation of the productive forces of the Anglo-American economy.
One of the sorely neglected and cruel ironies of what has come to be
called modernity was that its rudiments—capitalism and early republicanism—were simultaneously a catastrophic fiasco for Africa and
Africans.[18]

Planters as a class were not wholly supportive of "free trade" in
Africans, arguing that it benefited merchants or "Negro traders"—not
themselves. From Barbados in 1709 came an appeal from seventy-five
of this group, complaining of the "late high prices" of Africans, which
"has risen from no other cause but the liberty given to Separate Traders, which unless remedied in time is like[ly] to prove fatal, not only
to us but to the British Trade upon the [African] Coast." They claimed
to hold "at least two thirds of all the land and Negroes" in Barbados;
a competing petition from "Separate Traders" was signed, they huffed,
"mostly by a number of mean, inferior persons." In the good old days
when RAC had less competition—"before the Revolution"—it bought
Africans at three pounds and could even resell them at sixteen, but
since 1697, when "the Interlopers" arrived, the price has "arisen gradually to such a height" that now they were being bought for eight to ten
pounds and resold at near sixty—which was crippling their business, as
it was enriching a class that could quickly become their betters.[19]

A number of colonial planters thought that diluting the RAC monopoly simultaneously debilitated the Crown and enhanced the strength of
rivals in Madrid and Paris most notably. "Interlopers" was the favorite
epithet they used for the private traders, as pro-RAC petitions railed at
the alleged strengthening of "French, Dutch, Danes, Portuguese" and
weakening of the Crown through their "unrestrain'd Liberty" that had
soared "for some years after the Revolution."[20] In 1710, petitioners from
Barbados backed the RAC, arguing that it did deliver cheap Africans,
but now the price was rising, "occasioned by different interests of the
Company and separate traders," facilitating the "natives of the [Afri-
can] coast taking an advantage," as they "raised the price."[21] Sir William
Dains and Bristol merchants begged to differ with their contrasting
petitions.[22]

A group in London agreed with this critique from Barbados, however, arguing that these private traders were also unpatriotic, willing to

cooperate with the foes of their homeland in pursuit of naked profit. Besides, deregulation of the trade had introduced chaos in West Africa, which also allowed African leaders to manipulate one European against another and the Dutch to manipulate them all. These European neighbors "have tried all the ways they could think of to render the people of [England] contemptible in the eyes of the [Africans]," with untold downstream consequences. The implication was that New York, still retaining a substantial population of Dutch descent and a growing center of the slave trade, was collaborating handsomely against London. Prices of Africans had risen, not fallen, meaning the prices of commodities produced—for example, sugar, cotton, and indigo—were rising too. Private traders were arguing otherwise, but they were forging figures, it was said: "liars ought to have good memories," they reminded, an eternal bit of sage advice frequently ignored.[23]

Suggestive of the immense stakes at play was the fact that even as the mid-18th century approached, arguments about events in the slave trade from many decades earlier were still erupting. One Londoner in 1744 recalled the attempt in 1660 by the Dutch "to gain the *entire possession* of the most valuable parts of the coast of *Africa* and to EXCLUDE *Great Britain* from any share . . . as they have done in *Spice Trade*," centered in what is now Indonesia and the Malay peninsula: this "brought on themselves a War with this Kingdom in 1664," thus illustrating neatly how the lust for foreign plunder, notably in Africa and Asia, brought war to Europe in a pattern that hardly had abated in the 20th century, notably in 1914 (emphasis original).[24]

The road from 1672 to the 1698 "reforms" was rocky. The RAC had been given an unrealistically optimistic term of one thousand years—not unlike the Reich it anticipated—suggestive of the ambition of this business and how uncooperative Africans disrupted ambitious plans. The RAC also immediately encountered strong headwinds in West Africa from the French and the Dutch and the Portuguese particularly, who had dreams of enrichment all their own. This turmoil and the resultant difficulty of the RAC in providing the shackled labor force that planters needed added to the pressure that led to "free trade" in Africans. But this did not end the debate in London over who was to pay for African fortifications, needed to fend off what was equally destabilizing in the colonies: African insurrection and foreign intervention.[25]

"Separate" or "private" traders were not up to the task, it was asserted forcefully, particularly by planters.[26]

Erupting in the streets and coffeehouses of London from the late 17th to the mid-18th centuries was a spirited debate which encompassed the future of Africa and the Americas. An irked commentator charged accusingly that "separate traders" brought as many Africans in a three-year period to Jamaica, Barbados, and Antigua as the RAC brought in many years to "all the colonies in America during the time" when the RAC's monopoly seemed firmer. Thanks to these traders, Maryland brought more "income into Her Majesty's Exchequer," not to mention the wealth generated by Virginia, "so precious a Jewel in the British Crown." It was unfair to allot such power to the RAC when it could not deliver the goods, leading to Negro shortages, price fluctuations, and advantage to European competitors, it was claimed. Reliance on the RAC and its "mismanagement" had almost led to the collapse of the entire colonial project.[27] RAC defenders claimed contrarily that it was actually the private traders whose entry into the market had been disruptive, accelerating inflation—triple in some cases, not least in Cabinda, theretofore a happy hunting ground for Africans—and forcing enhanced vigilance from European competitors, fomenting tensions: in 1723, the Portuguese in Angola had destroyed a RAC settlement in Cabinda.[28]

A key argument for expanding the trade in Africans was that if London did not pursue this bestial path, it would fall behind other European powers. These included not only the usual suspects—the French, the Spaniards, the Dutch, the Portuguese, et al.—but also the Turks, who too were producing sugar, a prime British commodity. There was also concern about the Africans seeking to keep all Europeans "under their command" via arbitrage and manipulation, propelling an impetus toward pan-European concord or "whiteness" as a binding and corrective measure. Unless stern measures were taken, said one Londoner in 1714, say "Adieu, not only to the African but to the plantation trade."[29] London was deluged with petitions in the late 17th century demanding a widening of the slave trade, particularly from planters hailing from Barbados and merchants on the mainland.[30] While this debate was roiling in London, there was a continuing conflict with France, Spain, and the Dutch—not to mention Scotland—or as one analyst put it, "Papists" and "Jacobites" and run-of-the-mill antagonists—that was increasing the developing idea that London could not compete effectively absent a robust trade in Africans.[31]

In a sense, the rising merchant class had the best of this argument, one of the many reasons they prevailed in the end. But their critics countered that dragooning more Africans came with a price—a moral argument increasingly was being made concerning the degradation of the African—but, as well, it was a danger to increase the number of Africans in the Caribbean, as history exemplified. It is possible to view the proliferating moral argument against slavery as a reflection of the reality that increased enslavement brought real danger to colonists and colonialism. It was easier for moralizing to occur when subduing Africans seemed to be encountering violent difficulty.

The explicit agenda of an unnamed Jamaican merchant in 1708 was animated by similar concerns: he complained of the "cruelty" targeting the "poor wretches, the Negroes," who were "really treated worse than brutes" via "an insupportable tyranny and oppression." His words contributed to a growing apprehension about the indomitable problem presented by mass enslavement. He lamented that the enslaved did "help to make [Jamaica merchants] some of the happiest people in the world," while the merchants did "in return make them [the enslaved] the most unhappy, the most wretched and miserable part of the Creation." He was so bold as to append remarks by an enslaved African who decried the "haughty cruel men" who "commit the blackest crimes without a blush."[32] What may have been weighing on this Jamaican merchant's moralizing mind was the tempest erupting on his island that same year, 1708, when on the twenty-ninth of July a plantation in the mountains was the scene of massive slave revolt that took some effort to repress.[33]

By 1712, the governor of Jamaica was seemingly furrowing his brow, wringing his hands, and gnashing his teeth about the racial ratios, which spelled danger, particularly given "how very small a force at best" was at his disposal to repress revolts on "so large and plentiful an island"; this, along with "a foreign enemy," the comprehensible "apprehensions" of the planter class—which they "could not conceal . . . from their Negroes"—and the obvious "insolence" of the Africans, which was "very great," was a blueprint for a debacle. He demanded from London "an addition of white people amongst us"—with this important category going undefined, quite typically, allowing for the arrival of more problems in the form of dissident Irish and Scots or disguised French Catholics—"or otherwise this island may be liable to some very unlucky disaster by an insurrection."[34]

"For the Negroes on the island" of Jamaica "being 80,000," it was said in 1714, and the "white people not above 2000," the former "may at any time rise and destroy the white people"; besides, Jamaica had a "formidable neighbour," referring to the "French on Hispaniola," which increased the peril, as the internal and external antagonists could combine. This meant "additional subsistence" to soldiers in the region "over and above their pay," increasing the cost to the Exchequer, which was bound to grow, since "the Negroes had lately cut in pieces two white men,"[35] a premonition of worse to come. One possible remedy was enunciated in 1709 when the British authorities in the Caribbean pledged to free Africans who fought against the Spanish and French— but was constructing a system that provided an incentive for fighting for freedom the proper way to inspire the oppressed?

A problem for these critics was that the Utrecht Treaty of 1713,[36] inter alia, allowed suppliers from the sceptered isles to supply Spanish colonies with Africans, thus opening the door further for the rising merchants— but this too led to further squabbling with Madrid over numbers, duties, smuggling, raw conflict, and the like, meaning more conflict and war and, inexorably, more attacks on Carolina.[37] Utrecht was a defeat for Madrid, which also ceded strategic Gibraltar to London, providing little incentive for Spain to cease arming Africans to attack fragile British mainland colonies; it also led to a defeat for the important region surrounding Barcelona—cynically betrayed by a London that had pledged assistance for separatism claims: both betrayal and defeat opened the door wider for Spain's and Britain's reliance on armed Africans, with huge consequences for colonialism. Yet by involving British merchants so heavily in Spanish-controlled territory, Utrecht signaled that RAC supporters had good reason to fret that the rise of "private" or "separate" traders meant a victory for the latter's apparent cavalier attitude toward national sovereignty. Clarence Munford argues that it was Utrecht and the Asiento, or the concord on the slave trade—more so than "reforms" of the slave trade in London in the late 17th century—that was the turning point for capitalism, since, he says, "at that juncture, capitalist relations of production predominated *only* [sic] in the Netherlands and perhaps in England after 1689."[38]

Whatever the case, the waves of history seemed to be moving in favor of the rising merchants and the capitalism that propelled them.

To be fair, squabbling over the rich bounty that was the enslaved predated 1713, with raids and invasions by foreign powers often serving as a cover for slave poaching.[39] In the late 17th century, opportunistic New York City merchants such as Frederick Philipse, Thomas Marston, Robert Glover, and John Johnson profited greedily from the piratical poaching in slaves during King William's War when the threat of naval attack prevented laborers from England and Europe from crossing the Atlantic in adequate numbers and the attendant labor shortage in the colony and throughout North America caused a rise in the price of enslaved Africans.[40] Still, as London got more deeply enmeshed in the slave trade to Spanish territories, older strains of bigotry flourished, as the Jewish population in Jamaica—somehow—was accused of pro-Madrid sentiments, given their Iberian origins, and attempts were made to tax them heavily.[41]

Londoners could look at the Spanish Empire and glimpse a reflection of what could befall their domain. In 1701, one Englishman recounted how scores of years earlier the notorious Sir Francis Drake encountered in Panama the local version of the then marauding Maroons of Jamaica: the "Symerons," or Cimmarones, a "black People who about eighty years past fled from the cruelty of their masters, the Spaniards; and grew since into a nation under two Kings of their own"—they "extremely hated the Spanish," which made them a mirror image of the Maroons and their relation to London. Bringing more Africans to the hemisphere could bring more allies for London, particularly if deposited on Spanish territory, but could bring more enemies too, making this commerce exceedingly problematic.[42] Such was the dilemma of the colonizer: the escalation of the slave trade in the wake of 1698 and 1713 brought head-spinning profits—and mortal danger alike.

So the issue was joined: on one side, a flowering movement critical of mass enslavement, not least because of the danger presented to settlers in islands such as Jamaica, Barbados, and Antigua and, on the other side, those who were seized with the notion of the Brobdingnagian profits to be accrued and the herculean task of taming a continent that, it was thought, could only occur with mass enslavement of Africans. But even this stark contrast does not capture the tensions within the pro-slavery bloc, for example, that between planters fearing the rising strength of merchants who controlled the main source of capital: Africans. And even some of those thought to be ardently pro-slavery were having second and third thoughts—particularly those smaller planters and merchants in the Caribbean itself, who had a firsthand view of the peril presented by skewed racial ratios, a perception that led inevitably to a compromise: accelerating the slave trade but depositing more Africans on the mainland, where racial ratios were more forgiving. By the spring of 1701, Africans were selling better in Virginia than in Jamaica.[43] As early as 1762, it is estimated that most of the enslaved in Virginia came to the colony directly from Africa and were never "seasoned" in the Caribbean, which itself was a mixed blessing since if they had come from the latter, they might have learned the basics of revolt in training schools in Jamaica, Barbados, and Antigua, and if they had come from Africa, they may not have been "acculturated" into not revolting.[44] But it was also in 1701 that the Virginia authorities pointed to their vaster territory, necessitating more Africans, as a possible liability, given the "large open frontier" they had to "defend by sea and land & the eminent dangers of an impending war and scarcity of freemen . . . and ye remoteness of [their] plantations one from another, together with the fears of an insurrection from [their] servants and slaves . . . in case of an invasion to join ye enemy."[45]

The flux brought by more Africans sheds light on what was revealed in Virginia on the first day of spring in 1709 when "happily discovered" was a "dangerous conspiracy formed and carryed on by great numbers of Negros and other slaves . . . for the destroying" of settlers.[46] Anxiety rose when officials "received intelligence of several illegal, unusual and unwarrantable concourses, meeting & assemblings [of] Negro, Mulatto & Indian slaves at quarters where there are no white or freemen overseers and more particularly" apparent plotting of a "Notorious Insurrection."[47] Then "happily discovered" was yet another "dangerous conspiracy formed and carried on by great numbers of Negros and other slaves for making their escape by force," while "destroying" Europeans in the process.[48] A few months later the Africans were "going away with arms" and the militia had to be roused to "pursue them."[49] A few months after that, the authorities there were debating laws "for preventing the insurrection of Negroes."[50]

Shortly thereafter, a top Virginia leader was opining that the "fear of enemys by sea (except pirates)" had been reduced, but "the insurrection of our own Negroes and invasions of the Indians are no less to be dreaded."[51] Nonetheless, Lieutenant Governor Alexander Spotswood thought in December 1710 that an "intended insurrection of the Negroes" might be in store, necessitating the need to "prevent the meetings and consultations" of this terribly disgruntled force.[52]

By 1711, officials were continuing to debate—and stressing—"*better securing . . . Governm[ent] and Her Majesty's subjects of this Colony [against] attempts of Negro and other slaves*" to revolt.[53] In the midst of this turmoil, the decision was taken to try "Salvadore an Indian and Scipio a Negro slave" for "High Treason," leading to a "sentence of death" on the premise that "their execution and exemplary punishment may have a due effect for deterring other slaves"—though this proved to be faulty reasoning. Still, the head of the African—along with "one of his quarters"—along with other selected body parts were placed conspicuously "in the most publick place."[54] Undeterred was the "Negro Will," who, a few months later, was accused of "levying war in this colony."[55]

Frantic officials in Virginia sought to "prevent Negro slaves assembling together" and targeted "a Negro slave notoriously active in stirring up Negroes in Surrey County to levy war against H.M. government."[56] It was there that the Council of Trade and Plantations was told that an "intended insurrection of the Negroes" was exposed, to have been executed on "Easter Day"—with the perpetrators executed in turn.[57]

The tug of war between the RAC and the private traders—with the latter emerging triumphant—did bring the long-awaited slaves to colonial plantations, but part of the package was a surge of instability brought by the arrival of more infuriated Africans. The instability was magnified by continually disturbing reports coming from the Caribbean and Panama about various fugitives and Maroons who had attained a degree of freedom and, it was feared, had murderous designs on settlers.[58] That the Africans being brought to provinces such as South Carolina often came from hot spots such as Jamaica and Barbados did little to erode nervousness.[59] Spotswood argued that the small farmer opposed bringing in so many Africans but powerful merchants and some planters—quite typically—steamrolled their sentiments.[60]

Undeniable was the point that despite the instability brought by an influx of Africans after the rise of "free trade" in their bodies, importers of this commodity railed at the notion of higher taxes, so as to curb their arrival and pay for the added costs of their presence. There was "violent opposition" to this, it was said, particularly by the "merchants in England" and even by the RAC, as their putative mutual enmity was exposed as overstated. This opposition occurred even though the final cost would be shifted to the planter, but, it was felt, this tax would reduce the overall shipments, thus harming sellers in whatever guise. And this would harm the colony, given the need for slave labor for what was described boldly as "rapid expansion westward": unsurprisingly, merchants triumphed once more,[61] not least since more land meant not only more slaves to sell but an attractive enticement to dangle before potential settlers, who were so necessary to overwhelm these same Africans and indigenes. Land grants, along with a complement of rights celebrated later as an emblem of the Enlightenment, were akin to offering a material incentive—"combat pay"—to a soldier about to enter a war zone, which is what a good deal of the settlements were at that juncture and for a considerable time thereafter.

Also difficult to refute was the suspicious timing of the waves of unrest in Virginia, coming as they did on the heels of the uncertainty leading up to the Act of Union bringing Scotland more firmly under London's dominion in 1707 and the wars and conflicts that led to the Treaty of Utrecht in 1713. It would have been difficult for Africans to pick a better opportunity to unnerve the settlers.[62] There was a dizzying array of alliances between and among European powers in the first few decades of the 18th century—not to mention betrayals of the most cynical type—all of which left settlers exposed and jumpily unsteady, not the strongest negotiating position for them in the face of militant indigenes and Africans.[63]

London kept a careful eye on the unavoidable fact that Jamaica, in some ways the jewel in the Caribbean crown, was increasingly producing great wealth and was "surrounded by Spanish and French settlements" which sat uneasily beside an island with a "great number of rebellious Negroes in the mountains who frequently do a great deal of mischief." These Maroons were accompanied by "apprehension of an insurrection of their own [settlers'] Negroes, being about 40,000 in number and very insolent and not 3000 whites able to bear arms in the militia."[64]

But it was not as if Jamaica was the only problem in the region. In St. Christopher's, it was felt that the leadership in neighboring Guadeloupe was "so weak that the Negroes tended to take advantage of it to plunder the whole colony"—a situation discovered at the last second, leading to "nearly 40 of the leaders punished by wheel and fire." Naturally, in St. Christopher's there was a desire to "profit by this occasion," up to and including "conquest of this island [i.e., Guadeloupe]," the kind of opportunism that symbolized the arbitrage opportunities open to Africans willing to manipulate one set of colonizers against another.[65]

Given the demonstrated instability in the Caribbean, a wise would-be planter would have set up stakes on the mainland—despite the fact that wealth seemed to flow more readily from the Caribbean isles. Thus, in Maryland, the enslaved population grew at an extraordinary rate between 1658 and 1710; in four key counties, there were about 100 slaves at the beginning of this era, perhaps 3% of the total population; by 1710, there were over 3,500 slaves there, constituting 24% of the total population—and from 1695 to 1708 alone, at least 4,022 slaves arrived in the province.[66]

In neighboring Pennsylvania, European servants were providing problems quite typically, with William Penn himself griping in 1683 about "complaints" that this group was so audacious as to "sell & dispose of the goods & moneys of their masters," a "great loss" facilitated by a phenotype advantage that Africans did not share.[67] Africans presented their own special problems too, as in 1705 in what was to become the Keystone State, it was observed that "difficulties have arisen . . . about the manner and trial of Negroes committing murther, manslaughter, buggery, burglary, rapes, attempts of rapes and other high and heinous . . . capital offenses."[68]

New York, which early on had become a center of slaving, also had developed searing attendant issues. In 1699, there were moans about "preventing abuses daily committed by Negro slaves and Indians." By 1700, there was legislation against such "abuses"—though agonizing quickly emerged about this bill and the alleged "greater liberty to Negroes" it provided, more so "than the law of England" gave to "English men," which thus "would encourage them in stealing and committing robberies and other villanies."[69] In 1702, the authorities carped that the number of slaves in the cities of "New York & Albany also in other towns within this province doth daily increased and they have been found often times guilty of confederating together" for various "ill practices," among which were seeking "to kill or destroy their master" or "burning of houses or barns or barracks or corn" or killing cattle. It was deemed illegal for three or more to confer—as opposed to five in Virginia, giving an idea of the fright at the risk: a "Common Whipper" was designated to address violators. It was a crime for a slave to assault any "free man or woman professing Christianity." The enslaved were also barred from fleeing to Quebec—which was "of great concern during this time of war with the French," for of late Africans had done precisely that, apparently carrying "Intelligence" with them, which was "of very pernicious consequence." By the early 1700s, a law was passed "for preventing the conspiracy of slaves," with the death penalty assigned to those who did so—with their masters reimbursed.[70] By 1703, the authorities felt compelled to debate "an act to prevent disorders in the night," with an informative predicate: "whereas great disorders, insolences and burglaries are at times raised and committed in the nighttime by Indians, Negro and Mulatto servants and slaves to the disquiet and hurt of Her Majesty's good subjects."[71]

*   *   *

As the foregoing suggests, France in Canada presented a challenge to New York and the region sprawling northward, just as Spain challenged South Carolina. In Albany in 1687, officials expressed "apprehensions of the French," a problem magnified since "there are so few of His Majesty's natural born subjects, the greater part being Dutch."[72] Two years later, in what was to become the Empire State, "in the midst of all these troubles," there was another difficulty: "we are daily alarmed with rumour of War with France."[73] Per usual, there was confluence of the foreign and domestic threats: by the late 17th century in Massachusetts, there was fear that enslaved Africans were little more than "Catholic agents," as apprehension rose that this seditious labor force would join an invasion force and wreak havoc on New England and would "distroy all the English and save none but only the Negro and Indian Servants."[74]

In the early 18th century, when war between Paris and London erupted yet again, the enslaved that reached Quebec were deemed to be free. Apart from the incentive this provided for the enslaved to flee, it affixed in the mind of the African for decades to come the idea of Canada as Canaan, the site of refuge for those fleeing the Union Jack, then the Stars and Stripes. So many embarked on this route to freedom that on 4 August 1705 a law was ratified punishing with death every African found above Saratoga. A pressured London complemented this draconian bill by mandating conversion and baptism of the enslaved—but this alleged sop was quickly followed by a 1707 law that made the 1705 law seem mild by comparison. Slaves, not assuaged, responded on Long Island: reacting to the deprivation of certain privileges, they murdered their master, his wife, and children.[75]

Yet London had a problem in seeking to bar Africans from fleeing to Canada, a point that emerged directly in mid-1711 when conflict—typically—exploded between London and Paris and an attempt was made by certain mainland colonists to recruit Africans to enlist in a force to invade Quebec. Yet the commanding officer announced peremptorily, "I immediately ordered them to be discharged."[76] Left unclear was how these British settlers could compete effectively with other European powers if Africans were treated with such cavalier disregard. Ultimately, London would have to yield on this front, but this simply created yet another problem with settlers whose model of development presupposed slave-labor encampments stocked to the brim with Africans and the gross brutality that inevitably accompanied them.

New York had a dual problem, however, for simultaneously, it was "recruiting" Africans as slaves at a formidable clip, which created problems of instability that neighboring Quebec could profit from, while discharging Africans who might want to aid in alleviating this prickly matter. For with the loosening of restrictions on the slave trade, lucrative contacts in Madagascar in the late 17th century, not to mention similar ties to South Carolina and Jamaica, were developed by some avaricious New Yorkers.[77] Moreover, there was a lingering fear in Manhattan that despite the reconquest of 1673, some of the Dutch there had not been fully assimilated into the developing identity of "whiteness," an apprehension confirmed when some of them refused to pledge their allegiance to the English. Governor Edmund Andros wanted them resettled upstate—but would that not simply move them closer to potential collaborators in Quebec? The reluctance of the authorities to allow Catholic priests in the colony also betrayed a certain apprehension. The religious Cold War waxed in Manhattan as King James II, previously the Duke of York and successor to the throne following the death of Charles II in 1685, vetoed New York's Charter of Liberties and commanded all churches there to conform to the Church of England liturgy. Leisler's Rebellion, the local manifestation of the Glorious

Revolution, revealed the volatility of a settler population that was torn by confessional, linguistic, natal, and social antagonisms—contradictions that were made to order for African manipulation, which may have been the case when congruent with Leisler's upsurge, Africans in 1689 rampaged through the then farming village that was Harlem, as if they were marking out territory for future conquest.[78]

Compounding the security problem faced in New York was the reality that when Irish troops dispatched from London arrived in New York in 1700, they immediately began brawling and causing injuries, resulting in a court martial that condemned four to be shot, two of whom were spared only seconds before the fatal volley.[79] When New York passed a bill seeking to prevent "Soldiers & Sailors from Deserting Her Majesties Service and Servants and Slaves Deserting their Masters or Mistresses," the yoking of these apparently disparate issues came clear and revealed why barring Africans from the armed forces in the face of a French and indigenous threat could be foolhardy.[80] Like South Carolina under siege from Spanish Florida,[81] the Northeast faced a similar challenge from Quebec.[82]

In 1709, it was thought proper in New York to reinforce a bill "for preventing the conspiracy of slaves" and to pass a similar bill a few years later.[83] That same year, anxious officials were seeking frantically to keep track of the Africans brought to the colony by "separate traders and at what rates sold," as apprehension was rising that an insuperable problem was being created. "Willful killing of Indians and Negroes" was to be "punished with death and a fit penalty imposed for the maiming of them," though it was doubtful if such solicitude would tamp down the rising fury of the oppressed. It was made clear that this initiative was in response to the oppressed "being seduced from their allegiance to [the New Yorkers] by French priests and Jesuits."[84] In 1710, in neighboring New Jersey, it was deemed necessary to enact "an act for deterring Negroes and other slaves from committing murder."[85]

In Connecticut, by 1680, the number of enslaved Africans was not great, but many of them had roots in tumultuous Barbados.[86] Earlier, despite their paltry numbers, Africans were barred from the militia. Already—as was to become the case regionally—opposition to slavery was congealing but not on moral grounds but on the basis that this institution harmed the interests of poor Europeans.[87] By 1708, suggestive of the increase of Africans in the hemisphere, legislation was debated to punish severely "any Negro or Mulatto servant or slave" who would "disturb the peace or shall offer to strike any white person."[88] By 1715, legislators in Connecticut were mulling various "conspiracies, outrages, . . . murders, burglaries, thefts and other notorious crimes at sundry times and especially of late" that "have been perpetrated by Indians and other slaves." They had thought there were "different circumstances of this colony" compared to the "plantations in the islands," which had a well-justified reputation for riotousness—but now they were not so sure, realizing that even supposedly favorable racial ratios were no savior.[89] Thus, by the mid-18th century, what became the Nutmeg State had several plantations larger than those in neighboring Rhode Island, which was already notorious as a site for dispatching of slavers.[90]

This was no small matter, since by 1730, southern Rhode Island was nearly one-third African, nearly all being slaves, and—as an outgrowth of this trend—a few decades later, nearly half of Newport's richest residents had an interest in the slave trade.[91] By 1755, only New York City and Charleston, South Carolina, had a greater percentage of slaves.[92] This was part of a regional trend. As early as 1687, a French Protestant writing from due north was observing that "there is not a house in Boston however small may be its means that has not one or two" slaves; "there are those that have five or six"—suggesting how extensive was this labor force.[93] Though slavery was to be centered south of what became the Mason-Dixon line, the extensive involvement in the slave trade of the region closer to Quebec meant that British settlers generally had to be alert to the growing reality of rebellious Africans.

*　　*　　*

Suggestive of how extensive enslavement had become since the entry into the market of private traders, in 1709, Emmanuel Barselia, "being a Spaniard," complained that he was sold at Roanoke as a slave, this after being "sold for a slave in New England," though he was a "Christian . . . born free."[94] Massachusetts, which had endured the massive bloodletting of vicious wars with the indigenes and was to endure more conflict with the French in coming years, was in serious need of replenishing its labor supply,[95] though a 1690 plot there that involved Negroes and indigenes collaborating with the French in an attack on the colony may have led to concern about the African presence.[96] Earlier, Africans and indigenes had been barred from bearing arms—but passing a bill is different from it becoming an all-encompassing reality.[97] The iconic figure of this colony, Cotton Mather, was not singular in living in deathly fear of a slave insurrection.[98] The other side of the coin was represented by his compatriot Samuel Sewall, who was inspired toward abolition after reading of similarly inclined Londoners.[99]

Thus, the determinative events of 1688 laid the groundwork for a great leap forward for capitalism, fueled by enslavement of Africans, not least in North America. Yet ironically, as the economy grew on the mainland, it also laid the groundwork for a Unilateral Declaration of Independence. The development of the forces of production also opened the door wider for a massive influx of Africans—a key component of capital—which could also be a potential gravedigger for all those so bold as to exploit their labor. This reality leaped to the forefront of consciousness in Manhattan in 1712 and, at the other end of the colonial chain, in South Carolina soon thereafter.

3

Revolt!

Africans Conspire with the French and Spanish

Early in the morning of a moonlit day on 6 April 1712, fires also illu-minated the sky in lower Manhattan. What had happened was that a few dozen determined Africans armed with guns, hatchets, knives, and other purloined weapons gathered in an orchard at the rear of a house in the city's East Ward, burst into an outhouse, set ablaze that building, and then ambushed the settlers who rushed to extinguish the fire. Pre-ferring death to capture, a number of the rebels fled to the countryside and committed suicide before they could be detained, while others were arrested (approximately seventy)—about twenty-one were executed subsequently. Nine settlers had been murdered, but this did not arrest the continuing plotting of Africans against the authorities, at times in league with the French and Spanish and the indigenous. Since the total population of this future metropolis was reportedly a mere 6,307 at the time, of whom no fewer than 945 were Negroes, disrupting the status quo violently was not as difficult as it was to become.[1]

The message delivered with a thump to colonists was that it did not require an African majority, for example, in Jamaica or a good deal of the Caribbean, for this dark-skinned population to wreak havoc. The great trek to the mainland from the islands had not brought a safe ref-uge from the burning rage of Africans. Perhaps if danger could have been contained on Manhattan, there would be lesser reason to worry. But subsequent events were to show that the "reforms" of the slave trade, while delivering more African labor designed to propel the main-land economy, also had delivered perils in a broad swath of territory stretching from Massachusetts to Carolina. London then had to deter-mine if the model of development involving mass enslavement of Afri-cans was viable—though this piercing thought had yet to penetrate the consciousness of most settlers.

Perhaps understandably, mainland colonies—notably Carolina—embarked on a desperate search for more "white" settlers in order to outweigh and countervail the presumed and actual threat posed by rebellious Africans. However, the ill-defined nature of "whiteness" could easily allow for the infiltration of putative or actual foes of London from Madrid and Paris, not to mention Dublin and Glasgow. Besides, who would want to accept a colonial assignment that could easily lead to butchering at the hands of Africans or the indigenous or both? Inducements had to be offered, emoluments that eventuated in a purported democratic republic that further clipped the wings of the monarchy in 1776. These benefits were an appropriate sequel to the "reforms" of the slave trade—which too had weakened the Crown—that had delivered a bounty of free labor to the mainland, serving to enrich some of those who had been simple commoners in Britain. Yet—contrary to subsequent generations of U.S. patriots—the rights offered to settlers hardly formed a template that could be extended easily to Africans, precisely because thwarting Africans was at the heart of this offering.

Understandably, Governor Robert Hunter of New York—who happened to be Scottish—was irate about the tumult of April 1712, denouncing this "bloody conspiracy" designed to "destroy as many of the inhabitants as they could." To be fair, the chief executive had wondered if brutalizing Africans had a downside. He knew that it was undefined "hard usage" of these slave laborers—"I can find no other cause," he confessed—which sparked this revolt, though he underlined that some of the conspirators were "prisoners taken in a Spanish prize" and "by reason of their color which is swarthy, they were said to be slaves and as such were sold." But this rough racist injustice, which came to characterize these colonies and their successor states, probably swept within its ambit those who did not carry the disfavored status that was slavery, and they revolted accordingly.[2] Such crude practices could only further inflame men of color under Madrid's rule—who played a key role in the military in this empire—to despise London and its colonies even more.

Governor Hunter was not remorseful, though he had received "petitions from several of these Spanish Indians as they are called, representing to [him] that they were free men, subjects to ye King of Spain but sold here as slaves." He did not apologize for the fact that among the disreputably handled detainees was "a woman with child," nor did it ruffle his sangfroid that "some were burnt, others were hanged and broke on ye wheele."[3]

Others sought to draw the appropriate lessons, as in Pennsylvania, where policymakers resorted to a kind of tariff war to curb the importation of a human commodity that had proven to be quite dangerous. But this only created further problems, with irritated merchants and employers generally forced to stare down suddenly expensive European workers, and since Africans were simply diverted to next-door New Jersey, it was unclear if this quasi-abolitionist tactic designed as a life-saving measure was as practical as it appeared.[4] Other colonial lawmakers sought to assuage both sides by discriminating in their exports in favor of Africans—against those with roots in the riotous Caribbean—but the 1713 granting of the Asiento to London tended to undermine this nervous policy,[5] as allowing British merchants entrance to slave markets in the Caribbean served to create a larger market for slaves that could easily be diverted to the mainland by smuggling or otherwise. There had been attempts in New York to lay duties on these African imports, but, as was evident, this had not solved the problem of their unruliness.[6] Nonetheless, post-1712 this tariff war continued, and in 1716 yet another tax was placed on this troublesome import.[7] As things turned out, this measure was just as ineffectual in limiting the presence of Africans as similar measures for "preventing [and] suppressing" the "conspiracy and insurrection of Negroes and other slaves" were in barring this disturbing eventuality.[8] For simultaneously in Massachusetts—not that far away—others were pressing for easing tariffs on imported Africans.[9]

There were other considerations that rattled settlers, not least being the alleged role of a Frenchman Elias Neau in stirring up the Africans. Actually this supposed perpetrator was a Protestant, which should have put him on the side of the angels, but with French Quebec sitting menacingly on the colony's northern border, could one be sure about his alleged religious affiliation? The authorities barred Africans from attending his school, though Neau persevered until the year 1722, when he died.[10] The man in question was said to have been confined several years in prison in his homeland and seven years in various galleys because of his Protestant faith. Upon release, he came to New York and became a trader and a—presumed—devotee of the Church of England. In 1704, the Society for the Propagation of the Gospel in Foreign Parts opened a branch in New York seeking to convert the enslaved. This Frenchman joined them and began going door to door beseeching the oppressed—but this was a tough assignment, not least because of the accurate perception that the converts would face continuing bias, even if Christian. He persevered, taking great pains to provide catechisms and the like—and he began to make headway: by 1708, the number of devotees was increasing, though when some asked to be baptized, they were threatened with being sold to the netherworld that was Virginia.

As this controversy was developing, the 1712 revolt happened, which was all the more troubling since the fearsome Coromantees were said to be involved, and like their counterparts in the Caribbean, it was said that their plot involved liquidating the entire settler class and taking power. As rumors flew about the role of missionary work in fomenting rebellion, Neau maintained a low profile—which only increased hysteria, as his school was blamed.[11] That there were French-speaking defense witnesses in and of itself was not reassuring, irrespective of the content of their testimony.[12]

In 1706, an act had been passed to encourage Christianity, though critics—who increased in number after April 1712—had argued that adopting this religion could backfire, facilitating the freedom of the enslaved because of apprehensions about these religionists in bondage.[13] New York's 1709 law "preventing the conspiracy of slaves" now seemed like an eerie anticipation of April 1712.[14] After April 1712, further legislation was enacted "to prevent the running away of Negro slaves out of the city and county of Albany to the French at Canada," a reflection of both internal and external threats.[15] That such a law was passed again in 1718 suggested that the colonists had either bad memories or a repetitive problem.[16] That the settlers sought to bar "Negro and Indian slaves above the age of fourteen years from going in the streets" without a "Lanthorn and a Lighted candle" only served to illuminate the intractable problem faced by a colony reliant upon a volatile labor force.[17]

Yet this colony, like others, faced a dilemma, as the case of Neau suggested. Weeks after April 1712, the legislators convened and reproved the "hellish attempt" that had swept through Manhattan. This "convinced" them of the "necessity" of "putting that sort of men under better regulation"—which was understandable—but the method suggested was questionable: "take away the Root of the Evil," it was exclaimed, by accelerating the "importation of White Servants." But from whence were they to come? Neighboring Quebec? Ireland? Scotland? There were only so many English available, after all.[18]

Besides, New York was not the only colony seeking "whites," who also were in demand in the Caribbean—Jamaica not least—for similar reasons. And would not the frantic scurrying for more "whites" simply allow Paris and Madrid to deposit their nationals in Manhattan and create more turmoil? Had they forgotten so soon the presumed lesson of the presence of Neau? And with the demand for "whites" skyrocketing, would not that mean offering this favored group more benefits—for example, land taken abruptly from indigenes—which could only spell more conflict?

The problem faced by colonists, particularly as the Africans learned the English language—a skill often useful in their arduous labor—was that it became harder to quarantine them and keep troubling news about Quebec and the indigenous away from their eager ears. Nor was it simple to keep the disturbing news of April 1712 away from other Africans on the mainland, particularly given New York's role as a busy port. It did not appear that officials in usually placid New Hampshire in 1714 blamed a rash of "great disorders, insolences and burglaries" said to be "committed in the night time by Indian, Negro and mulatto servants and slaves" on the fiery events of 1712—though it would have been understandable if they had.[19]

It was not just the area that came to be known as Dixie that was wrestling with the fraught matter of reconciling the perceived need for bonded African labor with the often homicidal reality of their embattled presence. In 1720, authorities in New York were eagerly awaiting an arrival of Africans from the Caribbean, though imports from there were all too familiar with plots designed to rout Europeans.[20] By 1721, there was intense worry in Manhattan about yet another "designed insurrection of the Negroes within this city."[21] By 1726, records reveal that 180 Africans were imported from the Caribbean—and none from Africa—a trend that had been duplicated roughly as early as 1701. Of course, there had been a period during these few decades when Africans were brought from Madagascar—tellingly, almost all by private traders and none by the RAC, yet another developing trend.[22] By 1727, hapless legislators were reduced to a catchall offering of a "reward to any" who might "apprehend any Indian or Negro Slaves offending . . . any acts" they had passed previously.[23]

But it was the other end of the chain of colonies—severely threatened South Carolina—which endured an ongoing spate of instability before and following April 1712. Months later, Dr. Francis Le Jau, then in Carolina, tellingly referred to the Manhattan turmoil. Later, in early 1714, he anxiously referred to what occurred "Christmas last" when a "rumor spread of an Intended Conspiracy of the Negroes against us all like that of New York"; the plot he referenced "had formed in Goose Creek, where there is a good number of fine Negroes"—"the matter has been examined very diligently by our government," he added reassuringly. Worrisome was that the assumed ringleader was from the Caribbean "and of a very stubborn temper" who "had [e]nticed some slaves to jo[i]n with him that they might [take] their liberty by force."[24] What may have frightened some Carolinians about the presence of "French Negroes" was the rabble-rousing role of an African from Martinique. He was "of a very stubborn temper," said Dr. Le Jau, and "had inticed some slaves to join with him." His execution did not necessarily squash the disaffections of the enslaved: that the perpetrator was from Martinique[25]—and not Spanish Cuba—may have been soothing. Less assuring was the Zelig-like presence of Le Jau—yet another French-born Anglican, not unlike Neau—who just happened to be at the scene of this simmering volcano. Le Jau actually had arrived there in 1706; that he spoke six languages suggests his ability to assay diverse communities. Still, he was in accord with sordid settler sentiment as it ricocheted through the centuries, as he estimated disdainfully that the Africans he encountered were "generally very bad men, chiefly those that [were] Scholars."[26]

In retrospect, it is easy to infer that the Africans arriving in droves in the mainland colonies were bringing with them a raucous instability that threatened the viability of the entire colonial project as they served to embolden the indigenous and the "Catholic Powers" alike. As early as 1698—the crucial year that witnessed "reforms" of the slave trade—colonial officials in the city that became Charleston expressed alarm at the number of Africans arriving in town and urged counterbalancing with the arrival of more Europeans—but, once more, the problem was from whence would they come?[27] Suggestive of the complex problem faced by the settlers was the point that in 1706 an African brought news of the landing of invading Spaniards—yet the colonists would have been justi-fied in suspecting that this news was a tricky feint designed to distract their attention disastrously or even that the African was a double agent of the invaders.[28] Actually, Madrid's men, dispatched from St. Augustine, were joined by those of Paris, dispatched from the Caribbean, all des-tined for the Carolina coast in a sizeable fleet that included hundreds of men—including considerable numbers of Africans and the indigenous.[29]

Slave-trade "reforms" were "successful" in delivering more chained laborers, but this did not seem to arrest growing anxieties among set-tlers. A year before the Manhattan uprising, the governor of South Car-olina spoke with halting anxiety about the "great quantities of Negroes that are daily brought" to the colony—and, just as important, "the small number of whites that come among us"; one result of this imbalance was "how insolent and mischievous the Negroes are become." His worst prognostication was corroborated when an African named Sebastian and a band of hearties raided plantations, burning and plundering as they moved along.[30] In the prelude to this tumult, there was the usual anguish about potential invasions by the Spanish.[31] As ever in official Charleston, there were misgivings about the "French and Spaniards," their "publick enemies" who had "attacked" only recently. So uncertain was officialdom that they decided, fatefully, it was "necessary to have all the Mulattoes banished" because of their alleged perfidy "in the late invasion,"[32] a maneuver that could only imperil the colony further. But they had few options, since the Spanish in Florida—who armed "Mulat-toes"—often waltzed into Carolina and wreaked chaos before depart-ing, and they felt they did not have the time to make fine distinctions among those who were not "pure white."[33]

Balefully acknowledging the horns of the dilemma on which they were hoisted, defenders of Carolina slaveholders in 1712 put forward a bill that in its preamble recognized the importance of bonded Afri-can labor but lamented that these workers were "barbarous, wild [and] savage," which meant extensive measures to "restrain the disor-ders, rapines and inhumanity to which they are naturally prone and inclined." Thus, perversely anticipating the import of their vaunted Bill of Rights, amending their sacred Constitution after the overthrow of British rule, it was ordered that "every owner or overseer must have his Negro houses searched every 114 days for runaway slaves and mischievous weapons"—no requirement for a warrant by a magistrate was mentioned.[34]

Curbing these dangerous imports enraged merchants and planters who profited from this dirty commerce, while bowing to these businessmen could threaten colonialism as a whole. That the Spanish in particular were not opposed to arming Africans placed competitive pressure on London to acquiesce in a similar fashion—though this too could serve to jeopardize colonialism, given the heated opposition to such a strategy by most settlers.

All of these strains—and more—came to a head in Charleston's vicinity in the early years of the 18th century. Already the slaveholders in 1708 had decided on what was thought to be unthinkable[35]—"in case of actual invasion," it was said, it would be necessary to "have assistance of our trusty slaves [in] service against our enemies."[36] Settlers were in a desperate bind. Doubtlessly they feared "actual invasion" by Spaniards or Frenchmen or the indigenous or a combination thereof. But how did concessions to "trusty slaves" comport with the routine brutalization of Africans? Or were settlers simply trapped between the internal foe that was the enslaved and the external foe that threatened invasion?

Unsurprisingly, it was then that there was a coinciding between banner years of importation of Africans and a war with the indigenous that threatened to wipe out the colony.[37] In 1710 in Virginia, reports trickled in of "some Negroes going away with arms," and "it was to be feared they were gone too long" for benign purposes and may have "meditated insurrection," necessitating a call to "raise the Militia," thus disrupting production.[38] In 1712, colonial authorities were also told about neighboring Virginia that just as "the militia of this Colony is perfectly useless without arms or ammunition," the "insurrection of our own Negroes and the Invasions of the Indians are no less to be dreaded."[39] Actually, as frightening was the former, it may have been outstripped by the latter.

In 1715, the so-called Yamasee War erupted in South Carolina; this mass uprising of the indigenous could have led to the elimination of the entire settlement. Settlers may have then agreed that both African and indigenous uprisings were similarly frightening. This insight may have been notably perceived by John Barnwell—referred to bluntly by his sympathetic biographer as an "Imperialist"—who hailed from Dublin and whose conversion from Catholicism to Protestantism seemed to enhance his ferocity toward his slaves, nine of whom were lost during this conflict as they departed for a presumed better life. Though Virginians knew what their fellow settlers were up against, they drove a hard bargain before lending assistance, agreeing to send one armed man southward in return for a Negro woman—whose ability to produce even more slaves enhanced her value, making the bargain seem more unequal than it initially appeared. But then Carolina reneged on the reasonable grounds that Negro men would have rebelled further if women had been dispatched northward.[40] This would have "been inviting a slave rebellion" is the conclusion of one analyst—not a result then desired by settlers.[41]

But Carolina then was the land of unappealing options,[42] for it was not long before the authorities there were contemplating the distasteful prospect of seeking further to "arm [the] Negroes" when faced with a "great emergency" presented by indigenous warriors: "by these means," it was added, perhaps over-confidently, "they will be impower'd to resist a greater force than the Indian enemy."[43] Yet was it also possible that these armed Africans could have fled into the willing embrace of either the indigenous or their fellow Africans in Spanish Florida, further debilitating the settlement's security?

So unattractive were the options in Carolina that it was also in 1715, though faced with an uprising of the indigenous, that some Carolina slaveholders began exporting Africans to New York, which was aided by the latter reducing taxes on these perilous imports, which may have been foolhardy considering what Manhattanites had endured only recently. On the other hand, getting rid of troublesome property made sense—though reducing the labor supply did not. Yet the colonists, as best they could, were grappling with an incompliant problem—how to exploit the labor of Africans shamelessly but not to the point where they would rise as one and destroy them all.[44]

Then, in 1720, as the embers of the Yamasee War had yet to be extinguished, Carolina was faced with "an insurrection of Negroes" that "had been happily suppressed"—though some of the perpetrators managed to escape to "the Spaniards at St. Augustine." Not unconnected was the frightful reality that "of late years the number of Negroes has much increased in proportion to that of white people in Carolina, the number of white men being computed at no more than from 1500 to 2000 and their Negroes at 14 or 15,000"—odds that were not enticing.[45]

This imbalance may have been inspiring to the Africans who intended to—once more—liquidate the European settlement.[46] Making this plot even more bone-chilling for settlers was that it was a combined "Negro-Indian" plan that had as its design seizing power and in May 1720 was launched with the murder of at least two—perhaps more—Europeans.[47]

During this murderous row, there had been reportedly a "very wicked and barbarous plot" of the Africans, who had plotted to "destroy all the white people in the country." This plan was squashed, with "many of them," meaning Africans, "taken prisoners and some burnt, some hang'd and some banish'd," but, as was hardly atypical of the era, their conspiracy was evidently coordinated with an offensive of the indigenous: for as the Africans were "playing the rogue"—or not playing their assigned role of bolstering colonizers—a "small war" involving the indigenous erupted with these same settlers. "We increase dayly in slaves but decrease in white men" was the coda to this cycle of conflict, but as long as merchants held sway in their determination to flood the colonies with Africans who then conspired to slaughter settlers, it was unrealistic to expect an increase in the number of Europeans.[48]

The "whole province" was "in danger of being massacred by their own slaves," it was reported mournfully, though the failure to succeed did not quench the militant thirst for freedom of the Africans. For in 1721, the monarch in London was informed that the Africans again had come close to "nearly succeeding in a New Revolution, which would probably have been attended by the utter extirpation of all Your Majesty's subjects in this province." There was a number of extermination plots, one in 1728 and yet another in 1730, which almost came to pass: according to one spectator on the scene, there was a "conspiracy among their Negro slaves to have murdered in one night every white man in the province, to have taken such of the white women as they liked. . . . the Negroes in each family should murder all the white men of the family they belonged to"[49]—but still, Africans kept arriving in Charleston, as if someone had a death wish.[50]

Actually, it was deeper than that: the perceived need for slave-labor camps was so profound and the profits from them were so mind-boggling that local elites felt they had little choice but to run the risk of mass murder. Thus, by 1734, it was estimated that the number of Africans in the province was about twenty-two thousand, about three times the number of European inhabitants. With settlers well aware of events due west in French-influenced territory and at the Quebec border, there was a constant apprehension that agents of Paris would instigate insurrection in Carolina. Cried the colonial governor in 1729, "nothing is so much wanted in Carolina as white inhabitants"—though his definition of this racial category probably did not include French or even Irish Catholics,[51] who could easily have exploited his fierce racist desire. Thus, a few years later in adjacent North Carolina, the governor was disconsolate about the perceived dearth of supplies of Africans from the continent itself, leaving his charges with the "necessity to buy the refuse, refractory and distemper[e]d" from "other Governments," though it was a fair inference by this juncture that each boatload of Africans from across the Atlantic too contained a fair amount of individuals eager to shed the warm blood of settlers.[52]

And even if there had been a desire to curtail the import of angry Africans, the British did not control the entire mainland, and rampant smuggling meant that it was not difficult for contraband to reach territory claimed by London. Thus, in June 1719, the first ship from West Africa was said to have arrived with hundreds of enslaved Africans in New Orleans.[53] By 1721 a steady stream of slave ships was arriving in Biloxi, and by 1737, up the Mississippi River in Illinois, the population of Africans had doubled in five years.[54]

Often the guilty flee when none pursue, and this may have been the case in this instance; for it is not evident that the murderous events of 1720 in Carolina were part of a much larger conspiracy, involving "Catholic powers" and diverse bands of the indigenous. Still, settlers felt they had cause to believe that their massacre was scheduled, and perception can be as caustically illuminating as reality in gauging psychological impact. Fears of mass poisoning and bloody insurrection were palpable, and inexorably a trust deficit was heightened between the erstwhile master and slave.

Africans continued to make their way to St. Augustine, where the possibility of devising successfully gruesome plots was not unlikely. Soon Spanish emissaries were on the ground in Carolina, presumably for diplomatic and commercial reasons, though colonists there suspected their motives were malignant. For by the 1730s, Africans had become the most stalwart component of the militia in Florida and were supposedly being compensated handsomely for Carolina scalps.[55] The dilemma faced by Carolina colonizers was glimpsed when during this same time evidence emerged that they had shifted from focus on the external threat coming from Florida to the internal one presented by Africans—though the fact was the two were tending toward merger: this shift became, according to one perceptive analyst, "perhaps the strongest influence in the province on public policy."[56]

As ever, legislative remedies were devised as if they were a magical amulet, though their deficiencies were symptomatic of the colony's weakness. Thus in 1725, it was mandated that every slaveholder with ten Africans should hire "one white Servant Man or boy of a proper age" as a kind of monitor over this troublesome property and that "all proper encouragement be given to any Merchant, Masters of Ships or others who will undertake to import such white Servants." Rowdy Irish—or French or Spanish—Catholics presumably did not fit the bill. Other measures called for retrieving Africans who had fled to Florida—which was as dangerous as it was risible.[57] On the one hand, colonists sought to limit the number of Africans, knowing full well that to do otherwise was a major threat to security; on the other hand, the lust for the profit Africans produced was so mesmerizing that it tended to override commonsensical judgment.

Actually, the authorities did pay attention to ethnic (and often closely related religious) origins—beyond their obsession with securing more "white" settlers. First of all, the Spanish and French gave them little choice in this regard (not to mention the oft-suspected Irish). A 1721 report noted the presence of Palatines in New York, "Lord Baltimore"— the "Papist"—in Maryland, Quakers in Pennsylvania, and others. Similarly, the number of Africans was tracked—(25,000 in Maryland in an overall population of 80,000, compared to 4,475 amid a population of 35,012 in 1704). But this report inferentially underscored the seemingly insurmountable obstacles faced by London on the mainland—too many unreliable Africans and not enough reliable "whites."[58]

As the foregoing suggests, the problem of troublesome Africans was not solely the province of Carolina, nor the South generally. Near the same time in faraway Massachusetts, there was a similar plan of "encouraging the import of White Male Servants and . . . preventing the clandestine bringing in of Negroes and Mulattos"—yet this effort too was not successful.[59] Even in what became the Bay State, there was recognition of the "audacious manner," the "great disturbance," the "many mischievous practices," and the "grievous damage" perpetrated particularly by "Negroes and Mulattoes"—but a similarly ineffective paralysis in stemming the problem at the root by blocking their arrival. Well aware of the security danger these groups represented, in 1723 lawmakers there were seeking to forbid them from serving militia duty at the most important fortifications.[60] Understandably so—for it was reported in late 1724 that Boston had been hit by an arson epidemic and it was "likewise well known that these villainies were carried on by Negro servants."[61]

The issue of including Africans in the militia when they were perceived widely—and correctly—as a threat to settlements was indicative of the hard dilemmas faced by colonists. That Africans so often disappointed those who had placed trust in their benign intentions was suggestive of the point that the entire colonial project—a project that presupposed enslavement of Africans—just might not be workable.

But Boston—like Charleston—faced inventive indigenous and European foes too, which provided few options beyond having to rely on Negro labor for onerous duties. By 1728, Bostonians were focused on "sundry Expeditions and Engagements with the Indian Enemy as well as the French"—and the not unrelated matter of taxes "on the Importation of Negroes and to encourage the Importation of White Servants."[62]

Occasional cries notwithstanding, British merchants continued to carp about such local legislation imposing duties on imported Africans, even when made payable by the importers. This meant the "discouragement" of this commerce, it was said sadly, a status to be exacerbated further if a proposal that future taxes be paid by "the purchaser and not by the importer" were to be effectuated.[63] In Massachusetts, the governor, Jonathan Belcher, received explicit instructions from the Crown in late 1731, opposing any local taxes on importation of Africans, since this was "to the Discouragement of Merchants trading thither from the Coast of Africa."[64]

Meanwhile, Carolina settlers persisted in their comforting belief that combative Spaniards were "detaining our Negroes at St. Augustine" against their will, as this nettlesome conflict showed no signs of abating.[65] Debated at length in 1726 was a bill "for the better securing this Province from Negro insurrections & encouraging of poor [European] people by employing them in Plantations"—but obtaining the latter was neither simple nor easy, and the wiser among them might have wondered why they should risk life itself by settling among a growing number of African insurrectionists.[66] Actually, there were signs that there were some Europeans designated as French who were willing to throw in their lot with Carolina—but the arrival of what may have been well-placed spies exemplified why this powerful category of "whiteness" was problematic and, even today, hardly interrogated relentlessly for fear of the dangers it carried.[67] It is not easy to naturalize, normalize, and make veritably invisible a potent racial category—for example, "whiteness"—while subjecting it to interrogation, thereby possibly exposing its frailties. Interrogating "whiteness" could easily lead to a tugging of the loose threads of class hierarchy that this racial category otherwise obscured, thereby helping to unravel the colonial project as a whole. It was as if these purblind settlers were emulating a child who in covering her eyes imagines that in turn no one can see her too.

Thus, in Carolina, there was a noticeable skepticism about the presence of "French Negroes"—even when slaves—as they were associated with "ill consequences," as if they were agents directed from Paris. "Transport them to some of His Majesties' plantations or elsewhere," it was announced almost frantically in mid-1731.[68] Carolina may have heard of the extraordinary militancy by Africans that was rocking French Louisiana, led by a remarkable man of Bambara descent, known simply as Samba. First, in West Africa, he fought the French and Dutch and then was condemned to slavery in North America. During his passage there, he planned a mutiny but was discovered and enchained. As a slave on the mainland, he became valuable as a multi-lingual interpreter and commander of Africans deployed by colonists—before leading yet another conspiracy of the enslaved in Louisiana that—he was reported to have said—included "a design [for the Africans] to rid themselves of all the French at once . . . by making themselves masters of the capitol," while expropriating "all the property of the French." Despite this danger, the settlers felt compelled to continue to maintain a Negro militia.[69]

Carolinians may also have heard of what had occurred in Natchez in 1729 when a calamitous revolt of Africans and the indigenous occurred: about 250 settlers were massacred, with others carried into captivity in one of the most dramatic episodes in mainland history.[70] That this was a joint African-Chickasaw crusade was perceived as noticeably disturbing, particularly since it was thought that the tables would be turned and the settlers would be enslaved.[71] This was followed by a similar conspiracy that was uncovered in New Orleans in 1731, which—like its counterparts to the east—aimed at eliminating every trace of the set-tlers; perhaps a dozen Africans were executed as a result—including at least one woman—with a number broken on the wheel.[72] In the same period, a shipboard insurrection took place on a vessel destined for New Orleans, with a group of nearly three hundred Africans coming within a whisper of triumphing, halted only by indiscriminate slaughter by the crew, who murdered forty-five of their cargo and wounded forty-seven more, with leaders hung unceremoniously: the relieved captain quickly sold the remainder in Hispaniola rather than spend more time aboard with them on the way to New Orleans.[73]

In 1730, a British traveler in the Caribbean informed a friend in London about goings-on in St. Vincent that provided a disturbing pattern for those who were involved in subjugation of Africans, for there Africans, due to their skill in subversion, were treated like "free people" by the French: "the French go [there] to trade and admit the Negroes to trade here and in their other islands and [treat] them everywhere with such justice, favour and complaisance that they have entirely won their hearts." This was a danger-ous complement to the "progress the French make in Hispaniola."[74]

Ultimately, London was forced to move closer to the praxis of Madrid and Paris as it pertained to Africans, but this understandable reform clashed sharply with the model of development on the mainland, which presupposed despotic enslavement of Africans. This fueled a secession-ist split—and also exposes the analytical debility of simply implanting today's often unsophisticated understanding of "whiteness" on a period defined by sharp clashes between and among European colonial powers and settlers alike.

In short, there was cause to be suspicious of Africans who carried the label "French." It was also true, as said emphatically at the time, that "securing this province against an enemy" was a high priority, and France was included in this frightening category—though why Africans with French provenance should be likewise included was reflective of an ongo-ing insecurity, when even the enemy of one's enemy could not be trusted.[75]

The problem for the Carolina settlement was that the other "Catholic power"—Spain—was even closer than territory ostensibly controlled by France. For a recent visitor to Havana could not help but notice that "three sixty gun ships of war were fitting out in order to destroy the fort at Port Royal in South Carolina"; and, assuredly, Africans with varying origins would be included on board, and others on the ground on the mainland would be expected to participate in the assault.[76] It had become almost routine to expect bombardment near the Christmas holidays, a time when Africans tended toward maximum disaffection amid settler celebration and frequent inebriation.[77]

Colonizers may have had reason to think there was a spreading pandemic. If only Carolina had been in jeopardy, then London could have dispatched more redcoats there to squash the insurgency. But surviving the Yamasee War did not mean all of the mainland settlements could now breathe easily. For it was in 1722 the lieutenant governor of Virginia, Hugh Drysdale, warned of an "intended insurrection of the Negroes in two or three counties," the "design" of which was to "cutt off their masters & possess themselves" of the province, a metronomic plan throughout the colonial era. This official could envision "no other consequence" except to "make more severe laws for keeping [the] slaves in greater subjection"[78]—which was a predictable but by no means effective response.

As ever, the authorities responded with legislation—as if passing a bill could alchemically make danger disappear—speaking dolefully of "very great and eminent dangers" that "have of late threatened . . . from the frequently disorderly meetings of great numbers of slaves in a riotous and tumultuous manner," involved in no less than "secret plotting and confederating among themselves" with the aim of "contriving to rise up arms and kill and destroy"—so, surviving alleged perpetrators were to be sent as punishment to Jamaica and Barbados, though it was not clear what this might mean for the health of the overall colonial project.[79] A great trek had been made by European settlers to the mainland to escape rebellious Africans in the Caribbean, and now rebellious Africans were being shipped to the Caribbean. It was not as if the colonizers were wrestling with amnesia. More to the point, the colonial project had embedded within it contradictions and snares that were hard to evade, and foremost among these was the presence of resolute Africans who did not readily cooperate.

Yet amnesia was about as sound an approach as any other, given the depth of the problem faced. Present laws, it was announced sadly in 1723, were "insufficient . . . to punish the secret plots and conspiracies" of Africans, all of which seemed to be proliferating.[80]

Thus, in 1729, William Gooch, a leading colonist, warned that Africans near the banks of the James River schemed to flee to "neighboring

Mountains" to a site where "they had already begun to clear the ground" with a cache of "Arms & Ammunition." An attack was mounted against these Africans, and they were subdued, though their ambitious plan "might have proved dangerous," as they mimicked "the Negroes in the Mountains of Jamaica" whose ructions had proved so inimical to the needs of the settlers. For it was "certain that" even a "very small number of Negroes once settled in those Parts, would very soon be increas[e] d by the Accession of other Runaways and prove dangerous Neighbours."[81] In short, as time passed and Africans poured into the colony as slave trade "reforms" asserted themselves, the colonizer had accomplished the feat of making the mainland seem more like Jamaica—not less—thereby eroding the import of the great trek.

Then in 1730, an insurrection of the enslaved was slated for a different part of Virginia; hundreds gathered in Norfolk and Princess Anne Counties in a military formation that included officers to command them, with many managing to escape to the Great Dismal Swamp after their plot was foiled.[82] The latter site suggested the possibility of a capacious "Maroon" encampment rivaling—if not surpassing—its counterpart in Jamaica.

These Africans, it was reported, "had the boldness to assemble on a Sunday while the people were at church," as the occasion to launch "their intended insurrection." Thus, it was now ordered that "every man" should "bring his arms to church on Sundays & Holydays lest they should be seized by the Slaves in their absence."[83]

Then in 1731, somehow a number of Africans—via "loose Discourses," according to a leading official—had thought that His Majesty had mandated that all among them who were Christian should be freed, but "the Order was Suppressed" by the nefarious settlers, whom the enslaved perpetually suspected for varied reasons. Slaveholders felt this was just another excuse "sufficient to incite them to rebellion," leading to the "severe whipping of the most Suspected," in turn leading to further insurrectionary plans.[84] The repetitive nature of these alarms had "occasioned a good deal of fatigue to the Militia and some loss in their crops," wailed Lieutenant Governor William Gooch.[85]

Actually, the plans of Africans may have been more far-reaching than even the worst-case scenarios envisioned, for at the same time, Virginia authorities were forwarding to London a "box full of roots and barks" that would "cure the most inveterate Venereal Disease" and that had been a "secret in the hands of a Negro"; praise was lavished since "only mankind will be the better for" his knowledge—typically in the process of being appropriated without compensation. Unacknowledged was that African knowledge of "roots and barks" also proved useful in the numerous poisoning plots that arose in coming years.[86]

That Africans in Virginia were being compared to their counterparts in Jamaica was inherently intimidating, for it was in this island of turmoil that contemporaneously the Duke of Newcastle was told that "rebellious Negroes"—if aided by Paris or Madrid—"might easily make themselves masters" of all they surveyed, which was not out of the question since these Africans were said "to keep constant correspondence with ye Spaniards" in Cuba.[87] The proliferating fear that Africans—perhaps in league with the indigenous or French or Spaniards, perhaps by themselves—could rise up, liquidate settlements, and take over was an animating fear during this era of tumult, and the idea that London would backslide on this fraught matter (or worse, aid such a plot) paved the way for the 1776 revolt.

Earlier the authorities had sought the repeated remedy of tariffs on imported Africans to restrain their growing presence, but the profits were so immense in this hateful commerce and the methods of smuggling so well honed that it seemed foolhardy to even try to curb their arrival. For example, no British warships patrolled the Delaware River in the 1720s, and thus, smuggling and piracy were frequent, including the clandestine arrival of Africans.[88] In fact, these Africans in Virginia were producing so much tobacco that there was apprehension about the toxic effect of a glut on the market.

Africans' swaggering and swashbuckling disregard for the life and limb of their would-be masters was no better illustrated than at the source: Africa itself. Like revolts on the mainland, revolts in Africa appeared too to be increasing in the wake of slave-trade "reforms" that increased the number of enchained Africans. The problem here was that more than mainland revolts, bloodshed at the source of supply tended to implicate more directly colonizers in New England and merchants in Bristol and Liverpool. This served to deepen fear and resentment of Africans, a deadly development for the enslaved on the mainland. Shipboard insurrections were becoming more common.[89]

It was in early 1731 that a captain in Africa was surprised by his captives, and all his crew but three were killed. Months later, another captain, this time in Guinea, was murdered by Africans; in another tense episode, both a vessel and cargo were seized in Gambia, as the crew came under fire by angry Africans, a fiery battle that lasted for hours on end. The reach of these incidents soared far beyond the Caribbean and the southern mainland, as it was a captain in Boston who was warned bluntly that "for your own safety," there must be "needful Guard over your Slaves and putt not too much confidence in the Women nor Children least they happen to be Instrumental to you being surprised which may be fatal."[90] It was also in 1731 that the captain of a Massachusetts slave ship and his crew were slain by would-be slaves off the coast of Africa, which was followed by a similar assault near what is now Sierra Leone. Before the 1731 murders, it was the turn of a Rhode Island vessel when Africans revolted, killed most of the crew, and adroitly navigated the ship back to Africa, where it was run aground and all aboard fled to freedom.[91]

William Snelgrave may have been lucky in that his slave trading near Dahomey in 1727 "only" led to his being detained for a lengthy period by would-be captives who became captors; the perils of this business were suggested by his meeting other European captives there during his forced stay.[92]

*　　*　　*

But the colonists were like sailors bailing water from a leaky vessel: once they thought they had one leakage attended to, another seemed to emerge. Virginia settlers were sufficiently perceptive to realize that the growing number of Africans in their midst was a real peril. The RAC objected to taxes on its "products," and the planters too, as was their wont, desired to have ever cheaper Africans. These tariffs, it was said, were "so great a burthen upon trade that it amounted to a prohibition," while others objected stridently to this reasoning. Posing as the defenders of "the poorer planters," the merchants of Bristol argued that such taxes would mean the "ruin" of these tobacco farmers and other agriculturalists who had yet to climb the greasy pole of success and eminence. An "instruction" was sent to Virginia "not to pass any act that might affect the trade or shipping of Great Britain," a measure that fueled the perception that London saw these colonists as disposable, not to mention feeding the idea that the settlers might be better off on their own—or that there was a haughty disregard for the danger of having so many Africans on the mainland.[93] But London felt compelled to act since Pennsylvania and Rhode Island had taken similar steps to limit import of Africans, to the detriment of powerful interests in Bristol and Liverpool.[94]

Overlaid on this conflict was the ongoing one between the private traders and the RAC—who often could unite in opposition to those who sought to restrain imports of Africans generally—and whether or not increased competition in this odious commerce drove down prices to the benefit of small and large planters alike. The RAC continued to insist that a central authority was needed, particularly to maintain forts along the West African coast, so needed to repress Africans with ideas of assaulting subjects of the Crown. By 1730, the RAC had a reported thirteen forts and castles along the coast of western Africa, which were thought essential for flummoxing the "exclusive pretensions and encroachments of such other European nations"; yet for years now, private traders had been profiting from the protection of these forts "without contributing anything" to their upkeep, said a RAC spokesman; this was harming the coffers of the RAC with untold consequence for the Crown—should not this burden be shared? And for those concerned about "independency" pretensions of mainland colonists, were they not simply snookering the Crown by evading expense for forts while benefiting from the arrival of enslaved Africans?[95] And did it make sense in the long term for the affluent to profit from government outlays without contributing meaningfully to government coffers?

The RAC reminded one and all in 1730 of the plight of Captain James Murrel, who, "when his Negroes rose upon him and ran his ship ashore"—it was emphasized—"took *Sanctuary* at *Cape Coast Castle* where he was *kindly received* and entertained"; then there was "Capt. Blincoe" trading at "*Whydah*, during the late Wars in that Country," who was "protected by the Company's *Fort* against the Insults of those" who wanted his scalp. Could the private traders, it was asked querulously, play a similar role?[96]

Continuing the debate sparked by 1688, there was continuing discussion as to whether or not the monarch could "without consent of Parliament" seek "to exclude any of his subjects from trading to any parts of Africa." Potent interests in Virginia and Maryland argued that they were well supplied with Africans—but no thanks to the RAC, as the cry against burdensome government regulations grew in intensity. A Marylander asserted that his colony could absorb "more Negroes if they could get them," particularly from "Gambia" and "Angola," the "chief parts of Africa from whence" his province was "supplied"; further, it was said, ousting the private traders would mean "Negroes would be dearer and the province worse supplied. That the price of Negroes had formerly been 40 [pounds],"[97] "but are now sold at 18 [pounds]," it was added.[98] Whether he knew it or not, this Marylander was arguing for a future when more Africans would be brought to the mainland, bringing more peril to this land.

Inevitably there was another agenda that this Marylander did not deign to note. For the RAC was said to be owed "great sums of money" from mainlanders, and this now besieged company was "much" hindered in collecting by local courts. By not paying the RAC while encouraging private traders, sly planters and merchants could benefit.[99] Eventually some Londoners would believe that escaping the reach of British creditors was a prime reason for the rebel revolt of 1776. The RAC was being crushed in a joint maneuver involving its debtors, who were loathe to pay their bills, and private traders, who were eager to steal business—with both parties ably aided by local magistrates. This was the kind of conflict between the metropolis and the provinces that, if not alleviated, could lead to rupture.

Taken alone, London and its mainland colonies might have been able to survive this argument—but there were others. In 1731, a Londoner complained of Britons' trans-Atlantic cousins that "the best of the fish they send to Spain, Portugal, Italy," while shipping their "surplus lumber, horses, provisions, fish and other commodities" to "the Dutch and French Sugar Islands."[100] This dispute, it was said, was "only with New England," for "Maryland, Virginia and the Carolinas are entirely unconcerned"—but the latter provinces had their own beefs with London, disagreements that the metropolis's relations with New England tended to reinforce. Still, the remedy suggested was "encouraging our Sugar Settlements"—Jamaica as opposed to Massachusetts—in which case it would "necessarily follow that there will be a greater Call for Negroes."[101]

But this kind of thinking seemed to be worse than amnesiac—it was more like delusional. The great trek to the mainland had occurred, not least because of the real threat posed by rebellious Africans, many of whom had arrived in the Caribbean in the aftermath of slave-trade "reforms." But these "reforms" also meant more Africans being deposited on the mainland, with predictable rowdy results—and now the remedy suggested was bringing more Africans to Jamaica. If history was any guide, Africans on that island would then rebel—or defect to the Maroons—and some colonial intellectual would devise the bright idea of yet another great trek to the mainland.

Actually, this was worse than the comedy of errors which it appeared to be. Increasingly, New England was perceived as being an adjunct of French Hispaniola—not the British isles—which was incompatible with the basic tenets of colonialism.[102]

London might have well asked who was in charge, as its colonies traded with those with which it was warring.[103] These disreputable colonists were even accused of sharing "intelligence" with "our Enemies" to the "great prejudice & Hazard of the British plantations"[104]—but profit tended to trump patriotism in the relation between province and metropolis.

Some colonists were playing a dangerous game in consorting with Paris and Madrid, when these two powers conceivably could destroy British mainland settlements and, instead, build their own colonies there in their stead. Or instead these British mainland settlers could simply stab London in the back and ally with His Majesty's implacable foes and build an independent republic that could then swallow the settlements of Paris and Madrid, expanding the base of support of their new regime by offering a better deal—than that offered by the European powers—to those who were defined as "white" (particularly non-affluent men).

*   *   *

As London surveyed the colonial scene, it was not hard to spot ever stiffer challenges emerging not only from its traditional competitors in Paris and Madrid but, increasingly, from its own erstwhile colonies on the mainland. Private traders from there were challenging the RAC likewise. Ultimately and ironically, London provided the rationale and wherewithal for its massive mainland loss by eliminating Paris and Madrid as threats to its colonies during the 1756–1763 war.

London pressed on, however, as the logic of colonial conquest seemingly provided no exit strategy. The RAC did not retreat in the face of this challenge. The African Slave Trade, it was argued in a public declaration in 1720, was "one of the most beneficial to this Nation," as the beleaguered African continent also "produce[d] gold, ivory, bees-wax, gums, dying and fine woods . . . for which we exchange great quantities of our woolen, linen, iron, pewter, copper"—all this "without exporting any money," for "above all, the said coast produce[d] great quantities of Negro Servants or slaves." It was stressed that "*the preservation and improvement of the British colonies and plantations in America depend upon the preservation of the trade to Africa*," which "*should be carefully preserved and protected*," a goal best protected and maintained with a coherent, cohesive, and united policy in the face of an unyielding French challenge and not the kind of anarchy said to be brought by private traders.[105]

There was a ferocious commercial war between the RAC and its private-trader competitors, with the complaint emerging that this was causing a precipitous drop in prices of Africans, to the detriment of certain moneyed interests. The RAC was accused of not fulfilling contracts for delivery to Jamaica, making planning of planting problematic at best. In turn, private traders were accused of a dearth of patriotism by supposedly threatening to deliver Africans not to Jamaica but to Spanish interests unless their prices were met.[106]

London had a problem. British subjects were profiting handsomely from the tidal wave of Africans that was coursing across the Atlantic to the mainland, but at the same time, slave labor was boosting the productive forces of these colonies to the point where these once rustic provinces were becoming formidable challengers to the metropolis, setting the stage for a lunge toward independence. Moreover, the presence of so many Africans provided a similar number of opportunities for these seditious laborers to conspire with the indigenous and other European powers alike to liquidate London's settlements. In early 1732, the former matter arose in Parliament, as legislators noted that "cheap fur" notably in "New England, New York, New Jersey" meant entrepreneurs there were "supplying hats and caps throughout the colonies and were also exporting these products to Spain and the West Indies"— despite ever strident "protests" from London.[107]

Just as slavery forced Carolina to construct better roads and ferries, if only to foil rebellion, the slave trade was unabashedly the mainstay for the New England shipping industry as well as the industries that fed this octopus. This in turn fed the productive forces as a whole of this region, driving conflict with London.[108]

But there was another conflict deeply embedded in that which bedeviled the colonies and the metropolis: in Maryland in 1729, lambasted were "several petit-treasons and cruel and horrid murders" executed by Africans: these "cruelties" by them, it was said, occurred because "they have no sense of shame," and London was commanded to allow ever more heinous punishments, for example, "to have the right hand cut off, to be hang'd in the usual manner, the head severed from the body, the body divided into four quarters and head and quarters set up in the most publick places of the county."[109] Official London, reclining in its cosseted parlors—or so it was thought—was insufficiently alert to the danger presented by the presence of so many rebellious Africans, and this perceived insensitivity to peril also contributed to the 1776 revolt.

There seemed to be a race to the bottom by settlers, a competition to ascertain who could devise the most ghoulish penalties for Africans. At that point, connecting the presence of so many uproarious Africans to slave-trade "reforms" which would boost the mainland economy was not a priority item for discussion. Instead, it was thought that simple survival meant repressing Africans by any means necessary. In Virginia in 1733, settler revulsion at "conspiracies and insurrections" among Africans meant revising "insufficient" punishments, leading to some being subjected to "one ear nailed to the pillory and there to stand for the space of one hour and then the said ear to be cut off; and thereafter the other ear nailed in like manner and cut off"—all this for providing false testimony; thirty-nine lashes "well laid on" were also recommended, while slaveholders were to be fined for acquiescing to meetings of "five Negroes or slaves," while settlers found at such meetings were to be fined or whipped: this was one of the most encyclopedic bills in the entire era of colonial slavery on the mainland.[110]

Slave revolts followed by ghastly punishments, fomenting more revolts with increasing intensity; destructive competition between the RAC and private traders, providing leverage to African leaders; slave traders flooding fragile settlements with Africans, thereby jeopardizing their existence; New England colonies undermining the Mother Country, while fortifying European foes; continuous plotting by the indigenous, Paris, and Madrid alike—London had reason to re-evaluate its colonial project in the first few decades of the 18th century and even pursue a different model of development: it was in this context that Georgia was born, as a firewall protecting the exposed flank of the Carolinas while challenging Spanish Florida and even Cuba, all of which could change the political and economic calculus in the hemisphere, not least in New England. That it was designed to develop without pesky and insurrectionist Africans only increased its attractiveness.

4

Building a "White" Pro-Slavery Wall

The Construction of Georgia

The drum was pounding and the words were flowing with like insistency.

It was November 1733 in St. Augustine in Spanish Florida, which had long since gained a justified reputation as a scourge of colonies to the north—notably, the Carolinas, from which the enslaved were fleeing in ever growing numbers southward, where they often wound up in Madrid's military, eager to inflict mayhem on their former captors. But now an edict was being read to pulsating rhythms thought to be favored by Africans—it just so happened that Carolina ships with Africans aboard were in the harbor—which proclaimed that His Catholic Majesty Himself was promising liberty and protection to all slaves that deserted to his realm. Supposedly measures were taken to ensure that this seditious message would receive a wide audience.[1]

It did not take long before Carolinians began to condemn the reality of the steady stream of Africans fleeing southward, some committing murders "and other mischiefs" in their wake. There was a "dayly desertion," it was announced in 1738, which meant the "decrease of [the Carolinians'] produce of rice and naval stores" which was "the product wholly of these slaves." This edict, it was said forebodingly, was "intended to cause an insurrection of . . . slaves at the same time," causing them to "massacre their masters and then to desert"—an eventuality that did occur.[2]

This was all devastating news for Carolina settlers, though not unexpected since the Spaniards had long been seeking to unseat them, with Madrid's appeal to the enslaved as a major weapon. Actually, on 12 April 1731, the Council for the Indies in Madrid had arrived at a similar decision as that of 1733, and decades before that, Africans fleeing the Carolinas often found sanctuary in Florida.[3] By mid-1728, Carolinians were groaning about Florida "harbouring all our runaway Negroes," which meant a "new way of sending our own slaves against us to rob and plunder us; they are continually fitting out partys of Indians from St. Augustine to murder our white people"; these indigenes were "sometimes joined with Negroes." Then the dastardly Spaniards had promised "thirty pieces of eight per head for every live Negro" delivered from Carolina, incentivizing the greed of the ascending capitalists, turning slavery against itself.[4] By 1737, Spanish depredations in the Caribbean included "stealing" Africans away from British possessions.[5] Somehow Londoners and mainland planters infrequently paused to consider why it was that the enslaved were fleeing Carolina for Florida—and not vice versa.[6]

Some Carolinians had barely unpacked their bags from Barbados in 1686 when they were set upon by invading Spaniards in contingents that included Africans—which led to the seizing and carting away of even more Africans.[7] As early as 1713, it was mandated by the Carolina authorities that vessels "shall cruise between Port Royal and St. Augustine" on the lookout for fleeing Africans and advance contingents of Africans from St. Augustine, but the labyrinth waterways of the vicinity could not easily foil the determination to become runaways.[8]

The settler assault on St. Augustine in 1719 was one of a number of attempts to eradicate this perceived beehive of sedition.[9] As early as 1721, officialdom expressed mordant concern about South Carolina: "the frequent massacres" at "the instigation of the French and Spaniards" were worrisome, while the "manufactures of pitch and tar" meant an "increase [in] the number of Black Slaves," who had "lately attempted and were very near succeeding in a new Revolution which would probably have been attended by the utter extirpation of all [British] subjects on this Province." More military force was needed—no change there—but there was no answer as to where they would be commandeered. "No time should be lost," it was demanded, since "fortifications" were "but very few," which could mean "not only Carolina but Virginia" too could be lost. St. Augustine was a continuing menace, all of which demonstrated "the danger" faced by London's subjects. Surrender was not an option given the importance of pitch and tar to reducing reliance on the same commodity from the Baltic region, which had its own challenges, not least potential threats to London itself. But likewise threatening was the continuing problem of mainlanders with "thoughts of setting up manufactures of their own, interfering with those" of the motherland, not to mention "carrying on an illegal trade with foreigners," particularly the stalwart foes that were France and Spain.[10]

In September 1725, Charleston leaders found themselves debating once more their counterparts in St. Augustine about the failure to return escaped Africans, with Madrid's men willing to negotiate about the price but insisting that the Africans "must remain." This was an order, it was announced portentously, from His Catholic Majesty Himself. Dumbfounded Carolinians insisted—to no avail—that these Africans were "goods & estates" of themselves and the Spaniards were engaged in "robbing"—but their pleas were ignored.[11] For it was Madrid that thought that London's colonists were the interlopers: Spaniards had formulated elaborate claims to territory north of Florida claimed by the British.[12]

London's colonial project in the Americas already was floundering, with Jamaicans on the warpath, mainland settlers consorting with the French, Africans rebelling aboard ships, then on the ground—and now Spaniards were threatening the Achilles' heel of the mainland in the Carolinas, with a tempting Virginia not far distant.

*   *   *

Thus, it was thought that when in September 1739 the Africans in South Carolina erupted in what came to be called "Stono's Revolt," one of the bloodier episodes in mainland colonial history, the Spaniards had advanced further on the road to destabilizing their colonial competitor to the north. This was a contributing factor to a simmering conflict between London and Madrid, which overflowed in the following decade, then came to a combustible boil during the 1756–1763 war—which turned out to be a catastrophic victory for the British, weakening their European competitors as it emboldened their now liberated mainland colonists to revolt in 1776.

Yet even before the pounding drums of 1733 and the bloodlust of 1739, Madrid had revealed its intention not only by enticing Africans southward from Carolina but by forming a regiment of them, appointing officers from among them, allowing them the same pay and clothing them in the same uniform as the regular Spanish soldiers. It is probable that some Carolinians perceived this as little more than racial perfidy— or even a violation of the laws of war.[13]

The danger to the mainland colonies provided by Spanish Florida was a preoccupation of the founding father of Georgia, James Oglethorpe, whose colony was founded in 1733 in the midst of Carolina turmoil due north. He was no stranger to the perils brought by slavery, having served as a leader of the Royal African Company (perhaps a reason why he sought to block slavery in Georgia, as this commerce was growingly being driven by the RAC competitors: private traders).[14] In 1732, he opined that given the "proportion of Negroes" in South Carolina, this colony "would be in great danger of being lost in case of a war" with Spain or France. Thus, he thought, there was a felt need to "strengthen their Neighbourhood with large supplies of free-men," meaning Europeans.[15] In 1733, he announced that South Carolina had forty thousand Africans "worth at least a million of pounds sterling"—but poor Europeans might be a substitute for enslaved Africans in Georgia with the added bonus that (unlike Negroes) they could be "found useful" against the Spaniards.[16]

Oglethorpe had cause to seek an alternative to bonded African labor. During that tempestuous era, a Londoner denounced the "tragical accounts of plots and insurrections among the Negroes," which were so inimical to the interests of settlers; acknowledged freely was the unavoidable point that the harsh maltreatment of this bonded labor force gave them incentive to revolt—"the Yoke the Negroes wear," it was asserted, "will render them more exquisitely sensible of the Charms of Liberty [and] this Disproportion may encourage them to form Plots."[17] Always lurking as a threat was collaboration between Africans and indigenes, not a minor consideration on the southeast coast of the mainland,[18] as the Yamasee War had shown quite recently.

Nonetheless, despite the apprehension about the obvious danger provided by the increased presence of Africans, they continued to arrive in droves in South Carolina, a development that made all the more unlikely Oglethorpe's dream of a "white" pro-slavery wall in Georgia, bereft of Africans. Almost two thousand Africans were brought to South Carolina during the period stretching from September 1725 to September 1726, with annual importations doubling over the next decade.[19] A typical occurrence took place in May 1735. The Carolina merchant Samuel Everleigh arranged for a ship from Angola to arrive in his homeland with 318 enchained Africans aboard—even more were expected shortly from Guinea and even more from elsewhere on the beleaguered continent. Of the 318, virtually all were sold within two days, suggestive of the insatiable demand for slaves. Wanly there was an accompanying call for a "good number of whites to balance them," but this seemed more like self-deluding poppycock than anything else.[20]

The accelerating competition between the RAC and the private trad-ers had done its dirty work so devastatingly that even London itself by 1731 was having to confront a growing population of Africans,[21] a con-currence that eventuated in the earthshaking Somerset's case of 1772—and further reason to revolt on the mainland in 1776. The number of Africans in the North Atlantic region was growing mightily with little contemplation of the downside consequences. Even in New Hampshire, not renowned as a site of African presence, by the 1730s Negro slaves had become a sign of social status, as evidenced by their increasingly widespread usage and the skyrocketing growth in their numbers, more than doubling during this decade.[22]

Of course, it was London that often sought to block taxes on Afri-cans imported to the mainland—or at least to have these imposts paid by mainland buyers rather than Bristol merchants,[23] which inflamed some settlers, not necessarily on abolitionist grounds but on the basis of the metropolis's casual disregard for the havoc that could be wrought by a growing number of Africans and the Crown's apparent indifference to same.

Yet despite the danger signals, Carolina elites were reluctant to relent. In March 1734, a lengthy analysis moaned about the "intestine dangers from the great number of Negroes" that were now among them; the Negroes were "three to one of all [the Crown's] white subjects in this province. Insurrections," it was concluded morosely, "have often been attempted and would at any time prove fatal if the French should insti-gate them."[24] That same year, legislators mandated that patrols were "required to search [and] if necessary break open all Negro houses and to take away any guns, swords or weapons found there"—though how such contraband reached Africans was left unsaid.[25]

There were compelling reasons, in other words, to bar Africans altogether—particularly slaves—from Georgia, creating a presumed "white" wall of impenetrability blocking the militant thrusts from Span-ish Florida,[26] forming a catchment basin to ensnare fleeing Africans from Charleston, while placing more pressure on the presumed source

of the problem: St. Augustine. Intimidating the rich prize that was
Cuba, the strategically sited island that patrolled the approaches to the
mainland and the wealthy Spanish colony that was Mexico, was also a
relevant consideration. "No appearance of slavery, not even in *Negroes*,"
was to be allowed, it was said of Georgia by the colony's founder with
emphasis in 1733, while at the same time it was to be a blow in the ongoing religious cold war, serving as a refuge for fleeing Protestants—from
France and eastern Europe particularly—which also served to enhance
the developing and potent category that was "whiteness."[27]

Yet if bolstering "whiteness" was at issue in Georgia, the barring of
Africans simultaneously suggested that this important category had
been insufficiently theorized. For the absence of Africans would serve
to allow class and ethnic tensions among Europeans to fester, replicat-
ing Europe on the mainland, which was not exactly the goal of many
colonizers. Banning Africans would mean that Europeans would have
to perform tasks they might not otherwise, while being bossed—perhaps menaced—by other Europeans. Adding enslaved Africans, on the
other hand, meant that brute agricultural labor could be assigned to
the degraded dark folk, which would boost certain Europeans up the
class ladder and enrich others. Yet bringing bonded African labor to
Georgia—which is what eventually happened—would simply mean
extending Carolina's problems closer to St. Augustine. Except it would
be worse than before, for Georgia would be easier to overrun than Carolina, being weaker and closer to Florida.

Hence, the so-called Negro Act of 1735 explicitly barred slavery in
Georgia, since bitter experience had convinced settlers that it was only
Europeans "who alone can in case of a War be rel[i]ed for the Defence
and Security."[28] Any settlers so audacious as to employ Africans in
Georgia were to be fined.[29]

The fright in the region may have been so pervasive that few settlers bothered to deconstruct what was meant by "white," for as Georgia was being formed in the 1730s, Oglethorpe discovered that among
his troops were some who had served previously for His Catholic Majesty and others who were Roman Catholic and, ipso facto, suspect:
that they disclaimed allegiance to London and confessed to espionage
with the aim of exciting a mutiny in the ranks only served to increase
religious-cum-national hostility; Oglethorpe was forced to then foil an

assassination plot against himself—the bullet whizzed by his shoulder, leaving a scorch mark on his uniform.[30]

With the nervous elite in South Carolina recognizing belatedly the danger they had created, in 1737 they devised the "Negro Fund," which was a tax on imports of Africans to be used for "relief of the Poor Protestants" who had "arrived . . . lately from Europe with intent to settle"; they quickly discovered, however, that collecting this impost from "Negro Merchants and Factors" was not easy, leading to "many unsuccessful calls . . . made thereupon to the great disappointment of such Poor Protestants."[31] Of course, this reinforced—and accelerated—a preexisting pattern that was not to disappear after establishment of the post-1776 republic: burdening Africans in order to relieve Europeans in a way that frustrated class struggle across racial lines.

This idea that Africans—despite the outsized wealth they created—were more of a hassle than a bounty was not unique to Carolina, suggestive of how the security threat they posed was becoming a common concern. As Georgia was taking off as a refuge solely for Europeans, a New Yorker concurred that "honest, useful & laborious white people" were the "truest riches and Surest Strength" that could be provided—as opposed to "the disadvantages that attend the too great Importation of Negroes."[32]

When established in the 17th century, South Carolina had been hailed as not only one of the largest of London's colonies on the mainland but a site of synergy given its relative proximity to Jamaica, Barbados, and the emerging sugar colonies, thought by many observers to be more valuable still.[33] But the worm had turned, and now, given Carolina's proximity to Florida and Cuba, it was emerging as a vital threat to the entire colonial enterprise in the Americas that London had so assiduously maintained. This was particularly so given the utter turmoil that was coming to characterize the Caribbean and the Atlantic. Thus, in order to comprehend why a colony in Georgia was necessary, once more it is necessary to comprehend trends in the waters surrounding the mainland. The point is that the formation of Georgia was not only a response to inter-colonial conflict with Spain (and Florida and Cuba); it was also a response to growing rebelliousness of Africans in Jamaica and Antigua particularly. This restiveness suggested that these valuable islands could be lost forever, necessitating a redeployment of capital and managerial talent to the mainland. Fortifying the mainland by constructing a "white" pro-slavery wall in Georgia was the response.

*   *   *

In 1718, nautical miles away from Carolina in Bermuda, indigenes said to be Cherokee were causing an uproar; it was said they had made "inhabitants . . . very apprehensive" since they were said to be collaborating with "the Negroes (many already [had] run away from their masters into the woods)," and there was an incisive fear that this was a prelude to these antagonists seeking to "invade them."[34] As Georgia was just getting started, word came from the Bahamas of an "intended insurrection of the Negroes" there.[35]

As Africans were often valuable commodities and exiling them was often a remedy for their sedition, it became harder to contain epidemics of unrest. Already there was grumbling from Antigua about the decline of British trade in Africans by dint of importations from Dutch territories;[36] there were a "prodigious number of Negroes" brought to St. Christopher's, it was reported in 1726, from St. Eustatius.[37] What was going on in the region was symptomatic of the disastrous triumph brought by the increase in slave trading in the aftermath of 1688, for between this crucial date and 1707, Nevis, St. Christopher's, Antigua, and Montserrat had a similar experience with enslaved Africans, who once had constituted a minority or bare majority of the population but by the end of this era were surging to clear majorities of up to 80%—with predictable devastating consequence for the life expectancy of settlers.[38]

Simultaneously, Africans were fleeing Barbados for Martinique, though it was felt they were being poached improperly.[39] The RAC had reason to think it was the private traders up to their old tricks, for in 1726 this now withering body sought to prevent the "carrying off [of] any Negroes, Indian or Mulatto slaves" and "to inflict exemplary punishment upon masters [of] ships" who did so, particularly those who had been accused of "clandestinely" making off with "Barbados' slaves."[40] Perhaps these slaveholders should have left well enough alone, thankful that Africans with—possibly—felony in their hearts were fleeing, for it was also in 1726 that the governor in St. Christopher's traveled to neighboring Nevis, having been told there was an "intended insurrection of the Negroes there to destroy all the inhabitants"—two of the accused were executed,[41] which may not have been the best antidote to quell the anger of those remaining Africans.[42] Per usual in the colonies, sharp contention had emerged from "enemys from without and the Negro slaves within," requiring the urgent dispatching of "two Companys of soldiers," though if they had come from Barbados or Antigua or even parts of the mainland, these colonies too would have been dangerously exposed to unrest.[43] The Crown was forced to enact untenable measures to confront this threat, for example, mandating that all vessels trading near these disputatious islands should have no more than 25% passengers and crew of African ancestry—otherwise the vessel "shall be forfeited"—but this could empower unduly European laborers to the detriment of the grandees,[44] necessitating concessions to the former: these concessions ultimately took the form of herrenvolk democracy and its close relative: right-wing populism.

London had constructed a colonial problem for itself, the dimensions of which were often dimly realized. For the Caribbean colonies had far-reaching difficulties—beyond the obvious unforgiving racial ratios. In 1733, a commentator observed that in Hispaniola planters could go directly to foreign markets, facilitating hemispheric gains, while London's colonies had to trade through the metropolis. Then, as one dour commentator observed, there were too frequent hurricanes, "accidental fire" that could easily consume crops, high "mortality among the Negroes," deteriorating soil ("for sugar is the only thing of worth that his soil is capable of producing"), and "no timber"—and "to complete our Unhappy Situation we are every moment in Time of War to be devoured by the Enemies of our Mother Nation," often aided by "the Slaves [who] are really our Enemies." New England was a true Frankenstein monster, building up France and Spain, while Caribbean colonies could disappear at any moment.[45]

Though these complaints about the colonies were directed at both the mainland and the Caribbean, at least as of 1732 the latter seemed more valuable (though the risk of African insurrection and then collapse and total loss was probably greater). For it was then that one analyst detected that British exports to the Caribbean were "vastly greater than the Exports of like manufactures to New England"; likewise, imports from the West Indies were greater than those of New England. If this were so, then why should London strain the Exchequer to accommodate mainland colonies that seemed to be destined for "independency" in any case? This suggested that the "present advantage (if there be such) of New England to Great Britain must . . . decline," and ultimately its value will be "quite lost" to London, through "independency" or otherwise. Surely, the racial ratios in the Caribbean severely limited dreams of secession from the Crown, making settlers there more dependent on redcoats than were their counterparts on the mainland.[46]

If trade were barred between British North America and the French Caribbean—which was how a proper colonialism should operate—major gains to London would accrue, while simultaneously injuring the eternal foe across the channel. This improper tie between the mainland and France was also thought to strengthen Paris's interests in the all-important African market; similarly, said one Londoner, "by encouraging our Sugar Settlements it will necessarily follow that there will be a greater call for Negroes"—which mainland trade with the French was objectively blocking. As of this writing—1731—mainland ships were landing in Jamaica and "after selling their loading for money they carried it to Hispaniola and purchased molasses. That before this trade, the price of Slaves at Jamaica were not half the price they have been since." Besides, money was being made in Boston from lumber that really were "His Majesty's Pine trees," but instead this capital was flowing to Boston merchants with a dubious conception of patriotism.[47] Repeatedly—and mostly without tangible results—London condemned illicit trade between New England and the French.[48]

But it is difficult to move with determined purpose when disunity reigns, and such was the case in London, for with equal intensity there were those who felt the mainland colonies were "of much greater importance . . . than the Sugar Islands."[49] In summary, both the mainland and Caribbean colonies presented tough problems for London: the former were thought to be easing toward "independency," while simultaneously these presumed moochers were draining the Exchequer in order to prevent conquest by Spain or France or the indigenous in league with Africans, while the Caribbean isles—though valuable—faced a challenge that was probably more formidable given the forbidding racial ratios.

A gauge of the mind-bending instability brought by what was probably the most vexing problem—Africans—can be measured by the continuing unease about slavery expressed in the metropolis. In 1730, the Bishop of London expressed shock about the high mortality rate of Africans in Barbados—"out of their stock of eighty-thousand . . . there die every year five thousand Negroes more than are born in that island; in effect, this people is under a necessity of being entirely renewed every *Sixteen Years*" (emphasis original). Inevitably, he thought, this meant "alarming insurrections of the slaves," "now lately at Montserrat," which were "merciful warnings of that just temporal vengeance" which "in all probability" would "overtake" settlers. "The Sword has swung over their Heads by a very slender thread," he warned. For in the region there were "230,000 Negro slaves," and "upon the highest calculation"—probably too high in retrospect—the Europeans amounted to "ninety thousand souls," which suggested how they were "endangered, both from within and without" to the "assaults of a foreign enemy and to the insurrection of their own slaves." Yet "for the sake of a little private gain"—actually a lot in retrospect—enslavement by the colonist persisted rather than the "employment of a certain proportion of white Servants," making the "tenure of his life and possessions thereby daily more and more precarious."[50]

As if these events were not nerve-wracking enough, mainland settlers then had to contend with typically dispiriting news from Jamaica. This was no minor matter, for this colony—London's largest in the Caribbean—was seen as vital to all others. It could pose a challenge to Cuba and Hispaniola, not to mention Cartagena, and the price of Africans determined there could influence the whole region. Typically, private traders and their competitors were competing vigorously in this regard, with the former underselling the latter—"80 to 120 pieces of eight per head; whereas the Company sells from 250 to 300 pieces of eight" was the conclusion in 1728: the general commercial spin-off from being a slave-trade emporium (visiting merchants with bulging wallets ready to spend on food, lodging, and hospitality) was sufficiently attractive to make Jamaica a handsome prize.[51]

The problem for London was that the Africans refused to cooperate with this scenario. In 1716, His Royal Highness, the Prince of Wales, was informed that this colony was "in a dangerous state and almost defenceless" and that the number of "white people"—again curiously undefined—needed an increase to "prevent any insurrection of the Negroes."[52] By 1718, complaints emerged from this mountainous island about "rebellious and runaway slaves" who "formed themselves into several bodies; and of late have very much increased," while the presumed magic bullet—"several laws"—"proved ineffectual." Ominously, some of these former slaves had departed Jamaica for "French and Spanish colonies" nearby with unclear intentions.[53]

Matters had not improved by 1724 as a result of losses "occasioned by Pirates or rebellious Negroes" with—again—more settlers sought as a palliative.[54] By 1728, there was hysteria that Jamaica with its "commodious situation for trade" and "its many good harbours and bays" had become an attractive nuisance in great danger of being invaded, in case of any rupture between Great Britain and France or Spain.[55] By 1730, there was worry about the "dangers that arise from disguised as well as declared Papists" who could easily arrive in Jamaica given the desperation for a larger "white" presence; yet the bar on Catholic presence had served to "discourage Protestants" too, "which, as the number of white inhabitants are few, may be of very bad consequence."[56]

Barring bad consequence indeed was the motive behind attempts in 1730 to "prevent the selling of powder to rebellious or any other Negroes whatsoever," as this "tends to increasing their numbers," meaning the "robbing and plundering [of] the remote parts to the island to the great discouragement of new settlements."[57]

By 1733, Jamaican settlers seemed on the verge of surrendering the entire enterprise to the "rebellious and runaway slaves" whose population had "greatly increased" and "become more formidable in the North-east, North-west and South-west parts of this lands, to the great Terror of His Majesty's Subjects," who had "suffered by the frequent robberies, murders and depredations committed by" Africans. Soon it was expected that the "western parts of this island will soon become the seat of an intestine war as well as the eastern." The Africans had devised "considerable settlements" of their own, causing Europeans to flee, "to the great prejudice and diminution of His Majesty's Revenues." A hefty bounty was to be awarded to any settler so bold as to "kill or take alive" these rebels—"except where it shall be judged necessary to execute them, as an example and terror to others"; thus, each "barrack" was to be "duly provided with a sufficient gang of dogs" for unsavory purposes.[58]

As of 1734, Africans were in open revolt, planters were scurrying away in every direction, and there was a fear that the rebellious spirit of Jamaica was spreading to neighboring islands.[59] London was bracing for a possible invasion of the island by one of the nearby powers—probably Spain—and the colonists pleaded for reinforcements with little heed of the danger that other colonies might face if they were denuded of troops.[60] By July 1734, Richard Hemings of the assembly of Jamaica was embodying this trend, as he thought that to "dispose of the estate here . . . would be the best thing." Why? The "insecurity of our country," he told his aunt in London, "occasioned by our slaves in rebellion against us whose insolence is grown so great" was leading to a collapse of the colony. The miasma of fear was such that, he continued, "we are [not] sure of another day," for "robberys and murder [are] so common on our roads that it is with utmost hazard that we travel them"; for "the methods hitherto taken to suppress them have been attended with unsuccess and so vast an expense that I can safely say that two thirds of the inhabitants are already ruined."[61]

For decades, the settlers had been unleashing lethal force against the Maroons—forced to "arm the whole Colony," it was said in 1740: "every one began to despair" when this offensive proved unavailing. This occurred despite "inhuman cruelties" wielded against these bumptious Africans. "These runaways endured more near the space of a century," it was said with wonder, "than can be found on record of any State or People."[62]

The African known as "Cudjoe" and the Maroons he was said to represent embodied the runaway fears of settlers. History seemed to be repeating itself, for the Maroons who had so bedeviled the Spaniards in 1655 to the point that they contributed to Madrid's loss of the entire island were now seemingly engaging in a repeat performance—but with London this time as the victim. Cudjoe was thought to be aligned with a group known as the "Madagascars," suggestive of the expansive geographic reach of the ever-broadening slave trade. Finally, a treaty was brokered with these rebels in early 1738, as Maroon settlements were given de facto if not de jure diplomatic recognition—but what kind of signal did this send to nearby Africans, not to mention the Spaniards who might deduce that aligning with Africans suffering under the Union Jack could be a wise course?[63] Just as Madrid's surrender of Gibraltar to London was a telling sign of the correlation of the forces between the two powers, the treaty between Maroons in Jamaica and the Crown and the surrender of territory it mandated was an indication that British rule on this valuable island might not be eternal. And if Jamaica could be threatened by Africans, what did that mean for other possessions? Was the rise of the Maroons—and the de facto abolition they represented—simply a sign that the wiser policy was a Crown-directed abolition rather than a helter-skelter retreat in the face of angry Africans, perhaps in alliance with competing European powers? Would not the latter policy embody an even bigger loss than state-mandated abolition?

The naysayers disagreed. The treaty with the Maroons was deemed by some as a "humiliation" for London and a victory for "Captain Cudjoe" and his compatriots, who were, it was said, to be "in a perfect state of freedom"—not the kind of signal to send to a labor force based on brute coercion. Still, London could rest comfortably that it would escape the fate handed to Spain in 1655 in Jamaica since the Maroons had agreed that "in case this island be invaded by any foreign enemy, the said Captain Cudjoe and his successors" would fight alongside the redcoats.[64] No wonder London's critics were furious. The concession wrung from the Maroons was their pledge to kill Europeans—and even that could not be guaranteed, for "Captain Cudjoe" could just as easily betray London and ally with Madrid or Paris.

The situation, in short, was dicey for London in Jamaica. Would the rich colony be abandoned? What if the Spanish, in particular, worked out an entente with remaining Africans—after all, Madrid had ruled there just decades earlier: what might that mean for the overall balance in the region? Maroons were said to be in touch with Spaniards in neighboring Cuba, offering to invite their return on condition that their own freedom was guaranteed. When London dispatched two regiments from Gibraltar to bolster its deteriorating presence in the region, it may have occurred to Madrid to pounce on this colony on what was thought to be its land and punish the British further by aligning with the Maroons.[65]

Thus, did prudence then dictate London downsizing in the Caribbean and fortifying the mainland? But would that not play into the hands of mainland colonies there already leaning toward "independency"? And if London were forced to abandon Jamaica, what did that portend for the slavery project in the Americas as a whole? London was trapped in a maze of irreconcilable contradictions—though the elongated response was building a ("white") pro-slavery wall in Georgia, which could protect colonies to the north, while menacing competing colonial powers to the south.

Perhaps if the problem for colonialism could be localized in Jamaica, the wound that Maroons had begun to inflict decades earlier could be isolated and cauterized there, but such was not to be. For in 1733–1734,

Africans in the Danish Caribbean revolted with substantial military success over a period of months, endangering the entire colonial enterprise.[66] In 1729, a murderous plot of the enslaved was exposed in Antigua,[67] but it was in 1736 that an island-wide conspiracy of the Africans was uncovered there, which was the culmination of what had been a riotous spate of unrest since the slave-trade "reforms" decades earlier— for the enslaved intended to take the entire island and extirpate European settlement. London should not have been overly surprised, for as early as 1666 the problem of fugitive slaves had become so rampant that fear was cascading through the settlement.[68] Yet the quandary for the colonists was crystallized when after the 1729 tumult, the accused Africans were banished to the "northern colonies," where they could continue their mischief.[69] This banishment also exposed the colonial dilemma, since simply executing rebellious Africans was problematic given their value, while exiling them—often miles away from friends and familiar sights—would serve to alienate them further and would not necessarily convert the Africans left behind into pro-colonial advocates.

The news from Antigua in 1736 was startling nevertheless. By this troublesome year, there were reportedly three thousand Europeans and twenty-four thousand Africans on the island. The latter were reputedly inspired by the earlier turmoil of 1729 and the news of a similarly inspired revolt in the Danish Caribbean a few years later, when forty Europeans were massacred: this gave impetus to the gathering idea that Africans were increasingly acting in concert, a message hard to ignore on the mainland, where the African population was growing steadily. That the 1736 plot came so close to fruition after a long gestation was likewise worrisome.[70] If the trend of Africans acting in concert was on the uptick, despite the miles of ocean that separated them, then an impenetrable wall of "white" solidarity in Georgia was more desperately needed than first thought.

The prominent Carolinian Robert Pringle—a man with varied interests over a broadening expanse of territory—was certainly acting in concert, notably in early 1739 when he expressed frightful concern to a fellow European in St. Kitts about the "great mortality" of that island and the not disconnected reality of his interlocutor being "alarm'd for fear of an insurrection of the Negroes."[71]

Likewise, Europeans, it was reported in Antigua in 1736, were "to be murdered and a new form of Government to be established by the Slaves among themselves." There was concern that this "execrable conspiracy must reach the knowledge of distant countries and probably be animadverted upon with severity"—that is, reach the ears of Spaniards with a mutual interest in routing the British. Seeming regrets were expressed about the enslavement of Africans that was the root of this barely averted fiasco that led to forty-seven Africans executed on 15 December 1736: "we think it our duty," said this mealy-mouthed analyst, "to [advise] our fellow subjects of Great Britain to consider that slavery is not our choice but necessity; it being impossible to carry on our Sugar Manufactures by white Labourers"—a thesis then being challenged due north in Georgia.[72]

That this 1736 conspiracy was led by a valuable man, a "master carpenter" known as "Tomboy," was equally troubling. Born on the Gold Coast, his crew included reportedly "creoles of French parentage," with all being "initiated into the Roman Catholic religion," a troubling sign in the midst of a religious cold war (as was the reputed French angle). "The general tenour of the oath," it was announced tremulously, "was to kill whites"; an alleged cause illustrated the difficult straits of the colonial project: "we may say with certainty," said officialdom, "that the particular inducement to the slaves to set this plot on foot, next to the hope of freedom, was the inequality of numbers of white and black." A discourse that emerged on the legality of the enslaved being witnesses in court was the kind of development that would—simultaneously—enrage mainlanders beginning to worry about London's allegiance to bondage.[73]

Antigua 1736 was a paradigmatic event, informing one and all that colonies with overwhelming African majorities were unsustainable in the long run, thus hastening a redeployment of capital and personnel alike to the mainland—which in turn hastened the onset of the 1776 revolt, as tensions hurtled northward. Abraham Redwood—born in Antigua in 1709—was present in 1736: two of the chief conspirators were his slaves. Within months, he had sailed to the mainland, depositing his young family in Rhode Island, where—not coincidentally—the African population soon ballooned. Redwood became a major force in Newport, where the chief library today continues to carry his name and where his contribution to what became the United States continues to be celebrated.[74]

What was happening was not only capital—and managerial—flight to the mainland in the face of a none-too-slumbering volcano in the Caribbean but also moving the problem of slavery northward, which could only heighten the pace of change as Africans who had seen terror on the face of planters took up residence in North America. Thus, John Cleland, who had an Antigua plantation, applied to bring 120 Africans with him as he evacuated to South Carolina—which was not exactly a tranquil refuge for enslavement. He thought he could "employ" these laborers "much more to his advantage" in Carolina—and compared to Antigua, this was probably accurate.[75]

Nonetheless, it was not good news for mainland Africans and their destiny that by the end of the 18th century those arriving to form a new republic had been often driven to this point by the specter and reality of Europeans being slain by the enslaved. It may have been worse news when just as the authorities were sifting through the dire consequences of Antigua, they then had to contemplate requesting aid from the "French governor of St. Martin's" in order to "suppress a rebellion of Negroes in St. Bartholomew's"; evidently, this was a plot that involved more than one island, since "Anguilla Negroes went to join those in St. Martin's," and the colonizers felt compelled to cross boundaries in a similar manner.[76] But if the perpetual foe in Paris had to be called upon for aid, then what was the point of inter-colonial rivalry and war?

Given bloody revolt in the Caribbean, forming "white" Georgia can be seen as a way station by way of detour to abolition. That is, building a pro-slavery wall was a final and futile attempt to resolve the pulverizing dilemma delivered by mass employment of enslaved African labor. When "white" Georgia could not hold, conflicting and rupturing approaches were in order: abolition crept ever closer in London, along with secession and doubling down on enslavement by the settlers. Thus, the threat to stability said to be brought by enslaved Africans was so great that in 1736 even William Byrd—who become fabulously wealthy by dint of his avid participation in enslavement—was beginning to suspect that bringing more Africans to Virginia would only provide kindling for a conflagration.[77]

In sum, by the 1730s the suspicion was growing that slavery was morphing into a catastrophic success; that is, it had produced enormous riches and development while providing a huge opening for a stunning reversal of this model by way of African revolt, assisted by the indigenous,

European foes, or both. Georgia was the response: "the French are continually undermining us both in the East and West Indies," one Londoner
proclaimed in 1733, and this latest province could act as a buffer, particularly if there was "no appearance of slavery, not even in Negroes."[78]

But proclaiming a "white" colony was one thing—actualizing it was
quite another. Put simply, how could Georgia compete with the gravitational pull exerted by slave labor on working conditions—not to mention compensation—while its competitors luxuriated in this form of
bondage? The eminent settler Peter Gordon demanded enslaved Africans and dismissed European servants as "the very scum and refuse
of mankind, trained up in all sorts of vice, often loaded with bad dis-
tempers."[79] As early as 1735, one prominent settler was arguing that it
was "next to an impossibility" to proceed with the original blueprint.
The Europeans were unaccustomed to the "hot climate" and could not
"bear the scorching rays of the sun"; there was a "great deal of difference
between the expense of white servants and of Negroes, for Negroes
can endure this climate without any clothes"—yet another savings—
"whereas white men must be clothed." As for "diet," it cost less to feed
Africans. European poor were "generally indented for four or at most
five years," while Africans were in bondage eternally. "Frequent running
away" was easier for Europeans. Of course, said this settler, they did not
intend to commit the error of Charleston and allow for a "great number" of Africans—but excluding them altogether was ridiculous.[80]

By late 1738, clamor for Africans continued to build, despite the
"inconveniences and mischiefs" that accompanied their presence[81]—
since colonists were past masters in the devious art of smuggling,
barring Africans from Georgia would always be dubious in any case.
Oglethorpe—the leading colonist—objected strenuously, warning
bluntly that if Africans were to "be allowed, this colony must be immediately destroyed, for it would be impossible to prevent them deserting to the Spaniards, . . . who give freedom, land and protection to all
runaway Negroes"—who then might return arms in hand bent on furious revenge. Besides, overturning Georgia's original reason for being
would simply empower the "Negro merchants" who delivered Africans
and who had a penchant for flooding the market to the detriment of
security and who would then direct their ill-gotten gains to "lands in
the colony," thus eroding the fortunes of competing interests. "They

would pretend that there might be some limitation in numbers," it was announced perceptively. "But limitations cannot be put in practice, as experience has proved in other countries."[82]

Carolina's problem—an African majority—could soon become Georgia's problem, thus maximizing the perils faced by mainland colonies as a whole. For in the run-up to Stono's Revolt in September 1739—mainland Africans' imitation of their counterparts in Antigua 1736—the number of Africans in Carolina was increasing heedlessly, as if there were not a price in blood to be paid.[83] Carolinians were not alone in their insouciance, for by 1734 colonists in Mobile and New Orleans were demanding more Africans, apparently oblivious to the threat to life and limb that their presence seemed to promise: often they were getting them from Hispaniola, a frequent haunt of New Englanders, which suggested that these Gulf Coast Africans could soon wind up in Georgia or Carolina given this flexibly fluid market in slaves.[84] At the same time, the number of Africans in St. Augustine was rising correspondingly,[85] as debacle was courted by English-speaking settlers.

This London well knew, but the promise of holding vast colonial territory, with the enchanting dreams of profit it portended, was sufficient to squash doubts. But how could London responsibly initiate a colony in Georgia under the nose of a hostile Madrid, while its own colonists were bolstering this religious foe and colonial competitor?

It would have been understandable if London viewed its colonists as ungrateful wretches, demanding expenditure to protect against rampaging indigenes and Africans and European foes, while cutting deals with the latter in particular. "Our sugar islands are in a declining condition," warned one Londoner in 1738, "chiefly by the increase of the French settlements," buoyed by mainland treachery. If Caribbean colonies were weakened, the same fate could befall those on the mainland, which would then ricochet across the Atlantic to destabilize forts in Africa—which, like falling dominoes, could then endanger London itself. Yet colonial planters wondered why they could not send their produce directly to buyers, as they continued to question the very essence of colonialism itself.[86]

Carolina's proximity to the Caribbean now meant it had—in many ways—become the guardian blocking the path to Virginia heading northward, yet simultaneously this province with a growing African majority was subject to the machinations of the burgeoning threat posed by Spanish Florida and rampant instability in Jamaica. Georgia was the response—but was it sufficient even if the formidable obstacle of barring Africans could be attained?

Then there was the unstable internal situation in South Carolina itself. In late February 1733, a report was filed concerning "several large companys of Negroes meeting very lately at different places"—"three hundred met on Sunday last"—accompanied by "frequent robberies, insolences and unrestrained liberties of most slaves at this time." So far, so typical— but what was frightening was the perception that "there is some plot on foot, destructive to His Majesty's subjects in this province." The alarm was sounded: "no time may be lost" to intercept and crush this looming danger.[87] Africans, said the leading politicos, had "committed many outrages and robberys and lye in the swamp at the Head of Wando River where they bid defiance." To foil their "resistance," it was deemed necessary to "exercise military discipline either by shooting them or otherwise."[88]

It was almost as if the settler population could be diagnosed clinically with an advanced state of paranoia. But, as the saying goes, paranoids can have real enemies too, and such was the case for mainland settlers confronted daily by rebellious Africans determined to overturn the system they had been dragooned to build. When a free Negro arrived from Virginia—with "seven Negroes of his own"—he was greeted not with warmth as a class comrade whose existence could reassure the enslaved that eternal drudgery was not their destiny but with suspicious investigation.[89] In a shockingly clarifying moment in the immediate prelude to 1776, a similarly well-positioned African—Thomas Jeremiah—was executed by rebels in an unmistakable indicator that Africans generally would not be warmly embraced by the new republic.[90] The equivalence between African and slave and African and foe continued to build, a sobering development and not a predictor of racial harmony on the mainland.

*   *   *

Virginia, which was to become the hotbed of the rebel revolt in 1776, was likewise concerned about seditious slaves and their allies. In 1732, there were attempts to "make more effectual provision against invasions and insurrections," while by 1736 there were efforts to ensure "better regulation of the militia so as to render it more powerful for preventing

insurrections of slaves"—a campaign deemed necessary since "so
many Negroes are brought into the country."[91] As in neighboring Carolina, a tax was placed on the most valuable commodity—Africans—in
order to assure that any of their potential insurrectional plans would
be thwarted, the premise being that this would reduce the size of their
population. That parishioners should take arms to worship on Sundays
was mandated—a reflection of the time that Africans often chose to
revolt[92] and more than a "Hail Mary" (or, more realistically, a Protestant
prayer) ensuring that they would not do so.

Virginia, being a locus of valuable commerce, was unable to avoid
often disconcerting commerce with foreigners. In mid-1735, leaders
there were considering business dealings with the slave depot that Brazil
was becoming, a deal involving tobacco and other potentially lucrative
transactions in both Europe and Africa; ultimately, said William Gooch,
this arrangement meant "Trade to Africa should be increased"—the ultimate source of wealth—though the riches flowing into Williamsburg as
a result were bound to attract the eager attention of Spain.[93] It was also in
1735 that Gooch reminded London about the most recent war with Spain
when a Spanish prize was brought to his domain that included "several
Mulattos and Indians, said to be Spanish slaves," who may have been
sold in his jurisdiction, though he conceded their status was unclear;
such questionable sales invoking the more pinched approach to color
and slave status on the mainland often brought mainlanders into conflict
with His Catholic Majesty,[94] not to mention pushing the melanin rich
generally toward Madrid—and St. Augustine.

By 1735, London had begun to wonder if, perhaps, Virginians might
want to elasticize their notion of privilege by emulating the Spaniards—
as London would feel constrained to do by placing Africans among
the redcoats—by expanding the franchise to include free Negroes and
persons defined as "Mulattoes": this would erode an advantage held by
Madrid, thus enhancing the viability of Virginia itself. London's man
could not comprehend why "one *freeman* should be used worse than
another merely upon account of his complexion"; why "strip" these
groups of "those rights which are so justly valuable to every freeman,"
he wondered (emphasis original).[95]

Gooch was dumbfounded, reminding of a "conspiracy" of late among
those groups that the Crown wanted to reward, designed to eliminate

the settlement. Such plots, he pleaded, would "for ever be the case"—
"such was the insolence of the free Negroes at that time," he argued, "that
the next Assembly thought it necessary, not only to make the meetings
of slaves very penal, but to fix a perpetual brand upon free Negroes and
mulattos, . . . well knowing they always did and ever will adhere to and
favour the slaves." Yes, this did "seem to carry an air of severity," but slavery and colonialism were not for the fainthearted; and, in any case, as
"most of them are the bastards of some of the worst of our imported servants and convicts, it seems no ways impolitick, as well for discouraging
that kind of copulation as to preserve a better distinction between them
and their betters."[96] Such disputes reinforced the settler perception that
London was dangerously wobbly on the bedrock matter of persecution
of the "non-white," deepening the growing chasm between colony and
metropolis, bringing permanent rupture ever closer.

Mainland colonists were inviting disaster: they had been unable or
unwilling to stanch the seemingly ceaseless flow of Africans to their
shores, including those from rebellious Antigua with demonstrated
plans for mayhem in their hearts, who were joining those—notably in
Carolina—who were of like mind. Antigua was a mighty shot over the
bow by the Africans, inducing others besides Abraham Redwood to
contemplate abandoning ship, as it was apparent that Jamaica too—and
perhaps the Danish Caribbean and Anguilla and a spreading splotch
of turbulence in the region—was jeopardizing the colonial project as a
whole and even allowing European competitors to oust London altogether. Carolina had been the designated firewall protecting Virginia
and points north, but then the formation of Georgia was a damaging
admission that a new firewall had to be constructed and extended further south to the border with Spanish Florida. But this was a poisoned
chalice since now London's subjects were ever closer to armed brigades
of Africans, many of whom sought bloody revenge against these rapa-
cious settlers. London was forced to defend a profoundly unsettled
mainland with an unusual conception of patriotism that did not rule
out intimate relations with the Crown's bitterest enemies.

In September 1739, what came to be known as Stono's Revolt in South
Carolina exemplified the unavoidable fact that sterner measures would
have to be manufactured in order to conquer those who were now routinely referred to as "intestine" enemies: Africans.[97]

5

The Stono Uprising

Will the Africans Become Masters and the Europeans Slaves?

What was known as Stono's Revolt—a mass uprising of enslaved Africans in September 1739 in South Carolina that led to the massacre of dozens of settlers—took place at a time of rising tension with Spain and increased restiveness by Africans, suggesting that the newest firewall that was Georgia was proving to be quite porous. The authorities thought that what instigated this frightful upsurge was the repeated proclamations issued at St. Augustine by His Catholic Majesty promising freedom to all Africans who deserted from the north.[1] Perhaps if the massacres had been confined to the fiery border between Carolina and Georgia, the problem could have been contained. But Stono was simply part of a larger conflict between London and Madrid that stretched to Cartagena. London was unable to seize this city on the northern coast of South America, nor Cuba, while Madrid—despite significant aid from armed Africans—was unable to dislodge mainland settlers in Carolina and Georgia permanently. Nonetheless, one did not have to be far-sighted to envision that London had stumbled into a corrosive long-term problem unless it could neutralize or eviscerate the advantage accrued by His Catholic Majesty in arming Africans. Contrarily, heedlessly and perilously, manacled Africans continued arriving in the southeast quadrant of the mainland where the Union Jack fluttered, where they became ripe targets for recruitment by His Catholic Majesty.

*   *   *

After the slaughter of twenty-nine settlers[2] near the Stono River, viewed with stark suspicion was the delegation from Florida that had appeared just before this trailblazing event, supposedly with the aim of delivering a letter to General Oglethorpe—though it was generally known that

he was in Georgia. An official report, after stressing that the "insurrection" actually "depended on St. Augustine for a place of reception afterwards," pointed to the curiosity that the Spanish delegation bearing the
letter included an African who "spoke English very well" and, presumably, briefed the insurrectionists.[3]

Then shortly after the revolt, a Spaniard—said to be a priest—was
seized in Savannah; according to an official investigation, he was tasked
to "procure a *general insurrection* of the *Negroes*" (emphasis original).
"Every breast was filled with concern," it was averred with no little
veracity—and unbounded anger at St. Augustine, the "receptacle of
debtors, servants and slaves!"[4] Understandably, during the anxious
years of 1738–1739, Oglethorpe was obsessed with the threat from Spanish Florida—and eliminating it.[5]

Sifting through the ashes of revolt, Carolinians lamented the fact that
the Africans increasingly surrounding them were "brought from the
Kingdom of Angola," and "many of them speak Portuguese (which language is as near Spanish as Scotch is to English)"—providing Madrid
with an incalculable advantage, not least since the Africans were perceived as a multiple threat, as they were presumed to be Catholic too.
The Stono uprising was led by Angolans, it was concluded with discon-
solation. Worse, as the triumphant Africans headed southward to liberty, their numbers "increased every minute by new Negroes coming
to them, . . . some say a hundred"—there was rapturous "dancing, sing-
ing and beating drums to draw more Negroes to them"; tellingly, even
when "routed," the Africans "behaved boldly"—even as dozens of them
were systematically executed.[6] Perhaps it was a reflection of Carolinians'
arrogance—or ignorance—that reportedly they preferred the enslaved
to hail from Angola, though they might be conversant in a language
close to Spanish and might be Catholic besides.[7]

The Stono rebellion arrived at a supremely inopportune moment
for the settlers, for it was during those tense days that word arrived in
Charleston that war with Spain had erupted, and it did not require a
seer to imagine that the two events were connected.[8] The influential
William Stephens of the colony in Georgia, which was in the crosshairs,
moaned—as the scent of death still hung in the air from the Africans'
marauding—that "in the midst of these hostilities from abroad, it was
now [settlers'] great unhappiness to have a more dangerous enemy in

the heart of their country," a reference to the "Negroes [who] made an Insurrection." Carolina was "full of flames," he groaned.[9]

The Stono uprising struck terror in the hearts and minds of settlers,[10] solidifying the perception that though enslaved Africans were necessary for development, their presence was dangerous and, therefore, they must be even more brutally oppressed. But this bloodthirsty callousness would only serve to drive Africans further into the arms of the indigenous, Spaniards—or whoever appealed to them—which then heightened the oppressive strategy of the settlers, and so on and so on in an endless loop of destruction. When London seemed insensitive to this dilemma by seeming to take steps toward abolition, the already yawning gulf between the colonists and the metropolitans widened.

Stono also potentially jeopardized the entire colonial project in Carolina.[11] It was the culmination of years of turbulence, driven by fissures among elites and emerging doubts about their ability to govern. Unfortunately for them, Africans had a say about their future: when an African was hanged in a public square as an example after being compelled to make an unsteady oration urging slaves to be content with their desperate plight, it said more about the insecurities of his executioners than his forced words ever could.[12]

Carolinians were on edge for good reason, for in Charleston in August 1736 a visiting Hessian soldier observed that the entire "province was at the point of experiencing the most horrible Sicilian Vespers imaginable," referring to an awesomely furious mass slaughter of despised occupiers. "The entire Negro population . . . had conspired to assault their masters on a certain night, massacre all the [male] white population, make the women either their slaves or use them to gratify their desires, and sacrifice the rest." They intended to "attack the city, seize the magazines and massacre the inhabitants"—but were thwarted.[13]

More to the point, just before Stono, Don Manuel de Montiano, one of Madrid's chief delegates in St. Augustine, was chortling about the misfortune that had befallen London's settlers in the region. They had embarked, he said, with "100 Negroes to build a fort," but the enslaved "rose, slew all the English and hamstrung all the horses"—then "scattered." Supposedly, the runaways inquired about "the road to the Spaniards," a path trod by innumerable Africans previously.[14] On 31 May 1738, Montiano, in presaging this massacre and the enhanced tumult to come, reported elatedly that various fugitive Africans from the "English colonies" who somehow were ensnared in bondage in St. Augustine appeared before him and demanded their liberty—which was promptly granted over the adamant protests of their captors, a decision that was bound to increase his popularity among Negroes. On 16 February 1739, Montiano, in an evident escalation of the conflict with London, set aside an encampment near St. Augustine called Gracia Real de Santa Teresa de Mose—terrified Carolinians came to refer to it haltingly as Fort Mose or "Moosa," the site of a battle-hardened military unit composed of Africans.[15]

It is hard to separate the 1739 revolt from the ongoing contest between London and Madrid in the region. Madrid was "insolent," claimed one Londoner, adding, "the only method of reducing Spain to reason was first to make her feel our power."[16] Left unsaid was that at the root of this contestation was fierce jousting between the powers over the control of the fruits of the immensely lucrative African Slave Trade.[17] Perhaps even more troubling for Africans in the long term was the chauvinistic campaign launched by London against Madrid, seeking to prove the alleged superiority of supposedly fair-skinned, fair-haired Protestants, rather than the reputed dark, cruel, treacherous, and Catholic Spanish: this did not bode well for the abolitionist cause that presupposed a lessening of invidious discrimination targeting the dark-skinned.[18] Typically, such chauvinism targeting other Europeans was seemingly indifferent to the all-important cause of "whiteness," which served to complicate the colonialism of which it was a constituent element.

William Bull, a leader of Carolina, who had considerable military experience, warned days after the Stono revolt of the dire consequences of this event, as if he were reading Montiano's thoughts: "if such an attempt was made in a time of peace and tranquility," he asked, "what might be expected if an enemy should appear upon our frontier with a design to invade us"?—which, he well knew, was not a hypothetical concern.[19] Bull had been thinking along these lines even before the flames of Stono illuminated his thoughts: in early 1739, Bull recommended an "expedition against St. Augustine," prompted by the "dangers" provided by "the Spaniards giving open protection & encouragement to the Negroes"—"bombs, mortars & an engineer for the use of them" was demanded urgently.[20]

Weeks after Stono, policymakers in Charleston remained in an uproar, fretting that their "deserted slaves" now in St. Augustine might "rise in rebellion" against them: so "demolition of that place would free us from the like danger for the future."[21] "If we do not take this opportunity of attacking Augustine while it is weak," said Oglethorpe with sweeping portent, "all North America as well as Carolina and this province will feel it severely."[22] Their settlements could not long survive when "Negroes are encouraged" to massacre their masters. Quite sensitive to this crisis, Governor James Glen—a native of Scotland who served from 1738 to 1756—was obsessing about yet another fire in Charleston and wondering "how far this Accident may encourage our Negroes and other Enemies to form some dangerous Scheme."[23] The long-serving Glen was tautly alert to the threat imposed by Africans, considering them "more dangerous enemies" than either "Indians [or] Spaniards," since they were "ready to revolt on the first opportunity and are eight times as many in number as there are white men able to bear arms," a "danger" grown greater since Oglethorpe's "unhappy expedition to St. Augustine."[24]

These Africans, Glen emphasized, were "more formidable enemies than Indians can ever be, as they speak our language and would never be at a loss for intelligence."[25] That Africans were now ranked higher as a threat than "Indians or Spaniards" was quite telling, an indication of the dismal failure of the slave-trade "reforms," in that these measures had created a massive danger to security. If Africans were now the primary danger, would that mean more repression of them? Would it mean cutting a deal to subdue the Africans, even if it meant an entente with Madrid?

Spanish and African designs were no secret, since Carolinians were often in and out of St. Augustine. There stood the influential Caleb Davis early in 1739, in search of nineteen of Port Royal's most valuable Africans who had spirited away to Florida only recently. With temerity, he had demanded that the authorities in St. Augustine facilitate their capture, but to his dismay "the governor refused to deliver," ascribing his refusal to the edict of "His Catholick Majesty." Accusingly, Davis charged that this was a reneging on a bilateral accord between the province and Florida—but was rebuffed nonetheless.[26]

Neither the patience nor the capital—represented in the bodies of enslaved Africans—of Carolinians was inexhaustible. Spanish plans to attack Georgia in an attempt to suffocate the toddler of a colony, in a scheme that was said to involve a goodly number of armed Africans, were no secret either.[27] Havana was said to be the point of embarkation and battering Savannah the goal, which placed Georgia in a tizzy since fortifications were still paltry—what were described happily as "contrary winds" saved the settlement.[28] Pithily, the lieutenant governor of South Carolina spoke of the "designs formed by the Spaniards to invade and unsettle the colony of Georgia and to excite an insurrection of the Negroes of this province."[29] In what was thought to be faraway Virginia, there was awareness of the "considerable body of land forces" headed from Havana: "Spanish bravado," said William Gooch, was designed to "intimidate the people of Georgia from prosecuting their settlements."[30]

Feeling cornered, mere days after Stono, General Oglethorpe tried to arrange an attack on St. Augustine—"before more troops arrived there from [Cuba]," it was announced. But Carolina was reeling from smallpox and yellow fever—not to mention apprehension of what would occur and how Africans would react once armed settlers headed miles away. Oglethorpe may have had his opposition to the presence of Africans confirmed when he was forced to debate whether the enslaved should accompany his brigades and, if so, how many "white men sufficient to guard them & oversee them" would be needed. But this was a mere piffle compared to the basic matter of survival, for he knew that "they had to attack" Florida; if they did not, all British colonies on the mainland would be jeopardized. A "defensive war" had to be launched in order to free these colonies from St. Augustine, "from whence their *Negroes* were encouraged to *massacre* their masters" (emphasis original). This led to an uncomfortable, perhaps untenable decision: including Africans in an armed attack designed to bolster enslavement of Africans. Thus, "800 Negroes" would be included in the attacking force—and "160 white men to guard & oversee them," a cumbersome force at best. They were able to inflict some damage on St. Augustine in early 1740, though encountering fierce and former Carolina Negroes there was hardly uplifting. More to the point, after their initial success, they were constrained in following up, "having received advice from home that the Negroes were like to make another insurrection."[31]

Ultimately, it was determined that slaveholders who provided Africans to the armed forces would have their expenses subsidized, but in no case should the "proportion" of the militarized be more than "one third blacks to two thirds white."[32] Left unanswered was how effective an attacking force could be when it had to remain constantly on guard against a racial eruption within its own ranks. From London's viewpoint, did it make sense to expend the Exchequer on military missions involving Africans in bloody conflicts designed to preserve the enslavement of Africans? Would it not make more sense to involve free Africans in military missions designed simply to defeat despised European enemies, for example, Spain? But would settlers bow to the idea of free and militarized Africans in their midst? And what would a free and militarized African population on the mainland mean to the militarized identity politics that was "whiteness," which seemed to be based on this dark-skinned population's mass degradation?

By early 1740, Spanish troops were assaulting Georgia—"murdering the men there," according to Oglethorpe. "I pursued them into Florida," he said, where he noticed a fort peopled by Africans and the indigenous: they were "building a new one of Stone called Moosa to protect the Plantations they had granted to runaway Negroes who were armed and officered"—at that point there were an estimated "200 . . . armed Negroes" at this site,[33] and confrontation with them could easily inspire the Africans alongside him to his detriment.[34] Nevertheless, on 16 May 1740, Oglethorpe attacked Fort Mose, but this citadel was re-supplied from Cuba, which turned the tide against him, just as a similar effort had blunted a London offensive in 1702.[35] Oglethorpe's forces limped home, though one observer claimed they "fought like Lions"—yet still "lost their lives."[36]

It was then that settlers made an angst-ridden appeal to the Crown, recounting "smallpox" in 1738, then "pestilential fever" in 1739, and now "insurrection of our slaves," combined with "dangers from abroad"; there were "enemys very near and far too numerous and powerful for us," it was declared. Oglethorpe's forces had been "unsuccessful," and the prognosis was dire: "we are now exposed to [a] powerful enemy roused with resentment"—and that was not even taking the threat from the French into account.[37] Subsequently, Carolinians discovered that the night before the attack on Fort Mose, "many Negroes, Mulattoes and other slaves"—"between four and five hundred" all told—met with Florida's governor "and the Bishop," at which point they were informed that if they "swore by a cross" and "would fight well and drive the English out," they would benefit handsomely.[38]

Bull captured the fears of his settlement when he lamented how slave "property" had "become so very precarious and uncertain" to the point where "their Negroes" which had been "their chief support may in little time become their enemies if not their masters,"[39] and the ruling elite would be "unable to withstand it or prevent it"[40]—a plaintive cry that became ever more insistent as the two major mainland trends were revealed more dramatically: as London moved unsteadily toward abolition, settlers began thinking more and more that the Crown was at least unreliable and even capable of aligning with the Africans to corral the colonists. Surely, if influential colonists were mulling the wrenching possibility of the Africans becoming the "masters" of the settlers—a mind-boggling turn of events still difficult to imagine even today—it, minimally, presupposed that the redcoats would not ride to their rescue.

It was Bull who led the rhetorical charge against Spanish Florida and its encouragement of Negro restiveness, denouncing the unsettling reality that in mid-1740 "many [Africans] have already deserted and others [were] encouraged to do the same; and even those who have committed the most inhuman Murders are there harboured, entertained, and caressed."[41] Bull should have been forced to consider that if Spaniards were "caressing" Africans while his compatriots were lashing them, then elite Carolinians should have adopted a more benign approach—but this was incompatible with their obtaining colonial enterprise that mandated brutalizing of the enslaved.

*   *   *

Dealing with Florida and the insurgent Africans there was enough to deliver nightmares, but Bull also had to contend with "great apprehensions of Danger from the French & their Indians" on the colonists' back.[42] Bull well knew about the ever-present threat provided by the indigenous, while the French did not seem to be in the mood to disappear either. Earlier, one of Bull's fellow leaders, speaking from Barbados, wondered about the "exorbitant and surprising increase of the French in these parts"; it could easily be interpreted as a sign of weakness, driven by the unfolding fiasco with Maroons, when he proposed carving up the region with Paris—instead of driving them out—and even including in the bargain "Native Indians and free Negroes" in St.

Vincent, where they were in the process of gaining the upper hand. "If the French will not come into this," he said defiantly, "surely they have a premeditated design to circumvent and over run us"—to which an ordinary Parisian might nod sagely and approvingly.[43]

As years passed, this concern about French encroachment did not dissipate. There arose a dispute with Paris over control of St. Lucia, with France being advantaged, according to Governor Robert Dinwiddie of Virginia, since they "settled very fine plantations" there with "300 French families," which meshed nicely with their holdings in Dominica and their "settlement on St. Vincent." Though Virginia was many hundreds of miles away, Dinwiddie sensed that this French advance could in the long run threaten his own colony: "in a few years [France] will be so strong in those and other Sugar Islands (if the Crown of Great Britain does not interpose) that if we should have war with France, [I] am afraid that they will be able to invade and take all our Leeward Islands without any aid or assistance from Europe."[44]

"The great importance of the British Sugar Colonies to this Kingdom," said a Londoner shortly after Stono, "and the miserable circumstances they are reduced to" were even more remarkable given the "extraordinary progress France has of late years made"—a progress that was attributable in part, it was thought, to the privileged relationship of Paris's appendages to New England. The "pernicious practice of introducing French sugars into [the] Northern Colonies" was unjustifiable, if not treasonous. In order to obviate such a practice, the Crown felt compelled to bend prevailing racial praxis, which may have harmed further profit-making potential; that is, "coasting sloops" in the islands traditionally carried a Negro crew, but the latter could not provide "Evidence against a white person," a real demerit in an era of rampant piracy. Thus, it was mandated that "all coasting and trading vessels" should carry "a proportion of white men" instead—but the question lingered: from whence would they come? But something had to be done about "Northern Colonies" that had developed a "kind of Dependency on the French" to the "prejudice of Great Britain,"[45] according to one Londoner—and an oracle could have predicted an armed thrust toward independence by these provinces, ably assisted by France or, minimally, existential challenges to London's mainland possessions. And that same oracle might also have predicted that to bolster their ranks the anti-colonial rebels would elasticize the crucial identity that was "whiteness" to better confront Africans, indigenes, and other presumed foes by welcoming the huddled masses from all of Europe and not just those from the British isles.

For even before the thunderbolt that was Stono, the Africans had begun to upset the neat plan of building the mainland as a hedge against collapse in the Caribbean, for the distance between the two regions was insufficiently great to ensure that the flames of insurrection in Jamaica and Antigua could not be quarantined there. Carolina planters, ever alert to unrest in the Caribbean and what it might portend for their own livelihood—and lives—kept a close eye on this conflict-ridden region, and with the rise of Maroons and revolts, they had much to ponder. Early in 1739, the slaveholder Robert Pringle commiserated with a colleague in St. Kitts about mutual problems—the "fear of an insurrection of the Negroes" and the "hope" that their "wicked design will prove abortive & turn to their own Confusion."[46] Just before Stono, Pringle—ever alert to the machinations of Africans regionally—sympathized with another associate in Antigua about how (supposedly) that "island has already greatly suffered by putting too much trust in Negroes," whose most recent uproarious ructions had barely been put down.[47] Then Stono erupted, and Dixie slaveholders may have been excused if they had descended into feverish conniptions and the premonition that the end was nigh.

The perception was growing that London and the "Catholic powers" could not co-exist in North America. A sober Carolina investigation reviewed the sorry record: Coming, as it did, after Stono and after the failure to destroy Fort Mose, it appeared to be a summary of events pointing to a Copernican shift in London's approach to the mainland—perhaps not Africans becoming "masters," as Bull had hinted, but something similarly dire nonetheless. St. Augustine had been plundered in 1702 by redcoats and may have been taken altogether but for hurried aid from Havana. Then in 1704 and 1706, Spanish and French forces accompanied by "Mustees & Negroes and 200 Indians" retaliated in kind in Carolina. Then in 1715, the Yamasees were accompanied by Spaniards, leaving devastation in their wake. Then in 1727–1728, there was a repeat performance by the Spaniards, with luring slaves being a goal in all cases. Then there was the notorious edict from Madrid, transmitted by the beat of a drum in 1733—all culminating in Stono.

The conclusion? Something had to give. The antagonists of British settlers had to be defeated—and the Carolina elite much preferred to the see the backs of the Spaniards, the French, and their indigenous allies.[48] The problem was that the settlers' own harsh maltreatment of Africans made defeating the "Catholic powers" difficult. An entente with these powers, however, could open the door to a major victory for the settlers—while bewildering London and the enslaved simultaneously.

Shocks to a system, which is what Stono was, inexorably bring more far-reaching thinking, as the humdrum and the mundane are seen to be easily overturned. In sum, Spanish and French designs on London's holdings showed no signs of abating, which also meant that settlers' angst was not due for elimination either: Stono showed that Africans were straining to be free of the Union Jack as well, while profit-hungry settlers were willing to sell the rope that might be used to encircle their pasty necks. Suggestive of how the 1730s had marched the mainland to this turning point were the startling words of the powerful William Byrd of Virginia, who had bruited the similarly startling idea of curbing the slave trade: fear was a major reason, for as he acknowledged freely, "multiplying these Ethiopians amongst us" could ignite the always hovering "servile war."[49]

If a chain is only as strong as its weakest link, the fact was that the Carolina-Georgia-Florida border had become the weakest link in London's chain of mainland colonies, thereby jeopardizing them all. In June 1740, William Stephens received "intelligence again of another rising of the Negroes in Carolina, which, unless soon suppressed, has the appearance of greater danger than any of the former." This time Charleston was in the bull's-eye, and 150 furious Africans were on the march—"in defiance," he said. Reacting with brutal rage, the authorities again began executing them systematically—"they were daily hanging, ten in a day," said Stephens, though he still worried that the Africans might soon be "breaking open stores to find arms, as they did the last year." Given how "vastly disproportionate the number of white men is to theirs," he remained alarmed about how "precarious" things were.[50]

This worry was not misplaced, for it was not long before Oglethorpe himself had warned to "expect an Invasion from both French & Spaniards who if they succeed here [intend] to push their Conquest as far as Virginia," since "they may have too much reason to hope for success." Why? Because "all North & South Carolina being full of provisions and [containing] ten slaves to one white man[,] besides a very busy faction stirring at Carolina."[51]

Yet Byrd's words were destined to be ignored, for slavery and the slave trade had become a terribly addictive drug regularly delivering the mindless euphoria of stupendous profit—while simultaneously threatening survival of colonialism. Not long after Stono, Byrd's ostensible leader—Governor Robert Dinwiddie, the Glasgow-born executive responsible for pushing George Washington forward—announced beamingly the presence of "not less than one hundred thousand Negroes in the colonys on the main of America," with "two hundred and thirty one thousand Negro slaves belonging and employed in the British sugar colonys, which being valued 20 [pounds] sterling per head amounts to . . . 4,620,000 [pounds]." Yes, he said with the utmost satisfaction, "the British Empire of America is of inestimable value to the nation of Great Britain"—and given that, why not increase the capital that was Africans in order to increase wealth?[52]

Indicative of the crushing contradiction in which the mainland provinces found themselves was the reality that just as Byrd was considering curbs on this odious traffic, in Georgia—which had attracted the ravenous attention of Spaniards and Africans in Florida—there was already an attempt to remove the already leaky net constructed to exclude Africans. The Earl of Egmont dismissed these proponents in late 1737 as "malcontents" bent on "great mischief"—but that "many had been influenced to think with them" was indicative of the trajectory of the near future.[53] Oglethorpe, who railed against this veritable inevitability, found that the "poor people of Savannah[,] many of whom are deeply in debt" to a local merchant, felt obliged to "sign the Petition for Negroes which affirms that white men cannot work in this Province." Perhaps the "poor people" saw riches emerging from this deviation from the colony's origin, though Oglethorpe argued that "if the Petition is countenanced, the Province is ruined."[54]

Oglethorpe was not singular, for others also were concerned that more Africans "exposed" them all to "Domestick Treachery and Foreign Invasion," just to "gratify the greedy and ambitious views of a few Negro Merchants" who sought to "become sole owners of the province by introducing their baneful commodity"—with little awareness of the "Terror" this presented to "their unadvised Masters."[55] These Georgians thought it was madness to bring more Africans to their colony, given their propensity to revolt and ally with invaders. No, claimed those who were hungry for more enslaved Africans, what motivated them was something else: it was hypocrisy, they said, to "talk so much against slaves and slavery and at the same time oblige their fellow subjects, natives of the same land with themselves, to go through the same labour that the Negroes they are daily commiserating are employed."[56]

As so often happened for centuries to come, those who played this particular "race card" prevailed: to be against slavery of Africans meant you favored exploitation of Europeans. Or, to put it another way, those who favored lessening exploitation of Europeans should be in favor of enslavement of Africans. Those who prevailed were also implicitly arguing that "whiteness" itself would not be viable absent the presence of Africans to exploit shamelessly. Excluding enslaved Africans meant crass exploitation of European labor, which would mean class tensions and a dearth, by definition, of "white solidarity": this could be a greater threat to the colonial enterprise than enchained Africans—at least in theory.

Georgia was formed, as we have seen, to blunt Spanish Florida and Carolina Africans. By 1741, the cost of Africans was said to be about thirty pounds—the rough cost of passage from Europe to North America. Subsidizing this voyage, it was felt, offset the danger of larding the land with Africans. Plus, it was thought that enslaved Africans made settlers indolent and wasted time since so much effort was devoted to ensuring that bonded labor would not defect.

In effect, slavery placed the fate of the colony in the hands of those who were likely to revolt. Rice might mean African labor, but the silk to be developed in Georgia, it was said, needed only "women and children." Moreover, allowing African slavery meant a skewed class system, allowing "wealthy planters" and merchants to also lord it over "poor planters": the poor planter would feel the need to "mortgage his land to the Negro Merchant," allowing that merchant to gobble up readily the holdings of debtors. Besides, allowing slavery in Georgia would just move the problem of Africans fleeing ever closer to St. Augustine, thereby maximizing the problem that was supposed to be solved. These arguments were defeated.[57]

After 1776, it became quite fashionable in the new republic to blame London for the ills delivered by slavery, but what Georgia reveals—as one scholar noted—is that "if it was the aim of British policy to encourage trade in Negroes, the guidelines established for that colony could hardly have been less appropriate."[58] Buried in an avalanche of, perhaps, purposeful forgetfulness was a typical appeal made by one Georgia settler during this period, speaking of his compatriots: "Negroes, nothing but Negroes, is all the cry."[59]

Oglethorpe and his comrades were, in so many words, demanding a Georgia exception—"whiteness" in one colony. But how could this occur when on the Carolina border there was brutal slavery exerting a gravitational pull in one direction, while on the southern border there were armed Africans eager to invade? Ineluctably, Georgia would have to yield to the south or the north, and it did not require a sage to divine that yielding to the latter was more likely.

Repeatedly, Georgia's founding father—Oglethorpe—counseled that "Spanish emissarys are very busy stirring up Discontents among the People," and inexorably, "their principal point is Negroes," for he warned brusquely, "[there are] as many slaves as there are many Enemys to the Government and consequently friends to the Spaniard." What was to be done? "The way to overcome all this is to persist in allowing no Slaves, encourage the importation of Germans"[60]—but what if they were Catholic, which many were? Still, the pan-European project plodded ahead mercilessly.

For Oglethorpe would not budge. The Spanish, he opined, found "three insuperable obstacles in their way in driving out the English from this colony"—"the people being white and Protestants and no Negroes were naturally attached to the Government." True, there was the percolating matter of not only Spain but also France and other saboteurs seeking to entice Georgia to absorb more Africans, "being secure that Slaves would be either Recruits to an Enemy or Plunder for them."[61]

But Oglethorpe had proven to be a chess player who had difficulty in envisioning the consequences of his immediate moves: for it was not long after Stono that the authorities in Georgia noted pleasingly that since the formation of this colony, "the price of lands" had risen appreciably; as planned, the province was a "fine barrier for the Northern Provinces and especially for Carolina and is also a great security against the running away of Negroes from Carolina to Augustine." However, this was serving to make the province even more valuable than contemplated initially, which in the prevailing logic of the mainland had to mean increased demand for absurdly profitable enslaved Africans in Georgia,[62] a trend he opposed.

Oglethorpe had difficulty in factoring into this colonial equation the potency of stereotypes—or realities, as some of his peers would have it. Early on, one well-respected settler, while acknowledging the "inconveniences and mischief" that "the unlimited use of Negroes" delivered, felt their danger could be contained simply by limiting their numbers and proportions. For one thing, it was asserted, "their Constitutions are much stronger than white people and the heat in no way disagreeable nor hurtful to them."[63]

Initially South Carolina had been viewed as an extension of Barbados and the Caribbean generally, with Georgia belatedly organized as a protective membrane halting lancing offensives from Florida that could possibly reach the reward that was Virginia. But "reforms" of the slave trade sent more Africans to the region, complicating security profoundly, while developing the economy and bringing fabulous wealth to some colonists. Then Antigua 1736 and what was thought to be a humiliating settlement with Jamaican Maroons during the same era enhanced the value of mainland colonies—even though astute Londoners already had perceived that the Europeans and Africans arriving with regularity there were increasing the tendency toward "independency." But options for the Crown were narrowing: evidence was emerging that in light of the calamity in Jamaica, settlers were not only liquidating their holdings but were now selling Africans at fire-sale prices to Spaniards,[64] a clear signal from an important market that combined with French plans in the region indicated further pessimism about London's future in the hemisphere. Then Stono, related plots, and Madrid's penchant for collaborating effectively with Africans began to raise further doubts about the future of the mainland provinces. Tentative moves toward abolition by London could possibly checkmate Madrid (with the creation of a buffer class of "free Negroes" who could then be armed)— but would not this infuriate mainland settlers, impelling them recklessly toward "independency"?

*   *   *

Thus, the British Crown had to contend with an incipient abolitionist tendency—which the potential of losing the entire colonial investment through African revolt tended to bolster—yet this was a trend which was to enrage settlers in 1776. A British pastor traveled overland from Maryland to Georgia in late 1739 and was highly displeased with what he espied. The "miseries of the poor Negroes" angered him: "I think God has a quarrel," he thundered, "with you for your abuse of and cruelty to the poor Negroes." Given the atrocities perpetrated against them, he wondered why there were "not more instances of self-murder among the Negroes, or that they have not more frequently rose up in Arms against their owners. Virginia has once and Charlestown more than once been threatened in this way," he said in a manner that suggested he would welcome further revolts. He twisted the knife further by warning that a "foreign enemy is now threatening to invade you," which combined with African unrest could spell doom for the entire colonial project.[65] His words were mirrored by those of Samuel Johnson, who began to attack slavery as early as 1740.[66]

It needs to be considered that incipient abolitionism is hard to disconnect from comprehensible concern about the stability of the bloodily profitable slave system. This British cleric might have noticed in his peregrinations that there had been a large influx of Africans to Delaware after 1713 and about two decades later this group was almost 20% of the colony's population. At that juncture, as war with Spain loomed ominously, the Africans regionally revolted and aimed at uniting both the eastern and western shores of Maryland under their control, with an uncertain future designated for the settlers—who then proceeded to rally and head off this upsurge. As this desperate squashing unfolded, perspicacious settlers were aware that France too was beating furiously the drums of war, with London's settlements as a lush target. This was not disconnected, it was thought, from a spate of attacks on masters by the enslaved.[67]

It was then that Delaware's Lieutenant Governor George Thomas warned about the "domestick insurrections of the Negroes, spirited up by Emissarys from our enemies," which fomented—he noted with understatement—"melancholy reflections." That the administrative center that was New Castle was "without any guard at all" made the situation even more dire, particularly since "Spanish Privateers took many prisoners on the coast last summer."[68]

What to do? Like a mantra, Carolinians decided it was "absolutely necessary" to "get a sufficient number of persons into this Province," in light of the "unhappy accident at Stono"—treating as mere detail from whence in Europe they would come and how to bar Catholics and other presumed pro-Madrid forces from infiltrating under racial cover. Suspecting such a ruse, an early prominent settler in Georgia pointed to what he saw as the "strict connection between popery" and unrest among Africans, a frequent colonial-era complaint, which entente with Paris and Madrid post-1776 would tend to eliminate.[69]

Yet colonial leaders did not seem to understand that religious bigotry was at odds with the idea of bringing more "whites" to the mainland. Constructing a truer pan-Europeanism, which would erode the stain that was anti-Semitism, was a possible remedy, for example—but this too was not easy. Although Jewish migrants to Georgia had a justifiable concern about Spanish incursions in light of the Inquisition,[70] when Savannah settlers pleaded for the delivery of more enslaved Africans, their petition was signed by "above one hundred and seventeen free-holders" with a conspicuous exception: "the Jews applied for liberty to sign with us, but we did not think it proper to join them in any of our measures."[71] Further militarizing of the settler class was another remedy pursued with little consideration as to what this might mean for the culture created.[72] The "many late horrible and barbarous massacres" perpetrated against the "white inhabitants of this Province by Negro slaves who are generally prone to such cruel practices" made "it necessary that constant patrols should be established," it was announced by Carolina elites in late 1739.[73]

The authorities were so bold as to propose the ultimate sanction—curbing the importation of Africans—though well-honed smuggling techniques were not easy to overcome.[74] Weeks after Stono, the well-connected Robert Pringle was grousing about the proposed "very high duty on Negroes" but noted the gaping loophole that it would not "take place till Fifteen Months after it is [ratified]," so there remained "time to import a Pretty Many Negroes"—and, in any case, he thought he could still block this unwanted tax,[75] as resistance to taxation merged with hunger for slaves in a way that was to vex the mainland for years to come.

*   *   *

Despite the imminent threat to security brought by the presence of so many Africans, like hopelessly hooked addicts, there were those who were so enamored with the slave trade that they were willing to risk life itself in search of its magnificent profits. What is startling about the Carolina-Georgia border at this juncture is how droningly repetitive were the problems and how—just as repeatedly—there were concerted attempts to evade these same problems. The increased presence of Africans served to increase insecurity, inspire Madrid, heighten the military burden on London, and incite further secessionist strains with its colonies.

Dangers truly lurked: as Oglethorpe's expedition to St. Augustine suggested, Madrid and London had reached the snare of war, in a theater of conflict stretching from the mainland through the Caribbean to South America.[76] The events immediately preceding and following Stono were part of a larger tapestry of war between the two powers—colorfully abbreviated initially as the "War of Jenkins' Ear"—which included Admiral Edward Vernon attacking Porto-bello in July 1739, leaving London agog. Then there was the bombarding of Cartagena in March 1740, leaving major losses on both sides, before a retreat to Port Royal:[77] making Madrid play defense circumscribed its ability to launch an offensive against Georgia and Carolina.

In the short term, conflict with Spain brought opportunity (more privateers, driving up profits) and grumbling—certainly about conscription—though relieving pressure on mainland settlers was a prime cause of this anti-Madrid campaign. When Cuba was "taken," the Duke of Newcastle was told, "Great Britain will then be in the absolute possession of the key of the West Indies, of an island most valuable to her self and to these her northern colonies." The "whole Navy of England" could dock there. As to the "American levies," they were proceeding "briskly, even beyond what could have been expected," which was thought to be a positive sign for future efforts to oust European rivals altogether from the hemisphere—though this optimism did not take into full account that these "levies" or conscripts were increasingly sullen about what was befalling them.[78] Still, attacking Cuba indicated how seriously London took the idea of relieving the mainland by going to a major source of the difficulties endured by Carolina and Georgia.

It did not take long for this bright-eyed optimism of July 1740 to encounter sobering reality, with the Crown's chief military delegate in

New York reporting by September 1740 "desertions from His Majesty's Ships of War and Land Forces," which had "been so frequent" that it was reaching the point where his forces "may be unable to protect either . . . trade or country."[79] Upon landing in Jamaica, mainland draftees commenced promptly grousing about their pay.[80] Others all of a sudden had become "very sickly," with hundreds crowding into the island's already less-than-commodious hospitals.[81] To be fair, not long after landing, "nine officers and about one hundred men" from Virginia had been buried, suggestive of their difficulty in adjusting to the environment[82]—an adjustment Africans were thought to make with ease.

As noted, in addition to Havana, Cartagena was an attractive target for London, and here, Africans under the Union Jack could prove crucial, not only because of the presumed impact of the climate but also—as one analyst observed—because this importantly sited town contained "about 4000 Spanish inhabitants and near 20,000 Mulattos and Negroes who are all at their Ease and would be thought very rich in any other place." Ebony soldiers could infiltrate more effectively, it was believed. Similarly, Veracruz, also in the gun sight, was a city where, it was reported, "most of the inhabitants are Mulattos of a tawny dark colour," while there were a number of Africans there who had "become considerable merchants"—though little consideration was given to how the relatively deprived Africans under the Union Jack would react to what could only be considered surprising scenes.[83]

As things turned out, the 1741 Battle of Cartagena was a watershed moment in the mainland push toward separation from London, in that African troops were deployed promiscuously on both sides,[84] reminding the Crown that the mainland project of relentless despotism toward Africans had severe limitations; that mainlanders pursued this project while not being renowned for their competent martial skills in the field could only raise further questions in London as to whether following the settlers' unreconstructed anti-African policy was the wisest course. Yet Cartagena was a larger lesson for London, for in 1741 the redcoats seemed on the verge of a stunning victory, after seizing this port and fortifications—but then their attempted penetration of the town itself was repulsed, with Africans playing a major role in the defeat.[85]

Though this conflict was driven in no minor way by Madrid's quest to conquer London's mainland colonies, the denizens of the latter were not pleased when they were conscripted to fight—which was under-standable since so much filthy lucre could be garnered via slavery and the slave trade, which slogging through Cartagena could forestall. Worse for London was the Crown simultaneously recruiting and arm-ing Negroes for this war, which gave heft to the increasing plaint on the mainland that settlers were being treated like slaves—for in a certain way, they were.[86] When London moved to pay settlers at the same rate they compensated Jamaican Negroes, such a claim could more easily gain traction.[87] Africans from Jamaica were also authorized to share in the booty of plunder, alongside mainland settlers, which was the truly bounteous wages of war—but this too could launch the upsetting charge that the Euro-Americans were being treated like slaves.[88]

Early on, Lord Cathcart was optimistic, reporting in August 1740 of his "greatest joy" in "having at least three thousand" with him "from North America," which, he said, "heighten[s] greatly the hopes we have of success," particularly in taking the rich prize that was Havana, the presumed source of the rampant insecurity of the mainland.[89] But as the settlers began to desert their posts or suddenly fell into a "very bad state of health" or even "refuse[d] to serve," the Crown had to rely even more on Africans, which only magnified their ongoing problem.[90] In March 1740, Admiral Vernon told of the "scandalous desertions" that were a "shock," as subjects were "going over to the Enemies of our . . . Religion, as well as our Country"[91]—which some of his contempo-raries saw as indistinguishable. It did not take long before Admiral Vernon decamped to Jamaica with the aim of "raising a thousand cho-sen Negroes to serve" in a continuing attack on Cartagena. Planters in Jamaica, perhaps wishing to rid themselves of troublesome Africans, offered to raise "five thousand" instead.[92]

This increased reliance on Africans occurred not least because of reports from Havana that this city was armoring: a Spanish prisoner told the Royal Navy that "fortifications" had "greatly augmented," along with the "number of troops," which included a sizeable number of "the Negroes and Mulattoes."[93]

It is not evident that London considered the full impact of militariz-ing Africans—not least those from Jamaica, which had attained a justi-fiable reputation for fierce militancy—on their skittish colonists, who were not ignorant of Antigua 1736 and the recent bloodshed at Stono.

Nor did Londoners (or settlers for that matter) seem to fully comprehend the incongruity of recruiting Africans—armed and otherwise—to
fight on their side in the hemisphere, with the ultimate aim of preserving racist despotism on the mainland.[94] But with the competitive pressure placed on London by Madrid's long tradition of arming Africans,
it was also not evident if there was any viable alternative available. For
London's part, it seemed that the conscripted mainland settlers slot-
ted to fight in Cuba and Cartagena were more problematic than were
armed Africans, since the former required more tending and the latter
could be treated more roughly at less expense.[95]

Then there was the internal squabbling among the fractious mainland
settlers, complicated by differences in the value of their respective cur-
rencies and resultant disputes about who was being paid more—or less;
one settler could not avoid recalling 1716, when Virginians had to rush
to the rescue of South Carolina, and the stinging recollection that their
sacrifice was not compensated adequately.[96] Then London worried about
the political reliability of those who were—ostensibly—on their side,
since "many of the American soldiers," said one analyst, "were suspected
to be Irish Papists" and, ergo, not so closeted fans of His Catholic Majesty. Yet manpower deficits meant these suspects had to be deployed at
strategically sited Cartagena, though cautious voices advised to "employ
them principally on Board the Fleet": would not replacing these presumed "Papists" with Africans make more sense, since what was flaring
with Spain was more of a religious than a racial conflict?[97]

Moreover, as should be evident at this point, the settlers' model of
development—heavily dependent on tireless oppression of Africans—
was incongruent with London's developing global ambitions, which
did not rule out arming Africans. This settler model meant increasing appeals to London for rescue from Madrid's forces bolstered by
Africans, which could only mean diverting attention from what was
becoming a lucrative preoccupation: India. Thus, as the first anniversary of the Stono revolt approached, the authorities in Charleston and
Savannah urgently requested "protection & assistance" in anticipation
of yet another attack from St. Augustine—but what would have been
the response if armed Jamaicans had been deposited in their midst?[98]
Yet, as time passed, London was becoming more—not less—dependent
upon armed Africans.[99]

For to meet the Spanish challenge, Lord Cathcart and the Duke of Newcastle assembled a force that the former termed "the most considerable ever [s]ent from this Kingdom to the West Indies," a major logistical feat that could not have functioned optimally without the deployment of Africans.[100] The fleet assembled was "one of the largest ever seen in the new world," said one wondrous commentator, signaling the major stakes, with thirty-seven major vessels and thirteen others, carrying 1,820 guns, 15,000 sailors, and 12,000 land troops. Yet at Cartagena in 1741, Admiral Vernon suffered extremely heavy casualties among land forces with tropical fever—which some colonists thought Africans were immune to—cutting a prodigious swath through the redcoats; there was a near collapse of the siege, followed by a hasty retreat to Jamaica, then the launching of an equally fruitless attack on Santiago de Cuba, with the incurring of more significant losses. Initially, Admiral Vernon was contemptuous of the mainland conscripts, only deigning to use them as laborers, an insult that did not enhance their devotion to the Crown, particularly since settlers' losses had been staggering—Massachusetts alone had a mere fifty survivors out of its original five hundred volunteers.[101] The notion that Africans could more easily navigate the summer heat of Cartagena—and presumably Cuba too—took hold.[102]

London had rarely—if ever—conscripted so heavily among mainland settlers, and though a credible claim could be made that defeating Madrid's forces was in the colonists' interest, this view was occluded by the buckets of blood that were shed. When Londoners began referring to these draftees as "Americans," it helped to congeal an identity distinct from that of the sceptered isle, a kind of "emergent Americanism." When Admiral Vernon referred to them as "slothful," they keenly felt his scorn, and this did not increase their already dissipating patriotism. The conscripts may have taken umbrage at the idea of taking Cuba with the idea of re-settling these mainland settlers there, a thought that had occurred to leading Londoners. When the mainland draftees were referred to contemptuously as "fit only for cutting fascines [bundles of sticks] with Negroes," this may have curdled the emergent idea of "American" separateness verging on "independency" in a brew of pre-existent anti-London and anti-Negro sentiment.[103]

It is not as if British troops from Europe were excellent, as one witness termed them "raw, new raised, undisciplined"—"a fact known to everyone." Their officers were little better, being "either young gentlemen" of uncertain but suspicious provenance who "by way of reward" found themselves commanding men. Still, even this sharp-tongued observer was dismissive of "the American troops," who "were in general many degrees worse but the officers in particular were composed of black-smiths, taylors, shoemakers and all the Banditti that Country affords." As for the key posts they filled as "Engineers, Bombardiers and Gunners," well, "worse never bore the name or could be picked out of all Europe."[104]

While mainland settlers were bickering with the metropolitans and licking their wounds, Spaniards were mobilizing. In October 1741, the authorities in Madrid recalled that in 1737 "His Majesty" had mandated the "extirpation of the English from the new colony of Georgia," and the time was now "opportune to accomplish the destruction of Caro-lina and of its dependencies" and, in the process, to inflict "a damage that will ruin and terrify them." The orders were explicit: "devastate it by sacking and burning all the towns, posts, plantations and settle-ments."[105] By December 1741, the Royal Navy was advising that the coast of North Carolina "is very much infested with Spanish privateers, who have even landed in the country, and carried off hogs and black cat-tle to the great terror of the inhabitants of those parts."[106] By May 1742, Don Juan Francisco de Guemes y Horcasitas was coolly and confidently advising that he was "expecting at the very least" that his "forces will without the slightest . . . hindrance forthwith destroy all the plantations as far as Port Royal" in the process of seeking to "lay waste to Carolina and its dependencies." Part of his far-reaching plan involved trying to "find mean to notify the Negroes" so they could effectively collaborate in "the cause," effectuation of which would certainly mean "the com-plete success of [Madrid's] plans."[107]

By May 1742, eight thousand men had been dispatched from Cuba to invade Georgia and South Carolina, and they successfully reached the outskirts of Savannah. Seemingly crafted to intimidate these set-tlers was the presence of an entire regiment of Africans, staffed by Afri-can officers—and another similarly outfitted regiment of "Mulattos." Predictably, mainland Negroes fled to "enemy" lines, worsening the crisis.[108] One flustered Georgian concluded accurately that "the Span-iards depended much upon a Revolt of the Carolina Negroes" for vic-tory. He thought they had inserted "spies" and "Correspondents among the Negroes.[109] Oglethorpe agreed that the "Spaniards have intelligence amongst the Negroes," adding mournfully, "I know nothing can stop them" because of this distinct advantage.[110]

The metropolis too seemed stunned by the sight of armed and uniformed Africans assaulting mainland settlements. In distant London, there seemed to be shock at the heavy deployment of Africans by Spanish forces and, perhaps, more than a scintilla of nervousness, since this would inevitably place competitive pressure on redcoats to act similarly, which in turn would enrage mainland settlers. In the Spaniards' attack on Georgia and plan to seize Port Royal, they—said the **London Gazette**—"had a whole regiment of Negroes, with a company of Grenadiers." The reporter was astonished to see "Negro . . . officers walking along with the Governor of Augustine on shore and that they were dressed in Gold and Silver Lace Clothes like other officers and that they were kept in the Pay as the other regiments"—as if this were stranger than bizarre.[111] This conflict received maximum coverage in London, including the illuminating detail about the incorporation of former Carolina Negroes in Madrid's camp[112]—a trend that could spell doom for London's mainland settlements in the southeast, if not beyond.

Also scrutinized in London was an account of a Spaniard taken prisoner in Georgia who was interrogated about armed forces in Havana and replied that "half" were "Mulattoes and Negroes." Surprised interrogators asked if they were slaves and were informed, "no, they belonged to the militia."[113] After a knife was put to the throat of a British prisoner by the Spaniards, he somehow escaped and reported to the authorities that his captors had a "whole regiment of Negroes . . . commanded by Negro officers . . . cloathed in the same livery as the other Spanish regiments."[114]

Madrid felt that enslaved Africans in Georgia and the Carolinas would rise up and join the invaders and set the entire Southeast aflame. With victory, the plan was to enlarge the presidio at St. Augustine for further thrusts northward. Oglethorpe felt that forty thousand Carolina Africans "would be either an assistance to the invader or a Prize worth near Eight Hundred Pounds Sterling to them."[115] Observing from Virginia, Governor William Gooch anxiously noted the presence of Spanish forces that "landed somewhere to the Southward of Georgia" and perhaps, not coincidentally, evidence that had emerged of a "dangerous conspiracy formed by our Heathen Neighbours to attack Pensilvania and Maryland."[116] Eliza Lucas, the daughter of a former governor of Antigua, may have had a sense of déjà vu when in the summer of 1742 she found that "12 hundred" Spaniards had landed off the coast of Georgia, bringing with them "alarm" and "apprehension of danger immediately" concerning their plans for "the Negroes."[117]

There was understandable concern in Williamsburg for, according to Madrid's man in the region, "Carolina once ruined and destroyed[,] the extermination of [London's] colonial dependencies will follow." Thus, when Spain suffered a seemingly decisive setback in 1742–1743—blocked in its attempt to crush Carolina and Georgia—exhortations of pleasure poured in from the governors of New Jersey, New York, Pennsylvania, Maryland, North Carolina, and the Bahamas. In retrospect, this setback was momentous: it may not have been a true turning point in the struggle for hegemony on the mainland between Madrid and London; still, it was of no less import than the victory over France that was to come in Quebec thereafter.[118] Nonetheless, it was a harbinger of the reality that befell His Catholic Majesty from 1756 to 1763, when—in a truer turning point—Spain was ousted from Florida.

But for London, these proved to be calamitous victories, setting the stage for now less harried colonies to make a separate peace with Paris and Madrid against the interests of Britain, sly trickery that eventuated in the formation of the nation now known as the United States of America. Stunningly—for London—Carolina settlers persisted in trading with Spanish Florida, while fearsome attacks against them continued to be launched from this strategic peninsula.[119]

For Oglethorpe, this also proved to be a pyrrhic victory, for by July 1743 he had abandoned the colony he founded in Georgia—never to return; he had lost decisively the battle against African slavery, now a growing presence that was slated to increase with the punishment inflicted on Spanish forces. It was an ignominious conclusion for a man who had formerly been tied closely to the Royal African Company, whose fortunes were eroded by the rise of private traders, a group growing in importance on the mainland who then triumphed once more in the colony that he founded.[120] At best, he was an imperfect critic of slavery, since it was well-known that he had owned slaves and a plantation in Carolina, which compromised his faux abolitionism in Georgia.[121]

How could a "white" pro-slavery wall be constructed next door to Charleston, where Africans from the Caribbean and elsewhere were constantly arriving? On 8 January 1743, William Stephens of Georgia heard a "strong rumor" of "the Negroes rising and that 40 of them were . . . on horseback in Carolina"; weeks later, he heard "about 30 Negroes from Carolina [who] were by agreement to join the Enemy"—"if they could"—perhaps heading his way.[122] Seditious Africans could not be kept out of Georgia, so enslaved Africans might as well be allowed: this seemed to be the cockeyed reasoning among settlers.

In retrospect, it is easy to say that seeking to block enslaved Africans from Georgia was truly a fool's errand. It did not take into account how "whiteness" on the mainland could be easily torn asunder in a welter of religious and ethnic and class tensions among Europeans, unless enslaved Africans were there to solder and weld this otherwise unwieldy racial category.

Surely the retreat of the Spanish offensive on the mainland in the 1740s, blocked from taking over the southeast quadrant, made it easier to ignore Oglethorpe and introduce more enslaved Africans into Georgia in ever-increasing numbers.[123] By the spring of 1743, the border between Florida and territories to the north was not on fire—an eerie contrast with the constant fighting that had kept the border aflame almost continuously since Barbadians began to land in telling numbers in South Carolina in 1670.[124]

As quiet seemed to be descending on the border, enslaved Africans began arriving in greater numbers. The Earl of Egmont was informed of "overstocking " Georgia with slaves, to the point of "abuse"; this was not "consistent with the Safety of this Province," it was said, "yet because that trade [yielded] great profit, there was no end of importing." Indeed, as of March 1742, the writer continued, there were "several ships" that were "already commissioned" to "pour slaves upon us."[125] On cue, a Georgian cried out for even more Africans to arrive.[126] But Londoners were to find that as long as Africans were pouring into mainland settlements, this was tantamount to the delivery of more agents of Madrid bent on creating mischief. The Spanish challenge to the weakest link of London's chain of colonies—the Carolina-Georgia-Florida border, in other words—had suffered a setback but was far from being vanquished altogether.

6

Arson, Murders, Poisonings, Shipboard Insurrections

The Fruits of the Accelerating Slave Trade

If the threat to mainland colonies presented by the de facto African-Spanish alliance would have been contained on the Carolina-Georgia-Florida border, it may have been possible to downplay the existential threat to British North America.

However, just as London and Madrid were crossing swords in the area just north of St. Augustine—and beyond—a series of damaging fires in New York in 1741 raised the specter of taking this conflict into New England, Canada, and beyond, with potentially catastrophic consequences for the British Crown.[1] As an investigation announced tremblingly, there was a "wicked and dangerous conspiracy" "set on foot" by "white people & diverse Negro slaves and others to burn this whole town & city and to murder the inhabitants"—this "horrid conspiracy" was unraveled,[2] while leaving frightening memories of 1712.

What was worrisome for some New Yorkers about this reputed plot of enslaved Africans was—like Stono—it too tended to implicate the ubiquitous hand of Madrid. Yet since France in nearby Quebec could also lend a hand more readily in New York and New England than it could in Charleston or Savannah from its perch in Mobile and New Orleans, this also made these events particularly upsetting. London faced a dilemma: the derided "Catholic powers" were collaborating with Africans—many under the Union Jack—to destroy British North America. Nascent London abolitionists would have thwarted this design by becoming more solicitous to Africans, but this could only serve to enrage the settlers, pushing them toward "independency": either by being ousted forcibly by Madrid and Paris in league with armed Africans or being routed by settlers (in league with these very same "Catholic powers"), London seemed to be destined to relinquish many of its jealously guarded gains in North America.

An official investigation of the 1741 conspiracy in New York pointed the finger of accusation at Spain: "there was a cry among the people," it was stressed, "*the Spanish Negroes, the Spanish Negroes, take up the Spanish Negroes.*" Evidence was presented that these Africans with ties to Havana and Madrid "were talking of burning the town" down, and thus, "five Spanish Negroes [were] convicted of the conspiracy." One of these gentlemen had been noticeably busy, it was reported, having "been concerned in two conspiracies in the West Indies, the first at St. John's, the last at Antigua in the year 1736"—the latter being an especially blood-chilling plot that portended the total liquidation of European settlement. His punishment for 1736 was being ousted from Antigua, but this time no chances were being taken: it was declared that the "court sentenced him to be burnt at a stake." Yet the lesson was not learned altogether, for other defendants were punished by being shipped to Newfoundland. Perhaps a bit of water could have been the reasonable antidote to this fire plot thought to be centered in lower Manhattan, but investigators revealed a much larger "villainous design of a very extraordinary nature," that is, "the Spaniards had employed emissaries to burn all the magazines and considerable towns in English North America."[3] After all, there were "wicked white people" who with Africans sought to "lay this city in ashes and to murder and destroy the inhabitants" and who, too, had a hand in "the great number of publick houses in which Negroes have been entertained and encouraged by rum and other strong liquors," which was a "principal instrument to their diabolical villainies."[4]

The ominous presence in this plot of those who were defined as "white" also suggested to the most perspicacious settlers that an "independency" gambit had to be accompanied by attractive enticements for European recruits, lest they be seduced by incentives provided by antagonists of these budding republicans: land seized from indigenes and then allotted to recruits and, after much wrangling, a "Bill of Rights" was one response.

This was not the only insight illuminated by incendiarism. Belatedly, it was realized that the liquors that had been an essential element of a destabilizing trade offensive in Africa could boomerang, with even Oglethorpe warning that "Rum & Spirits" could "destroy the troops & labouring people here, as it hath done [to] the Armys in Jamaica & Cuba."[5]

Sufficiently spooked, the New York authorities sprung into action, "offering a reward to any white person that shall discover any person or persons concerned in setting fire[s]"—"one hundred pounds" was the sum offered.[6] "Jack a Negro Man," who had been convicted in this "late conspiracy," aided the state in ferreting out "discoveries" and was provided a pardon for his troubles.[7] Africans generally were terrorized in the wake of this plot: the chief victims included "Othello and Quack," who agreed to be hung, rather than immolated.[8] There were "five Spanish Negroes," it was said, who had arrived in New York only recently and had been "sold as slaves," though it was felt they were "pretending themselves as free men"—they too were convicted, then four were pardoned, with the fifth unlucky soul executed.[9]

This bloodlust was a priority since the authorities found it "dangerous and inconvenient at this juncture" for investigators to journey up the Hudson River to Albany in light of the presumed danger and the relative closeness to French Quebec—"especially," it was noted tremulously, "as they have great reason to be apprehensive that there are many white people and Negroes concerned in the said conspiracy not yet apprehended."[10] Already New York was nervous about the French presence in Cape Breton and Louisbourg,[11] while the Spanish incursion into Manhattan was so significant that their currency was not only circulated but coined there, though this was highly irregular.[12] France was known to harbor a corps of battle-tested Africans in Louisbourg,[13] which motivated the New York legislature to enact a bill "to prevent the running away of slaves out of the city and county of Albany to the French at Canada."[14] Still, despite the real nervousness about the presence of Africans, New York settlers continued to be major players in the slave trade, which guaranteed that disobedient captives would continue to arrive.[15]

Mainland settlers were repetitively clamoring for more "whites," though rarely considering how this layered identity opened the door for pernicious infiltration by Spaniards and Frenchmen. Did they not fully understand the import of this relatively recent racial identity? Or were they so frightened that they flailed and opted for what appeared to be the simplest remedy? Did the growing salience of "whiteness" tend to ease these religious conflicts? On the other hand, since African slavery was at the root of their enterprise, this sorely limited officialdom's choices for residents and, probably, intensified the terror aimed at these unfortunate Negroes, who, unlike their European allies, could not hide in plain sight—and were visibly obvious embodiments of sedition.

In the prelude to 1741, officials in neighboring New Jersey were fielding complaints about "much damage and molestation from piratical vessels, especially from vessels fitted out from the Spanish islands in the West Indies," particularly Cuba, where armed Africans were known to proliferate.[16] These Spaniards had a growing number of African minds to influence, for the latter's numbers were growing not only in New York but also in New Jersey. In 1737, there were almost four thousand Africans in New Jersey, and over the next eight years, this number increased sharply.[17] The spate of fires that hit Manhattan spread across the river to Hackensack, as two slaves were convicted of setting fire to seven farms in 1741 and were sentenced to be burned at the stake.[18] By 1744, there was an attempt to curb this influx by placing a tariff on "imported Indian, Negro and Mulatto slaves," an attempt to raise revenue and heighten security.[19]

What made 1741 so intimidating to mainland settlers was not only the breadth of the plot and the context of raging war with Spain in the hemisphere but the preceding events as well. In September 1730, a New York City brigantine returned with a terrified crew after a number of "Spanish Mulatto" and African pirates had boarded the vessel and seized its cargo as it sailed through the Windward Passage. In 1736 in Manhattan, a suspicious blaze caused severe damage, which was said to be the handiwork of disgruntled Africans. As with other parts of the mainland, the numbers of Africans were surging in New York with little sensitivity to the downstream consequences. According to one source, between 1732 and 1754, more than 35% of those who disembarked at the port of New York were Africans: with the 1740s war with Spain hampering arrivals from the British isles, the role of Africans in the labor force assumed even greater importance. As the number of disaffected Africans increased, also growing were reports of arson: suspicious blazes had become Manhattan's frequent companion, as alleged acts of arson were thought to be lit by discontented Africans, with women playing a leading role. In short, the conflict with Spain exacerbated ordinary tenseness, for in addition to the routine hardships visited upon the downtrodden when war arrives, the deployment of armed forces from Manhattan to the Caribbean left this future metropolis vulnerable to the compounded vexation of servile insurrection and foreign invasion.

Not only did 1741 bring a potentially devastating conspiracy, but it also brought an unsolved crime wave and yet another spate of mysterious fires. Typically panic-stricken colonists turned vigilante and began seizing Africans in the streets indiscriminately and escorting them rudely to the city jailer: recalled was the reputed participation of Spanish-speaking Africans in the tumult of 1712. If it was any consolation, Catholics of various ancestries too came under heavy pressure—but that only meant that Angolans, who were well represented in Manhattan, would receive extra scrutiny. The nervous Manhattanites were not reassured when during the trial of the accused in the wake of the 1741 plot, discussion emerged about how the defendants had been discussing Admiral Vernon's assault on Porto-bello, with firm allegiance to London not confirmed.[20]

"If the truth were ever known," claimed one high-level official, "there are not many innocent Negro men," an opinion that hardened over the decades, if not centuries. They were thought to be inspired by priests, sent by Madrid.[21] After this plot was detected, the authorities in New York continued to rail against "the encouragement of Popery" and its "dreadful effects," which were also perceived in the propagations of the "Moravians."[22] This only worsened an anti-Catholic bias that already was persistent. By then, in many mainland settlements, followers of this faith were doubly taxed, unable to vote or hold office, possess arms or decent horses, have churches or schools—and in Virginia, they were not even allowed to be witnesses in any case, civil or criminal. By 1741, about a quarter of New York's population of about eleven thousand was African—and, understandably, they were seen as prime targets for recruitment by Catholics, who at times were treated like them.[23]

This bias led to a severe clampdown on Africans from heavily Catholic Cuba sojourning in Manhattan, which in turn deepened their hostility toward the settlers; but the settlers felt they had little choice, not only because of the ongoing tension with Spain but also because if these particular Africans were adjudged to be free, then it would be difficult to have testimony of slaves admitted against them—for example, in the trials of the accused in the 1741 plot.[24] Settler apprehensions were confirmed when an African confessed in the aftermath of the uncovering of the 1741 plot that only recently he had been walking and talking with an African from Cuba, and they decided to repair to a tavern for a beer—where he was introduced to this vast conspiracy and asked to take an oath involving setting afire houses and killing slaveholders.[25]

The tendency of mainlanders to improperly dragoon Africans who were subjects of His Catholic Majesty, then enslave them, repeatedly roiled relations between London and Madrid and deepened the animosity of Negroes, particularly in Cuba, toward their northern neighbors[26]—particularly in the incendiary year of 1741.[27] It seemed that there was a presumption in favor of the alleged slaveholder in mainland courts when an African—or "Mulatto" or indigene—was brought before jurists and claimed as property.[28] This facilitated slavery but did little for London's reputation among these aggrieved groupings. It was as if London's settlers were telling the world that not only would they refuse to accept an enhanced status for Africans, but they would not accept other powers doing so as well. This may have benefited the settlers, but it could only serve to heighten Africans' antipathy to London, which was not helpful in hemispheric struggles for power. When during this tumultuous era Africans were even fleeing French rule in New Orleans for a presumed better life in Havana, this should have emitted a gusty indicator to London as to the direction of political winds.[29]

This last point was hard to ignore, for as one contemporary analyst put it, "Spanish Negroes" were "crucial" to Madrid's "enterprise because they had gained fighting experience while serving in the Spanish fleet. In fact, [it was] assumed that the Spanish would assault the port" of New York.[30] Perhaps in response to competitive pressure from Spanish forces, by the 1740s, London was employing ever more African regiments, notably in Jamaica, at a time when increasingly African sailors were being employed in many of the major European navies and merchant marines.[31]

With mainland draftees continuing to display a noticeable dearth of enthusiasm for fighting abroad, London's choices were narrowing. As flames were erupting in Manhattan, an officer of the Royal Navy was baleful about not having "sailed sooner" to Jamaica "for want of men," as "between 30 and 50 having deserted by the enticements of the people of Boston and the large wages given by the merchants."[32] Nonetheless, just before this, there was sober debate about taking Havana—a "place of very great strength"—according to one British official. Jamaica was to be the launching pad, with "already 500 men raised in Virginia," though little evident thought was devoted to how normally rebellious

Jamaicans might react to the presence on their territory of mainland settlers with a substantially different attitude toward those of the darkest hue.[33]

Yet despite this deteriorating situation from the Caribbean to Quebec, with the northeastern mainland colonies being outflanked, Massachusetts was reluctant to move away from moth-eaten policies. "No Indian, Negro or Mulatto, except one Servant of the Captain's" was allowed to be "inlisted or retained" to serve at "His Majesty's Castle" guarding the entrance to the main port. Though friction with Spain was increasing, Massachusetts lawmakers found it necessary to debate a bill designed to "prevent Mutiny and Desertion" yet stepped up efforts to bar Africans. A call was made to recruit a "Thousand Men" to send to the Caribbean, with a "bounty" dangled as an emolument. In fact, the Exchequer was strained by further inducements, for example, more "Billeting Money," as the original sum was deemed "insufficient." Two men petitioned for more funds in light of their "extraordinary Experience in raising Companies of Volunteers for the Expedition to the Spanish West Indies"— though there was still reluctance to deploy Africans at the prime "Castle" in Boston, a port city thought to be more civilized than Charleston.[34]

As intensified pressure was placed on Africans in Manhattan in the aftermath of the 1741 plot, due north in Boston there were groans about the "defenceless Condition" of "a Fortress of the utmost importance to the Safeguard of the Province." This was the case, though simultaneously it was reported that "Two Thousand Four Hundred" of His Majesty's finest men from this province were involved in hostilities in Cuba; it was felt appropriate to dispatch "One Thousand Negroes" to this distant clime. However, this latter move could cause this victimized group to espy a group of their type facing different circumstances than within the Bay Colony, possibly implanting seditious ideas or causing them to be less prone to accept bigotry after jeopardizing life and limb on behalf of the Crown. Since it was acknowledged that more men were needed for this Cuban venture, this could only increase the importance of Africans, who were less able to demand more funds, more "Billeting Money" and the like.[35]

Thus, as the battle in the Caribbean was coming to a head, one "white" soldier successfully petitioned to be granted "one hundred acres of the unappropriated lands of the Province in full Satisfaction in enlisting Soldiers for the Expedition against the *Spaniards*"—though this could have well brought the colony into further conflict with expropriated indigenes: Africans were hardly in a position to demand as much.[36]

Telling was that even local policymakers had "taken great pains to discourage" conscription, an indicator of a growing separateness from the Crown.[37] Simultaneously, one Scottish writer recalled that when the time arrived for Admiral Vernon and his officers to attack the Spanish Caribbean in the early 1740s, "the 1000 Negroes they carried from Jamaica on that expedition was sufficient force to have taken the town of St. Jago de Cuba,"[38] which, if true, upgraded the importance of Africans as it downgraded the need for enlisting mainland settlers.

Furthermore, some local leaders were objecting to the enlistment in the Crown's forces of the indigenous, though they had acquitted themselves well in combat in Canada in 1711. Apparently there was both racist and pragmatic concern about these potential recruits, the latter grounded in reluctance to see a group that had yet to be subjugated wholly to receive military training.[39] In short, settlers were both resisting fighting and seeking to block others from doing so, calling into question their viability as subjects.

Still, one outgrowth of the developing political trend was the opening of more opportunity for mainland settlers, with the entire province of Georgia, for example, desiring Africans. For example, Rhode Island's reputation as a headquarters for the trade in Africans increased after this turning point of the 1740s, as Spanish interests absorbed mighty blows, despite (or perhaps because of) Spain's Manhattan offensive; this included more Africans being brought to Newport, not to mention others being dragged to the southern colonies and beyond, particularly to the Caribbean. This profit in turn stimulated more dreams of "independency."[40] A not atypical Rhode Islander was Godfrey Malbone, who had major interests in both Newport and the base of "independency"—Virginia, where he owned fifty enslaved Africans.[41] This association of Newport with the slaveholders' dominion that was Virginia was hardly happenstance since the former harbor town at this juncture was as busy—or busier—than Boston or New York, engaged in a highly prosperous trade with the Caribbean and Africa (the first of the enslaved arrived there in 1690—the profit on one journey to Africa could be as much as $6,500).[42]

The middle of the 18th century marked a turning point for the mainland, as represented by the reality that in 1730 Rhode Island had an

African population of 1,648, but by 1755 this number had almost tripled, and then represented 11% of the province's population.[43] As the number of Africans in the northeast increased, this made this region ever more similar to the southeast, uniting the two, providing both with further reason to support slavery, to resist slave revolts, and to question the trend in London to rely upon Africans to confront Madrid: all of this was occurring as the Crown was beginning to place more emphasis on its mainland investments, as Jamaican Maroons and Antiguan sedition-ists continued to give Caribbean settlers reason to make the great trek to the mainland.

Thus, ships from this ocean-bound colony anchored by Newport suffered frequently from shipboard slave uprisings probably because it was the leader among the provinces in this hateful commerce: the "first mover's advantage" it gained in the aftermath of slave trade "reforms" continued to be felt.[44] A revealing incident occurred well before the acceleration of the slave trade in the middle of the 18th century when a Newport vessel headed for the Caribbean with almost one hundred enslaved Africans aboard—and suffered a devastating revolt. Perhaps as a result, there was significant pressure internally for Rhode Island to move toward European indentured labor, as the province's chief executive argued that the "unruly tempers" of the Africans made them unsuitable as a mass labor force.[45] Of course, such a shift did not pre-clude the reality of Newport slave ships continuing to dump Africans in the Southeast.

The assimilation of Africans in the province proceeded fitfully, which should have alerted wary settlers of the perils of Africans' alienation: the eminent Ezra Stiles was disturbed to find that the majority of Afri-cans in Newport refrained from attending local Christian churches,[46] for reasons he found hard to fathom. Nevertheless, if there was a chal-lenger to Rhode Island in the dubious category of insurrections aboard slave ships, it may have been Massachusetts. This province was a leader in both slave trading and falling victim to shipboard insurrections, all of which engendered further hatred of Africans on the part of fami-lies of murdered ship crews, their communities, and others as ripples of resentment continued to flow.[47]

* * *

There was a noticeable acceleration of shipboard revolts beginning at the midpoint of the 18th century, when commercial interests were in the process of retreating from—or being chased away by—rebellious Africans in the Caribbean to the mainland and were seeking to bring along more enslaved Africans to develop North America. To the credit of the Africans involved, their contumaciousness probably helped to decrease the number of Africans who were to be enslaved, as their militancy placed a high premium on slavery that many Europeans were unwilling to pay.[48] This was discovered by the Irishman Nicholas Owens when in December 1750 he set out from Liverpool to enchain Africans as slaves. Arriving in West Africa, he quickly arranged for the detention of eighty unfortunate souls, who were packed inside a vessel with a cargo of ivory. But then he had the misfortune of encountering a (former) French ship staffed by Africans who had slain their captors and commandeered the vessel. Owens and his crew tried to overawe these Africans, but as he recounted, "The slaves behaved so as to make us give over the attempt with loss on our side." Then Owens and several of his mates were seized by Africans and enslaved in retaliation before escaping.[49]

Similarly, the Caribbean—notably Jamaica and Antigua—had garnered a well-deserved reputation for developing African bellicosity and came to be disfavored in this regard by the notorious "Negro Merchants," who began increasing their commerce in Africa itself rather than engaging in transshipments of human cargo from these islands. Disrupting the link between the Caribbean islands and the mainland drove the latter provinces closer together, solidifying bonds, which too stimulated more dreams of "independency."[50]

Traveling to Africa for slaves meant the ensuing of more venomous discord, bolstering more anti-African bias, jeopardizing the flexibility of London if it contemplated heeding nascent abolitionism by seeking to better confront Madrid by co-opting Africans. Thus, by May 1747 off the coast of Guinea, Africans rose against their European captors and killed a number of them, though two of the crew jumped overboard to escape.[51] In 1754, there was an uprising of Africans aboard a Bermuda slave vessel: strikingly, an individual identified as a Spanish slave was said to have murdered the captain and other European mariners. Since Robert Pringle, Henry Laurens, and numerous other mainland entrepreneurs used Bermudian vessels to correspond with their counterparts elsewhere and since mainland periodicals routinely credited Bermudian captains with reporting major events—the 1712 revolt in Manhattan, for example—this revolt was not easy to ignore.[52]

This was particularly true for Laurens, who was to become a leading rebel against London's rule rather shortly and whose immense slave holdings would be jeopardized if abolitionist stirrings and increased solicitude toward Africans became reality. He was one of the mainland's largest slave traders and had close ties to Newport and Philadelphia. As the slave markets of the Caribbean were transformed in the mid-1750s, he played a key role as Africans were sent to his homeland, South Carolina, from French slavers. He controlled a vast business empire, but trade in Africans was at the center of his many dealings.[53]

London's colonies in the hemisphere were not one wholly unitary unit, but it was fair to say that events in one portion reverberated in another, as suggested by the exodus to the mainland after Antigua 1736 and the impact on the mainland of the contemporaneous ongoing revolt of the Maroons of Jamaica. Thus, when in 1753 a major uprising of Africans rocked Barbados, which involved, inter alia, beating to death a European man, the case received somber headlines due north, especially in Halifax, Nova Scotia. The settlers on this sugar island were lucky in a sense since the uprising was aborted before the enslaved had launched their intended total "destruction" of the settlers.[54]

The acceleration of the slave trade as the middle of the 18th century approached revived the old argument about the Royal African Company versus private or separate traders, and to that extent it was proper for colonists, be they in Barbados or Bermuda or Baltimore, to see their fates as conjoined, since the fuel for their development—Africans—arrived from the same source. "Will not every British Planter in America and every West India Merchant," it was argued in 1745, "grant that the Negro Trade on the Coast of Africa is the chief and fundamental support of the British colonies and plantations in America?" What if London's "most formidable rivals," for example, Paris, "monopolize the whole African Trade to Themselves, will they not naturally furnish their own Colonies with the best of Negroes, and suffer Englishmen to purchase their Refuse only; and that too at an exorbitant rate"? Was it not true that the "Wealth and naval power of Great Britain is, in a great measure, owing to the extensive Commerce and navigation to and from

[its] American Colonies and Plantations; and that these must be totally ruin'd and undone if unsupplied with Negroes"? What would happen if Paris made alliances with local Africans—just as it had been doing with mainland Africans: would a bunch of diffuse private traders be capable of mounting a counter-offensive like the Crown could?[55]

But the RAC had been losing momentum steadily since the late 17th century: by 1749, the forts on the coast of Africa, so needed for the propulsion of this odious commerce, "were in great distress," it was reported. The idea was taking hold in certain London quarters that the homeland was losing the race for wealth and influence to Paris because of the latter's supposed advantage in dominating the African Slave Trade. And this, it was said, was due to the erosion of strength of the RAC— "dissolved to the great Joy of both of the Dutch and French," which was a "scandal." The "Negroe-Trade alone" was "of a most prodigious consequence" and during the heyday of the RAC was "the most flourishing of any in the Kingdom" and "the most beneficial to this Island of all the Companies that ever were formed by [British] Merchants." This trade was of momentous significance for the Caribbean holdings of London, which could hardly be maintained if France dominated the commerce in Africans from its bases in West Africa and Hispaniola (and, it could have been added, aided by mainland settlers). This French upsurge had "laid a sure foundation to supplant" Britain in its "whole American Commerce in general." With urgency, it was asked rhetorically, "are we not indebted to those valuable People, the Africans, for our Sugars, Tobaccoes, Rice, Rum and all other Plantation produce? And the greater number of Negroes imported into our Colonies from Africa, will not the exportation of British Manufactures among the Africans be in proportion; they being paid for in such commodities only?" Was it not true that the "general Navigation of Great Britain owes all its Encrease and Splendor to the Commerce of its American and African colonies"?[56]

Yet the French had the upper hand in Africa, it was maintained, since in the parts of Africa where they resided, they were "the only Purchasers of Negroes," and "consequently having no bidders against them," they were able to "make their own market." Contrarily, "the case is quite otherwise on those parts of the coast where the British Company have settlements" because of the competition brought by the "separate purchasers" or private traders. "This naturally raises the price of Negroes" to the detriment of London's overall interests. Moreover, Paris did not tax enslaved African imports to its colonies as much as London did, perhaps providing another advantage. Hence, if Paris gained the upper hand in the slave trade, London's colonies would be obliged to "depend on the labour of the *White Men* to supply their place," which would not be competitive, and perhaps worse, "they will either soon be undone or shake off their dependency on the Crown of England. For White Men cannot be obtained near so cheap," a point recently thrashed out in Georgia (emphasis original). Further, if this were to occur and "White Men" supplanted "Negroes in planting," this would mean the "drain" of the country's "Husbandmen, Mechanics, and Manufacturers too," ruining Britain's economy. The provincial tail wagging the metropolitan dog (and being savaged by a French mutt) was what was envisioned, and the decline of the RAC was an essential part of this nightmare.[57]

London was trapped in a rickety contraption of contradictions that all seemed to point toward shedding—perhaps involuntarily—a good deal of its holdings in North America. There was a tendency in London—and certainly among the settlers—to see enslavement of Africans and its inevitable complement, the slave trade, as essential to a robust confrontation with its European antagonists.[58] But the kind of slavery being imposed in London's settlements was even more repugnant to many Africans than the situation in Havana and Cape Breton, which were more willing to erect a buffer of free Negroes. This may have been an acceptable burden for London except that its crafty colonists were busily cutting deals with those same antagonists, France most notably, which was to eventuate in 1776—and these manipulative settlers decreased the maneuverability of the Crown when they railed at the idea of such a buffer besides.

It was not as if Londoners were unaware of the dangerous path the settlers (and they themselves) were pursuing. The Earl of Egmont was told as much by a premier settler, William Byrd of Virginia, when the latter observed that growing numbers of Africans "make them insolent & foul means must do, what fair will not," creating a "publick danger" or the fearsome "servile war." So, he said as early as 1736, consider "an end to this unchristian traffick . . . lest they prove as troublesome & dangerous everywhere as they have been lately in Jamaica," site of the militant Maroons: "we have mountains too," he reminded London, "and so as much mischief as they do in Jamaica" could arrive on the mainland.[59]

Byrd's words were comprehensible since there were an estimated 6,000 Africans in Virginia in 1700, but by 1756 there were more than 120,000.[60] There were about 1,000 Africans next door in North Carolina in 1700; by 1730 there were 6,000 and by 1765 about 65,000.[61]

As the number of Africans grew, measures to bar their insurrection were passed, with their subversive activity deepening enmity toward them,[62] lubricating the path to both opposition to incipient abolitionism and increasing enmity toward Londoners who moved in that direction. After a knock-down battle in Georgia, the enslaved African population increased dramatically: between 1750 and 1766, the number of the province's Negro denizens grew from around 500 to about 7,800.[63] Even the powerful Byrd and the Earl of Egmont seemed powerless in the face of those merchants and planters who refused adamantly to halt the slave trade, which was to create momentum for secession.[64]

The wider point was that as the number of enchained Africans grew, the number of furious Africans grew too, meaning the plotting against slavery also increased at a frenetic pace. This intensified the anxiety of settlers, which was not assuaged when signs of incipient abolitionism— or even recruiting and arming Africans to better confront His Catholic Majesty—began to surface in London. Instead of bowing to this sentiment, some settlers moved in an opposing direction. In North Carolina in 1754, there was a concerted effort to hamper those who were seeking to curb the trade in human beings. Even the "clandestine" trade from the Cape of Good Hope to Madagascar was approved since to do otherwise—it was said—violated the rights of major merchants.[65] Curbing the slave trade to the mainland in the mid-18th century was difficult at best, and whether these barriers failed or succeeded, the subsequent momentum created was tending to facilitate "independency."

The larger point was that, to a degree, the region sprawling from the northeastern part of North America through the Caribbean to South America was a unitary theater of conflict, and the obdurate attitudes toward Africans that had calcified in the area stretching from Savannah to Boston were often counter-productive to London's larger schemes, notably the need to divert capital and troops to India. This thought may have occurred to the New York merchant Charles Hicks, who had been residing in South Carolina for years, before arriving in St. Augustine at an emotionally charged moment between London and Madrid. There he saw hundreds of armed Africans, including some who had fled Carolina and others from Veracruz; in fact, he thought the Spaniards there had a "great dependence upon the Negroes" and, therefore, were "very desirous of another expedition" to Charleston, assuming that Africans there would join their assault. Indeed, he well knew that former Spanish prisoners in Carolina "used to tell the Negroes" there that "they would come for them"—and "the Negroes seemed well pleased."[66]

However, London found that despite the cost in lives and funds, the easier course was to wage war against Spain and eliminate this threat, rather than to seek to alter the policies and attitudes of mainland settlers. Thus, in 1743—when it had been thought that the southern border had been pacified—leaders were still being "annoyed by the Spaniards," who were urging Africans across the border to "commit massacres and assassinations and the burning of houses," for example, what had transpired in Manhattan: this was "proof," said officialdom, that "His Majesty's subjects are never like[ly] to be free from their horrible and mischievous endeavours until an Enemy so barbarous be removed."[67]

But London, which already controlled a gigantic and growing empire, could hardly afford to shun indefinitely the idea of arming Africans en masse, not least when mainland settlers often seemed so reluctant to enter into combat. Moreover, unrest was already bubbling over in Scotland and manifesting itself in Boston, leading to a grand revolt north of England in the 1740s at a time when London was seeking to confront a daunting challenge from Spain.[68] The epochal battle of Culloden in 1745 caused some Scots to look back in anger at the Act of Union of 1707 bringing Scotland more firmly into the United Kingdom, with one acerbic critic arguing that the concord was corrupted since it was "brought about by the distribution of a sum of money among the Scots' aristocracy" and "greatly against the wishes of the Scottish nation in general." Recalled was a 1719 plot hatched in Spain to invade and overturn the 1707 pact (with plenty of Scottish aid, it was thought), which was only nipped in the bud at the final moment,[69] a complement to London's plan a few years earlier to aid Catalonians in revolt against Madrid. A Scot visiting Jamaica in the 1740s noted knowingly that "the Scots abroad aver very remarkable for standing by their Country-men. . . . most of all the Scots I knew in Jamaica," he reminded resolutely, "were Jacobites"—not necessarily good news for the Crown.[70] Some of those who were defeated at Culloden were exiled to Maryland, where they could enjoy a further opportunity to make devilment at the Crown's expense.[71]

Thus, writing in 1747, a Scot visiting Jamaica espied "a conspiracy among the Negroes, for a general insurrection to destroy all the white people." The Africans he encountered were "stubborn, resolute and revengeful Creatures in their own Way," exhibiting "low-cunning which they employ in Theft or revenge." There were "computed to be about 100,000 Negroes" there, and "by a law of the country, for every 10 Negroes, there ought to be one white Man but this had been so little observed that" he found only one "white man for fifty Negroes; and the white servants that come, or are sent thither, are the very Scum of the Earth, and, generally speaking, prove good for nothing." Worse, in Cuba there were "much better Government and Discipline among the Negroes." This Scot seemed as if he wanted to opt for the Spanish model when he spoke of meeting a Jamaican, "of Negro parents, educated in England," who was a "superior genius," leading him to conclude that "it is not color but genius and education that makes the man"—a thought that would not necessarily be embraced on the mainland. Yet even this thoughtful Scot drew the line at Jews, opting for a less forthcoming attitude, which could only narrow the base of support for London in the region.[72]

This was all very worrisome. But given that it was a Scot writing at a time of unrest in Scotland, London justifiably could have viewed his words with jaundice. Was he simply seeking to mislead? Was his implicit praise of Spanish Cuba an indirect indicator of his true loyalties? Was his anti-Semitism a further way to undermine the Crown? If London had to look askance at reports from a perpetually restive Jamaica that indicated brewing troubles—just because it emerged from a Scot—might this be an indication to pull back altogether from this island and relocate to the mainland? Or perhaps it meant that the Crown should rely more heavily on Africans and less on potentially disloyal "whites" who happened to be Scottish? It was estimated subsequently that one-third of "whites" in Jamaica were Scottish, suggestive of the Crown's perplexities.[73] If Scots were considered to be unreliable politically, then London would be inched ever closer to the remedy of increased arming of Africans, which would then serve to jeopardize further the allegiance of mainland colonies.[74]

Compounding the dilemma was the point that London also had to be concerned about the presence of Dutch residing in its mainland colonies, not only in Manhattan but in Savannah also.[75] Holland had been ousted from ruling Manhattan and the vicinity merely decades before, and London had reason to believe that not all in this province had been reconciled to British rule (not to mention the perception that Spain's previous rule of part of the Netherlands had left a deep imprint there inimical to London's interest, which could be transferred across the Atlantic). In elite colonial circles, analyzing and unpacking "whiteness" appeared to be anathema, which could only allow festering problems to flourish—ethnic and religious tensions between and among Scots and Irish and English and the Dutch in the first place. Such tensions weakened the colonies, making them easier to fall prey to foreign invasion or insurrectionary Africans—or both.

Thus, London routinely demanded more "white" settlers in its provinces in the Americas, while it was well understood that this did not mean all who fit this description—for example, those with sympathies to Madrid and Paris; but this was hardly articulated. It was as if the elite did not interrogate "whiteness," then no one else would either, and the inherent frailty of this unstable category would somehow magically disappear.

By 1745, the question of how to protect the colonies while some settlers were bent on flooding the streets and plantations with Africans had been broached in the streets of London. At this juncture, the Cartagena debacle and calamitous events such as the Stono and Manhattan revolts—all of which implicated the destabilizing role of Africans—were well-known. By that point, South Carolina was in a familiar pose, on its knees begging the Crown to send more troops to confront its multiplying internal and external foes. Of course, said one Londoner skeptically, these troops were to be "paid from Great Britain but under the command of the governor," though this combination had hardly eliminated the threat from abroad and at home. "It is very certain that South Carolina is overstock'd with blacks in proportion to the number of white people," said this astringent critic. After data from customs there were examined, it was noted that Charleston was bringing "from two to three thousand [Africans] annually" to its shores. As George Burrington saw things, if the will and means could be galvanized to "make proper laws and regulations to restrain the rich planters from keeping dangerous numbers of Negroes," then London would not "be at the expense of paying a standing force to keep them in obedience." There was a certain logic to this view, but it clashed sharply with the hegemonic views of "the rich," not least Henry Laurens, who within years was to be revered as a Founding Father of the new republic.[76]

Burrington's point was echoed in Georgia, where one settler observed that "Negroes would be hurtful in Georgia as long as there is a War with Spain"; the problem was, said John Dobell, that some of his fellow Georgians were "stark mad after Negroes" and, quite literally, were willing to risk "poison" in order to effectuate their demented schemes.[77] Yet, in what was to be a commonplace in the post-1776 republic, there was an astonishingly broad "white" united front demanding more slaves in Georgia. "I find that all from the highest to the lowest vote for Negroes," Dobell was told by a comrade, "and look upon me as a stone in their way toward which they direct all their spite"; dirty tricks were suspected in pursuit of their goal, as this correspondent had "fear" that his "letters may be intercepted." His opponents were "so exceedingly bold as to bring over Black slaves" in "defiance" of "the King" and "express orders" and at "this dangerous time of War," when Africans were known to be unwilling to defend the Union Jack.[78]

Moreover, Burrington and Dobell could have mentioned that it was not only Charleston that was clamoring for more redcoats—a presence that would subsequently be scorned when billeted in local residences, helping to shape the successful rebels' vaunted constitution. For Delaware also demanded more British military men—they were "absolutely necessary" too, it was added, to supply the "West India islands with bread, meat, lumber and many other things" involved in an "extensive" bilateral "trade" involving "400 ships or more," which enriched the Exchequer in London—though there was nearby "not any fortification," which jeopardized Philadelphia.[79] In Maryland in 1745, there was fear of invasion from the French and Spanish, which was bound up with religious politics and the crisis in Scotland, and a resultant request for fully manned battleships.[80] Due south in North Carolina, the governor was pleading for more British troops in 1753, since if redcoats were visible, "the Negroes who have lately attempted an insurrection . . . will have the less to discourage them to repeat their attempts"; plus, "fortifications at the mouth of this river" near Wilmington were "in a defenceless condition." There was also a growing "contraband trade, particularly of French rum & molasses," which was fortifying the Parisian foe.[81]

This was not a unique problem. Georgia was formed in large part to blunt Spanish Florida, but its formation extended London's border dangerously close to the French domain in Mobile. By 1754, the governor of Georgia was irately demanding troops since the French were conspiring to "persuade the Indians to attack the English."[82] As ever, there was suspicion about the French since they were not perceived as being sufficiently anti-African and were willing, like Madrid, it was thought, to dispatch African agents to stir up the enslaved on the mainland.[83]

Burrington's fellow British subject Henry Ellis, who had served the Crown as a governor on the mainland, also sought a remedy for the fix in which the settlers found themselves. It was Ellis who recommended forming a buffer class of free Negroes and "Mulattos" between Europeans and Africans, not unlike what was evolving in southern Africa and parts of Latin America. He proposed that enslaved Africans should be freed at the age of thirty in the Georgia he ruled—but, as with a similar proposal in Virginia, it met with a stone wall of resistance by settlers determined to construct a racist despotism.[84] This was also a course of action that complicated the effort to checkmate the more expansive attitude toward Africans that obtained just across the border in St. Augustine.

Africans, in short, were a major antagonist, but mainlanders were reluctant to curb the seemingly ceaseless flow of Africans who were arriving, which was raising searching questions in London about their judgment, if not their sanity. It was still true that in the 1740s in Charleston there was a search for revenue combined with apprehension about racial ratios that led to an attempt to tax slave imports. According to policymakers, the supposed "barbarous and savage disposition" of these Africans "may hereafter prove of very dangerous consequence to the Peace and safety of this province," a concern driven by memories of Stono and their "barbarously murdering" settlers: the only question to decide was if the "purchaser" or the "importer" should pay these duties, though if history was any guide, this province would continue its proven ruinous course.[85] Charleston, as a major port of entry for enchained Africans on the mainland, often set the pace for its slave-owning neighbors.

So, yes, there were mainland leaders who realized that unleashing more Africans in their midst was a recipe for a debacle, but with planters retreating from Antigua and Jamaica to the mainland and a continent to conquer, alternatives to the present course were few. Before being ousted, Oglethorpe had warned of the "mutinous temper" in Savannah, "fomented by the Spaniards," which was "but part of their scheme for raising a general disturbance through all North America. Their corre-spondence with the Negroes," he advised, "too fatally manifested itself in the fires of New York"—but his was a voice hardly heeded.[86]

Yet by early 1744, some elite Carolinians were soberly pensive: the Africans were "quiet but they [had] not always been so," and in any case, recent stormy events they had spawned in "Antigua, New York and Jamaica" were "sufficient warnings" of the danger of this "force that may be turned against" them. Like others of that time, they recognized that they had to be alert to events not only in their backyard but also in colonies thought to be distant.[87] Most likely, Madrid felt that as long as there were Africans in the colonies north of Florida, there was a chance that London's rule could be toppled, for a few months later, a Georgian was counseling that "the Spaniards intend to invade," as a "great number of vessels & troops were expected" from Havana and St. Augustine.[88]

A troubling sign arose when a few Carolinians actually began to defect to Florida, Africans in tow, in an act considered to be "Treason."[89] After all, slavery appeared more stable in what was to become the Sun-shine State than due north. When these fleeing settlers voted with their feet in favor of Madrid and not London, they tended to indicate that the latter's model of colonial development would have difficulty surviving in a head-to-head contest with His Catholic Majesty's provinces.

The bind in which Carolina found itself was exposed when Afri-cans were sold to merchants in Florida. This too, it was thought, could bring "fatal consequences," not only denuding the province of labor but strengthening a foe and meaning "taxes fall heavily on those who remained"—though the overriding concern was that the Africans "so sold to the Spaniards might be employed in the murdering & plundering [of] His Majesty's subjects."[90] Buying Africans, selling Africans—every turn seemed to bring peril. Likewise, Carolina policymakers were debating bills to "prevent the stealing, carrying, enticing & inveigling away Negroes and other slaves," though one would think that reducing this population's sizeable numbers would be their goal.[91] The gravamen of this law was not unique to Charleston, for simultaneously in Delaware, Spaniards were landing and carrying off enslaved Africans while plundering plantations.[92]

Those Africans still stuck in Carolina proved to be so conspiratorial that it would have been understandable if the authorities felt they had sold the wrong slaves to Spaniards. For in early 1747, a plot by Africans to poison fellow residents was revealed,[93] just one of many such plots that seemed to increase along with the slave trade.[94] Poisoning proved to be a recurring crime in colonial North Carolina, perhaps exceeding that other favorite: arson. Nevertheless, consistent with Stono, murder or attempted murder occasioned almost 25% of the executions of enslaved Africans in what was to emerge as the Tarheel State, and most of their victims were of European origin.[95]

Thus, as Africans began—once more—surging into the mainland in greater numbers, increased disorder and combustibility accompanied their presence. And—once more—the authorities raised the alarm. This repetitive cycle—dragooning more handcuffed Africans, then warning dejectedly about their presence—suggested that these settlers were either playing a dangerous game or wagering that in the end they could effectively squash an African insurgency by sheer force of arms. Thus, in late 1748, officials in Virginia acknowledged that it was "absolutely necessary that effectual provision should be made for the better of ordering and governing of slaves, free Negroes, Mulattoes and Indians and detecting and punishing their secret plots and dangerous combinations." Indicatively, it was noted that "many Negroes, under pretense of practicing physic have prepared and exhibited poisonous medicines, by which many persons have been murdered."[96]

African herbalists in South Carolina too knew far more about plants than most local doctors did, and, unsurprisingly, by the early 1750s the province was gripped with hysteria over stories about poisonings by Africans "practicing physic." Evidently some Africans knew of botanical poisons so lethal that even the most competent—official—physicians in the colony had no effective antidotes. The local press argued that the "horrid practice of poisoning white people, by the Negroes, has lately become so common, that within a few days past, several executions" of these alleged herb manipulators "have taken place in different parts of the country," "by burning, hanging, and gibbeting."[97] Similar executions also befell Africans in Georgia who near the same time were accused of attempting to poison slaveholders.[98]

During this same period, a prominent slaveholder, Charles Purry, was murdered in his home in Beaufort, South Carolina, by "his" slaves. Reflecting the brutality of the slave system that had ensnared these Africans, he was stabbed in the eye and the chest and thrown into the river, his body weighed down with various items. Only the accidental recovery of his body the following day prevented the planned murder of two other prominent planters. A similar fate befell the father-in-law of William Drayton—the latter man was also part of the elite. Another African accused of poisoning his master was sold to Jamaica in May 1750[99]—an island where his belligerence would fit nicely.[100] The fright about poison was so pervasive that those Africans who purported to devise antidotes could gain freedom.[101]

A traveler in 1750 conceded that the "dangerous art of poisoning is known to the Negroes in North America, as has been frequently experienced"; the fact that some of their poisons did not "kill immediately" made their handiwork even more effective and hard to detect.[102] Indeed, if subsequently enacted slave codes in Georgia and South Carolina can withstand reasonable inference, they cry out with the conclusion that slaveholders in both provinces had become obsessed with the notion that they might be poisoned by enslaved Africans.[103]

Troubling for the colonists was the idea that poisoning slaveholders had spread to Massachusetts by 1755, as two Africans—male and female—were executed in Charlestown for doing so.[104] In faraway Louisiana, the authorities passed a bill forbidding the import of Africans from Hispaniola because so many deaths of Europeans of that island had occurred because of poisons administered by Africans.[105]

But these plots by Africans may have been minor in conception compared to what occurred in 1748, when an African in South Carolina issued an astounding confession about a conspiracy of him and his comrades to "rise and cut off. . . .[and] kill the . . . white people of this province and then to make their escape to St. Augustine"—but first they would "set the town and magazine afire." They would also "murder all the Negroes that would not join them." One enslaved woman in discussing her purported role in the plot said she wanted to "live as well as white people with a good deal more." Another corroborated the overall contours of the conspiracy, though adding that Antigua might be their ultimate destination,[106] a barely comforting substitution.

But what made this plot soar—in a sense—beyond Stono and revealed the uncouth seams of London's colonial project was the alleged participation of an Irishman (and presumed Catholic), Lawrence Kelly, who hailed from Pennsylvania and had been in Carolina for fifteen years; when queried, to the relief of the settlers, he asserted that he knew no one in St. Augustine—though this response could not erode the possibility that the desperate search for "whites" had led to the inevitable: "sleeper" or long-term agents of Madrid stirring up Africans. Then Thomas Russ, "one of the white people charged," was interrogated and revealed that he was born in New England, which could be seen as suggestive of regional strain that would implode in the next century, in 1861. Then John Matthews, also "white," was charged and responded that, yes, he knew Russ—but knew nothing of the conspiracy.[107]

Several Africans conceded that this plot had been hatched in concert with others of their status from surrounding plantations—and that "some white persons" too were involved, which widened the circle of mistrust.[108] That their design was taken seriously was demonstrated when the governor took time out from his busy schedule to query witnesses himself. It was then that "Kate," a "Negro woman," declared that "a boat with white men" was to rest nearby "in order to carry off" the Africans after they had perpetrated their bold deeds.[109] The targeted slaveholder, James Akins, was understandably outraged by this plot, while Henry Laurens—whose ministrations in aiding the arrival of so many Africans to Charleston branded him as a veritable accomplice—confirmed the existence of a "horrible Insurrection intended by the Negroes there."[110]

It would have been understandable if the governor had inferred that the participation of an Irish Catholic meant that the ubiquitous hand of His Catholic Majesty was asserting itself. If so, what did this mean for the policy encouraging "whites" generally to become settlers? Was this not just further invitation to Madrid and Paris to create deviltry? And since "whites" were thought to have been involved in the Manhattan conflagration of 1741, did this episode in Carolina suggest that the increase in the number of Africans on the mainland also meant an increase in the kind of plotting of which they were so obviously capable? If those who were defined as "white" were conspiring against slavery, did this mean that London's incipient abolitionism had to be confronted more directly? If so, what did that mean for tranquil relations between the provinces and the metropolis? And did this also mean that, perhaps, incipient republicanism had to make itself more attractive precisely to foil the prospect of the germ of abolitionism spreading into the ranks of ever more Europeans?

The broader point was that the proliferation of poisoning schemes, gruesome murders of slaveholders, and participation of Irish—or "white"—men in slave revolts all pointed to an escalating crisis on the mainland. As imports of the enslaved rose—notably to Georgia, with pent-up demand for this valuable commodity which rested uneasily and dangerously close to vulnerable Carolina—revolts of the enslaved rose accordingly. And as these two yoked elements rose, a third rose in turn: incipient abolitionism. And as incipient abolitionism began to flower, settler confidence in London's ultimate intentions fell correspondingly.

When Africans continued fleeing to Florida, as they did repeatedly in the 1740s,[111] it was apparent that more firepower would be required to eliminate the Spanish threat and safeguard London's settlements. By this juncture, the ban on slavery in Georgia was a virtual dead letter, eroding Oglethorpe's dream of building a "white" pro-slavery wall to block this mass flight. With inauthentic courage, Georgia mandated that each planter should employ one adult European male capable of bearing arms for every four African male slaves[112]—but even if this had been sufficient to tie down the Africans, it was not clear what that would mean in case of a Spanish invasion.

Thus, Georgia had evolved from being a putative firewall into a trans-mission belt for Spanish thrusts into London's settlements. In the same year as the abortive 1748 plot in South Carolina, lawmakers in Virginia felt it nec-essary to legislate further about raising a competent militia, in light of the fact that they were "exposed to the invasions of foreign enemies by sea and incursions of Indians at land, and great dangers may likewise happen by the insurrection of Negroes and others."[113] By 1749, it seemed that the view a few years earlier that the subversion from Spaniards had been eliminated was bizarrely inaccurate. From St. Augustine, said one writer reporting from Charleston, they "seduced and encouraged our Negroes (or slaves) to des-ert" from Carolina, then "gave them freedom": "there is hardly a week," it was said with distress, "but a dozen of them go off at a time in canoes."[114]

The rabid confusion this turn of events was creating was indicated when in 1755 Georgia enacted a slave code that simultaneously sought to pulverize Africans while allowing them to join the militia. Why the contradiction? It was simply a reflection of a painfully redundant prob-lem: how to enslave Africans so as to develop the economy, while hinder-ing their ability to rebel in league with settlers' antagonists.[115] Countering these Africans was made all the more difficult because of the terrifyingly close proximity of Spanish St. Augustine and French Mobile.

Yet despite this implanted fissure of placing Africans in the militia[116]—a cure that was arguably worse than the illness—through this same period, London was continuing to receive reports about Georgians trading with these very same putative enemies: Spain and France. The same accusation was laid at the doorstep of the affluent Carolinian James Edward Powell.[117] In 1756, there was an unusual number of Spanish ships docking in Charleston on voyages from Cuba, said to be involved in an illicit tobacco trade.[118]

Perhaps, rather than seeing these men as having a novel conception of allegiance to London or even as ungrateful hypocrites, it might be better to see them as "premature" U.S. patriots; that is, economic logic was impelling them like a swift river current toward secession: while London was seeking to restrain their business dealings driven by the luscious bounty of African enslavement, Paris and Madrid had burst the dam and were more than willing to encourage settlers' shady bargains, and, thus, these mainland men chose not to fight this trend but embrace it, along with the pretty profits it delivered. The combined strength of Paris and Madrid could outweigh that of London and could preserve the existence of a new republic which would then call for a temporary cease-fire in the religious wars by enshrining in its constitution freedom of faith, bringing hosannas of praise from the presumably enlightened. The presumed enlightened then could cheer as the new republic garroted the "divine right" of monarchs, while undermining the challenge provided by a rising population of enslaved—and the feisty indigenous—by opening the floodgates and admitting a tidal wave of European (or "white") migrants. The latter, overjoyed by the opportunity to be reaped in a new continent—and their Enlightenment cheerleaders[119]—could then readily turn a blind eye to the existence of enslaved Africans (and even their frequent revolts), which had propelled the lunge toward secession in the first instance.

This blindness also made it difficult to acknowledge that the fire-lit skies of Manhattan were also enlightening and that the repetitive poisoning plots provided a foretaste of what fate still awaited many settlers unless there was a radical course correction, which arrived duly during the years stretching from 1756 to 1763.

7

The Biggest Losers

Africans and the Seven Years' War

The beginning of what has been called the Seven Years' War in 1756 (also denoted as the French and Indian War) between London and mainland settlers on the one hand (with some indigenes and Africans) and the usual antagonists (European foes, the indigenous, and Africans) on the other hand was a continuation of what had become a decades-long conflict.[1] For our purposes here,[2] what is critically important is the impact of this conflict on the tangled issues of slavery and the slave trade and the growth of secessionist sentiment. In short, this war led to Madrid being ousted from Florida—and for a brief period, Cuba—as Paris was evicted from Quebec. But, once more, this proved to be a catastrophic victory for London, for when pressure was eased on mainland settlers as a result, they seized the opportunity to revolt against the Crown with ample aid from the "Catholic powers." Ultimately, this led to creation of a slaveholders' republic that then ousted the European powers from leadership in the African Slave Trade and gobbled their mainland provinces in the process—meaning Africans were the biggest losers (along with their indigenous comrades).

*   *   *

Though it had been thought that Spain, a noticeable nemesis of London, had been defeated decisively in the 1740s, in 1750, Carolinians were negotiating futilely with St. Augustine on a pact guaranteeing the mutual return of escaped Africans—or capital flight[3]—but since the flow of Africans was generally one way (headed southward), there was little incentive for Madrid to negotiate in good faith. Even though—supposedly—there had been a cessation of hostilities between London and Madrid as of 1748 in the wake of their latest combativeness, 1752 saw Spanish privateers seizing a sloop sailing from Antigua (perhaps the most problematic of colonies) to New York and taken to Puerto Rico. "Restitution" was demanded by the powerful governor of Virginia, though odds were that this demand would be rebuffed.[4]

As ever, the external threat made the internal one appear even more fearsome. In mid-1755, Governor Robert Dinwiddie was irate about the "villainy of the Negroes" when the province faced "any Emergency": this was "always fear[e]d," which was no exaggeration.[5]

Near that same time, Spaniards were brazenly committing acts of piracy against ships sailing from Jamaica to Virginia, seizing rum, coffee, wine, silks, sugar—and slaves. Similarly frightening for mainlanders was that the Spanish crew in this instance included an Irishman,[6] giving sustenance to the suspicion that the slave conspiracy a few years earlier in Carolina may have involved Madrid. Subsequently, Virginia's governor was informed that the colony's militia "does not amount to 7000 men" and was "thinly spread over a widely extended country." If there was a foreign invasion, the province contained "50,000 Negro slaves to whom (no doubt) an Invader would proclaim liberty upon their joining them."[7] Governor Dinwiddie was forced to admit that what had bamboozled mainland colonies in the 17th century was persisting in the 18th also: the combined danger of Negro insurrection and foreign invasion.[8] The only change was that the flood of arriving Africans in the wake of slave-trade "reforms" simply made the danger more palpable.

In the immediate prelude to 1756—suggestive of how on edge the settlers were—Virginians were debating whether they should "arm some of the most trusty" of their slaves and were considering how to "keep" and "increase" the "aversion which happily subsists between Negroes and Indians."[9] Stoking enmity between the latter two was a strategic initiative by colonists. By 1756, the cry arose from Hanover, Virginia, that "[there are] so many black foreigners among ourselves as may justly alarm our fears and in [South] Carolina they are much more numerous than the county militia. Now if the French should invade our frontiers" and "if the Indians that are now neuter . . . should join with them and if these united forces should pour down upon us and meet with the welcome reception and assistance from so powerful an enemy among ourselves," then "scenes of blood, cruelty and devastation would open in our country"—for the doubters, it was added ominously, "it is not so improbable as we could wish."[10] These "black foreigners" could very well be followers or sympathizers of His Catholic Majesty—if recent history were a guide—thus compounding the perils discerned.

Yet symptomatic of the stiff challenges faced by mainland settlers was the fact that by 1760 even Georgia—where allergies to abolition and Africans seemed interchangeable—there was spirited discussion concerning "Negroes that may be trusted with arms" in the militia.[11] The colony had opened the floodgates, and Africans had flowed in accordingly: the overall population tripled between 1760 and 1773 while the population of slaves almost quintupled, and as had been predicted since 1733, the security of the province plummeted accordingly, a situation hardly assuaged by considering the arming of Africans. Mainland colonies had become the land of limited alternatives. Repetitive wars with indigenes and Europeans alike and the constant bleeding of slave resistance had taken an appalling toll on settlers, which was exacerbated by the calloused brutality of military discipline, which fueled desertions and mutinies—and the occasional strike.[12] Arming Africans to guard a system based on enslavement of Africans was both a non sequitur and emblematic of a system being ripped apart by multiplying contradictions. Something had to be done, particularly since competitors were placing more—not less—pressure on mainland settlements with every passing day. Just as Spain placed pressure on British settlers to arm Africans when it pursued this policy, France's policy of providing ever more lavish presents to the indigenous provided a similar motivation for Britain.[13]

Thus, once more, London was forced into the breach, shedding blood and treasure in copious amounts for seven long years, not least because settlers' disastrous policies toward Africans created enormous opportunities for Madrid and Paris to exploit handsomely. What resulted was a disastrous victory: for pushing the Spanish out of Florida and the French out of Quebec by 1763 eased pressure on mainland settlers and infuriated Paris and Madrid, which now had incentive to bolster a rebellion against British rule. That London felt it necessary to tax the settlers (in a real sense, this war was for their benefit) combined with the already yawning economic chasm between colony and metropolis to create conditions for the rise of a new republic: certainly taxing of imports of slaves, which was also of military significance, further eroded London's support both on the mainland and within important centers such as Bristol as well.

In other words, the 1756 war was both a solution and a problem. Yes, ousting Spain and France from their North American strongholds was a plus for London—but it arrived with a profound cost. Settlers too were running a grave risk whenever the specter of all-out war was bruited. The eminent Carolinian Charles Pinckney—like others—felt that the 1756 war would mean that the Africans would take advantage of the flux and, as had been their habit, "rise upon their masters and cut their throats in hopes of obtaining freedom."[14] This thought may have occurred to Samuel Davies of Virginia, who in 1757 was reduced to beseeching "his" Africans to remain loyal to him in the face of a possible French invasion; as if the same did not apply to his class, he denounced the potential invaders as "cruel, barbarous people" who punished Africans with "death in the most shocking manner."[15]

Colonial Philadelphia—in many ways the leading mainland city—was typical in that 1756 marked the onset of a decade in which slavery reached a zenith, as the assorted accumulated factors of the rise of private traders, the retreat from the Caribbean to the mainland, and the generating economic engine of these colonies now seemingly running on all cylinders all began to assert themselves forcefully. Feeding this phenomenon was the drying up of the supply of indentured German and Scotch-Irish laborers, a process driven in part by events in Europe and by London's vigorous recruiting for its war machine. Thus, 1762 was the peak year of importation of Africans in Philadelphia's history to that point, and it also happened to be the year when in a remarkable development, London ousted Madrid from the key colony that was Cuba, a major fruit of the war. Yet, while the mainland was heading toward a rosy dawn of renewed enslavement, London was inching toward abolition: even among Quakers, virtually isolated in Philadelphia as vigorous opponents of enslavement, manumissions were rare until the eve of 1776.[16] Many settlers—even those with abolitionist stirrings—had yet to grasp the unavoidable tie between exploitation of the enslaved and expropriation of native lands and how one fed the other.[17] Yet in Britain, William Hogarth—whose fame as a painter had yet to evaporate when he passed away in 1764—in his illuminating art had associated the servitude of Africans with moral corruption, while portraying the darker skinned as independent personalities.[18] It was this view that was rising in London, as an opposing viewpoint was ascending in mainland provinces.

As the population of Africans increased in Pennsylvania, so grew the diversity of their origins in a manner that emitted troubling signals. By 1762, there were advertisements calling for the return of fleeing Africans with roots in Guadeloupe and facility in a multiplicity of languages, not to mention "Spanish Negroe[s]," whose record of stirring unrest was well-known.[19]

The number of Africans in the colony of New York doubled between 1723 and 1756 and, with the French and Spanish threats then dissipated, ultimately tripled during the six decades between 1731 and 1790.[20] The African population in New York City increased by over 20% every year between 1756 and 1771.[21] It was during the heat of war that New York merchants began to increase investments in the African Slave Trade, as if they anticipated the ultimate result in 1763. Shipboard insurrections too received more prominence as a result, which may have had the impact of accelerating antipathy toward Africans, thereby paradoxically hastening the trade's acceleration.[22] Yet shipboard insurrections were precisely the violently distasteful acts that fueled the abolitionist sentiments of Londoners who held dear Hogarth's images of Africans.

In 1761, West Africans on board a vessel departing the Gold Coast launched a bloody revolt, with twenty of their number murdered as a result. But increasingly, such bloodshed was seen on the west bank of the Atlantic as a mere cost of doing important business. Despite the clear difficulty in delivering Africans to Manhattan, by 1756 there were almost twenty thousand slaves who lived within a fifty-mile radius of New York City. At that moment, slaves constituted about 25% of the total population of what is now New York City and the present-day suburbs of Westchester and Suffolk Counties, as well as Bergen County, New Jersey. Male slaves were about 60% of the total enslaved population in these agricultural regions, which was not a prescription for stability.[23]

Nonetheless, there was a gift to slavery on the mainland delivered by London's vigorous prosecution of the 1756 war: this was accompanied by an incompatibility of growing abolitionism within the British isles and growing enslavement in its provinces. Naturally, the emblematic province that was South Carolina did not elude this trend—that

is, the irrepressibly turbulent scare about the African presence following the Stono revolt had dissipated by the mid-1750s, when imports of
Africans began to creep up steadily again.[24] As the number of Africans
grew—along with crazed agitation about their ultimate intentions—
political discord was muted among the settler elite, as merchants who
owned plantations cooperated with planters who were dependent on
the export trade, a tendency that rose with the war.[25] The mirror image
of their concord was an extraordinary number of plots by the enslaved
leading up to and continuing during the 1756 war.[26]

As the 1756 war was winding down, one key low-country district was
all too typical of the surroundings: of the adult males there between
the ages of sixteen and sixty, there were 1,064 Africans but only 76 persons defined as "white." Yet when hundreds of Acadian refugees poured
into Carolina, Governor James Glen was among those who expressed
"utmost uneasiness" since, it was felt, they "may watch opportunitys
and join with the Negroes." Among the opportunities was the fear that
Negro chimney sweeps were thought to be preparing the ground for
mass immolation of the slaveholding elite and their allies.[27]

Still, why not embrace fellow "whites," particularly given the numerous Africans all around? There was still a kind of religious war at play,
and "whiteness" was hardly a hard fact but akin to a fervent projection;
in other words, when the provinces demanded more "white" settlers,
they hardly had patriotic French Catholics in mind. What they had in
mind was what was to evolve—Europeans willing to tolerate African
enslavement and unwilling to conspire with foreign antagonists against
their slave society. Hence, since France was at war with Britain, it was
felt this would override all else, particularly since these Catholics were
an early victim of ethnic cleansing. In 1756, a prominent slave dealer
observed that religious liberty extended to all (meaning, for example,
"the High Church, Low Church, Quakers, New Lights, Old Lights, Ana-
Baptists," et al.)—all "save the Roman Catholic, who is utterly denied
the publick use of his profession in almost all parts of America."[28] The
unease at the arrival of the Acadians could have created more suspicion
of London—how dare the Crown dump potential subversives and religious oddballs in their province!—which suggested the dilemma faced
by the Crown in that even seeking to bolster the "white" population
might lead to exasperating attitudes among mainlanders.

The question was not trusting "whites" but trusting the French. Consider that during the war it was suspected widely—redolent of decades of history—that London's foes were enticing Africans in the colonies with promises of freedom in return for aid. In the pivotal New York–New Jersey region, a 1756 report expressed anxiety about "too great intimacy between the Negro slaves and the French neutrals in this province which may at this time tend to stir up the Negroes to an insurrection when such numbers of [the province's] militia are detached to the frontiers against the French."[29] This was not a trivial matter since during this war enslaved African men were enlisted in the New York militia through various means and accompanied redcoats to distant frontiers where Frenchmen were prevalent.[30]

A metropolis edging closer to abolition and colonies moving in the opposite direction, a paradigmatic colony frowning on the arrival of what today would be considered racial brethren to countervail a disproportionate number of Africans—such factors were creating an unsustainable relationship that collapsed by 1776.

*   *   *

As ever, the infighting between the private traders and the now withering RAC seemed to overshadow the overarching conflict with the European powers. Looking back from 1744, one Londoner saw nothing but negative and little but the advance of European competitors from the time the RAC monopoly eroded in the late 1690s up to that present moment.[31] Private traders may have benefited from this erosion, but as one analyst argued in 1748, it was "necessary" to "keep up the Awe and respect of the barbarous natives, by a Power that can punish or protect them"[32]—and private traders were not sufficiently cohesive to do this, compared to an entity akin to the once formidable RAC: this argument did not prevail[33] and, according to some observers, served to pave the way for the rise in this important commerce of European competitors,[34] which could only mean harming London's interests in the colonies and making warfare in 1756 inexorable. Thus, from Barbados—in some ways a more valuable colony than Jamaica—came the 1752 report that there had been "no Negroes" supplied "by the Royal African Company for many years": they were all "furnished by separate traders."[35]

Thus, although it appeared that Britain and its colonial appendages were acquitting themselves well in the race to enchain Africans, a growing chorus of voices in London and the Americas disagreed, asserting that actually the race was being lost to European competitors. A tendency was rising that came to define the emerging republic: as retrograde forces grew in strength, they complained and whined paradoxically about their weakness—as if they realized deep in their hearts that the reactionary nature of their conquests would inexorably generate a fierce and debilitating response. Thus, these flesh peddlers felt that their opponents were grabbing the hearty Africans, leaving to London—it was emphasized— the *"tender, effeminate"* Negroes, who were "absolutely unfit for the *hard labour* of the Sugar Colonies," meaning these slaves "must always be a *loss and disappointment* to the Planters." For the planters, this also meant *"one great cause of their being now deeply in debt; and must be their ruin."* London was losing, it was thought, in the race to enslave *"Gold Coast"* and *"Whydah* Negroes," places where the French were "powerful competitors" of the British and "by the various encouragements given" in Paris "are enabled to pay a higher price than [British] private traders."[36]

These latter West Africans, it was reported, were "the most valuable and so necessary for the subsistence of sugar plantations," as they were "hardy and are [i]nured to labor," which was "not the case with other Negroes from Angola [and] Calabar" and those from Gambia—leftovers then were consigned to London's settlements.[37] If London was actually losing to Paris in a battle for such a valuable resource as Africans perceived as the most worthy of the enslaved, this could mean further momentum for war to reverse this gathering debacle, which would also mean taxes on settlers to pay for the war—since Africans were the essential coin of their realm. For as one propagandist argued, the settlements were "an inexhaustible fund of wealth and naval power to this nation," while the erosion of the RAC's monopoly had served simply to erode British power and empower European rivals;[38] but this propagandist, like others, seemed befuddled by the rise of private traders and merchants and the newly enhanced age of capitalism they represented.

The controversy about increased taxes also affected that most valuable of commodities—Africans—with some Virginia interests objecting in stern terms in the pivotal year that was 1756 about the prospect of such a policy,[39] which was nothing new.[40] By 1760, objections to such imposts had hardly budged, though the preamble of proposed legislation in the dominion noted that due to "insults and incroachments of the French," there was a need to raise "twenty thousand pounds," so an "additional duty of ten percent was imposed upon all slaves imported or brought into this colony and dominion for sale"; but this was a "great disadvantage to the settlement and improvement of the lands in this colony," as it "prevents the importation of slaves and thereby lessens the fund arising from the duties upon slaves"—so this law was "hereby repealed."[41] This meant the arrival of more Africans in the middle of war, though this troublesome property had a demonstrated propensity to take advantage of the encroachments of the French—and Spanish.

Importing more Africans and throwing caution to the winds was part of the culture of mainland colonists. After all, though an objective naysayer could argue that bringing more Africans was folly, the settlements were still standing and, by some measures, thriving, which was hardly a reason to change course (or culture). What upset many settlers was taxes on imported Africans, not the presence of this valued commodity:[42] associating the lifeblood of government—taxes—with fearsome Africans was destined to complicate future administrations on the mainland.

Thus, the danger notwithstanding, by 1747 Governor Gooch of Virginia was gloating about the two thousand Africans "imported the last summer" from "the coast of Africa."[43] Yet simultaneously he was moaning about the "misfortune of having the capitol of this city," speaking of Williamsburg, "burnt down, whether by accident or design, has not yet been discovered, tho' from the Circumstances, there is Reason to suspect the latter."[44] The estimable Gooch had difficulty in connecting the influx of Africans with the rise of instability.

In the midst of the 1756 war, potential migrants in Britain were apprised of the attractions of South Carolina. They were told of a tax that was "so heavy" on imported Africans "that it amounted to a prohibition" and, thus, was forced out of existence, but now "the war" too had "prevented any from being imported"—at least officially: "I do not find that in above nine years time," it was announced in 1761, "our number of Negroes is diminished, but on the contrary increased." This growth had reached the point where "the Negroes bred from our own stock will continually recruit and keep it up, if not enable us to supply the Sugar colonies with a small number of Negroes"—which could thwart presumed French control of the most bountiful slave territories. Left unsaid was what means—particularly crude means—were used to engender procreation. Also left unsaid was whether the growth of shipboard insurrections had created an incentive for settlers to breed their "own stock." Yet, when the Exchequer turned to raise revenue to pay for this war, it would be hard-pressed to avoid taxing the growing number of Africans, irrespective of how they arrived in Carolina. Thus, it was reported, in 1724 there were fourteen thousand "white people" in the colony and "about" thirty-two thousand slaves, "mostly Negroes," while as of that writing, the former had grown to twenty-five thousand and "the number of Negroes" amounted to thirty-nine thousand (though the latter figure was more precise "because a tax is paid for them").[45]

As some Londoners saw things, Madrid was seeking to reverse the logic of history by seizing Georgia and Carolina,[46] but the strategic problem hardly addressed frontally was whether bringing more Africans to Charleston and Savannah could more readily effectuate Spain's dream. As late as 1762, Benjamin Martyn, a leading colonist, was ranting that the "frontier to the Southern Province of North America" was "exposed" to "danger" by the Spaniards, who laid claim "to all the lands from St. Augustine, as far as Charles Town"; the "Southern Provinces of North America are now become objects of the highest consequence of the French also," from their lair in nearby Mobile.[47]

Paris and Madrid were also, it was thought, denying Bristol and Liverpool merchants their due in the slave trade. As one self-described "proprietor" put it, this security threat was aided immeasurably by "the French, our most dangerous trading rivals." Parisians were challenging these settlers on all fronts, particularly in the realm of control of human capital, since "whatever deprives the American planters of Slaves, or enhances the Price of them," he said, "is essentially detrimental to the Colonies."[48] But even this candid assessment ignored what others well knew: mainland settlers were busily engaged in mutually profitable business deals with London's most "dangerous" rivals, as Britain was engaged in what was thought to be a battle for supremacy, if not survival, in a death match with these rivals.

*   *   *

War had recurred yet again, but, once more, in order to gain a fuller picture of its manifestation on the mainland, more background on events in the Caribbean in the period leading up to 1756 is necessary. For the 1756 war was about the future not only of the mainland but also of the Caribbean. French strength in Hispaniola and Spanish strength in Cuba were more than a match for London's Jamaican bastion. Underlying all of these empires of slavery was the African Slave Trade, the fruits of which had helped to drive conflict between the European powers in the 1740s: rather than being a departure, 1756 was a continuation.[49]

That is, as London's settlers felt compelled to retreat from the Caribbean to the mainland in the face of Maroons and various liquidation plots engineered by Africans,[50] this was only increasing the Crown's headaches. In 1754, some voices in London were still begging for more "white people" to settle in Jamaica, "so as to be able to defend that great island"—but any who scanned headlines regularly would view such a proposal with extreme skepticism. In the middle of the conflict with Maroons, a similar call was made in order to "form a barrier against the rebellious Negroes for the security of the old planters"—and fell on deaf ears. It was truly "remarkable," it was conceded, that the "lands" appropriated for these would-be settlers in Jamaica was "in the neighbourhood of the rebel Negroes," as if proponents were actually seeking to discourage settlement. Besides, the remaining planters in Jamaica wanted to send their sugar and produce directly to foreign markets, "without being obliged to bring them first to Great Britain," which was "opposed by the manufacturers," as these planters too sought to have their profiteering trump allegiance to the Crown and its closest allies in London. Even during the "late war," London found "Smugglers from Jamaica" were dealing with "Spanish Dominions," à la mainlanders. Indeed, it was charged, war with Spain was "profitable to the island of Jamaica"—elites at least—"as all war with Spain is, tho' ruinous for Great Britain." But despite the contribution to the Exchequer, Jamaica was not the mainland; it could not as easily flout prerogatives of the Crown—not least because mobilized Maroons limited planters' options.[51] Perhaps London (or even colonists) would draw the obvious inference that mobilized Africans on the mainland could limit "independency" options similarly.

Of course, it was improbable that Jamaica or the other sugar colonies would be abandoned altogether, particularly since these territories allowed for a more forthright and proximate challenge to Cuba and Hispaniola. Moreover, there was a kind of integration between and among London's colonies, with events in the Caribbean reverberating on the mainland. David Cutter Braddock was an example; he spent a good deal of time in Savannah, where he was a major landholder, but also was in and out of Jamaica, the Turks Islands, New England, and Charleston on a regular basis.[52]

The ampler point was that African rebelliousness was serving to drive settlers from the Caribbean to the mainland, which increased the importance of the latter, helping to contribute to the 1756 war. In Jamaica, Braddock may have heard that planters were complaining about the cost of Africans—which was rising. And even if there was concern in London about adding to the ungovernable supply of this island, perhaps greater concern remained about the impact of their presence in terms of the conflict with Madrid and Paris and their ally-ing with these powers. Pressure from these powers had hampered trade with the mainland—for example, the "supply of horses from North America, especially from [Rhode] Island." Horses were now "twice the price" as before, and "unless [the] price of sugar rises," the planter "can't go on, he must be ruin'd." But there were two particular matters that had concentrated this former Jamaican planter's mind more than oth-ers—the price of slaves and the burden of taxes, which were linked: for if the latter increased, the planters would be "disabled from purchasing every year a fresh supply of Negroes." Slaves were bought "chiefly with the produce of manufacturers," including "fire arms, . . . gunpowder, . . . spirits, tallow, . . . some India goods, . . . woolen goods." But paying more taxes meant buying fewer Africans, which meant producing fewer manufacturing goods. Yet if Africans were still being snatched and could not be disposed of in London's various settlements, then the "sur-plus" would be sent to "the Spanish Coast for gold and silver," allowing more Africans to populate "Spanish settlements," which seemed con-trary to London's long-term interests.[53]

Worsening London's strategic dilemma was that some Jamaican Afri-cans were fleeing to Cuba (as their counterparts in Carolina were fleeing to Florida): the "consequences to this island will be very fatal," opined one subject in 1751.[54] By 1760, yet another significant slave rebellion rocked Jamaica, the only surprise being that the planters were caught unawares, with agitated undulations from this revolt flowing like molten lava in coming years.[55] While still confronting boiling unrest in Jamaica in the middle of a war, London then had to deal with what was described as "an intended insurrection of the Negroes" in Bermuda, which was repressed barely.[56] This had been preceded by acute food shortages caused by a spate of French privateering, which was thought to have motivated the Africans there, suggesting their objective alliance with London's enemies.[57]

Paris had its problems too, for in the late 1750s a major slave conspiracy erupted in Hispaniola. As had been the pattern, Africans chose the time of war between the major powers to assert and leverage their own power and influence, which put them in a better military position. The problem for London was that concessions to Africans to foil such conspiracies would not be accepted happily on the mainland and could serve to accelerate the incipient push to independence.

Of course, disposing of these Africans on the mainland was one way out—which is what occurred in Manhattan, Philadelphia, and various other North American sites—but such transfers were not an ideal remedy given Africans' demonstrated restiveness. Moreover, since planters and governors worried that pulsating unrest in one colony was a boon to another, African subversion probably increased fractiousness between and among the provinces, to the detriment of London's overall colonial project.[58]

It remains true that in the 1760s in Massachusetts, the argument rose more forcefully that security meant getting rid of slavery—and, perhaps, Africans too—a conclusion that was driven largely by reaction to events beyond its shores, for example, Manhattan 1741 and Jamaica 1760. It was evident by then that there was an irreconcilable clash between how British settlers chose to maltreat Africans and the reaction of this besieged group, which was thereby incentivized to ally with European rivals and the indigenous alike, to the detriment of these same settlers. As the 1756 war was concluding, there were more sales of Africans from Massachusetts to far-flung sites,[59] a kind of ersatz abolitionism that was to become au courant in the republic: ultimately, there was a conflation on the mainland of getting rid of both slaves and Africans generally, since the latter—in whatever guise—were perceived as a threat to internal security.

In the immediate aftermath of the war, legislation was introduced in Boston to bar the importation of enslaved Africans,[60] while another was designed to tax imports.[61] Similarly, in Delaware, measures were introduced to bar importing of slaves in the aftermath of war, alongside more draconian regulation of those who remained (including proscribing "profane swearing").[62] Still, the market for Africans was so deep and liquid that it was unclear if Boston (or New Castle or Wilmington) could be a real mover of the market. On the other hand, a scant century later, forces from Massachusetts were battling vociferously their erstwhile mainland compatriots in Dixie, and the issue of the future of African bondage hung in the balance, as the complicated saga of capitalism propelled by slavery entered its terminal phase.

Again, ready alternatives were not perceived by settlers as being readily available in the mid-18th century. During the summer of 1757, a mainland slave trader was moaning about the "great decay of trade in these parts," speaking of coastal West Africa, "occasion'd by the French war and scarcity of English shipping," which had affected dramatically the price for Africans. The Africans purchased were as difficult as ever, he thought, straining to retain "their ancient customs without alteration," while treating attempts to impose Christianity upon them—thought to be a condition precedent to assimilating them successfully to enslavement—with "ridicule or laughter" despite his most strenuous efforts.[63] Repeatedly, France was denounced during this war for having its vessels lying in wait for the slave traders who sped from Newport with cargoes of rum destined for Africa and thence to the Caribbean with Africans in chains.[64] With the African trade hampered, obtaining Africans in the Caribbean, despite their manifest tendency to create disturbance, at times seemed like the least horrible option. Massachusetts was simply not a market maker in this regard.

But as long as Madrid and Paris, as was their wont, were determined to collaborate with Africans against mainlanders, the neat solution of reliance on the Caribbean market remained problematic at best. Bringing Africans from Antigua to the mainland, which was occurring in the prelude to 1756,[65] also brought an uncertain benefit to those who were poised to rebel against London, while it reminded the metropolis that, perhaps, a different policy toward Africans and enslavement might be warranted.

Wiping out Spanish settlements in Florida—and even Cuba—and ousting the French from Quebec would slice the Gordian knot, it was thought. Nonetheless, there was a recognition in London that the Caribbean and settlements generally were hardly stable and were replete with unforeseen circumstances; thus, it was said in 1753, "Cromwell's war with Spain, though it procured to us Jamaica, weakened our other islands by the numbers drawn out of them for the St. Domingo expedition." Would the ouster of France from Quebec and Spain from Florida lead to a similar result? More than this, what was acknowledged then has been little recognized since; that is, "the Negroes are ever true to their own interests, without being at all slow in apprehending them," and they were hardly wedded to London—as Antigua 1736 and Carolina 1739 well showed—but, in a pinch, would align with Paris, Madrid, the indigenous, or all of the foregoing.[66]

But London too was encased in a trap of its own making: more slaves to the colonies meant more opportunity for European competitors to weaken or overthrow British rule. Taxing African imports so as to restrain their presence and raise revenue to better confront competitors meant alienating mainland planters or Bristol or both. Thus, at the midpoint of the 18th century, London's prospects in the Americas were not as bright as they seemed. Relocation from the Caribbean to the mainland and driving more Africans to the latter can be seen in retrospect as analogously disastrous as Napoleon's invasion of and then retreat from Russia. The 1756 war, however it turned out, was unlikely to reverse this dim picture, as even a victory simply delivered a further disaster.

*   *   *

Massachusetts, which was a cradle of revolt against the Crown, symbolized this problem, for it had formidable problems in confronting its population of Africans, while keeping a wary eye on Quebec, a problem that accelerated in the prelude to the 1756 war. Actually, this was just the flip side of solving the knotty matter of having within one's borders numerous European settlers who were determined to get on with the nasty business of ousting the indigenous and making fortunes and, thus, were not as inclined to participate in ambitious ventures that might take one to Cartagena or Santiago de Cuba. Before the war, these male settlers were hassling the authorities with various and creative means of avoiding conscription,[67] to the point where elites were thinking the unthinkable and emphasizing the *"great Number of Negro men"* there who *"may be made very useful in Case of an Invasion."* Now "obliging the said Negroes" to take up arms was being pursued.[68]

But the Africans might have been less enthusiastic than those who were seeking to command them, for by 1747 there were "riotous Proceedings" involving "armed Seamen, Servants, Negroes and others in the Town of Boston, tending to the Destruction of all Government and Order . . . following impressments."[69] By 1748, both problems merged when Africans were jailed for arson and European settlers were still proving to be troublesome soldiers.[70]

Settlers were absconding and deserting,[71] and those who remained, said Governor William Shirley, were engaged in "riot and Insult upon the King's Government"; this "extraordinary" revolt by a "Mob" was occasioned by conscription: the revolt against the draft was slated to be crushed "by force," with the "need" to "fire upon 'em." Unimpressed, the accused rioters threatened to "burn a Twenty gun ship" being built for "His Majesty." This "outrageous Tumult," this "inexcusable . . . insurrection" was worrisome, particularly since the militia charged with the crushing of it was "very tardy" in responding. Perhaps worse, the reason for this unrest was disturbing since the "uneasiness" was propelled by the "difference made between the Sugar Colony Islands and His Majesty's Colonies Upon the Northern Continent" insofar as London was "exempting the former from" the kind of conscription visited upon the mainland.[72] Evidently the rioters did not accept the idea that the "Sugar Colonies" had a deficit of "whites" and could not spare them because of a surplus of mutinous Africans, which meant that Boston would have to carry an extra burden, providing yet another rationale for 1776 and disassociating from a dangerous Caribbean: in Philadelphia, even indentured servants of European descent were putting forward what were described as "cogent" and "strong" reasons why they should not face "inlistment."[73]

Sooner rather than later, these rioters were taking up arms—against the Crown. Sooner than that, jurists in London could point to policy reasons as to why it might be wise to move toward abolition, to display more solicitude toward the abhorred African so as to better confront European competitors.

But indentured servants may have objected to being transported to the Caribbean to fight in a war whose strategic implications for the Crown may not have been well understood by them or even seen as being in their direct interest. Easier to understand were the labor shortages that hit Pennsylvania, once these laborers found themselves in

Cuba—a development which led to the bringing of more Africans to this colony, which was like trying to douse a fire with gasoline. But as the 1756 war unfolded, Governor Shirley would have none of this, feeling that survival itself was at stake, arguing that "when a country is in danger of being lost to the Enemy, it is not a time for the Government of it, to enter into critical dissertations" as to "whether the inlisting of Indented Servants" for defense could mean promoting a "Tendency to lessen the Importation of them into the Country for future Tillage of the Land, and to increase that of Slaves."[74]

Yet the French had not taken a vacation while their antagonists to the south of Quebec and to the east of Mobile were ensconced in internecine conflict, as border raids and boundary disputes continued to rage.[75] As late as 1756, Quakers and others were seeking military exemptions,[76] while other Europeans were forcing an exemption of sorts by deserting and mutinying. When a decision was made to take a census of enslaved Africans in Massachusetts,[77] it was easy to infer that the authorities wanted to ascertain where potential enemies—or contrarily, potential defenders—might reside: a paradox that neatly summarized a problematic dilemma. If Negro defenders were sought, this could contravene the provincial policy of racist autocracy, and it was too ghastly to digest fully the consequences of taking a census of potential enemies. By 1758, one slaveholder was petitioning for compensation after his "Negro Servant" had joined the military but was now sickly and no longer "[of] service nor ever like[ly] to be," illustrating that defending the province would be costly.[78]

This petition was not singular, suggesting a number of explanations, including masters, quite typically, gaming the system at a time of crisis.[79] Africans themselves were petitioning for compensation after joining in "the expedition against Canada," compensation that was being refused to them,[80] which could make their brethren less willing to defend the Crown—or to attack its foes. This was no minor matter when European settlers were devising all manner of excuses to avoid military service.

If Massachusetts had been unique, perhaps the problem of settlers' reluctance to fight could have been downplayed, but in Virginia too, Governor William Gooch was carping about events in Albany, where there was "great desertion among the troops, occasioned . . . by their want of pay, the several provinces, Virginia excepted not having advanced that Payment for them."[81] By 1758, George Washington, who was particularly hostile to the idea of arming Africans, was reporting that smallpox was devastating his troops, providing an "unpromising circumstance."[82] By 1759, mutiny and mass desertion had become the hallmark of mainland soldiers; entire regiments simply refused to perform any duty whatsoever. On 29 May 1759, a Rhode Islander was shot for desertion, and a fellow settler from Connecticut faced a similar destiny on 15 June—a trend which could hardly inspire their loved ones or, perhaps, others to swear allegiance to the Crown.[83]

Reporting in 1761 from Martinique, where the French governor had just been taken prisoner and "articles of capitulation" had been drafted, the leading redcoat invader, General Robert Monckton, was waiting impatiently for "troops from Carolina" that had yet to arrive, while "vessels" that he expected "from New York" were already deemed to be not "adequate" even before touching the shore. "I have already been obliged to buy some provisions" as a result, he lamented, and he was requesting "some from England"—though London might well have asked, what about the closer mainland?[84]

This had to be taken seriously since the 1756 war was not a cakewalk for London, as a 1757 meeting between the governors of North Carolina, Virginia, Maryland, and Pennsylvania demonstrated. Conferring with the Earl of Loudon, grave concern was expressed about the "danger of the enemy's making an attack on the province of South Carolina, either by sea from St. Domingo, or from the Alabama Fort [of] the Creek Indians on the head of the Mobile, for which reason they have agreed that there ought to be two thousand men employed in the defence of that valuable province of South Carolina and to secure Georgia."[85] The worst fears of these executives may have been realized when in mid-1759 John Pendarvis of South Carolina, described as a "free mulatto," expended a hefty "sum of seven hundred pounds currency for arms and ammunition" for the intended purpose of waging "insurrection against the white people."[86]

By 1760, Governor Henry Ellis of Georgia thought he had found the remedy to this problem of "intrigues" of the French—"I have been able to set the Chickasaws upon the Cherokees"—but with little contemplation of the long-term consequences of stirring ethnic antagonism.[87] This diabolical tactic proved unavailing in his Carolina neighbor, for by late 1761, the authorities were complaining that military contingents had been "reduced so low by desertion" and the like that the province had become dangerously vulnerable.[88]

Old habits—particularly profitable ones—die hard, however, and in the heat of the 1756 war London's pre-eminent William Pitt was remonstrating Virginia's governor about the "intelligence" he had received "of an illegal & most pernicious Trade, carried on by the King's Subjects in North America, & the West Indies, as well as the French islands," not to mention "the French settlements on the Continent of America & particularly to the Rivers Mobile & Mississippi." This "enabled" and served to "sustain & protract this long and expensive War," as "large Sums in Bullion" were being sent by "the King's subjects" to French hands: this "ignominious trade" was a "danger,"[89] it was pronounced correctly— the only trouble was that already these Virginians were swiftly moving beyond seeing themselves as true "King's subjects."

Actually, a dominant theme of the 1756 war, which makes it a virtual dress rehearsal for the 1776 conflict, was the repeated accusation that settlers were double-dealing, collaborating with the French, as redcoats fought them. "I have undoubted proofs," said the leading redcoat, Lord Jeffrey Amherst, in 1762, "of the Enemy being supplied with Provisions from almost every port on the Continent of North America," though at that precise moment there was "the greatest demand for provisions to supply the King's Troops."[90] While the redcoats were battling to seize Cuba and relieve pressure on beleaguered settlers, Lord Jeffrey knew that "merchants . . . particularly those of Pennsylvania and New York were entering into schemes for supplying the Havannah with provisions."[91] Pitt had also heard from Governor Shirley of Massachusetts, who too was outraged by the "pernicious trade carried on by the northern British colonies to the French settlement in Hispaniola."[92] Shirley, who had traveled from South Carolina to the Bahamas by early 1760, found this to be a "very large trade" and "very lucrative," involving about "80 or 90" vessels.[93]

Settlers had their own complaints. Affluent Carolinians could not have been pleased when European settlers were dispatched in late 1761 to Barbados, where they had a chance to witness the spectacle of "great exertion in raising five hundred volunteers completely armed & clothed and five hundred Negroes" similarly outfitted; there were "three hundred Negroes at Antigua" and an expectation that "other islands will raise their proportions."[94] In Barbados, Carolina's progenitor, any master with thirty or more slaves was obliged to contribute one man to the armed force, with fines for non-compliance.[95] Carolina settlers may have wondered understandably about the long-term viability of their prized investment in human commodities when these Africans were arming nearby.

Such conscription was even more necessary in light of shortfalls among mainland settlers. Reporting from Barbados, James Douglas in 1761 was waiting anxiously for "forces from America," which, quite typically, had yet to materialize. Yet "His Excellency and the gentlem[e]n of this island," who had a more severe security challenge, were nevertheless "very zealous in having voted and raised 500 white men and 600 Negroes" to sustain the Crown's forces—which "Antigua and the other islands will also do," Douglas added. This was crucial since he was expecting momentarily enemy "privateers" while his troops were "busy in the intended attack."[96]

As the pivotal year that was 1762 dawned, leading redcoats—not least due to resistance to military service on the mainland—were raising a "corps of Negroes" for "service in . . . Jamaica" with the aim of attacking Cuba and marauding as far afield as New Orleans. Thousands of men were involved, though still expected was a "detachment from North America" of "provincials." Exquisitely detailed instructions were devised for the care and feeding of the latter—"special care" should be taken to ensure that they "be treated with all such proper attention and humanity, that they may not return home disgusted with the service, but on the contrary," will feel motivated to engage militarily on "future occasions." But little attention was devoted to the problem created of having settlers serving in a similar capacity as those whom they viewed as slaves—like an associative law of mathematics, did not that imply that these colonists were no more than despised Africans? In a stunning misunderstanding of "provincials," London decided that the settlers and the Africans "should have an equal share in all Booty gained from the enemy in common with . . . regular troops" and "in proportion to their respective numbers, rank and pay." In retrospect, given such a mandate, what may be shocking is that the revolt against British rule on the mainland commenced formally in 1776 and not 1762 (or earlier, when this idea was first ventilated).[97]

But did London have an alternative? Mainlanders were objecting strenuously to fighting, while the major population center of Africans that was Jamaica was typically afire, all this in the midst of a crucial war.

In May 1762, Lord Albermarle spoke freely of "the great utility of the slaves to Major General Monckton's army": "I believe he had near 3000 from His Majesty's Islands," made all the more important given the "great uncertainty" of his "receiving any from Jamaica, as that island has been so much alarmed for some time past," compelling the redcoats to go on a buying spree: "I purchased near 100 Blacks at Martinique," with others bought at St. Kitts and Antigua. He wanted even more and was considering "raising" a "corps of Free Negroes" besides, which could only give this group leverage that could be wielded in favor of abolition.[98]

London was in a bind. Jamaica, it was said, "alone" could "easily raise a great number" of armed Africans, since there were "four Negro towns" and "at least [six] hundred who are all good marksmen being the remains of the Negroes who were formerly in rebellion, . . . bush fighting being their principal forte." Resorting to reliance upon Africans who had exacted more than their share of British blood was indicative of the quandary faced by London.[99]

Mainlanders were not the only "whites" upset by the turn that this war was taking. As the siege of Havana was accelerating in August 1762, troops in nearby Guadeloupe focused on something else altogether. "Subaltern officers" were irked that they were to be deprived of rich spoils of war—slaves: it was a "subject of discontent," the Lords of the Treasury were informed. It was unclear if mainlanders were among the grousers, but surely their outlook was reflected among these malcontents, which suggested to London the problem of their inclusion within the ranks.[100]

As the war gained momentum and the fecklessness of mainland settlers became more evident, Henry Ellis, who had served as governor in Georgia and knew well of the hair-pulling about slavery that occurred there, was toting up the changing situation. With Florida taken, London could then "deprive the Negro of an asylum," a Spanish policy which had "ruined many of the King's subjects in America" and had left the southern "frontier" in a "weak and unsettled" condition, though the "soil and climate" were "excellent." It was a single step from this realization to its complement: that a more forthcoming attitude toward Africans could reduce the need for "asylum," transform the "weak and unsettled" frontier, and develop a more bountiful colonialism—except this would have undercut the established policy of the settlers.[101] "Gaining the Negroes to our interest," Ellis argued, "by assuring them ample liberty and promising them lands [on] one of the neutral islands, where a black colony might be settled," would be "highly useful to this nation," speaking of Britain—though he did not consider that this prospect could terrify mainland settlers, who had been intimidated by St. Augustine for decades and were to be hounded by Haiti for decades to come. As for the settlers, he saw them as an attacking force against Havana, cannon fodder in a sense, since they were "entirely free from danger"— an opinion not widely shared on the mainland.[102]

A 1756 law in troublesome Antigua illustrated the challenge to which Ellis responded. "The small number of our able men and the nearness and populousness of the French islands make it absolutely necessary that our whole force should be constantly preserved in a good posture"; and this could be accomplished by dint of the "many free Negroes" theretofore "not incorporated into any of the Regiments of this island." Yes, "several fatal accidents" had ensued previously from entrusting "arms and ammunition with Negroes," but the present crisis did not admit many alternatives. With the need to curb restlessness among the unabashedly gladiatorial Africans of Antigua by building a buffer of "free Negroes" and the continuing security threat posed by European competitors, London was moving in a direction on this island that would have found favor with Ellis.[103]

* * *

The 1756 war seemed to conclude with a smashing victory for London. Though popularly much of the subsequent analysis has focused on the ouster of France from Quebec, in terms of the slavery that provided propulsion to the mainland, the ouster of Spain from Florida (and from Cuba for a while) was decidedly more profound. The rear base and material aid for fleeing Africans was decimated, opening the door to increased importation of Africans to Georgia and Carolina particularly. The apparent eradication of the threat from both Spain and France to the mainland set the stage for the North American colonies to follow up aggressively on their wartime intimate dealings with London's European antagonists and forge what amounted to a de facto alliance against Britain, as was reflected in 1776. This was occurring as London was a few years away from a judicial ruling that seemed to suggest that abolition was arriving within the empire, and if Henry Ellis is to be believed, a reordering of the role of Africans in certain colonies was also in store, which would place them at odds with mainland provinces. Colonists paying attention may have noticed that beginning in the 1760s there were a string of cases in English courts concerning slavery in England.[104]

France's ability to appeal to indigenes had provided sustenance for this war, and in its aftermath London chose to try to hinder settlers from moving further west, seizing their land and compelling Africans to work it.[105] These measures infuriated land speculators, notably in Virginia, including George Washington,[106] Thomas Jefferson, Arthur Lee, and Patrick Henry—that is, a murderer's row of rebels. Choctaws and other indigenes were undermined—akin to Africans—when European powers were ousted: this was good news for settlers, who could now take the land of the indigenes and deepen enslavement of the Africans.[107]

The Virginia elite was also taken aback by the cooperation between Africans and indigenes during the war: what caused "general Consternation," according to a correspondent of the lieutenant governor, was indigenes' "saving & Caressing all the Negroes," which seemed to be a prelude to "an insurrection" with "the most serious consequences."[108] It was also noted with concern that the enslaved were convinced, as one Euro-Virginian admitted, that the French "will give them their freedom," and the concomitant threat of slave uprisings shaped indelibly the colony's wartime mobilization.[109] The 1756 war, in short, lit a fuse that then exploded in a revolt against the Crown in 1776. Likewise— and not unrelated—was the changed circumstance for captive Africans, who continued arriving by the boatload on the mainland but now found weakened rear bases in Quebec and St. Augustine, previously used to launch punishing attacks against British settlements.

8

From Havana to Newport, Slavery Transformed

Settlers Rebel against London

By 1762, London had been at war for six years with France—but also Austria and Russia—and had suffered draining losses, worsened by mainlander desertions, mutinies, and general dissent, though the conflict in North America was, to a certain extent, for their benefit. During this time, Spain had been far from neutral, as its privateers preyed upon vessels sailing from New York to Jamaica in particular—then Madrid chose to throw in its lot formally with the eventual losers and joined their ranks.[1]

The moral, political, and economic impact of the resultant fall of Havana in 1762 to British forces was incalculable. It was a mighty blow to Madrid's entire position in the hemisphere and, for our purposes here, was a major step toward the 1776 revolt.[2] Early in the climactic battle, a British officer noticed that those Cubans he was confronting were "mostly Mulattos and Negros."[3] London had its share too (as did the provinces)[4]—the Earl of Albermarle was, he lamented, "in despair" because of a perceived deficit in this crucial sphere and emphasized the need to "raise as many Negroes *at any price* as I cannot do without them": left for further deliberation was how to forge cohesion among the diverse combatants.[5] The point was that both sides were enlisting armed Africans, which did not augur well for the mainland policy of intensified racist tyranny.

Indeed, it would have been comprehensible if alert pro-slavery mainland settlers had been ringing dissonant alarm bells and shouting from the rooftops about this policy of arming Africans as a matter of state policy. Combined with creeping abolitionism in London and growing disgust there with provincial trading with the avowed enemies of the Crown, these were ominous signals that the colonial status quo was not sustainable.

Furthermore, free trade in Africans mandated a deep and liquid market for this valuable commodity and often meant easing the sale of Africans throughout the Caribbean—this was one way to get rid of troublesome slaves, but those in this category were often in rude good health and robustly creative, so deporting them to a competitor made little sense at a time of conflict between empires:[6] one way out was to crush an opposing empire, hence the 1762 siege of Havana. Thus, the capture of Havana was greeted rhapsodically by some colonists on the mainland. The "capacious harbour" of Havana, where the "galleons from Porto-Bello and Vera Cruz rendezvous on their return to Spain," was a true El Dorado, thought the militant Boston cleric Joseph Sewall.[7]

Other colonists acknowledged that they were aware that this venture was not in their best interest since they were not necessarily apprecia-tive of the world-historical significance of this campaign. Instead, many of them were angry, noticeably about the major casualties endured— it is estimated that about half of the provincials fell victim to various camp and tropical diseases, and a third of the entire force perished from such causes. The division of the booty was particularly outraging—not just sharing with Africans, but the lion's share was taken by redcoat offi-cers; for example, a whopping 40% of the thousand men who departed Connecticut died, while those who returned to this colony took home about a pound for each private.[8] This paltry sum was doled out, though it was estimated that when Havana was conquered, as much as ten mil-lion pounds in goods and the like were seized, adding to a dissatisfac-tion that grew further in 1763 when the Crown sought to block colonists moving further westward.[9]

In Pennsylvania, settlers in 1763 launched a paroxysm of violence tar-geting the indigenous, a trend that, according to one observer, evolved to the point leading up to and following 1776 whereby "exterminating Indians became an act of patriotism." London's mandates against mov-ing further westward and avoiding yet another conflict with indigenes was ignored—flagrantly.[10] Fueling the growing anti-London revolt was the feverish hunger for the land of the indigenous that combined with the rapt desire to enslave Africans to toil on this very same land. Yet post-1763 London was perceived as a formidable hurdle to this remu-nerative process. In faraway Michigan, a reason—besides the obvious: seizure of land—for this obsessive concern for indigenes was glimpsed.

The Hurons were being pressed to "deliver up" Africans for various "misdeeds" with little tangible result, as evidence emerged of deepening collaboration between the two subordinate groups,[11] a tie that regurgitated the dire memories of the Yamasee War, decades earlier in Carolina. In the long run, an alliance between these two groups yoked to London could threaten settlers as a whole—as the 1812 war, a few decades later, demonstrated.[12]

While colonists saw their profit-making thwarted, British royalty and leading officers reaped handsome dividends from the plunder of Cuba. The Earl of Albermarle and Admiral George Pocock took home hundreds of thousands of pounds by themselves. This division incensed provincials, while many Londoners found it hard to understand why the outcome of the 1756 war mandated that Florida would be retained and Cuba returned.[13] From the settler viewpoint, the maddening juxtaposition was the sight of Londoners reaping a beautiful bounty in Cuba, while they were barred from doing the same in the furthest reaches of the mainland.

Outraging the colonists further was that after being blocked in what was deemed to be a fair share of the plunder of Cuba, they petitioned for land grants in the territory stretching west from Georgia and the Carolinas—but the Crown balked at what amounted to yet another war against the indigenous. This refusal was yet another step toward 1776, as the settlers ditched the Crown, embraced republicanism—which widened their base of support by retreating from rule by hereditary ancestry and moving toward rule by "race"—then moved aggressively to execute their land grab on territory to be worked by even more captive Africans.[14]

In a series of swaps, London returned Cuba—but ousted Madrid from Florida, which had a devastating impact on the fortunes of Africans in the region. When Spaniards departed in 1763, they were joined by numerous indigenes and Africans who wanted no part of Anglo-American colonialism. Though Negro freedom became a remote possibility in Florida during the following twenty years of British occupation, it is striking that this "14th colony" did not revolt successfully in the years following 1776, and this may have been attributable to the lingering legacy of Fort Mose and St. Augustine and the militant legacy that railed against the pro-slavery project of the rebels.[15]

Still, there was a discernible tension between mainland colonies now freed to pursue pro-slavery policies with gusto and London, which was more susceptible to hemispheric trends and had begun tip-toeing toward the antipode of 1776: 1772 and tentative abolitionism. After all, London had made extensive use of armed Africans during the 1756–1763 war[16]—not least during the all-important siege of Havana—and, unlike colonists, did not have to fret about this policy backfiring on the banks of the Thames, in contrast to settlers, who were jousting for influence with Africans and the indigenous along the James River and other tributaries.

*   *   *

London had its eye on Cuba for some time, as this strategically sited island commanded the entrance to the Gulf of Mexico and, appropriately, was shaped like a pistol pointing at the mainland. Havana supplied St. Augustine, which in turn threatened Georgia, Carolina, and points north and, thus, was targeted by the redcoats in years immediately following the Stono revolt. On 8 June 1742, a flotilla left Havana with a sizeable complement of armed Africans; according to a witness, "the design is to enter the province of Georgia," then proceed to the Carolinas and "destroy whatever they can" along the way, with "the whole country to be sacked," inflicting a "heavy blow on England."[17]

There was also continuing concern about Africans in Jamaica deserting and receiving succor in Cuba to London's disadvantage, and as an outgrowth, the redcoats sought to attract Africans from Cuba, which necessitated pursuing policies that would not necessarily be embraced on the mainland.[18] Throughout the 1740s, Havana remained in the crosshairs,[19] and in response, Spanish Cuba showed no surcease in arming Africans,[20] which left London few choices beyond responding similarly. A problem for London, however, was that colonists often refused to accept the concept of Africans under Spanish jurisdiction being free and not enslaved; that is, if one from this category arrived at a mainland port, he was liable to be enslaved and sold, which was harmful to British-Spanish bilateral relations, not to mention giving these men even more incentive to desire war against the mainland.[21]

The broader context was the transition from the Crown's emphasis on the Caribbean colonies to the mainland colonies—but the former were not to be dispensed with until the 20th century, and until that point, London found it difficult to pursue the kind of rigidly racist policies pursued in Georgia northward. Cuba, the largest Caribbean island by far, exerted magnetic pull on its neighbors, and the Crown found this hard to resist. By 1763, propagandists in London were assessing this context, and there was still no unanimity of opinion as to whether the mainland was more valuable than the Caribbean—to that extent, it became easier to bend to the Havana model. One analyst sought to split the difference and declare that both the mainland and the islands were equally valuable to London, though it was added purposively, "all possible care should be taken to prevent His Majesty's subjects [from] purchasing sugar, rum and particularly molasses in the French islands . . . by prohibiting their importation into North America." When pursued, such an approach was destined to alienate mainland merchants who had profited handsomely over the years from thumbing their noses at such policies. As this analyst saw it, there was a seamless garment that linked "Great Britain, Ireland, North America, the West India islands and Africa," and this integrated commerce—with the slave trade as the essential glue—was "of greater advantage to this country, than all our trades whatsoever." It was hoped that the war with France would provide the Crown with more leverage in obtaining the Africans deemed to be most valuable—from the "Gold Coast, Popo and Whidah"—who were "most valuable for the laborious cultivation of sugar cane," since their experience in "very barren" areas made them ideal and exceedingly adaptable workers for "extremely fertile" areas: besides, this part of West Africa may have contained more gold than Brazil, increasing its value.

The 1756–1763 war was critical in hammering Paris and Madrid in the region—and, if French Hispaniola could be detached from the mainland, this would improve the fortunes of London's sugar colonies. Moreover, with the defeat of Spain in Cuba, London could begin to challenge in the lucrative metals market, in which Peru and similar colonies had become hegemonic.[22]

At this juncture, ever greater victories seemed to loom for the Crown, with France and Spain humiliated. Madrid was denuded of about 20% of its entire navy with its 1762 defeat, undermining its ability to defend Cartagena and points southward. The relative ease with which Havana was taken left little doubt as to which European power was destined for hemispheric—perhaps global—hegemony.

But a closer look revealed that this immense victory contained the seeds of an immense setback. The British plan to take Havana involved a combined force of four thousand redcoats and provincials, a regiment of five hundred free Negroes and two thousand enslaved Africans from Jamaica, and a number of pilots from the Bahamas who were familiar with the north coast of Cuba.[23] One did not have to be a sociologist to envision that it would not be easy to mesh such a force—particularly the provincials with the Africans.

The plan of attack was well considered also: before the actual assault, London informed Governor William Henry Lyttleton of Jamaica of the need to recruit a "certain proportion of free Negroes" in this "expedition," since such would "greatly contribute to the success of the enterprise"; a "considerable number of slaves" too had "been found extremely useful in the late war with Spain." So, Lyttleton was instructed to rustle up "two thousand slaves at Jamaica" for "immediate service"[24]—sending them abroad did seem a better idea than allowing them to create a ruckus at home, particularly considering that as of 1760 Jamaica was, per usual, aflame. Besides, as of June 1762, the Earl of Albermarle was issuing a typical plaint—"I wish the North Americans were arrived."[25]

As the moment approached to storm the beaches of Cuba, the cry rose, "the more Negroes . . . we have the better,"[26] as they were "much wanted."[27] Recalled fondly by one leader was "the great utility of the slaves to Major General Monckton's army at the reduction of Martinique (I believe he had near 3000 from His Majesty's islands)."[28] These Africans from Martinique also proved to be valuable in the taking of Havana.[29]

This absence of mainlanders was even more inopportune, for at a crucial moment of empires clashing, some of His Majesty's most important subjects were missing in action. Moreover, free Negroes in Jamaica, perhaps smarting from previous mistreatment by the Crown, did not seem enthusiastic about joining this expedition. Perhaps they realized that if captured in battle, they could easily be re-enslaved or that, by foul means, some who marched beside them under the Union Jack might devise the devious idea of seeking to manacle them. In addition, Jamaican planters were at that point reluctant to commit their most valuable property, fearing losses and inadequate compensation. So the Crown was reduced to heading to Martinique to buy Africans there, which was not the ideal way to build an invading force.[30]

When the mainlanders did finally turn up, according to Lieutenant General David Dundas, they were more prone to retreat than advance and "were more sickly than most," as they wilted under the summer heat of Cuba.[31] To be fair, the Earl of Albermarle, who may have been more dedicated to this mission than most, confessed in June 1762 that "a hot climate does not agree at any time with my constitution,"[32] so he too was melting in the warmth. There was a perception that Africans fared better than Europeans in warmer weather—an environment that characterized the Caribbean and a good deal of South America—and with that idea in mind, a farsighted Londoner could easily envision the continued deployment of Africans to wrest territory away from Madrid. In July 1762, redcoats were busily bombarding Havana and its "obstinate and gallant defense," but this burdensome task was complicated by "increasing sickness of the troops, the intense heat of the weather and the approaching rainy season"; this obviated, said the Earl of Albermarle, "my being so sanguine as to our future success against the town particularly as we have no news of American reinforcement."[33] After Havana had been conquered, the Earl of Albermarle, "now better acquainted with the climate," found it to be "certain that the only season in the year for troops to act is from the beginning of November to the latter end of March."[34]

It was stressed to Admiral Pocock that he should purchase Africans at "*any price*" and obtain "as many Negroes as possible," which gave automatic leverage to counter-parties,[35] Africans not least. Thus, His Majesty's finest officers in the spring of 1762 were scurrying about the Caribbean, not just to Martinique but to St. Kitts and Antigua too, seeking Africans for an important invasion; a number of them were to be armed.[36] "This want of men makes our situation rather ticklish," said one British leader, as at a critical moment he was reduced to trying to "hope for the best."[37]

By June 1762, Admiral Pocock was told that "armed Negroes" under the Union Jack had "landed" in Cuba, though in "disguise."[38] But at that point, the redcoats realized they may have been outfoxed, for it was then that Admiral Pocock was informed that their foes had seized the opportunity to attack the Crown from the north; that is, Spanish and French battleships were spotted near Newfoundland at a time when "protection of this coast" was "entirely bare" from Canada to Florida. This was "incomprehensible" to General Amherst since "parts of their own dominions are at stake" in the Caribbean, though he recognized instinctively that his foes were capable of creating "great mischief."[39] Alarmingly, cried Sir Francis Bernard, "there is not a man of war north of Virginia."[40] This emergency meant that the redcoats scrambled to divert forces to the north,[41] possibly jeopardizing the potent Cuban mission. This had to be done since a report from Halifax revealed that "internal enemies, the Indians and Acadians,"[42] were on the march, all of which enhanced the need for more Africans, as it led to searching questions as to why settlers could not protect adequately His Majesty's colonies.

Meanwhile, back in Cuba, a spirited defense had been mounted. A "detachment of armed Negroes and Mulattoes with each corps" was spotted under the Spanish flag.[43] Finally, in August 1762, troops from New York arrived in the theater of conflict, the excuse for their tardiness being "they had fallen in with three French men of war and some frigates" and suffered a "great loss," which "would have been much greater had the French acted with vigour and judgment."[44] It was hard to ignore the reality that by the time these mainland malingerers arrived, Havana grandees were already contemplating the wording of the articles of capitulation.

Provincial tardiness notwithstanding, Havana was taken. It was a "glorious conquest," said the beribboned Robert Monckton, who was uniquely qualified to make such a pronouncement.[45] Actually, said another interlocutor, it was "the most glorious stroke that ever was struck by . . . British arms."[46] "The attack was so vigorous and impetuous," said the Earl of Albermarle, "that the Enemy was instantaneously [driven] from the breach."[47] The Spanish endured a "considerable" loss, he added, with "upwards of three thousand sick and wounded" jammed "in the churches and convents," as bodies were being buried hurriedly. Bursting with ambition, he targeted New Orleans next, though he acknowledged, "my army is very much reduced" and needed more than "a little rest and good food," which he thought "will soon recover them." Cuba needed to be "properly secured" too, which required even more troops.[48]

Still, it was unclear when another time would arise when veritable eternal foes would be so frantically on the run, and the Earl of Albermarle was baying for blood. Why not take St. Augustine and Pensacola? "I should imagine that a conquest might easily be made," he opined. As for the eastern end of Cuba, it was a mere "thorn in the side of the Jamaican people" that should be "removed."[49] Also slated to be removed, he thought, was the "Bishop of Cuba," whom he found to be a "very dangerous man," equal parts "troublesome and impertinently litigious."[50]

These were ambitious plans, and if history were a guide, armed Africans would be required, though official London did not seem to contemplate fully the danger of arming Africans to guard a system based on enslavement of Africans. Perhaps, like some analysts in the 21st century, elite Londoners were probably thinking excessively in class and ideological terms, assuming that armed and adequately compensated Africans would not necessarily sympathize with enslaved Africans. The Somerset case was now less than a decade away, and the Earl of Albermarle did not issue an edict freeing the enslaved. What he did do, however, was promulgate a measure bound to irk slave traders and others who were fans of free trade in Africans.

Descending upon Havana were men from the mainland who had shown little compunction about enslaving just about any African within sight, and they may have thought that this island could absorb many more slaves. At that moment, there may have been about thirty-two thousand slaves in Cuba and about four thousand in Havana.[51] The measure crafted by the Earl of Albermarle pandered to this sentiment before adding carefully that in order to "prevent many evils and abuses that would arise from an unrestrained importation [of Africans] it is absolutely necessary to limit the number annually to be introduced"; to do otherwise, he said, would be "hurtful and prejudicial" to London's "other sugar colonies." Thus, John Kennion was allocated the "sole license and liberty of importing Negroes into the island of Cuba," which "shall not exceed two thousand," that is, "fifteen hundred males and five hundred females"—with "imprisonment" for those colonists so audacious as to disobey this edict.[52]

This may have been seen as a sign of good faith by Africans instrumental in taking Havana, but it was not viewed similarly by many mainland settlers. It was a throwback to the era preceding the rise of the "separate" and "private" traders, an enhancement of the Crown and a blow to the proliferating class of merchants. It was a defeat for free trade and the sweet magic of the marketplace it was thought to bring. It was the kind of burdensome regulation and government interference in commerce that was to leave republicans drunk with rage for years to come.

Nevertheless, the Crown had reason to be disappointed with the response of the planter class regionally—whose interests were now being protected by limiting imports of Africans to Cuba—since they either held back on committing the enslaved to battle or charged a pretty penny for their services or sought to finagle unwarranted compensation in the event of casualties.[53] Mainland settlers were lollygagging and seemed in no hurry to join the fray and were blocking the integration of Acadians into their community, while some Irish and Scots were deemed to be of questionable reliability. Besides, there had already been loud mutterings about "independency" in North America. Recruiting armed Africans was, in a sense, the least bad option. Yet even this seemingly shrewd calculation elided the overriding contradiction: considerations of class and ideology aside, how long could one depend upon armed Africans to protect a despotism based on battering Africans? For as long as mainlanders were determined to equate "African" with "slave," even well-compensated men of ebony would be in jeopardy.

The settlers evaded this aching anomaly when after independence, they moved to open the doors wide to further migration to their shores of Europeans from the Atlantic to the Urals, thereby eluding the religious cold war, hastening the forging of a truer "whiteness" (though still marred by a disuniting anti-Catholicism and a continuously eroding anti-Semitism) and trying to make sure that weapons were kept far distant from the eager arms of Africans. In short, the option that prevailed in the republic was securing "white" men in arms to protect a system based on enslavement of Africans while expropriating indigenes' land.

*　　*　　*

The upshot of the 1756–1763 war was to provide an energy boost for the slave system—which is why there was so much anger on the mainland about London's decision to limit the slave trade to Cuba during its brief rule. Compared to the island, by the 1770s heavy importations to the mainland meant the market for the enslaved there was (in a sense) glutted.[54] This suggested that a bounteous profit could have been made by exporting Africans from the mainland to the island.

Thus, shortly after the war ended, a London bureaucrat noticed that "the number of Negroes is constantly increasing in America," particularly since there was "more care in breeding them than is taken in the West Indies." Their number had doubled in recent years in Rhode Island, while those in New York had grown to about fourteen thousand and Pennsylvania's was reaching toward twenty thousand. This bureaucrat concluded that if their growing number was taxed, it would both decrease their growth and encourage the deployment of more European servants.[55] But bureaucratic blather about limiting the number of mainland Africans had been spilling forth for years with little visible impact, which suggested that the Crown was not in touch with reality.

Hence, despite this bureaucratic admonition, by the early 1770s Africans were flooding into the mainland, particularly to Virginia, the Carolinas, and Georgia. Part of this trend was a rush to acquire the enslaved in response to the non-importation agreements targeting London: that is, mainland rebels disgusted with London not least because of taxes imposed to pay for the costs of the 1756 war had moved to curb trade with the British isles (which had the not accidental impact of strengthening mainland merchants and weakening metropolitan competitors). Naturally, after Madrid was ousted from Florida, imports of Africans gyrated upward—since flight southward was curbed—which should have conciliated those colonists upset with the Cuban limitations.[56] But this too brought complication since this peninsular province was close to the Bahamas, and there were mostly "Blacks" and "Mulattoes," it was reported in 1768, who possessed a "very bold and daring spirit which makes it necessary to have a proper force," that is, a "Garrison as soon as possible."[57] The 19th century would reveal that the Bahamas presented a threat to mainland slavery just as Spanish Florida had earlier.[58]

For ineluctably, those Bahamians with arms would include Africans, complicating the existence of slavery there and in Florida. And since Cuba was back in Spanish hands, the opportunity was re-ignited for Havana to resume its noisome meddling in the internal affairs of British colonies. Africans were continuing to flee from British soil—now the Bahamas—to Havana, which, said a leading official, was "very detrimental to His Majesty's subjects here whose property chiefly consists of their slaves," a practice worsened by Cuba's claim that sanctuary was provided "under the ridiculous pretense of their becoming Catholic."[59] Those who had fled, he said, were "engaged in turtling" and had managed to get within "ten leagues distance" from Cuba.[60] Thus, by 1769, the Captain-General in Havana was arguing that he had "no authority to deliver up the fugitive Negroes" of the island, which suggested that the problem of fugitive slaves from Georgia had migrated even more from Florida to Cuba.[61]

A further complication was the evident discord that accompanied the British takeover in St. Augustine, where the African presence was easily detectable. Whenever a fire broke out or a robbery occurred, the Negroes were immediately suspected.[62] It did not take long for a British subject to counsel the arrival of more "Germans from the Rhine" and "Protestants from the southern provinces of France," not to mention migrants from the "islands of Greece."[63] But would bringing in more nationals from the eternal foe across the channel—in the shaky name of "whiteness"—actually resolve or exacerbate Britain's underlying security problem?

For consistent with past practice, the victory in the war just seemed to be a timeout before the "Catholic" powers reloaded. Even after Havana had been seized and Spain was reeling, Whitehall—that is to say, official London—continued to warn leaders in Virginia that "the French and Spaniards in Florida & Louisiana have long, and too successfully inculcated an idea amongst the Indians, that the English entertain a settled Design of extirpating the whole Indian race, with a view to possess & enjoy their lands."[64] This was a perceptive prediction as things turned out, but it also outlined neatly how venturesome settlers' dreams were seemingly designed to deliver war, while draining London's pocketbook. Thousands of miles to the south, Madrid and London clashed over control of what came to be referred to as the Falklands by the latter and the Malvinas by the former[65]—a controversy that stretched into the 21st century. By late 1770, William Bull of South Carolina was being warned that "a declaration of war" with Spain "was daily expected,"[66] which meant renewal of what it had been thought the war had solved— that is, Madrid's encouragement of slave revolts, along with more frazzled nerves leading to hasty and ill-measured decisions by provincials.

Spain's aggressiveness and the supposed inability of the war that had concluded in 1763 to resolve matters satisfactorily can be overstated. For fortunately—for slave owners—those in Georgia found that the pursuit and return of fugitive slaves was much simpler and easier once London took over Florida.[67] The African population of Georgia was growing steadily and with it the inevitable: revolt. By 1765, a number of fugitives banded together and withdrew into the swamps along the Savannah River and at times made marauding forays into neighboring colonies. A few years later, Africans fresh off the boat from their homeland went on a rampage and slaughtered their overseer in the field, killed three more Europeans, and wounded others before being overwhelmed.[68]

Confident that capital loss in the form of fleeing Africans would now be curtailed, slaveholders in Georgia went on a frantic buying spree, despite the danger of such a course. The Caribbean was the principal source for those Africans entering by sea via Savannah and Sunbury, a reflection of the retrenchment from that region driven in no small part by the seeming inability to suppress Maroons in Jamaica and plotters in Antigua and elsewhere. John Laurens, member of both a prominent republican and leading slave-dealing family in Carolina, in the late 1760s warned hirelings bringing Africans from Jamaica, "be very careful to guard against insurrection. Never put your life in their power for a moment," since "slaves were antagonists who could never be fully trusted."[69] This tempestuous—though not inaccurate—advice was a reflection of the turmoil brought by steady arrivals from a rebellious region.[70] Thus, the enslaved population increased exponentially, growing from six hundred in 1751 to fifteen thousand in 1775, with the Caribbean being the major source in the early period and Africa in the later. With such an increase arrived a destabilizing delirium driven by fear of the ultimate intentions of this abused property, frenzy that was hardly assuaged when it appeared that London was moving either toward abolition or conciliating Africans—or both.

Strikingly, it was in Jamaica that a trend also arose that was to sweep the mainland: planters and merchants analogizing their relationship to London as that of slave to master.[71] Astute Londoners came to realize that there was a dialectical connection between the extraordinary brutalizing of Africans by planters and merchants and the concomitant fear that a worse fate would befall these elites. Surely, the growing spate of slave conspiracies that accompanied and followed the 1756 war were designed to provide these entrepreneurs with an indication that their worst phantasms could easily become realities. Apparent overtures by the Crown to the Africans did little to dissipate these febrile fears.

In retrospect, the elites' real trepidations about being overrun by Africans might have driven this fear of their becoming enslaved, a trend that was also evident on the mainland. In the mid-1760s, North American slave dealers began importing Africans from Martinique despite their widespread reputation for hell-raising—causing official-dom to force the return to the island of some of them.[72] One scholar has asserted that this massive influx from the Caribbean "changed the culture" of the mainland enslaved;[73] if so, it contributed immeasurably to a pre-existing combativeness, adding to the colonists' malaise as they faced off with London—and its growing abolitionism. The arrival on the mainland of Africans from the Caribbean was even more remark-able since there was a general and understandable suspicion of Africans arriving from this tumultuous region.[74]

The high-strung dread of slaveholders was not altogether misguided. For example, in what was to become the British colony of Guiana, an Akan leader from West Africa—known simply as "Cuffy"—led a fierce revolt of twenty-five hundred of the enslaved, who were well armed and—for a while—claimed to have seized power in the 1760s.[75] This rebellion in Berbice on the northern coast of South America was thus subject to manipulation by Madrid: Africans visited bloody retribution on the most odious of slaveholders.[76] There were two destructive fires of suspicious origins in Barbados in 1766 in a colony where European set-tlers were outnumbered by Africans by at least four to one.[77] In Tobago, the years 1770–1774 were each marked by violent slave revolts, with rebels holding out for periods ranging from eleven days to six weeks, with eighty Europeans all told being slain. In Dominica, Africans were poisoning Europeans with hugely fatal effects, while in the British Windward Islands, there were numerous instances of Africans slaying their masters with knives and other weapons.[78] By 1773, redcoats were strapped while seeking to overturn a fierce rebellion of the enslaved in the nation that became Belize.[79] Like a firefighter besieged by a corps of energetically dedicated arsonists, redcoats were scurrying from pillar to post in a vain attempt to dampen flames, while—as some Londoners saw things—mainlanders were busily bringing even more pyromaniacs to town.

Uneasiness about the Caribbean meant that some Georgians also established their own trans-Atlantic connections and participated directly in the slave trade following the war and the years leading up to 1776. Thus, nearly as many enslaved Africans arrived there in 1765 as had reached the colony from overseas during the preceding fifteen years. In each of the years stretching from 1770 to 1774, over eleven hundred enslaved Africans arrived—with the apex arriving in 1774. It was Georgia that in 1774 opposed initially and adamantly a provision put forward by the rebels in their Continental Congress—establishment of which was a concrete step toward "independency"—which would have discontinued the slave trade. In coming decades, mainland slave traders were to replace their British counterparts as champions of the slave trade and, thus, had a financial incentive to break decisively with the Crown. Some Georgians in the days following the colony's establishment in 1733 had warned that allowing the wicked "Negro Merchants" to establish a toehold would turn into a foothold as they used their heft in crop production to dominate the entire economy. Predictably, slave dealers leveraged their clear advantages at settlement time following harvests to strengthen their overall position in other commercial endeavors, a trend which was of great moment for the future of the rebels.[80]

In neighboring South Carolina, there was so much concern about the mass arrivals of Africans in the 1760s that one settler thought it would be unwise to continue eliminating the indigenous since their lands would soon be reoccupied by runaway Africans, who would soon become even more formidable enemies than the indigenes. These Africans—this "*Internal* enemy," it was emphasized—were "daily" increasing, and "over these we ought to keep a very watchful Eye, lest they surprise us," leading to the settlers' "Common Death."[81] Charleston had the largest Negro population of any city on the mainland, constituting about half of the city's population by 1765 and 61% of the entire colony. Adding to the flux was the importation of forty-two thousand Africans between 1760 and 1774. Characteristically, in December 1765, rumors spread through Charleston of an impending revolt of the enslaved.[82]

Imports of Africans were especially high in 1765, and there were several encampments of runaways near the Savannah River for these recent arrivals to reside in, if they had the gumption.[83] Hefty rewards for these subversives were offered, with little noticeable impact on their running amok,[84] as they were reported as continuing in their "Depredations on the Inhabitants in that Neighbourhood with Impunity," setting fires—a "White Child was burnt to death"—stealing, firing weapons randomly at settlers, and the like.[85]

By one estimate, between 1769 and 1773, the African population of this colony leapt from 80,000 to 110,000, bringing with it difficult adjustments for all. Newly arrived immigrants, journeymen, apprentices, even slave-holding master mechanics were not completely satisfied with a system whereby their livelihood was being challenged and undercut by a flood of slave labor. This cutthroat competition brought unsteady employment for many of them—but this did not necessarily turn them against slavery, as there was an outweighing fear of an actual cutthroat revolt of the enslaved; instead, it formed a basis for dissatisfaction with London, which was seeking to restrain these same men from moving westward—it also brought unity with other elites, who were difficult to cross in any case.[86] There was a similar concern about how slavery was distorting the labor force in Virginia[87]—which did not seem to produce abolitionists either.

The leading anti-London rebel, Christopher Gadsden—like Laurens, his fellow Carolinian—was immersed in the issue of slavery. He was a trailblazer in terms of forging "white unity"—bonds forged between and among European settlers across class and, at times, ethnic and religious lines—in the face of a Negro majority. It was a variation of the longstanding argument that the—actual—cutthroat threat from Africans should be sufficient for such unity, that is, that the prospect of slave insurrection should remind the white poor of their presumed identity of interests with their racial brethren, who happened to be filthily wealthy planters and merchants. Gadsden's view was that the elite should at least be seen as fulfilling obligations to those who were less affluent. Without this maneuver, he said, it would be "little less than madness" to keep importing Africans.[88] Thus, in South Carolina near the same time, far-reaching apprehension was expressed about the presence of so many Africans, referred to by one observer as "an Internal Enemy that one day may be the total Ruin" of the province.[89]

Brouhahas about taxes and revolts were spreading in the aftermath of the 1756 war, indicating that a crisis was morphing into something far more dangerous. In North Carolina, strenuous objection was raised in 1765 to taxes to be imposed upon imported Africans—an impost that helped to ignite revolt.[90] The objectors did not seem to connect the continuing influx of Africans with what was confronted in 1766—a "general Insurrection of our Negroes," as Lord Charles Greville Montagu of South Carolina put it. The preceding Christmas of 1765, many of the

Africans had fled to the swamps, and he then sensed that a "dangerous Conspiracy and Insurrection was intended." Heedlessly, Africans kept arriving, which—said one Carolinian—"must render" the settlers "less formidable to a foreign or an Indian enemy."[91] By 1767, reports trickled in from one key county about armed runaways raising a ruckus.[92]

Similar apprehensions about revolt had occurred to Virginians, notably when in 1765 legislators found it necessary to pass five bills concerning "slaves committing capital crimes and for the more effectual punishing [of] conspiracies and insurrections of them."[93] Just before that, an African by the name of "Bob" was on trial for administering poison to a physician.[94] In 1767, a man described as "a respectable member of the community" warned bluntly that enslaving Africans was "dangerous," pointing to ongoing "insurrections in Jamaica"; to "imagine," he concluded, "that we shall be forever exempted from this calamity . . . is an infatuation as astonishing as it will be surely fatal."[95] This "respectable" man may have been reacting to contemporaneous news from the unbridled isles due south, wherein elites were requesting reinforcements for "protection and security from rebellious and runaway Negroes" and an "invasion" by "foreign enemies in case of a war."[96] In 1770, an insurrection was detonated in Hanover County, resulting in a pitched battle between fifteen settlers and almost fifty Africans.[97] That same year, there was a huge and raging fire at Shadwell Plantation in this province, thought to be set by the enslaved: Thomas Jefferson's prized violin was barely rescued.[98]

There was a great increase in the number of Africans in Jefferson's homeland between 1727 and 1769, but after 1772 these numbers began to decline. Most of these Africans were arriving from Africa, not the Caribbean, but—as is apparent—this did not seem to suggest that they were less willing to revolt.[99] In Virginia, Founding Father George Mason echoed this viewpoint, reminding that the "primary cause" of the decline of Rome was "introduction of great numbers of slaves."[100] Subsequently, it was Mason who raised the specter of the reviled Oliver Cromwell and his instructions sent to Virginia to arm the enslaved if need be, to restrain the settlers, and the long-ago dangerous insurrections of the enslaved in Greece and Sicily.[101] Such sobering sentiment recurred on the mainland as settlers began to contemplate the idea that London would arm Africans in order to crush their bubbling revolt.

It has been acknowledged that in South Carolina the decision to revolt against London was made simpler by the sentiment that the Crown could no longer ensure domestic tranquility and was, in essence, seeking to turn slaves against their low-country masters, leaving slaveholders with no choice but to create a new authority—not least to more effectively suppress Africans.[102] The point here is that this feeling was not exclusive to South Carolina alone. For in Boston, there were weighty concerns about Africans too, this time of the armed variety, for the Crown had dispatched Negro troops there at a moment when there was already proliferating bigotry. In 1768, redcoat officers encouraged some of these Africans to attack their masters and, in a final flourish, asserted that "they should be able to drive all the Liberty Boys to the devil." Outraged, several Bostonians lodged complaints about a "dangerous conspiracy." Unsurprisingly, this incident stirred acidulous consternation and caustic concern about London's long-term plans. Unsurprisingly still was the reality that among the leading slaveholders—and rebels— were Samuel Adams, John Hancock, and James Otis. New England had been the epicenter of the slave trade for decades, and it was the region's leading personality—John Adams—who, it was reported, "resorted to racis[m]" in opposing the "Stamp Act of 1765."[103] Not incongruous was the fact that before 1770 the majority of pro-slavery rebuttals—seeking to refute a growing stream of British abolitionist propaganda—emerged from the mainland colonies, particularly those of the north.[104]

Hence, when in the postwar era Massachusetts—and other colonies—moved to bar the further importation of enslaved Africans into the province,[105] arguably this was due to prejudice and unease about the continuing and dangerous presence of this stigmatized group as much as humanitarianism. In Connecticut in the early 1770s, attempts were made to limit the presence of enslaved Africans because it was "injurious to the poor and inconvenient," with fines assessed to those who disobeyed.[106] Inconsistent with Boston, in any case, was the haughty rebuff in 1767 given to a bill shaped by the Quakers introduced in New Castle, Delaware, designed to ban the further importation of Africans.[107] Rhode Island revealed the Janus-faced approach of the colonies to the slave trade, as voyages from Newport reached their apex in 1772.[108]

As 1776 approached, colonists were torn about slavery and the slave trade. What has been represented subsequently as abolitionist sentiment was more of a fear about the dangerous presence of so many Africans perceived as agents of various powers and their impact—as Connect-icut suggested—on the "poor," that is, Europeans with little means of support. On the other hand, slavery was a major source of wealth, and repudiating it meant repudiation of powerful elites, which would be dif-ficult at best. Thus, in the spring of 1772, official Virginia railed against "importation of slaves," particularly since "it greatly retards the settle-ment of the colonies with more useful inhabitants and may in time have the most destructive influence."[109] This latter point was notably true—but this did not necessarily suggest abolitionist influence but pointed to a future when the "Old Dominion" would gain added notoriety as a "breeder" and exporter of Africans.

Colonists were upset with the taxes imposed by London to pay for the costs of war and colonization[110]—though, as we have seen, objections to taxes in (and by) the colonies long preceded 1763.[111] Understandably, enslaved Africans were a major target for taxation since they were one of the most significant repositories of wealth; besides, taxation could restrain importation of a force liable to ally with indigenes and foreign invaders alike, to the detriment of settlers.[112] However, such taxes were at times seen as cutting into the profits of powerful slave traders and hampering further economic development, for which slave labor was seen as the ne plus ultra.[113] Thus, His Majesty was told that increased taxes on slaves were a "prejudice and obstruction" to commerce, nota-bly "discouraging the culture of tobacco and by raising its price to lessen its consumption and consequently the national revenue."[114]

Some men in the Rhode Island elite argued passionately that the Sugar Act hindered severely their capacity to engage in slave trading to Africa.[115] Naturally, some men within this elite chose this moment—as they did during the war—to engage in arbitrage as between this elite and London. This list included Aaron Lopez, a whaler, smuggler, and slave trader in Newport, who capitalized handsomely as a battle raged between conservative anti-London merchants and wealthy landown-ers, on the one hand, and another group of merchants, on the other. In 1765, the Sons of Liberty declared a non-importation initiative targeting the receipt of all British goods to protest the Stamp Act, promulgated in London—but this did not deter Lopez and others.[116] Disunity within the elite did not necessarily stultify secessionist plans; instead, such fractiousness may have contributed to increased desperation, ill feeling, and impaired judgment.

Meanwhile, in London, colloquies erupted in 1766 concerning the Stamp Act. One lawmaker argued that "the price of an effective male" slave had fallen from eighty pounds to fifty since this bill was enacted—but this was countered by the allegation that the number of ships heading to Africa had fallen virtually to zero. It was suggested that "not a vessel will go as long as the sugar duty and molasses [duty] continue. The exportation of lumber and British manufactures must fall in proportion."[117]

*   *   *

Postwar euphoria had given way to gloom and doom. The torrential inundation of Africans crashing onto the shores of the mainland, bringing with them more horrid scenes of inhumanity and the reality that Madrid in particular held an advantage over London because of its differing attitude toward the Negro and eagerness to arm him, all served to propel a transformative abolitionist movement.[118] This in turn served to heighten apprehensions on the mainland as to what was London's ultimate intention concerning Africans and settlers—that is, would the former be deployed to impose discipline on the latter, an abrupt turnabout from the tyrannical bigotry and slave-labor camps that had become de rigueur?

In that context, June 1772 proved to be a watershed, clarifying—in the eyes of many settlers—that London was moving toward abolition, which could jeopardize fortunes, if not lives, as Africans seeking retribution were unleashed. This was the import of Somerset's case, but, likewise, the same could be said of the *Gaspee* Affair, which took place days before this important ruling was made in London.

There had long been an illicit trade carried on in Narragansett Bay in Rhode Island. Taking note of the trade carried on by some settlers during the war with the French and as part of the postwar dispensation, London placed armed vessels there in 1764, which was not accepted with equanimity by settlers, particularly when the Crown's military began stopping vessels and seizing some as complaints increased. As London saw things, this was all about piracy and illicit dealings—the settlers saw an attack upon commerce. A climax was reached on 10 June 1772 in the wee hours of the morning, when a brig arriving from Africa, the *Gaspee*, entered Newport and was boarded by officers of the Crown. In response, a mob of about five hundred male settlers rioted, burning the British ship. Yet what seemed to inflame the settlers was not only that the miscreants were to be tried in London but that the chief witness against them was a Negro, raising unsettling questions about the presumed equality of this mudsill group.

The rioters had conscripted Aaron Briggs for their escapade, oblivious to the growing idea that he might have more in common with the Crown than with the settlers. He was to serve as a witness against one of the colony's elite and a prominent pro-slavery advocate—John Brown— whose surname was bestowed upon a university in Providence. "I saw John Brown fire a musket," said Briggs, and "the captain of the schooner immediately fell from the place he was standing." The proclamation of King George III said that members of the crew of the vessel were "dangerously wounded and barbarously treated." The Earl of Hillsborough apparently did not grasp the graveness of what his comrade on the scene told him about the Browns, the "principal people of that place," the "ringleaders in this piratical proceeding"—that is, should they "arrest the parties charged by the Negro Aaron?" Briggs, described variously as a "mulatto lad of about sixteen years of age"—he may have been eighteen—was at the heart of a dispute that deepened the schism between the Crown and the mainland.

Speaking from Boston, Governor Thomas Hutchinson was enraged by "so daring an insult," which was guaranteed to "rouse the British lion, which has been asleep these four or five years." Brown and his companions should be arrested and tried, he concluded. Settlers were equally furious, with one local writer—calling himself "Americanus"—carping about a "star chamber inquisition" and adding that "to be tried by one's peers is the greatest privilege a subject can wish for." Indeed, it was said, "to live a life of slaves is to die by inches."

The youth who actually knew something about slavery, Briggs, had been bound as an apprentice at the age of five—until reaching twenty-four—as a laborer on a farm. He was carrying out a task near the shore when he was beckoned by those who were about to riot. He was given a handspike—the rest were armed with cutlasses and muskets. It was then that he spotted Brown and watched aghast as the attack unfolded.

Daniel Hormanden, who was on the scene when Manhattan went up in flames in 1741, was dispatched to adjudicate in Rhode Island and found himself amidst a similar conflagration; he promptly informed London that the "Negro evidence" was at "the foundation of this inquiry" and had "much plausibility." Worrisome was the "state of anarchy" that he espied not only in Rhode Island but, as well, in "their sister colony Connecticut." In fact, the Crown knew that this case "attracted great attention throughout the English colonies"; the House of Burgesses in Virginia was among the official bodies that were up in arms, with Thomas Jefferson and Patrick Henry among those leading the clamor. Interestingly—and in a dramatic illustration of the contrasting dreams of Africans and Europeans on the mainland—Briggs may not have been forcibly drafted, as suggested, but saw rowing to the *Gaspee* and boarding it as a way to escape bondage, just as those who were with him saw attacking the Crown as a step toward liberation.[119]

Understandably, some analysts have concluded that this inflammatory incident was a crucial moment leading to an enhanced revolt against British rule. London long had been concerned with settlers' commercial activity, notably with France; then there was the issue of being taken to London to be tried—but the accelerant that made this blaze difficult to contain was the presence of Aaron Briggs as the chief witness, signaling that the Crown was moving in a direction different from the settlers' on the touchy question of Africans, which helped to solidify the gathering notion that London was moving toward having this despised group impose discipline on settlers. The *Gaspee*, a vessel sixty-eight feet in length with eight guns and a crew of about thirty, became a tangible symbol of what settlers viewed as oppression.

Interestingly, Rhode Island—where the slave trade had reached new heights and where smuggling was probably more developed than in all of North America[120]—reacted most strongly to this incident and, thus, could fairly be considered the actual cradle of revolt against the Crown, more than Boston or Lexington or Massachusetts as a whole. Apparently His Majesty Himself took a personal interest in this case, and he may have been rattled by the fact that the decision was made to try the defendants in London precisely because it was felt that no Rhode Island jury would convict the defendants. It was this incident that led directly to the formation of the Committees of Correspondence and the Continental Congress. It was the "First Blow for Freedom," crows one historian, "greater perhaps than the more famous Boston Tea Party, which occurred over a year later," as "many of those involved in burning the 'Gaspee' later turned out to be important patriots."[121]

Ezra Stiles, who also became a prominent patriot, confided to his diary that there was "nothing more alarming" and that "nothing more contributed" to "establish a Union and Confederacy of the Colonies" than this incident. It was "obnoxious, alarming and arbitrary," he spat out, adding noticeably acerbic words about Briggs—"the Negro-Indian Witness" who seemed curiously "Tutored and instructed"—adding to the perception that Africans were being used to bludgeon colonists.[122]

Stiles's ire was a reflection of the growing conflict between the local elite—flush with profits from the slave trade—and the Crown. Besides Stiles, Nathaniel Greene, regarded as second to George Washington as a rebel military leader, was also involved. This was no scruffy mob that struck what could fairly be called the first sturdy blow for "independency" but the local elite. Yet they were backed by others, insofar as the Crown's investigators could find hardly any to testify against them—except, quite tellingly, Briggs.[123]

By the fall of 1774, the revolt against British rule was evident, and the attack on the *Gaspee* was still at issue. A "petition" from the "American General Congress to His Majesty" objected to colonists being tried in London for offenses committed in the colonies, which was both a harbinger of the U.S. argument about "states' rights" (vis-à-vis Washington) and an indicator that the productive forces, fueled by slavery, had grown to such a point in North America that it was viewing itself as a separate jurisdiction. But this petition, driven by the *Gaspee*, went further in its bill of particulars by questioning Parliament's moves in Quebec in "abolishing the English and restoring the French laws" and not cracking down more on "the Roman Catholic religion throughout those vast regions that border of the westerly and northerly boundaries of the free Protestant English settlements." Also questioned was the continuing presence of the British army in the colonies; and though it was not noted, racial incidents such as those that occurred in Boston in 1768 may have been a factor here too, for in full-throated declamation, the petition thanked the "Creator" since they were "born the heirs of freedom" and not "in a land of slavery," that is, "degraded into a state of servitude."[124] The more colonists analogized themselves to slaves, the more they revealed the nature of the society they sought to construct and how sensitive they were to tampering with its chauvinistic dynamics.

The case of the *Gaspee*, according to one scholar, was a "proximate cause" that led straight to 1776 in that it led directly to "the formation of the inter-colonial web" of alliances, "the activities of which led relentlessly to colonial union and finally to successful collaboration in resisting British rule."[125] But standing in for Africans as a class, Aaron Briggs veered in a different direction. For just before the *Gaspee*, Lieutenant Governor William Bull of South Carolina had warned advisedly of the danger of seeming to place Africans "on a footing of equality" with "their masters as it might tempt slaves to make resistance and deter masters and managers from inflicting punishment with an exemplary severity" which was "so necessary." Thus, contrary to "royal humanity," which argued otherwise, Bull demanded that a settler charged with slaying a slave should be spared the death penalty.[126] There was good reason for Briggs to side with London against the settlers—and good reason for the latter to do otherwise.

In the siege of Havana, the Crown confronted energized African troops who fought Africans under the Union Jack, as mainland settlers were deserting and mutinying. Allowing these Africans to share in the booty infuriated settlers, a state of mind that was worsened when the slave trade to Cuba was circumscribed and further movement westward in North America was obstructed. Then to top it off, London sought to impose taxes on slaves and scuttle a profitable smuggling business (which often involved the slave trade)—while seemingly, as with their booty decision, appearing to equate Africans with settlers in the case of Aaron Briggs, a proposition that still nettled decades later.[127]

A disproportionate share of the colonies' traffic in slaves was borne by Newport's ships, and striking at the ocean province could easily be seen as a blow against the entire slave system. Then in the 1770s, as anger at London was rising, the legislature in this maritime colony moved to penalize those who freed their slaves, as if to send a message to burgeoning abolitionist sentiment in London and to a future Aaron Briggs.[128]

As the crisis with London accelerated, an opportunity arose for Africans to engage in arbitrage, playing upon the contradictions between the colonizing power and the settlers,[129] just as they had taken advantage in the past of contradictions between settlers and the "Catholic powers." But this proved to be a dangerous ploy when the settlers revolted successfully, driving London from the thirteen colonies and leaving the Africans to confront the none-too-tender mercies of self-righteous republicans. These premonitory settler apprehensions flowing from Rhode Island may have dissipated in the fullness of time but, instead, seemed to be realized when in June 1772, as the *Gaspee* was still being digested, the Crown appeared to be taking a step toward abolition of slavery within the empire, which marked yet another step toward "independency" of the mainland colonies.

9

Abolition in London

Somerset's Case and the North American Aftermath

As things turned out, June 1772 was not only on a level with July 1776 as a determinant of the future of British North America but, in a sense, was a necessary stepping-stone to the latter, better recognized date. Slaveholders had long felt uncomfortable in London, objecting to disapproval there of their brutal floggings of their Africans and the perceived laggardness in retrieving runaways. As Somerset's case dragged on, more antipathy to slavery was engendered in the British isles, further outraging colonists who had normalized this form of property as any other, like a steed or a parrot. When the abolitionist Granville Sharp bashed colonists in this regard, Benjamin Franklin struck back vigorously. When days after *Gaspee* the decision was rendered in Somerset's case and it was reported as ending slavery, the insecurity of slaveholders increased, while the self-assertion of the enslaved had a similar uptick. Some of the enslaved took the case as a cue to flee—with some seeking to make it all the way to London—while Charles Carroll of Maryland, one of the richest men in the colonies, experienced difficulty in disciplining his cocksure property almost from the time the case was rendered. Influential personalities in the metropolis were beginning to recoil at the enslaving habit of the colonists, spawning mutual rage that was not restrained when the latter began to argue that they—the settlers—were being treated like slaves by London.[1]

Lost in the furor was the judge's limited decision freeing an enslaved African belonging to a settler, who had escaped to the metropolis. The Crown and the colonies might have been able to downplay this decision, taken alone, but given the preceding real and imagined slights—non-importation agreements; reluctant mainland conscripts; the specter of unleashing armed Africans against the settlers—it was not easy for an already tattered relationship to survive. Colonists refused to be short-sighted and insisted rightfully that just because the decision was limited to England did not mean that London would refuse for all time to extend its substance across the Atlantic.

James Somerset—the ostensible cause of this turmoil—though catapulted to fame in London, was born in Africa and was carted to Virginia by a slaver in 1749, at which time Charles Steuart, a merchant of Scottish origin residing in Norfolk, purchased him. Somerset then moved at Steuart's behest to Boston, then to Britain. That this case was seen as influencing the fate of slavery as a whole is evidenced by Steuart's revelation that not himself but the "West Indian Planters and Merchants" were paying the fees for this case.[2] That this case was seen as embodying multiple ramifications was suggested by Somerset's multiple domiciles and, especially, his four-year stay in Boston, where African insurgency seemed to be rising.[3] Steuart, on the other hand, had distinguished himself earlier in the eyes of London, by performing "civilities to the Spaniards" in 1763, after which Francis Fauquier told him, "[I will provide] notice of your Intention of going to London who I doubt not will sh[o]w you all civilities"—which in retrospect, seems like anticipatory sarcasm.[4]

The case that in June 1772 prompted a tsunami of abolitionism started innocently enough, according to counsel for the enslaved. It was on 3 December 1771 that the slave known as James Somerset was found to be shackled on a ship in the Thames bound for a westward destination—when this matter was revealed to anti-bondage advocates. He had been bought in Virginia originally, but his tendency to bolt led his master to seek to sell him to Jamaica, hence his being found on the Thames. A writ of habeas corpus was drawn up demanding that the "body" be produced before the courts. Somerset's consul did little to suppress the concerns of slaveholders about the far-reaching nature of this case. Slavery produced a "horrid train of evils," he argued, and if not checked, would proliferate in London, not just spreading from "our own colonies," said consul, but from eastern Europe and Africa too, with "destructive consequences," quite "dangerous to the state." In words that colonists should have heeded, he warned that those who are "excluded from the common benefits of the constitution, are interested in scheming its destruction"—and anybody familiar with the Maroon Wars in Jamaica or the history of South Carolina would know why he referred contemptuously to this "pernicious institution" that was slavery.[5]

This case, as much as any other, demarcated the yawning gap between the colonies and the metropolis, underlining an identity in the former that was boldly different from the latter. This case, as much as any other, defined the emerging view which was to characterize the republic's key leaders: a defense of slavery—which confronted awkwardly the Crown's long-term interests in Cartagena, Havana, and St. Augustine.[6] This case, combined with the November 1775 bombshell dropped by Lord Dunmore in Virginia when he threatened to unleash armed Africans on a brewing revolt against the Crown,[7] solidified opposition to London, ushered into existence a new republic, and ossified for decades to come a caste-like status for Africans, seen widely among settlers as thinly disguised revolutionaries eager to collaborate with foes of all sort to subvert the status quo.[8] Understandably, the only fitting rebuke for revolutionaries bent on abolishing private property—albeit in themselves—was a steely counter-revolution.

The reading public had plenty of opportunity to parse the details of what came to be referred to as Somerset's case, which helped to harden the notion that London favored the enslaved over the slaveholder. This was understandable since, as the historian James Walvin sees it, this case "in effect" meant that enslavement was "outlawed" in England,[9] which illuminates why so many Africans were familiar with Lord Mansfield's opinion.[10] Thus, understandably, the case was much discussed in Virginia, both in the press and face to face;[11] it was reported in at least thirteen British newspapers, several widely circulated magazines, and almost two dozen newspapers in North America. Contemporary analysts felt it had implications not just for the British isles but its possessions too, and it is this perception that served to fuel anti-London sentiment, which was to detonate in 1776.[12] Historian Steven N. Wise argues that this case "was even more influential in America" than in London—with one observer at that time concurring, while moaning that the case would "cheat an honest American of his slave."[13] Historian Michael Groth has a point in asserting that "in one sense, slaveholding Patriots went to war in 1775 and declared independence in 1776 to defend their rights to own slaves."[14]

Actually, newspaper readers had much to ponder generally, notably in the keystone colony that was Virginia, for there headlines blared about Africans being armed by London[15] and Paris,[16] suing for freedom in Scotland,[17] and, naturally, plotting revolt in Jamaica.[18] It would be easy for settlers to perceive that the worm was turning, that they were surrounded by Africans who could easily be enlisted by the colonizer to squash their incipient revolt—a perception that seemed to be realized in November 1775 with the remarkable edict of Lord Dunmore.

* * *

Unsurprisingly, the momentous decision of 22 June 1772 was not embraced warmly by the majority of settlers. On the other hand, a Manhattan journal reported with skepticism about how on that pivotal day in London "a great many other blacks" came before Lord Mansfield, who had delivered the opinion of the court, and bowed first to the judges and then to the bar, with "symptoms of the most extravagant joy."[19] This appreciation of Mansfield may have been a personal signal to this jurist who had a young Negro woman living as a member of his family—generally unthinkable in North America—not to mention his being a powerful Scot, a part of the kingdom that was to distinguish itself as a fount of abolition. Following Mansfield's opinion, more cases followed his precedent, indicating that the appreciation of these Africans was well placed.[20]

A self-described "West Indian" said in 1772 that the case was of "full concern to America; and it had engrossed much of general expectation"—which could have well applied to both the Caribbean and the mainland. For, it was announced portentously, this was a case not of slavery but of "property," more than this, a type of property authorized by Parliament, and "if property, therefore in Negroes, was repugnant to the law of England, it could not be the law of America." What next? Judicial activism abolishing private property in general? What was needed was both a strengthening of the demos—or at least those who were property owners and slaveholders—and strengthening of parliamentary-style bodies, both of which were to be calling cards for rebels in 1776. Moreover, it was announced forebodingly, this case could well stir "insurrections in America." And what about the impact in the homeland? This writer had traveled to France and saw hardly any Africans, a result of a conscious policy, since Paris was concerned that "otherwise the race of Frenchmen would in time to come, be changed"—in stark contrast to London—but now with this decision, the sluice gates would be opened and Africans would now arrive in waves, meaning "stain and contamination," not to mention the undoing of revenue-producing colonies.[21]

Edward Long of Jamaica, who knew more than most how easy it was to rile up slaves, argued passionately that with this legal decision, "slave holding might perhaps be very well discontinued in every province of the North American continent," and surely it would harm profitability. More than this, it was a "direct invitation" to the Africans in the hemisphere "to mutiny" or flee to London. They would bribe captains to flee, thereby corrupting the well-wrought and profoundly crucial system of transport. It would empower competitors, especially Paris, and tear the empire apart.[22]

A newspaper in Boston was among those that worried about the case's implications.[23] Journalists there may have learned about the enthusiastic reception for the Negro poet Phillis Wheatley in London, which astonished even her. Samuel Estwick, not known to be one of her supporters and a confidant of planters in Barbados, felt that the case would inspire slave insurrections, which was understandable since they had been spurred by much less.[24] Another pro-slavery advocate said that slavery in the Americas was just a form of villenage, and this institution continued in full bloom even after the Magna Carta; besides, Georgia was a negative example of societies that barred slavery, bringing economic stagnation, and in any case, it did not deter other powers from pursuing enslavement.[25] But in the long run, it was Wheatley—not Estwick—whose perception about London's attitudes were more incisive, for it was in England that abolitionists pressed for her freedom. And her wariness about how this new status would be viewed in Boston was underscored when she requested that a copy of her document of liberty be safely stowed in Europe, which could allow her to escape the benighted colonies for a more enlightened home.[26]

Other Africans in the colonies exceeded Wheatley in actually seeking to escape to London, with their erstwhile masters left behind arguing that this London decision had spurred their wanderlust.[27] One in this group was Abel, forty years old, six feet tall, literate, a violinist and pilot. "I have whipped him," his "master" confessed unashamedly: "I believe scars may be seen upon his body" as a result. He had been to England—and now wanted to return.[28] This attempted flight to freedom was reflective of the anomaly of the era: settlers saw escaping from London as the goal, while Africans saw escaping to London as the objective.[29] One scholar of this era, has argued that in this volatile context it "was often the slaves who incited the British. African American initiatives began in the fall of 1774 when very few white Americans were angry enough at Britain to favor independence." Before that Abigail Adams found that a group of enslaved Africans in her province planned to make a proposal that if they were freed, they would take up arms against the settlers.[30] There was a "conspiracy of the Negroes," she warned her spouse, the future U.S. president.[31] The enslaved in Bristol County, Rhode Island, joined the loyalists too.[32] John Adams should not have been surprised by this turn of events. After all, he had served long and faithfully as a counsel for slaveholders and once argued that Massachusetts presumed all Africans to be slaves.[33]

In the fall of 1774, James Madison had anticipated Dunmore's edict, noting that only recently "a few of those unhappy wretches," meaning Africans, "met together" to conspire with redcoats on the premise that "by revolting," then "they should be rewarded with their freedom."[34] Madison's interlocutor, William Bradford, agreed that there was a "well founded" apprehension about an "insurrection" being "excited among the slaves"—but hoped against hope that London would disdain such a "slavish way of Conquering."[35]

Coincidence or not, it did seem that Africans were spurred to heightened activism after June 1772. In Boston in early 1773, a group of Africans in petitioning for freedom contrasted sharply their treatment with the treatment of Africans by "the Spaniards"—who supposedly did not possess the "sublime ideas of freedom that Englishmen have" and yet acquitted themselves better in this regard; speaking "in behalf of" their "fellow slaves in this province," they expressed a desire to return to Africa.[36] Peter Bestes and his much-besieged African comrades would have found that in Boston, those who were pro-London often represented the enslaved in court, while rebels routinely represented masters.[37]

Repeatedly, Africans in Boston and their backers denounced the anomaly of rebels prattling about "liberty" while endorsing enslavement. Why, said one commentator in 1773, this was a sheer "solecism of language." There was "not a Right to bring them from their own country," it was said of the beleaguered Africans, and, thus, "they ought to be returned thereto, at the public Expense, if they chuse [choose] it, which, doubtless, would be the case with many."[38] Appealing directly to the province's governor, the Africans—in a cry that resonated even more insistently after the founding of the republic—seemed desperate enough to throw in their lot with the Crown in return for concessions: "We have no property! We have no wives! No children! We have no city! No country!"[39]

Manhattan in particular had good reason to worry about the turbulent drift of events. For much of the 18th century, New York City held the largest percentage and the second-largest absolute number of enslaved Africans of any port town in British North America. This demographic imbalance fed shivers about the long-range ambitions of Africans. When in 1774, amid violent scenes of loyalist reprisals against rebels, two slaves murdered their masters, known supporters of the rebel cause, fright rose about a crushing maneuver by a London-African axis.[40]

*   *   *

Some settlers were beginning to see the revolt against British rule not only as a thrust toward "independency," opening even more the growingly profitable trade with Hispaniola and France, but as a simple attempt at survival in the face of a perceived attempt at their liquidation propelled by London and Africans alike. The planter class was explosively angry about Lord Mansfield's demarche as a result, with one among them claiming that now "slave holding might perhaps be very well discontinued in every province of the North American continent situated to the north of the Carolinas." What would now befall the slave traders who had piled into this odious business with the shriveling of the Royal African Company? Echoing the democratic-sounding rhetoric emanating from the mainland, it was stated that the legal opinion thwarted Parliament and was a kind of unwarranted judicial activism. Worse, it was thought, the end result would be miscegenation, creating individuals like the "Portuguese and Moriscos in complexion of skin and basement of mind," a "venomous and dangerous ulcer," in other words. The result would be "bloodshed" and a "spirit of mutiny" and untold horrors.[41]

Even before June 1772, one Londoner complained that Africans "do not certainly consider themselves to be slaves in this country, nor will they put up with inequality of treatment." The number of Africans in the isles was estimated to be fifteen thousand—but Granville Sharp, the abolitionist, thought it was higher, perhaps twenty thousand. Some

Londoners found it disturbing that some of these African men were marrying Englishwomen, while the major planter Edward Long complained that "the lower class of women in England are remarkably fond of the blacks," raising the dreaded specter of miscegenation[42]—contrary to Long's fondest hope, this was (in a conservative sense) an indication of the danger of allowing slavery to fester.

Anticipating conflicts between London and Washington that would animate the early 19th century, a propagandist wondered what would happen if a slave ship bound for the mainland from Africa somehow was blown into England. Would this "property" be confiscated? Was it not dangerous to have one set of laws in the metropolis and another in the colonies? Was this not simply deepening a split, virtually mandating formal separation? And what about the reputed fifteen thousand Africans in the British isles? Would not their numbers increase to the point where the kingdom would be transformed?[43]

To close observers, it may have seemed already that London's emissaries on the mainland were exhibiting shakiness on the bedrock issue of slavery. When an African was sold in Boston, Governor Thomas Hutchinson of Massachusetts displayed a remarkable solicitude toward this man's claim that he was actually born free in Lisbon. Instead of dismissing the claim peremptorily, Hutchinson sought the aid of the Earl of Dartmouth in resolving the matter.[44]

Yet another London-based analyst observed that though "the number of Negroes in the Southern Colonies of North America is equal, if not superior, to that of the white men—their condition is truly pitiable; their labour excessively hard, their diet poor and scanty; their treatment cruel and oppressive." In itself, this was simple quotidian truth (though rarely acknowledged on the mainland), but the conclusion was the point that was driving thoroughgoing change: "They [slaves] cannot but be," it was reported ominously, "a subject of terror to those who so inhumanly terrorize over them."[45] James Swan, a Scot writing in Boston, also spoke of the "odious" nature of slavery "in the eyes of every British subject." With eloquence, he denounced the "crimes attending the slave trade" and the "extreme cruel usage the Negroes meet with in the plantations." Virginia was singled out. "My blood run[s] cold" at the thought, he declaimed. In a growing trend signaling a growing dispute, he assailed bitterly the hypocrisy of slaveholders bemoaning lack of freedom. Why, one could just as well, he stressed, start "making slaves of *British* subjects" if this dirty business were not halted. "Setting at liberty" those who were enslaved was his abolitionist demand, though his failure to detail compensation for slaveholders reified the view that those of his ilk were the dangerous radicals whose jurisdiction settlers must escape.[46]

In these scalding analyses of slavery, these opinion molders were simply reflecting the considered opinion among a goodly number of Africans, including the soon-to-be-renowned memoirist Olaudah Equiano.[47] This fabled African arrived in London weeks after the Somerset case was rendered, providing him with a ringside seat at the making of history.[48] Equiano also spent a good deal of time in Belfast, and, not coincidentally, by the late 1760s anti-slavery sentiment there had hardened.[49] Like Equiano, Ignatius Sancho wanted a harder line taken against the rebels.[50] Sancho was so hostile to the rebels that he seemed to skew reality to make it fit his fond hope that they would be defeated.[51] Equiano's and Sancho's anti-rebel sentiments were mirrored at the highest levels, for it was Maurice Morgan, top aide to Sir Guy Carleton, who in 1772 published one of the first proposals for gradual abolition.[52]

It was becoming commonplace for leading intellectuals in London to find it painfully ironic that brutalizing mainland slaveholders were in the vanguard of those yelping for liberty.[53] Quite typically, these abolitionists—most notably, the heroic James Ramsay—were often quite hostile to what were seen as hypocritical cries for liberty by slaveholders.[54] Their anger may have come to a boil when Virginia's eminent Richard Henry Lee compared the situation of his fellow colonists to "Egyptian bondage," which could very well "become the fate of every inhabitant of America," that is, every "white" inhabitant.[55] Ramsay, says one scholar, "hated American rebels."[56] According to a Nigerian authority on these matters, "Englishmen who had not lived in the West Indies and America had not been so depraved by plantation mentality" and were thus enabled to accord some degree of humanity to black "chattels"—hence Lord Mansfield's decision and the negative reaction to it due west.[57]

The Somerset case both reflected and propelled this growing abolitionist sentiment in London. Plans for abolition were being devised, as well as plans to circumscribe the slave trade. One bold Londoner envisioned a time "when the blacks of the southern colonies on the continent of America shall be numerous enough to throw off at once the yoke of tyranny to revenge their wrongs in the blood of their oppressors and carry terror and destruction to the more northern settlements." This "insurrection on the continent" would then provide "incitement in the islands and a signal for a general and . . . merited carnage," featuring "horrible cruelties and the most furious revenge," which "may end to the disadvantage of the whites." The issue was bruited of settling free Africans in Florida, which would have re-created the pre-1763 problem faced in Georgia and the Carolinas of slaves north of St. Augustine finding refuge: "colonies of free Negroes" tied to London would "shake the power of Spain to its foundation"—that is, settlers' foundational interests were to be sacrificed in the process.[58]

If settlers had gotten hold of this inflammatory pamphlet, they would have been justified in viewing it as an ominously dangerous straw in the wind. Now it was not just the enslaved of Antigua contemplating the liquidation of settlements. This chilling denouement was now being discussed in ostensibly more respectable sites in London. In such a context, "independency"—ousting London, adopting a truer "whiteness" by calling for a formal truce in the religious cold war, and, thereby, broadening the base of support for a new republic—seemed like common sense driven by the mandate to survive. With a bow to predictability, London's interests were sacrificed in 1776 by the settlers. Still, this fiery rhetoric was becoming the rage among London's abolitionists, who found it easier to clamor for total abolition of slavery, while their mainland counterparts leaned toward gradualism.[59]

Nonetheless, there was a relationship between abolitionists on both sides of the Atlantic, particularly the tie between Granville Sharp and Anthony Benezet. The latter thought that the rebelliousness of Africans meant that "some of the colonies" could fall "under the dominion of their slaves" in the Caribbean and could awaken settlers to the "alarms of danger" they faced.[60] But Benezet also knew that the cost of an African was increasing along with growth in rice and indigo production in South Carolina and Georgia, meaning the arrival of even more Africans—"ten thousand were expected," he said in the spring of 1773 tellingly exposing his justifiable concern. "These colonies appear so stupefied and their hearts so hardened by the love of gain," he moaned, "that it is feared nothing less than a blow from heaven will [rouse] them from their lethargy."[61] Actually, it was the double blow from Somerset and Dunmore that roused them—though not necessarily for the better.

The rage of settlers notwithstanding, Lord Mansfield's decision was not necessarily a radical break from the train of history but, more, a logical progression. The siege of Havana and previous battles in Cartagena had shown that in the immediate future, London would need more—not fewer—Africans in its contestation with the "Catholic powers," and it did not require a fortune-teller to discern that arming Africans in order to keep other Africans enslaved was not a sustainable project in the long term. Moreover, the Maroon Wars in Jamaica showed that if something sufficiently severe was not done, the entire colonial project could be lost. The fecklessness of mainlanders when it came to fighting—deserting, mutinying, trading with the enemy, hinting broadly about "independency"—indicated that other options should be explored, and undercutting the source of their wealth which had boosted "independency" in the first place, that is, enslaving Africans, did seem to be an appropriate rejoinder. Then there was the growth of abolitionist sentiment in London and Scotland, which seemed to be gaining in strength with every passing day and was driven in no small measure by the riotous obstreperousness of Africans themselves.

In any case, as early as 1748, Virginians had reason to argue that just because a mainland slave was in London did not mean manumission ipso facto.[62] In 1749, Dudley Crofts, a Caribbean slaveholder, had asked if the status of his slave property was altered as a result of his being in England. Lord Mansfield's ruling was two decades away—but the fact that the question had to be asked then was indicative of changing times.[63] About a decade after Crofts's inquiry, a verbal war had erupted in London between the pro-slavery lobby and its growing list of detractors; in a sense this was a reflection of the reality that as the slave trade surged in the prelude to 1776, more Africans were turning up in the isles, further stoking debate.[64] The legal status of slavery in London was contested long before 1776—as suggested by the clandestine sneaking of Equiano into town in 1762, underscoring the reality that the "master" did not feel he had an unquestioned right to sell his "property."[65]

*   *   *

Given the venom directed at Lord Dunmore subsequently, the momentous year of 1775 had begun ironically with public addresses of praise to the governor for his determined attitude toward the indigenous in Virginia.[66] Lord Dunmore had not stinted in confronting indigenes, but as a faithful servant of the Crown, he diligently opposed efforts of colonists to move westward, seizing land of the indigenes—to the consternation of settlers.[67] But as Lord Dunmore became the first full-fledged villain of the rebels, denizens of the dominion came to believe that he was seeking to incite indigenes against them too,[68] which may have stemmed from the perception that he was obstructing land grabs.

In assessing Lord Dunmore, colonists had a lengthy record to draw upon. Even before his abolitionist proclamation, he opined—auspiciously in retrospect—that the Africans were "on the side of the Government." A leading redcoat general concurred and added, "we must avail ourselves of every resource, even to raise the Negroes, in our cause."[69] Just before June 1772, he was acknowledging that "the people of this colony are very anxious," this time about a bill to "lay an additional duty upon the importation of slaves," a measure devised because there was already "just cause to apprehend the most dangerous consequences" of demographic projections. Actually, the issue was not only "lessening [Africans'] number" but even the "total expulsion of them," since the proportion of Africans was growing spectacularly, thus imperiling the colonial project; this disproportion was said to be "sufficient to alarm not only this colony but all the colonies of America," since "in case of a war . . . with Spain" the "people with great reason tremble" at the prospect of this external force aided by an internal foe. Finding the "proper means of averting a calamity so alarming" was a priority, he thought—but how could this be done when planters demanded slaves and merchants profited from same (and as Lord Dunmore was to find, London too might find a specific need for Africans)?[70]

Colonists should have applauded in 1772 when the regime in Virginia sought to impose taxes on imported Africans, even if they were arriving from Maryland and the Carolinas, for this was effectively limiting the numbers of those who could slit their throats—but some were too blind to see.[71] Surely, there was still a profit to be made via bonded labor, and this factor tended to override all else.

But even before the edict of November 1775, Lord Dunmore had made decisions that settlers found difficult to applaud. On 1 May 1775, for example, as revolt was percolating in Williamsburg, he warned apocalyptically, "I shall be forced and it is my fixed purpose to arm all my own Negroes and receive all others that will come to me whom I shall declare free," unless colonists halted their unrest.[72] Like Somerset, this was a direct threat to exalted private property, a threat not only to "nationalize" this wealth but to deploy it in armed assaults. It is difficult to imagine words better designed to ignite revolt among a class of settlers who had grown affluent on the basis of tyrannical bigotry.

Lord Dunmore, on the other hand, was focused on those who he thought would have been satisfied to cut his own throat. This was part and parcel of the "threats" against him, Dunmore said, complaining of the "dangerous measures pursued" by his detractors. "If not treasonable," he thundered, it was minimally "one of the highest insults" imaginable. Speaking in May 1775, he knew then that his opponents were "apprehensive of insurrections amongst their Slaves (some Reports having prevailed to this effect)." Seeking to "soothe them," he purred that he had made gunpowder less accessible not because of his opponents' behavior but to keep the Africans from seizing it. Not being dupes, the enraged settlers were not buying this notion and, instead, their "fury" then became "uncontrollable."[73]

In June 1775, Lord Dunmore refused assent to a bill for paying militia with a duty on slaves, a maneuver subject to various interpretations,[74] not all of which left him in a positive light among settlers. His Excellency should have considered events in South Carolina, where the debts of a number of "gentlemen" escalated when they felt compelled to pay "Negro merchants" for slaves, while stiffing "dry goods merchants." This not only hindered overall economic growth; it signaled the peril involved in being perceived as tampering with the interests of powerful human traffickers—for example, taxing their commodities as London had done. Even discussing taxes to be imposed by a growingly unpopular leader—not least taxes on enslaved Africans—was bound to excite passion.[75]

Typically, as November 1775 approached, rumors of slave conspiracies poured into Williamsburg, and by July 1775 word had reached there about events in neighboring North Carolina and the allegation that Governor Martin was plotting in league with Africans.[76] As these unnerving events were unwinding, Virginia periodicals were bulging with similarly disturbing reports about Africans joining London's navy in Newport, site of the heralded *Gaspee* controversy, while other Africans were joining the redcoats in Boston.[77] Concomitantly, there was a widespread belief among Africans that somehow it was their fate that was driving this tumult and it was their freedom that settlers wanted to block and that London was on their side.[78] Surely the articulate Negroes of that era were appalled by the hypocrisy of slaveholders yelping for liberty while continuing to enchain slaves[79] and, thus, leaned toward London.[80]

Thus, when in November 1775 Lord Dunmore in Virginia issued his famous—or infamous, in the view of settlers—edict offering to free and arm Africans to squash an anti-colonial revolt, he entered a pre-existing maelstrom of insecurity about the fate of slavery and London's intentions. For some settlers, this stirred savaging memories of slave insurrections and poisonings and the overriding concern, stretching back to Oliver Cromwell, that somehow London would sacrifice settler interests on an altar with Africans wielding a sword of retribution. As 1776 approached, the idea was growing in London that if settlers persisted in their escapades, they could be brought to their knees by inciting Africans against them.[81]

That Lord Dunmore accompanied his proclamation with a declaration of "martial law" to confront "treasonable" settlers and "traitors" was viewed with malignity by settlers. Viewed similarly by the governor's ostensible constituents was his threat of "reducing" their "houses to ashes and spreading devastation" wherever he could reach. By speaking so bluntly, the governor helped to convert moderates into radicals. Of course, in November 1775, he was responding to disturbing signs of armed resistance to the Crown that had been in motion for more than a year.[82] Thus, when the influential planter Landon Carter got wind of a "Scheme for the Negro Command," he was "incredulous," refusing to accord the "least credit to a thing so inhuman as well as so dangerous"—then with resignation he accepted the bitter reality.[83]

November 1775 was preceded by 19 April 1775: it was then, announced South Carolina rebels, that "the actual commencement of hostilities" erupted with the Crown, at the behest of "the British troops in the bloody scene . . . near Boston." But quite tellingly, these patriots instantly linked this fraught moment with the "dread of instigated insurrections in the colonies"—which Lord Dunmore had foreshadowed—and this inciteful factor provided "causes sufficient to drive an oppressed people to the use of arms." By June 1775, the rebels' Continental Congress, a direct challenge to London's sovereignty on the mainland, chose to "make inquiry concerning insurrections of slaves."[84]

Settlers from what became the Palmetto State knew that a military attack upon their ranks was often accompanied by an insurrection of the enslaved, eager to take advantage of the resultant flux. Josiah Quincy arrived there just before the epochal battle at Lexington and remarked pointedly on the "great fears of insurrection" that were abundant.[85] In May 1775—as highly motivated delegates assembled at the Continental Congress—one of Charleston's leading figures received word from Arthur Lee, then in London, to the effect that the Crown was planning not only to deploy indigenous allies against the colonists but, as well, to encourage "an insurrection amongst the slaves." Similar fears arose in Georgia, all of which served to forge in the crucible of independence the entirely understandable idea that Africans were hostile to formation of the republic.[86]

On 29 May 1775, a local periodical reported a purported plan in London to ship "seventy eight thousand guns and bayonets" to the colonies for use by Africans, indigenes, "Roman Catholics," and "Canadians" in order to subdue settlers. When the royal governor arrived in Charleston on 19 June 1775, he was told that it was believed universally that the ship that brought him had on board thousands of arms for Africans to effectuate an insurrection.[87]

Influenced by events in South Carolina, similar fears arose in Georgia, since by 1775 nearly half of the population was African.[88] Thus, in May 1775, Georgia's governor received news of a skirmish in Boston with alarm, as the report was accompanied by the news that redcoats were on their way to South Carolina and that slaves were being liberated, with the entire region in an uproar of ferment. Colonists were turning en masse against him, and he could envision no other result except an anti-colonial rebellion.[89]

Setting aside the veracity of these swirling rumors and allegations, they certainly suggest that an anxiety-ridden state of mind was descending on many settlers as 1776 approached. Frazzled nerves led to hasty decisions, at times wrongheaded, and often violent retribution visited upon those who were seen as a source of insecurity: Africans, for example.

Even before the Dunmore proclamation, colonists were up in arms in light of alleged attempts by the Crown to incite the Africans against them.[90] Of course, the Africans hardly needed external assistance to rebel, as events in Norfolk months earlier suggested.[91] Nevertheless, when two hundred Africans instantaneously flocked to the Union Jack after Lord Dunmore's call, panic set in among settlers, with their erst-while governor denounced as a tyrant, while Africans viewed him as a liberator—not the last time that a racial divide emerged over a fundamental matter on the mainland.[92] The edict was far from trivial since at the time it was estimated that as many as two thousand Africans would fight under the Union Jack in response to Lord Dunmore's proclamation. The rebels in response felt obliged to reverse field and allowed Negro enlistment in their ranks, as in a repetitive pattern, the alleged tribunes of liberty were moved toward practicing what they preached by those whom they accused of suppressing their liberty.[93]

Thus, this edict, says one historian, "did more than any other British measure to spur uncommitted white Americans into the camp of rebellion." (The competition in this sweepstakes may have been Lord Mansfield's controversial opinion.) Even in New York, where Lord Dunmore once served, angry Long Island farmers burned him in effigy as they fretted about Africans "being too fond of British troops." Contrastingly, the edict reinforced a pre-existing pro-London tendency among Africans, manifested most directly when more of this group fought alongside the redcoats post-1776 than alongside the successful rebels.[94]

Thomas Jefferson claimed that as of July 1775 separation from Great Britain was not on the settler agenda, but the proclamation was said to have changed all this, turning the temperate toward zealotry. Ironically, this proclamation had a similar impact on what was becoming war, as the Emancipation Proclamation did on another war decades hence.[95] Jefferson had reason to know, as he was informed directly that "great numbers" of Africans had flocked to Lord Dunmore, and as a result, "the person of no Man in the Colony is safe, when marked as an Object of their Vengeance."[96]

Certainly, Jefferson's comrade Patrick Henry was vociferous in his reproach of Lord Dunmore, whose edict was said to be "fatal to the public safety" and "dangerous" besides.[97] Dunmore was no fan of Henry, terming him a "man of desperate circumstance" who in May 1775 had "advanced" near the governor's abode and "there encamped with all the appearances of actual war."[98] There was growing anarchistic rebellion in the colony, with Lord Dunmore himself barely escaping detention by the rebels.[99]

However, Patrick Henry and his comrades thought they had reason to wage "actual war" against the Crown, for in August 1775 a patriot preacher in Maryland warned that Lord Dunmore was "tampering with" the settlers' "Negroes, . . . all for the glorious purpose of enticing them to cut their masters' throats while they are asleep. Gracious God!"[100] Somehow, a revolt against London was morphing into a revolt against Africans, in a repetitive pattern that was to stain the resultant republic for decades to come.

*　*　*

There were other, more personal motivations that led to this momentous month. The rowdy rebels had detained Lord Dunmore's spouse, causing her to flee to London by August 1775, while he was hiding out on a ship offshore.[101] Virtually as much as any individual, Lord Dunmore—along with Africans in Antigua and Jamaica who chased settlers to the mainland—could well be considered a Founding Father of the republic. So much loyalist recruiting was occurring among Africans as a result of his edict—to the fury of rebels—that a Connecticut slaveholder advertised that his "Negro Wench" was "now pregnant and bids fair to make more recruits for Lord Dunmore."[102] On the eve of 1776, there were about sixteen thousand persons of African descent in New England, who were thought to be potential foes of the anti-London revolt. That slavery was firmly entrenched in this region in 1776 made these fears understandable.[103] Further south in Philadelphia, a headquarters of anti-London feelings, the anger toward Lord Dunmore had attained hyperbolically stratospheric heights,[104] adding highly inflammable fuel to the fires of rebellion: that such rhetoric was echoed in Maryland was indicative of the trepidation induced by his notorious edict.[105]

On the east bank of the Atlantic, the feeling was that Lord Dunmore was seen as a "nobleman of a firm and resolute disposition" who was treated with "respect" initially by Virginians—before he became "engaged in a violent altercation" with them over the "whole militia law," which could be seen as a pre-emptive measure on his part to weaken those who were opposed to London's rule, then to bludgeon them with armed Africans. This supporter of His Excellency knew that the province had a "prodigious multitude of Negro slaves," which by his counting "amounted to twice the number of the white inhabitants." This imbalance, it was thought, left the latter fearful and desperately desiring a measure that would allow each county to "raise a company for its pro-tection," which the Crown sought to block, leaving colonists fearful that London and Dunmore were conspiring against their interests.[106]

With the growth in population of Africans and the resultant sense of incipient settler revolt, Dunmore's edict came at a sensitive moment. If his edict could have been seen as a purely local matter denuded of wider consequence, the toxic fallout could have been more easily contained. But alas, this was not so, for what motivated Dunmore was part of a larger mainland pattern. The pro-London Thomas Hutchinson knew that in South Carolina "the Negroes are very insolent"; he then referred to a controversial case wherein the settlers had "tried a free Negro for saying that if the King should send troops, he would join them." Thomas Jeremiah may have been innocent of this charge, but his ancestry and the colonists' incitement helped to condemn him: he was found "guilty of exciting the Negroes to an insurrection," then executed. When the colonial governor began to raise an objection, the settlers bluntly informed him that "if he offered to stay execution, they would erect gallows before his door and make him the executioner of the Negro," in a kind of blood oath that came to solidify the construction of "whiteness" when lynching became a blood sport decades later. But on one detail Hutchinson was wrong—or at least premature: "surely," he concluded, "such a tyranny cannot last."[107]

In a pattern that was to be repeated after the coming of the republic, it was London that sought aggressively to save the life of this African Jeremiah—before he was hung and cremated on 18 August 1775. The royal governor thought his only crime was being a prosperous and free African in a city filled with poor and destitute Europeans—making this episode a harbinger of the lynchings that scarred the landscape in Dixie a century later. Yet since the governor was warned bluntly that if he intervened, he too might be in jeopardy, his hand was stayed.[108]

Nevertheless, one contemporary scholar has a point in asserting that as matters evolved, the "invading British army and low-country blacks shared a common foe in the republican slave masters of the low country,"[109] shedding further light on Jeremiah's execution—his class status as a property owner notwithstanding. In South Carolina in 1775, Africans were thought to outnumber settlers to the ratio of five to three, which only increased the skittish insecurity of the settlers.[110] But it was even more skewed than this, for according to one source by 1776, in the three low-county districts of Georgetown, Charles Town (including the city), and Beaufort, there were fifty-three slaves to three settlers.[111]

Reputedly a leading redcoat played upon this sensitive factor, reminding these settlers of their vulnerability, asserting that if their rebelling continued, "it may happen that your rice and indigo will be brought to market by Negroes instead of white people." That is, they could be ousted from their high perches and in a reversal of fortune become subject to the diktat of those whom they were accustomed to ruling. That was in March 1775. In May, South Carolina dispatched energized delegates to the Continental Congress in Philadelphia.[112] Unwittingly (perhaps), London had helped to construct a "Black Scare" that propelled settlers toward secession, with untoward and unhappy consequences for the Africans left behind when the Crown was defeated.

From Philadelphia, William Bradford informed James Madison about a recent "Negro conspiracy" in Charleston and worried that Virginia would witness the same. Bradford's panic was exacerbated when he considered that Africans thought that the conflict between settlers and London was all about their enslavement—which was not altogether wrong. As for the condemned Thomas Jeremiah, Bradford recited to Madison the chilling words of leading rebel and slave trader Henry Laurens, who thought it to be true that the accused was "guilty of a design & attempt to encourage our Negroes to Rebellion & joining the King's Troops if any had been sent there."[113] The point was not necessarily if Laurens was accurate in his sentiment—the point was the state of mind of rebels who were coming to believe that a London-African combine was mounting against them, leaving secession—a Unilateral Declaration of Independence—as the only way out.

Already the other prong of revolt—settlers' growing economic strength fettered by London—was asserting itself in that the decision had been taken by the rebels that no commodities should be exported from the mainland to the British isles or British Caribbean.[114] This was further transforming the political economy, as one slaveholder in 1775 mandated that no "clothing" for his property should be imported from the isles: instead, "ten Black Females" were "to be employed in spinning solely."[115] Still, by making his plantation more dependent upon often seditious slaves, this "master" was opting for a sour alternative—which was why months later Robert Carter decided that this enterprise was "to be carried on by Whites only."[116]

Lord Dunmore's bold move stirred the pot of unrest irately—on all sides—quickening the pace leading to the 1776 revolt. Yet his edict should not be viewed in isolation but as part of a broad tapestry that both illustrated and prefigured his startling words. For in neighboring North Carolina, the governor had outraged settlers when the rumor was floated that he intended to imitate Lord Dunmore and unleash the Africans against them. Actually and in private, Governor Josiah Martin conceded that armed Africans could be quite useful in crushing revolt.[117] But he undercut his case among settlers when he suggested that he was against "giving encouragement to the Negroes"—unless there was an "actual and declared rebellion" by the dissidents.[118] That these words emerged in August 1775, just weeks before Dunmore's stinging demarche, only contributed to the growing panic among settlers that they were to be overrun shortly, leaving them with few options beyond revolting and tossing aside the Crown. The Earl of Dartmouth was correct when he averred that "the situation of Governor Martin" was "in many respects similar" to that in Virginia[119]—with the prospect of an inter-colonial contagion.

Irrespective of whether London planned to incite Africans to thrash settlers, many among the latter certainly thought this to be so. Whether theirs was a guilty fear borne by cruel exploitation of Africans is another story altogether. Arthur Lee, as noted, had made a similar rabble-rousing claim, and because he had been educated in Edinburgh and had practiced law in London, it was assumed widely that there was something to this story. Yet a colonial official branded his assertion "fictitious," though it had "inflamed the populace"[120]—that the republic was called into being in part by fear of African insurgency did not bode well for the population that became U.S. Negroes, then "African Americans."

Still, the proliferating sentiment that Governor Martin was entertaining such utterly inflaming notions helped to tip the scales against him among settlers. The presence there of thousands of Africans, many of them relatively recent arrivals and hardly "assimilated" to non-violence was hardly reassuring to settlers.[121] Not for the last time, mainland settlers sought to unite Europeans upon the basis of fear and hatred of Africans, part of the connective tissue that knitted together the identity that was "whiteness." What gave such disquieting claims weight, however, was the unavoidable reality that Somerset had set aloft the notion that London was moving toward abolition—and the settlers not so much. Slave pilots, for example, so useful in navigating the numerous inlets in North Carolina, were among the first to ally with London in its dispute with the settlers.[122]

Janet Schaw was passing through North Carolina then and noted that an edict of the Crown on 12 June 1775 had offered a pardon to all rebelling settlers who sought conciliation—but somehow, this was not what they heard. Instead, she recalled, they were told London "was ordering the Tories to murder the Whigs and promising every Negro that would murder his Master and family that he should have his Master's plantation"—and, she said, somehow the Africans believed this to be true, which meant that a heavy "price" would be paid. She was stunned to ascertain that "an insurrection was hourly expected. There had been a great number of them," meaning Africans, "discovered in the adjoining woods the night before, most of them with arms." This had forged a remarkably high level of solidarity among settlers—and terror against Africans. She was told that this Negro-phobic "artifice" was a wily "trick intended in the first place to inflame the minds of the populace and in the next place to get those who had not before taken up arms to do it now and form an association for the safety of the town," even though by this juncture she found it likely that "the Negroes will revolt."[123] Whatever the case, a signal factor in instigating presumed loyal subjects to become fire-breathing radicals was the very idea that London was stirring a dreaded "servile revolt."[124]

Convincing settlers that Africans would rise and murder them all was a charge that did not seem far-fetched in light of Manhattan 1712, Antigua 1736, Stono 1739, Manhattan 1741, Jamaican Maroons, and all the rest. That London seemed to be moving toward abolition in 1772, which had been preceded by arming Africans to fight in the Caribbean, gave ballast to the claims made against Governor Martin.

Settlers in North Carolina already were rattled when an enslaved African named Sanders was found guilty of having shot a colonist; the defendant, though worth a considerable eighty pounds, was accorded a wrenching verdict: "burn the said Negro alive."[125] Such alarms were consistent with what James Madison thought he knew, for it was in January 1775 that he was informed of a plan by London to emulate Martin and Dunmore by arming the enslaved to squash his revolt.[126] A few months later, the future president shakily referred to "tampering with the slaves," as he alluded to Dunmore's plan "to make great use of them" in case of escalating conflict. The "truth" was, said this diminutive and bookish Virginian, that Dunmore was meddling in the "only part in which this Colony is vulnerable; if we should be subdued," he warned gravely, "we shall fall like Achilles by the hand of one that knows that secret."[127]

In retrospect, it is hardly stunning how many rebels either anticipated Lord Dunmore's edict before it was written or predicted something similar, all before November 1775,[128] suggesting that it was a logical outgrowth of ongoing trends, including the increasing use of Negro troops from Cartagena to Havana, the perceived unreliability of certain Irish and Scots, the negative reviews of mainlanders' fighting capabilities on behalf of London, the import of Somerset's case, and the like.

From the opposite shore, settlers reprimanded Lord Dunmore's proclamation for providing "encouragement to a general insurrection," which they threatened unsubtly could mean "inflicting the severest punishment" upon Africans; making it plain, any Africans so bold as to be involved in "conspiring to rebel"—a "wicked step"—were promised "death" while being "excluded all benefit of clergy."[129] Those African soldiers captured in battle were designated for sale as slaves in the Caribbean[130]—surely an incentive, if any were needed, for the Africans to fight even more ferociously against the settler revolt. Dunmore was accused of a major sin—he had "rendered insecure" property and had "exposed" settlers "to the dangers of a general insurrection."[131] Dunmore and Martin had become the twin towers of treachery, embodying the direst fears of settlers. They were lumped together with the rebels' sternest London critic: Samuel Johnson, whose words, said Benjamin Franklin, were "applauded" in Parliament. Supposedly, "Lord Dunmore & Governor Martin [were] already carrying one part of the [Johnson] Project into Execution, by exciting an insurrection among the Blacks."[132]

There is little doubt that Lord Dunmore had tossed shale oil on a raging fire in November 1775.[133] Lord Dunmore's "Ethiopians," as they were termed, garnered a form of revenge when they inflicted damage in Virginia, a "grand sack" of a number of homes, as one observer put it.[134] All this was unfolding in an overheated atmosphere with rebels worrying that an "Indian War is not improbable," alongside the typically dreaded "insurrection of Slaves."[135]

Thus, in early November 1775, Lord Dunmore landed at Norfolk with dozens of grenadiers and a band of loyalists and Africans; there they confronted successfully rebel militia. Quickly he issued his edict—and it was downhill from there. By December, a declaration of war by the rebels was promulgated. The animosity Dunmore engendered was captured by the Virginian John Norton, who denounced the "cruelty" and "wicked" acts of the Crown's forces: "after pillaging the plantations on the rivers for some months past, taking Negroes, burning houses," and "like depredations," Lord Dunmore capped it all off by issuing a "damned, infernal, diabolical proclamation declaring freedom to all our slaves who will join him."[136]

With a "few Scotch excepted," boasted Richard Henry Lee of Virginia, Dunmore had "united every man in the Colony." Indeed, if London had "searched the world" for the man best suited to wreck its cause "and procure union and success" for the rebels, it "could not have found a more complete Agent."[137] He was not far wrong. (Intriguingly, one writer also thought that those few who backed Governor Martin in North Carolina also included "Highlanders" of Scotland, a "brave and hardy race.")[138] Lee could afford to brag because as of early October 1775, the rebels had received by land from Baltimore and other sites substantial amounts of gunpowder which had been purchased in the Caribbean.[139]

Lee was not wrong in his implication that Dunmore was no outlier or loose cannon but was operating well within the bounds of leadership thinking set down in London. A proposal emerged in Parliament as early as January 1775 calling for the abolition of slavery and thus "humbling the high aristocratic spirit of Virginia and the southern colonies."[140] It was also in November 1775 that a remarkable debate erupted in Parliament as to whether "all the slaves in America should have the trial by jury." A formal motion was introduced on this terribly fraught matter, accompanied by a proviso to "annul all laws" on the mainland to the contrary. Amidst pained remarks about a "civil war" under way, the "vice" of slavery was denounced, and though instant abolition was not yet on the agenda, clearly designated way stations along the way were. This jury measure then was seen as "an auspicious beginning" to that end, which was to "extirpate slavery from the face of the earth." Tossing down the gauntlet before mainlanders, it was announced brazenly, "let the only contention henceforward between Great Britain and America be, which shall exceed the other in zeal for establishing the fundamental rights of liberty to all mankind"—a contest in which London was confident it could easily best those who were enamored with enslavement. But more than noble aims were involved. One official compared the mainland to a "chain, the upper part of which was strong and the lower weak," referring to Virginia southward, "on account of the number of Negroes in them." It was intimated that "if a few regiments were sent" to the latter provinces, "the Negroes would rise and embrue their hands in the blood of their masters," which did not seem overly perturbing and probably underlined why there was opposition expressed to "conciliatory offers" to the rebels.[141]

What fueled the intensity of this conflict was the perception in London that the rebels were little more than hypocritical gasbags, a perception fueled by the bruised (human) property of the latter. It was also in the south, it was said in Parliament, where the "spirit of liberty" was "more high and haughty" than elsewhere, that is, precisely where there was a "vast multitude of slaves. Where that is the case in any part of the world, those who are free, are by far the most proud and jealous of their freedom. Freedom to them," it was said wisely, "is not only an enjoyment but a kind of rank and privilege," increasing exponentially the profundity of this state. "In such a people," it was stated, "the haughtiness of domination combines with the spirit of freedom, fortifies it and renders it invincible." What to do then? Suggesting that Lord Dunmore might actually have been less radical than some London counterparts, it was suggested to "reduce" the mainlanders "by declaring a general enfranchisement of their slaves," with jury trials being a first step:[142] these were radical measures that most U.S. Negroes would not enjoy for decades. Suggestive of the growing chasm between the metropolis and the provinces was that trial by jury for Africans—discussed in London in 1775—was miles ahead of the civil rights discourse in the emergent republic.

In a way, some of the more trenchant critiques of the colonists and their motives for revolt were confirmed by them. The important rebel James Iredell responded angrily in June 1776 to a purported "diabolical" plan by London of "exciting" the enslaved "to cut [colonists'] throats" and to perpetrate "universal massacre"; with bitterness, he said knowingly, "resentment for such cruel usage had added spurs to our Patriotism." To a degree, by seeking to enlist the Africans, London accelerated the resentment of the settlers, leading directly to its substantial losses in what had been a mighty British North America.[143]

Thus, one leading slaveholder had a point in arguing that "late Acts of Parliament" were "tending to create a might[y] difference between His Majesty's subjects" on the mainland and London, leaving settlers with the choice of seeking to "continue" as "free-men" or to "become Slaves."[144] The slave trope emerged too in May 1775 at the Continental Congress in Philadelphia, which embattled South Carolinians attended, along with John Hancock and other leaders. London's alleged attempt to "convert" colonists "from freemen to slaves" was decried heartily. The *Gaspee* was alluded to in referring to "hardy" efforts to "seize Americans and carry them to Great Britain, to be tried for offenses committed in the Colonies"—yet the overarching fright was the "horrors of domestic insurrection."[145]

Subsequently, John Adams mused about the "melancholy account" he heard from Georgians and Carolinians, particularly their apprehension that a redcoat offensive would mean that "20,000 Negroes would join" them, since the "Negroes have a wonderful Art of communicating Intelligence among themselves." The saving grace for the rebels was that many allies of the Crown too were slaveholders and were reluctant to unsheathe the weapon of abolition.[146]

Florida, then under British rule, did not join wholly the 1776 revolt and provides an indicator of why the Dunmore edict and the specter of arming Africans was taken so seriously. Because of the Spanish heritage, it became simpler for the governor to create four militia companies composed of Africans. During the post-1776 conflict, Africans played a significant role in Florida's defense and in launching offensive raids against Georgia.[147]

June 1772 and November 1775 were powerfully important landmarks on the road to 4 July 1776. Compelling loyal subjects to revolt against the Crown required a pervasively profound threat to the colonists' status quo—and the rapidly changing status of the African was tantamount to such a threat. The dilemma for Africans who sensed that freedom and an enhanced life were more likely to come from the metropolis, as opposed to the rebels who had devised a model of development based on their mass enslavement, was that if their understandable alliance with London did not pan out as conflict with the rebels sharpened, they would be bereft, surrounded by a sea of hostile U.S. patriots eager to pulverize those who, in their mind, had engaged in the darkest of betrayals.

10

The Counter-Revolution of 1776

Lord Dunmore's proclamation effectively barred any possibility of rebel reconciliation with London. As one subsequent analyst put it, "the people rose in revolt at the idea of an army composed" of Africans, "many fresh from the wilds of Africa" tromping through North America. The "reign of terror" this augured did "arouse the entire colony as nothing else could have done" and, in so many words, "forced war."[1] In response to this controversial edict, Virginia militarized further, forming thirty-two new volunteer companies and embarking irrevocably on the road to revolt.[2] Even the Duke of Manchester in May 1776 conceded that the "Americans were greatly incensed against the King" for "giving orders to arm the Indian tribes against them; and encouraging the blacks slaves to rise and cut the throats of their masters."[3] Lord Dunmore's edict appeared in full in many British newspapers, and Parliament debated it. Although the point is at times lost sight of in the glow of rebel victory, the fact was that there was staunch opposition to secession in London—and for good anti-slavery reason.[4]

London may have misjudged the virulence with which the colonists would view this edict, as suggested by a 1770s encounter in England endured by Josiah Quincy of Massachusetts, who was admired by both John Adams and Benjamin Franklin. A "Whig sympathizer" observed "how lucky it was that Quincy had come, since more than 'two thirds at that time thought the Americans were all Negroes!'" Perhaps thinking North America was demographically akin to the Caribbean helped bolster the controversial edict. An angered Quincy, in turn, reverted to the now familiar—and effective—rallying cry of the rebels, replying that the "majority" in the isles not only "thought" they were mostly Negroes but "still treated them as such."[5]

Lord Dunmore's proclamation should not have been viewed as overly shocking. Since Somerset's case, there had been growing polarization, with some pro-slavery militants beginning to develop ever more racially colored justifications for slavery in response to incipient abolitionism. In early 1775, some anti-rebel advocates had anticipated Lord Dunmore by proposing an armed assault on the southern colonies since Africans would instinctively back the redcoats, bringing a quick end to the conflict. Even Edmund Burke had mulled the explosive idea of "general enfranchisement" of the enslaved in order to "reduce" the South. Samuel Johnson had toasted the "next insurrection of the Negroes in the West Indies" and declared himself quite willing to "love all men except an American." Earlier he had referred contemptuously to mainland settlers as a "race of convicts" who sought to convert Africans to Christianity in order to make them docile.[6] Settlers in South Carolina and Georgia acknowledged in 1775 that if a mere one thousand redcoats had landed in the latter province and if their commander had handed out a few enticements to Africans—accompanied by a declaration of freedom for them—he would be instantly joined by twenty thousand Africans, including those fleeing from South Carolina.[7] All the while, colonists were grousing about being treated like "slaves" and yearning for secession.

*   *   *

During the first week of December in 1775, rebels convened, and the white hot rhetoric flowed with passion about "despotism," focused heavily on the edict. Lord Dunmore, it was said, was "assuming powers which the King himself cannot exercise"; strategically, their first "resolve" chose to offer a "pardon" to those Africans who "shall return in their duty," though it was unclear how many accepted this offer. Tactlessly, this was accompanied by another resolution promising "death" to those Africans who followed Lord Dunmore's "wicked step," which "excited our slaves to rebellion."[8] Lord Dunmore had "startled the insurgents," said Governor Thomas Gage in Boston, leaving him with "few" who were "Friends" and leaving the "opposite Party numerous, active and violent."[9]

"Plantations had been ravaged," claimed rebels in early 1776, at the behest of "a lawless plundering soldiery and the more savage slave," with the "wives and children stripped almost to nakedness, their very bed-chambers invaded," as they were "treated with every indignity."[10] By

March 1776, Lord Dunmore was "endeavouring to raise two Regiments here, one of White people, the other of Black"—he should not have been surprised to ascertain that recruitment for "the former" proceeded "very slowly," while "the latter" proceeded "very well."[11] By April 1776, Major General Henry Clinton, a leading redcoat, was gloating alongside the Cape Fear River about the "forty or fifty Negroes" that had joined his forces: "I have determined to form a company of them," he said.[12]

The rebel response was swift, retributive, and, as noted, angrily vengeful: Africans captured after fighting alongside redcoats were to be "properly valued," then dispatched to the Caribbean or Central America, "there to be sold" with the proceeds "repaid to their respective owners, provided they are not unfriendly to American liberty."[13]

But luckily for the rebels, many of Lord Dunmore's African forces were felled by smallpox—"nine or ten of his black regiments every day," said one observer.[14] A stunning "150" of these "Negro forces" had "died within a short time," said one journalist,[15] and the fact that other Africans were fleeing en masse to British lines could not compensate for the shortfall.[16]

By May 1776, Thomas Jefferson was informed that these "shattered remains of the Ethiopian Regiment" were still planning an "attack," but now the prognosis for success was decidedly grim.[17] In response, Lord Dunmore's detractors charged that in addition to speedily "inoculating the blacks for the smallpox," "His Lordship" also "sent ashore" affected "wretches . . . in order to spread the infection, but it was happily prevented."[18] Lord Dunmore soldiered on, but depleted forces were not a prescription for strangling the infant of revolt in its cradle:[19] this outbreak of smallpox arguably foiled the plan to deploy Africans to squash the settlers' rebellion. Thus, by June 1776, the British mariner A.S. Hamond acknowledged bluntly that "Lord Dunmore and his fleet" were "in much danger from the enemy"—but if there had been more healthy Africans, he boasted, "I do not think it would be in the power of the Rebels to dispossess us." But such was not to be, and by August the same Hamond was lamenting the "sickly and weak state of the troops under Lord Dunmore's command,"[20] which doomed him to failure. If that were not enough, anti-London forces displayed remarkable unity, with Hamond marveling that "not a single man of any sort of consideration left the Rebels[']" ranks.[21] He did not connect rebel cohesiveness directly to the November 1775 edict of Lord Dunmore.

Intentionally or not, Lord Dunmore had poked a stick into a hornet's nest. One historian has observed that as early as the 1760s in Virginia it was "likely" that "every white person in the eastern counties knew of a free person who had been killed by a slave"; thus, "individual whites had nightmares about waking up amid slaves or feeling the first spasms of a stomach contorted by poison." They had just endured a remarkable spate of slave plots driven by the flux brought by the Seven Years' War[22]—and now it was being suggested that Africans armed by the state were going to be unleashed. Colonists had endured actual poisonings by the enslaved, had to squash slave revolts instigated by Spaniards, and now confronted Africans armed by London. It is little wonder that the settlers rose as one to oust London's rule.

Still, the rebels faced a real problem in launching war when so many within their ranks had counseled theretofore policies that meant bringing more Africans to North America, thus hampering their chances of prevailing against London. Thus, by December 1775, George Washington had endured a change of heart and now was willing to allow Africans in his ranks, a policy switch that was blamed on the British. There was a class element in this reversal, however, in that free Negroes were to be allowed, not the enslaved.[23] Still, given settlers' veritable phobia toward Africans of any sort, this was a breakthrough. However, as suggested by the aftermath of their victory, which led to a curtailment of the rights of even free Negroes, this was a temporary change of heart at best, driven by the relentless exigency of conflict.

Apparently when Washington arrived in Boston to confront the redcoats, he was shocked to find so many armed Africans,[24] and even during the dark days of early 1779 he resisted the "policy of arming our slaves."[25] Lord Dunmore had forced the hand of an outraged Washington and clearly influenced his reversal, as Africans too numerous to mention were in the process of fleeing to British lines. On the other hand, wittingly or not, London became identified with what one scholar has described as "race war" and "black supremacy,"[26] ideas which united settlers irreversibly as it complicated the postwar future of Africans insufficiently blessed to escape the charnel house of North America that had been created to entrap them. The conclusion stressed by one perspicacious writer, that the Negro was viewed as "*not* an American," a permanent outlier, an eternal alien, should be viewed in this context.[27]

*   *   *

Washington was joined by Jefferson in reversing field in that in the heralded Declaration of Independence of 4 July 1776 he sought to include
language upbraiding the Crown for inciting enslaved Africans—but this
incendiary language was stricken.[28] Also deep-sixed by Jefferson was
language he described as "reprobating the enslaving" of Africans, but
representatives of South Carolina and Georgia objected strenuously,
though he admitted that "Our Northern brethren," many of whom profited enormously from the slave trade, also dissented: "they had been
pretty considerable carriers of [Africans] to others," said the future president with accuracy.[29] Like many Africans, the exiled Thomas Hutchinson, the last colonial governor of Massachusetts, found Jefferson's Declaration to be the epitome of casuistry. If the rights enumerated were
so "absolutely inalienable," he asked querulously, how could the august
delegates reconcile depriving so many Africans "of their rights to liberty"?[30] One astonished resident in Bristol, England, remarked after
reading the Declaration that "one would imagine that the Parliament
of Great Britain . . . had treated" the rebels "with as great cruelty and as
much injustice as they [rebels] . . . treat their Negro slaves."[31]

    As for the final member of the founding troika, John Adams, as the
unveiling of Jefferson's handiwork approached, he was in intense dialogue about events in North Carolina, whose governor, Josiah Martin, was
deemed to be Lord Dunmore's companion in perfidy. The future president's interlocutor informed him in April 1776 that this governor's reputed
"wicked" maneuvers had "totally changed the Temper and disposition of
the Inhabitants that are Friends to Liberty," meaning rebels; support for
the Crown virtually disintegrated—"a total separation is what they want,"
Adams was told. "Independence is the word most used," with "in many
Counties not one dissenting voice."[32] Adams found this to be "very encouraging," as he renounced the "baseness and cruelty" of his correspondent's
"Enemies" and embraced the "Wisdom, Virtue and Valour of North Carolina."[33] It was in June 1775 that the feasibility of neutering London's advantage among Africans by taking abolitionist steps was recommended to
Adams, though worry was expressed that this could simultaneously wreck
the rebel cause among the all-important slaving lobby. Thus, this step was
to prove to be a bridge too far for all concerned.[34] This also indicates why

observers should view with skeptical restraint the crassly pragmatic post-1776 attempt by rebels to recruit and assuage Africans—as suggested by Washington's overtures to free Negroes—a solicitude that virtually disintegrated on cue after London was ousted from the thirteen colonies.

Adams was a savvy politician in that he was able to ride the wave generated by Governor Martin—though Africans were the losers in almost every respect.[35] Echoing the perverse motto of the era, it was Adams who bluntly informed the Crown that the settlers "won't be their [London's] Negroes."[36] Yet the dilemma of the settlers there was exposed when it was revealed that within months of Governor Martin's perceived perfidy, enslaved Africans were still pouring into the colony from abroad.[37]

Governor Martin was accused by his opponents of "arming the slaves against their masters," and they advised that this claim be "published as an alarm to the people" about the "horrid and barbarous designs of the enemies."[38] Governor Martin was outraged by the assertions "falsely imputed" to him, though by this point he had lost credibility with his supposed constituency.[39] By April 1776, what Governor Martin allegedly had proposed had been transformed into the more expansive proposal that "Governors in different colonies have declared protection to slaves who should imbrue their hands in the blood of their masters."[40]

Unfortunately for Martin, Africans in North Carolina were in the process of rebelling—which was the problem with rebutting the idea that they were aligned with London; for once this latter idea took off, it became captive to the plans of unruly Africans who did not necessarily coordinate closely with the Crown but whose plans were ascribed to London nonetheless. Just as settlers earlier had pointed to the supposed ubiquitous hand of Madrid in explicating African rebelliousness—which had the advantage of evading responsibility for their own awful maltreatment of slaves—with their armed revolt against His Majesty, it was now the ubiquitous hand of London that was the despised culprit.

For Governor Martin's denials seemed hollow when in July 1775 an "Intended Negro Insurrection" was uncovered in his backyard, a revolt bent on "destroying the inhabitants of this province without respect to age or sex." Reputedly, the combatants were to be "armed" by the state and, said rebel leadership, "settled in a free government of their own." Reportedly, "considerable ammunition" was found among those formulating this "accursed plan," designed to make settlers "easy prey."[41] Thus, by July 1775, one settler in this colony seemed on the verge of a nervous collapse: "Sound the alarm," cried John Simpson.[42] That a number of Africans said to be instigated by the Crown to revolt had secreted themselves in a fort near New Bern did not aid London's cause.[43] Once more there was a contagion at play, for in the months leading up to July 1776 there were various disturbances and alarms among the enslaved in Georgia, the Carolinas, Virginia, Pennsylvania, New Jersey, and New York, which alarmed and dismayed settlers accordingly.[44]

Increasingly, the bill of indictment against London was the perception that it had aligned with Africans against the settlers, confirming the calcified biases of those who long held a conception of Perfidious Albion, not least in South Carolina, where the longstanding African majority had kept colonists on edge.[45] Gabriel Manigault, a leading member of a leading family in the future Palmetto State—seemingly seeking to reassure himself, as much as others—asserted in September 1775 that there was "not so much reason to be afraid of the Negroes as was at first suspected"[46]—but, understandably, this was hardly a unanimous opinion. A keener indication of the trend that eventuated during the war emerged when George Washington was told in 1776 that in Charleston redcoats were quite deftly and successfully "encouraging our slaves to desert to them."[47] Others in Charleston were stunned by the "curious fact" that during this time of tumult "Negroes were engaged with white persons in wholesale robbery," reminiscent of a role often played by colonists: "pirates."[48]

So as the new year of 1776 was unfolding, a panicked rebel leadership found that a determined force of runaway Africans had gathered on Sullivan's Island, hard by what is now Charleston, to harass the patriot war effort allegedly in conjunction with British warships. For London and the Africans, this was a double-edged sword, associating the former with the horrors of Negro revolt, while associating the latter with resistance to what was coming to be seen as a sacred cause.

Suppressing African resistance became a crucial component of forging settler unity—and the solidifying identity that was "whiteness," which cut prodigiously across religious, ethnic, class, and gender lines. The forging of settler unity and the congealing identity that was "whiteness" also consolidated the developing connection between settlers' fear of alleged British enslavement, their own possession of Africans as chattel, and the fear that the relationship between master and slave could be reversed to their crushing detriment.[49] Again, these perceptions did not arise in a vacuum but were bolstered by the preceding decades of insecurity, often brought by Africans aided by a external forces—the "Catholic powers" and then London almost effortlessly assuming this villain's role.

Though the Charleston elite had good reason to suspect that bringing more Africans to their vicinity was inimical to the prospects for a victorious anti-London revolt, the enslaved kept arriving nonetheless.[50] Months before the Declaration of Independence, the Continental Congress meeting in Philadelphia forbade slave importations "into any of the thirteen United Colonies"[51]—which was wise since many of these Africans could be converted into redcoats—but this measure proved difficult to enforce given perceived production needs and skillful smuggling talents.[52]

Enslaved Africans continued to arrive in the colonies regularly, as the rebels continued to natter on about "liberty," and as evidenced by the thwarting of Jefferson's words to rebuff this trend, powerful interests seemed to envision no alternative to this mortal danger. More Africans were arriving and being implanted in fertile soil that associated their presence with an increasingly discredited foe in London—though, evidently, their presence was deemed necessary nonetheless. These contradictory strains were creating a symbiotic loathing and reliance upon Africans, with murderous surveillance deemed necessary to ensure they were at all times under control, a trend that did not necessarily abate with the founding of the new republic.

In addition, the continued importation of this problem people was costing hundreds of thousands of pounds sterling, driving a portion of the colony's elite into debt. Though this was understandably viewed as necessary for the economy, it was also the equivalent of continued importation of potential enemies. On the other hand, the slave trade had to be reconfigured, since relying upon Liverpool and Bristol was made more difficult by war. Why should human traffickers in Britain send slave labor to those who were rebelling against the Crown? Moreover, rebelling against foreign creditors can at times make smart business sense, particularly if you can outgun them. That the embattled settlers ultimately succeeded in ousting the British from the astronomically lucrative slave trade indicated they were astute assessors of a prime factor in developing capitalism: risk.[53]

Samuel Johnson may have had this issue in mind when he claimed that the rebels' revolt was driven in part by "associations of fraud to rob their creditors." As he saw it, this meretricious method defined their rebellion in that they boasted of their "contributions to the last war, a war incited by their outcries and continued for their protection, a war by which none but themselves were gainers"—but which they did not want to pay for in taxes. Above all, he was flabbergasted by their constant prating about liberty while continuing the enslavement of tens of thousands—"how is it that we hear the loudest yelps for liberty among the drivers of Negroes?" he asked mischievously. In words that could only deepen the schism with the rebels, in 1775 he counseled abolition of slavery and added none too diplomatically about the Africans, "if they are furnished with firearms for defense and utensils for husbandry and settled in some simple form of government within the country, they may be more grateful and honest than their masters."[54] Arm the Africans and indigenes to combat the rebels, he declaimed.[55] Naturally, Johnson was rebuked sharply by the rebels and their supporters, with a denunciation of Lord Mansfield also included for good pro-slavery measure.[56]

A London parliamentarian had suggested that if the settler revolt was successful, the then-profitable relationship between the Caribbean and the mainland would be disrupted, meaning the "inevitable ruin" of the former, thereby jeopardizing the slave trade and slavery.[57] This was prescient in a sense, for it is striking that after the revolt succeeded—and republicans surged to leadership in captaining the slave trade—abolition deepened its hold on London, which led inexorably to the destruction of slavery in the Caribbean.

When the republic was established, slave traders there, coincidentally enough, assumed control over one of the most important markets for the enslaved—that is, the mainland—which could then be leveraged for expansion into allied markets in Cuba, Brazil, and elsewhere (not to mention North America itself), while London was left with (mostly) small Caribbean islands.[58] By the early 1790s, republicans held a majority position in supplying Africans to Havana, placing them far ahead of those who had been the leaders: Madrid and London.[59] This development explicitly rebuked the irksome 1762 declaration of London concerning Cuba that had circumscribed mainlanders' participation in what was to become a deliciously profitable trade in human flesh.

This also carried implications for Cuba's neighborhood: In 1770, there were about 250,000 Africans in Hispaniola, and by 1790 this figure had doubled: what needs to be considered in this context as well is the extent to which Euro-American slave dealers provided the demographic imbalance that led to the Haitian Revolution.[60] "Gentry was the war's clear victor," says one perceptive historian of the eruption in Virginia that led to the founding of the U.S.:[61] he could well have added the overlapping but distinct category of slave traders.

Other than Virginia, South Carolina too had a major problem in launching an anti-London revolt, while worrying that its chances could be snuffed out easily by a rebellion of the enslaved. As in North Carolina, the border with Georgia was also afire, with the rumor that leading royal officials were plotting to ensure that slaves would become masters and masters would become slaves,[62] a rumor given weight by the controversies involving Lord Dunmore and Governor Martin. John Stuart, London's man in St. Augustine, dismissed this notion—though his very residence echoed memories of a time when organizing Africans to attack settlers was par for the course; he admitted that "nothing can be more alarming to the Carolinas" than arming Africans, while conceding the instrumental nature of such a claim in that its repetition meant that "Leaders of the disaffected Parties easily carried into execution their plan of arming the People," meaning settlers, instead.[63]

Stuart's residence in Florida may have given him a warped view, for this province was the dog that didn't bark, though it was under London's rule, like those thirteen to the north. Why did Florida not join the secessionists? Arguably, the legacy of Spanish Florida had not dissipated, that is, the presence of a corps of armed Africans and what had become an industry of annoying Georgia by providing refuge to escaping Africans. Still, there was worriment about arming Africans to confront rebels, though this was hardly avoidable. Moreover, Seminoles and Creeks had pledged to back the Crown. As things turned out, scores of armed Africans prevented the defection of Florida.[64] It is possible too that anti-Catholicism also hampered the attempt by the rebels to triumph in Florida,[65] a factor that may explicate the failure to bark of another conspicuously silent canine: perpetually restive Quebec, still smarting over perceived "Anglo" domination to this very day. A century earlier in the aftermath of Bacon's Rebellion, elites had accelerated the deployment of "race" and religion to sanctify rule through "whiteness," but Florida and Quebec suggested that by 1776 this remained a work in progress.

Whatever the case, weeks after 4 July 1776, Africans were flooding into St. Augustine from Georgia and the Carolinas, in a replay of what had occurred when Madrid was in control of this strategically sited port.[66] Simultaneously, with the pressure eased on that front, British official-dom was able to dispatch forces from St. Augustine to Virginia, a force that likely included Africans, for as one rebel noted at the time, the pres-ence of these redcoats had brought "exceeding bad effects . . . among the blacks."[67] For a year after these words had been uttered, rebel leadership in Georgia spoke nervously about the "British troops in Saint Augustine" and what that portended for the "vast numbers of Negroes" there, who were "sufficient to subdue" them. "In point of number the blacks exceed the whites and the ready channel of supply and secure retreat which Saint Augustine affords, render them much to be dreaded."[68]

Also hampering London's response was a factor that should have been anticipated, a factor that had caused the Crown to retrench to the mainland in the first place—Africans in Jamaica were on the warpath, necessitating the dispatching of troops that could have been helpful in smashing the rebels' revolt.[69] At a crucial moment in 1776 when London needed to concentrate its forces on the mainland, Sir Basil Keith, the governor, was alarmed by the "amazing and dangerous disproportion" of the slaves there,[70] which merited immediate attention. Thus, weeks after Jefferson's Declaration, Vice Admiral Clark Gayton of the Crown's forces confessed that mariners had to be diverted to suppress a "general Insurrection of the Negroes," forcing "martial law" and mandating that a flotilla be kept in the Caribbean—instead of heading northward—"for the safety" of Jamaica: this was deemed prudent since the "Rebellion" there "was to have been general throughout the island."[71] Seemingly pleased, one mainland periodical reported breathlessly that in Jamaica "provisions have become very scarce" since "the Negroes had actually rose and cut off several plantations"; derided were the "humane Butch-ers of Britain" who in 1772 had ordered forces redeployed from the island to the mainland in order "to cut [mainland settlers'] throats" and now were reaping the whirlwind.[72]

Ironically, a mainland revolt driven in no small part by opposition to abolition and perceived friendliness of the Crown to the Africans was aided immeasurably by a revolt against the Crown by Africans. Ironically still, just before the Africans revolted, the elite in Jamaica—not unlike their mainland counterparts—were complaining bitterly about taxes imposed upon the importation of the enslaved, though these imposts may have saved their lives.[73]

For a good deal of the post-1776 conflict with the rebels, London had to monitor carefully the unruliness of the Africans in the Caribbean—not least their combining with their counterparts in what was to become Haiti—which hindered the ability to suppress the rebels.[74] At the same time, London was becoming increasingly dependent on Africans, but because of the demographic imbalance racially in its colonies, the Crown was being forced in a direction contrary to that of the rebels.[75] With Paris aiding the rebels, London was rebuffed when it turned to France with a proposal to form a "cartel" against the Africans[76]—thereby compelling the Crown to pursue few options beyond working out an entente with Negroes.

*   *   *

There were many ups and downs on the road to formation of the new republic, but the die was cast with Somerset's case and Lord Dunmore's edict—and the decades of history that undergirded both: as the rebels cut deals with the once-derided "Catholic powers," especially France, the Crown's destiny was sealed. In a sense, London was lucky to escape with Canada. Yet all of the years in which London complained about settlers' trade with Paris and Madrid was an ironic premonition of what such commerce would lead to in the post-1776 era.

What one insightful historian has defined as a "white settler revolt" and the "white American War of Independence" was triumphant; Thelma Wills Foote adds that for many Africans, "it was their relocation to the British side, not the long march" to victory in the U.S., that meant moving from "slavery to freedom." For the upshot of the triumph of 1776, she says, "brought about the reassertion of slaveowner control over the enslaved black population in the new republic."[77] How many Africans fought on the "wrong" or losing side is open to debate,[78] though it is evident that—for the most part and understandably—Africans did not see their best interests vindicated by the establishment of the republic.[79] When the import of Somerset's case was extended to Scotland in 1778—and expanded—the perspicacity of these Africans was vindicated further.[80] According to one commentator, enslaved Africans on the mainland "secretly wished the British army might win, for then all Negro slaves will gain their freedom. It is said that sentiment is universal amongst all the Negroes in America"[81]—and this pro-London sentiment continued virtually until the surrender of the forces of Robert E. Lee, distinguished scion of a founding family who thought he was simply solidifying their legacy.[82]

Thus, the Connecticut legislature was not atypical in never demanding that masters free their slaves who fought in the anti-London revolt.[83] Delegates at the first constitutional convention in the state of New York deemed it to be "highly inexpedient" to debate slavery.[84] At the constitutional convention that encompassed the states, it was future president James Madison who argued that the still-bothersome Somerset's case necessitated that the U.S. Constitution include a rigorous clause mandating the return of enslaved fugitives, a policy that irritated relations between the republic and the Crown for decades to come.[85]

Both sides—but particularly the Crown, fighting thousands of miles away from headquarters—found that African soldiers often were more disciplined than others, perhaps because they had more at stake. Few Africans—unlike Europeans—had farms to tend during the harvest season, a time when the desertion rate among those with this obligation soared, as London discovered when it was conscripting forces for Havana and Cartagena years earlier.[86] Few Africans had Africans to monitor on said farms either, making it easier for them to focus on the tasks at hand. Few Europeans had to worry about being sold into slavery if captured on the battlefield. Those with such troublesome property had further reason to despise London when after the revolt's success, the Crown refused to compensate numerous republican slaveholders after "their" Africans fled.[87] According to one account, about twenty thousand enslaved Africans joined the redcoats, roughly the same number of European loyalists who joined regiments[88]—which does not account for free Negroes who acted similarly. Among the latter was Benjamin Whitcuff, a free Negro from Long Island, who joined the redcoats early on and spied for nearly two years—before the rebels caught him and hung him—though British troops arrived minutes after the rope was tightened, cut him down, and saved his life. He was joined in his pro-London crusade by an unnamed Negro who participated in a plot to kidnap George Washington.[89] Another free Negro, Samuel Burke, claimed that he personally slew ten rebels in one battle in North Carolina.[90]

The presence of so many enslaved Africans handicapped the rebels, particularly in South Carolina. In March 1779, a theme was sounded at the Continental Congress that was to resound throughout this conflict: Carolinians, it was reported, were "unable to make any effectual efforts with militia, by reason of the great proportion of citizens necessary to remain at home to prevent insurrections among the Negroes and prevent the desertion of them to the enemy." Because "great numbers" of the Africans were susceptible "either to revolt or to desert," rebels defensively and explicitly, in the crude practicality that became their hallmark, sought to form their own Negro regiment, if only to "lessen the danger from revolts and desertions by detaching the most vigorous and enterprising from among the Negroes."[91] That same year—1779—a French diplomat captured the dilemma of the rebels and, ultimately, why the Africans were to suffer so grievously for decades to come: the Africans, he said, repeating a phrase that had become tellingly common, "are the intestine enemies of this colony," he opined, "but the number of white men is too small in proportion to raise an outcry against the emancipation proposed [by] the English."[92]

It appeared that the repudiation of the Crown by the rebels had evoked the patriotic temper of the British while causing them to cast a jaundiced eye upon the repudiators. Noted writer and anti-slavery advocate Thomas Day captured this mood when he proclaimed that slavery was a "a crime so monstrous against the human species that all those who practice it deserve to be extirpated from the earth."[93]

Even today there are those in the isles who have refused to accept the glorious narrative that encapsulates the rebels' revolt in the U.S. Charles Hazzell of Tipperary, Ireland, recently pointed to the "Royal Proclamation of 1763" as the ignition for rebellion in 1776, since it "expressly forbade land ownership and settlement beyond the line of the Appalachian mountains," which was "to be reserved for Indian country" but which the settlers desired, along with a generous stocking of slaves. "For some colonials," he says, "this was hard to stomach," a lengthening list that included George Washington.[94] "The real flaws of the U.S. founding fathers," according to David Paul of the United Kingdom, writing recently, "were inherent in their motivation for the revolt against

British rule," since "they objected to a government that sought to protect peaceful Indians from the theft of their land and feared a court
system that had started to have grave doubts about enforcing slavery,"
that is, Somerset's case. "They therefore had to create a devolved structure that would stop central government interfering with local courts'
enforcement of land grabs or enforcement of slavery," he asserts.[95]

Whatever the case, it is evident that there is a disjuncture between
the supposed progressive and avant-garde import of 1776 and the worsening of conditions for Africans and the indigenous that followed upon
the triumph of the rebels. Moreover, despite the alleged revolutionary and progressive impulse of 1776, the victors went on from there to
crush indigenous polities, then moved overseas to do something similar in Hawaii, Cuba, and the Philippines, then unleashed its counter-
revolutionary force in 20th-century Guatemala, Vietnam, Laos, Cam-
bodia, Indonesia, Angola, South Africa, Iran, Grenada, Nicaragua, and
other tortured sites too numerous to mention.

*   *   *

It is also worth reiterating that the potent concept that is racism is necessary but insufficient in explaining the past and present plight of those
who are now designated as "African-American."[96] More to the point,
this beleaguered grouping has endured the misfortune of fighting and
losing a struggle that led to the formation of a slaveholding republic,[97]
then a Jim Crow regime,[98] and then becoming enmeshed in the inevitable structural inequality that flowed from indecisive victories over
powerful antagonists determined to implant bondage and apartheid.[99]
Of course, there have been self-inflicted wounds over the decades,
poorly understood, foremost being some U.S. Negroes' participation
in the assault on Native American sovereignty as Reconstruction was
writhing in its death throes.[100] Nevertheless, it has been inadequately
comprehended that those of African descent in North America have
suffered grievously from economic-cum-political persecution too, their
clumsy attempts to adhere to the diktat of Euro-American elites notwithstanding: the simple term "racism" does not necessarily encompass
this multi-headed hydra. This is the sad destiny of those who have not
triumphed wholly over powerful foes.

It is also the case that it is much too generous to conclude that the former slaveholding republic has suffered from a tragic flaw: it is more accurate to aver that this polity has suffered from a design flaw, that is, that it was not accidental that the fabled founders somehow "forgot" to include all of the former colonies' denizens in its bounty. Unavoidably, this design flaw led to a blazing conflagration that concluded formally in 1865.

In some ways, 1776 was an outgrowth of 1688: the result of "free trade in Africans" and resultant restiveness of overwhelming slave majorities in the Caribbean that drove the Crown to retrench on the mainland and the concomitant growth of the productive forces there, allowing North American colonies to strain at the leash held by the colonizer. Likewise, 1861 was an extension of 1776: the failure to resolve the nettlesome matter of slavery—indeed, augmenting this atrocious institution—culminated in bloody civil war. Strikingly, the supposed trailblazing republic and its allegedly wondrous Constitution had a fatal design flaw in the form of enhanced slavery, which caused it to crash and burn by 1861. As with Lincoln's anti-slavery edict, Lord Dunmore's offer applied most directly to Africans whose masters were not on his side. Like Lincoln, Lord Dunmore faced a strategic disadvantage on the battlefield which forced his hand. Williamsburg had an African majority—but was also a tinderbox of rebel enthusiasm. In this context, his edict was too attractive to resist since London's forces were stretched thin, reaching deep into the Caribbean not least: the long history of Africans rebelling against colonists was a lore that Lord Dunmore could hardly ignore.[101] But for the Africans who sided with London and Lord Dunmore, their decision—though understandable—was catastrophic, as the victorious rebels were able to claim the high ground of the Enlightenment, making their foes (even enslaved ones) appear to be misguided counter-revolutionaries.

The dilemma for those tarred as pro-London Negroes—which in the eyes of some meant the entire population of the enslaved—metastasized when the new republic flung open the doors for immigration. Thus, the first Congress in 1790 enacted a naturalization rule that made citizenship relatively simple to attain—for Europeans. "Free white persons" who resided in the United States for as little as two years could be naturalized. Subsequently, nativists complained bitterly that some of those gaining citizenship "scarcely knew" of the republic's existence before arriving at a mainland port. Yet, like starry-eyed devotees of the

"Enlightenment," they failed to note how this naturalization process aided republicans in overcoming the demographic challenge delivered by so many Africans and indigenes.[102]

Of course, to be fair, 1776 with its determined assault on the divine right of monarchs was inspirational globally, even to those who sparred combatively with the republic, such as Ho Chi Minh[103] and V.I. Lenin.[104] This foreign embrace of 1776 may be more a result of diplomatic niceties and protocol than anything else. The anti-monarchial emphasis of the republican revolt pragmatically forged a wider base of support by which the Crown could be attacked. It is not self-evident that the aristocracy of class and ancestry that obtained in London was less humane and more retrograde than the aristocracy of "race" that emerged in the aftermath of 1776 in the territory stretching south from Canada.

Speaking of Canada, this massive nation is a kind of control group allowing for a measurement of the fruits of 1776: is it the case that those groups—for example, Africans and the indigenous in the first place—who have been disfavored south of the St. Lawrence Seaway have fared worse than those of like ancestry north of this artery, notably in a way that would justify and sacralize the bloodletting that created the republic?

And speaking of more "loyal" appendages of an erstwhile empire, it is quite telling that Australia, so similar to the U.S. in so many ways, has endured a raging controversy about its origins as a violently implanted redoubt of white supremacy in a way that dwarfs and overshadows any such conversation in the presumed revolutionary republic.[105]

It is also true that the republic became a welcome refuge for asylum seekers fleeing barbarism in Europe. But context is necessary here too: the despotic dictatorship of Rafael Trujillo in Santo Domingo played a similar role—particularly for Jewish refugees who were turned aside elsewhere in the 1930s[106]—but few would downplay his meretricious motives in seeking to perfume via whitening his malodorous misrule by doing so, or would fail to consider his contemporaneously complementary massacring of darker-skinned Haitians in the thousands.[107] It would be ironic indeed if a perverse form of affirmative action were deployed to excuse or rationalize the misdeeds of a budding superpower, while trumpeting racially questionable offers of refuge, then simply castigating similar misdeeds of a developing nation.

Yet, though the creating of revolutionary regimes in France, China, and Russia—among others—has been subjected to withering analysis of their respective real and imagined debilities, the United States of America largely has escaped similar scrutiny of its origins, though it has been apparent for some time that the blessings of liberty escaped the grasp of the Africans and the indigenous most terribly: and this was hardly a matter of happenstance. And to suggest blithely, as some have, that 1776 created a template for the subsequent extensions of liberty to those who were initially excluded is similar to giving the jailers of apartheid credit for the enfranchisement of Nelson Mandela, while eliding neatly the stark commonalities that have linked white supremacy on both sides of the Atlantic.[108]

Indeed, given the braiding of slavery with independence in the origins of 1776 and the emergence of a superpower as a result, it is unavoidable that those who are concerned with overturning the toxic legacy thereby created have to build more consciously and forthrightly an anti-racist, pro-equality movement of global proportions. Sadly, simply tinkering legislatively and judicially in the domestic realm, given the current balance of forces, is plainly not up to the gargantuan task at hand.

This conclusion also derives from the many years I have spent as a political activist, as executive director of the National Conference of Black Lawyers, and as counsel to the premier hospital workers union now headquartered in Manhattan. After voting in—and participating in[109]—numerous U.S. elections including that of 2012, I find it striking that today the pundits are buzzing about the imminent decline of the Republican Party in light of the fact that this entity depends heavily on the "white" vote in a nation where this group's percentage of the electorate is declining.[110] Yet, remarkably, few are those who actually inquire as to why this sector tends to lean in a conservative direction[111] and, least of all, the deep historical roots of this phenomenon in a nation where not only was citizenship determined on a racist basis, but, furthermore, benefits were dispensed by the state in a similar fashion—and not just to elites.[112]

Few of the pundits have wondered if conservatism among Euro-Americans—notably in the working class and middle class—may hark back to the founding of the republic and a time when opportunity included becoming the owner of land once controlled by indigenes and stocked with enslaved Africans:[113] many in these classes likewise scrutinize with skepticism the opportunity today for multi-racial, multi-class coalitions which have advanced considerably beyond this troubled though still blindly heralded era. After all, when a comfortable majority of Euro-Americans voted across class lines for a Klansman and Nazi—David Duke—for governor of Louisiana in 1991, was this a simple display of "false consciousness" or a cagey wager that the clock of history can be reversed, particularly when there is glorification of the grimy origins of a former slaveholding republic?[114] Surely, the pro-Nazi majority had little incentive to dismiss the "Black Scare" which helped to propel a good deal of Duke's success, when this phenomenon helped to propel the founding of the tendentiously glorified republic in the first place.

Meanwhile, the descendants of enslaved Africans continue to suffer astronomical rates of incarceration, are disproportionately accorded the death penalty, and endure all manner of ills—with few scrutinizing the origins of the republic in search of a reason why. As I write, the ills just noted, which can fairly be seen as part of the legacy of slavery and Jim Crow, continue to be worked out in the most advanced capitalist nation, where I happen to reside. This is a cautionary note when contemplating the trajectory of the alternative modernity: socialism. It would have been premature to administer last rites to capitalism on the basis of the horrors of slavery, and, similarly, the well-known human rights violations that accompanied the rise of socialism should not be interpreted to mean that this project too is destined for permanent interment.

These ills which continue to afflict the descendants of enslaved Africans in North America—and the reasons why which stretch back to the republic's founding—are an issue that should animate study of and activism within what is now the U.S. as the 21st century unwinds.

NOTES

1. The primary value of this collection is that it assembles in one convenient spot a valuable compendium on colonial slavery from various archives.

2. The same desire to make the path smoother for future generations of scholars explains why—in some instances—I have provided in the following pages the location for some published (though rare) books. As practitioners know well, writing today about colonial slavery carries the heavy burden of having to rely profoundly on non-African sources produced by rulers, settlers, travelers, and the like. Still, this "defect" has the "advantage" of demonstrating the nervous apprehension of these forces about African militancy and how it shaped their resultant actions; though it is also fair to infer that the bias of such sources may magnify and heighten the "ordinary" panic felt by officialdom.

3. Hispaniola was a mini-version of the mainland in this regard and, thus, was to give rise to what I view as the abolitionist antipode of 1776—the Haitian Revolution.

4. Since this book concerns Africans who often were "commodities" and, thus, may have been resident in London one month and Charleston the next and Spanish Florida thereafter, the now normative term—"African- American"—is not always appropriate in this context. Thus, variously, such terms as "black" or "Negro"—or "African"—will be used to designate a population with roots on the African continent. Moreover, the term "African-American" used casually across the centuries to describe a grouping whose well-being varied wildly can be misleading and, ultimately, obscure a diminished (or nonexistent) citizenship status. Similarly, those whom I quote often use such terms as "Mulatto" and similar designations now viewed widely as archaic.

5. Christopher P. Iannini, **Fatal Revolutions: Natural History, West Indian Slavery, and the Routes of American Literature**, Chapel Hill: University of North Carolina Press, 2012, 282–283. See also Paul Pressly, **On the Rim of the Caribbean: Colonial Georgia and the British Atlantic World**, Athens: University of Georgia Press, 2013.

6. Gerald Horne, **The Deepest South: The United States, Brazil, and the African Slave Trade**, New York: NYU Press, 2007. See also Gerald Horne, **Exporting Slavery and Jim Crow: The U.S. and Cuba and the Road to Revolution**, forthcoming.

7. See, e.g., Gordon S. Wood, **The American Revolution: A History**, New York: Modern Library, 2001; Joseph J. Ellis, **Founding Brothers: The Revolutionary Generation**, New York: Knopf, 2000; Richard Brookhiser, **Founding Father: Rediscovering George Washington**, New York: Free Press, 1996. Cf. Herbert Aptheker, **The American Revolution, 1763–1783: A History of the American People: An Interpretation**, New York: International, 1960; and Howard Zinn, **A People's History of the United States: 1492–Present**, New York: HarperCollins, 2003. Ironically, the U.S. in a sense has emulated today's Cuba insofar as the operative slogan seems to be "within the Revolution everything, against the Revolution nothing." In other words, one can

quarrel about the destiny of the republic but—generally—not the eternal verity it is said to have created. Of course, left-wing republicans tend to emphasize the role of less grand Europeans in 1776 (those not of the left wing tend to stress the role of the Olympian Founding Fathers). Some of these historians tend to see the plight of Africans as the "original sin" of the republic (which begs the question of the dispossession of the indigenous). In any case, as I suggest in the concluding pages of this book, the left wing's misestimating of the founding is of a piece with their misestimating of the present: this includes a reluctance to theorize or historicize the hegemony of conservatism among the Euro-American majority—and an overestimation of the strength of the left wing among this same majority—which has meant difficulty in constructing the kind of global movement that has been essential in rescuing Africans particularly from the violent depredations that have inhered in the republic.

8. Kevin Phillips, **The Cousins' War: Religion, Politics, and the Triumph of Anglo-America**, New York: Basic Books, 1999.

9. Kevin Phillips, **1775: A Good Year for Revolution**, New York: Viking, 2012.

10. See, e.g., Joseph E. Inikori, **Africans and the Industrial Revolution in England: A Study in International Trade and Economic Development**, New York: Cambridge University Press, 2002. See also Eric Eustace Williams, **Capitalism and Slavery**, Chapel Hill: University of North Carolina Press, 1994. For slavery's contribution to the development of capitalism in Scotland, see T.M. Devine, **To the Ends of the Earth: Scotland's Global Diaspora**, London: Allen Lane, 2011. For a perspective on African resistance in North America to the development of capitalism, see, e.g., Christopher N. Matthews, **The Archaeology of American Capitalism**, Gainesville: University Press of Florida, 2010.

11. Edmund S. Morgan, **American Slavery, American Freedom: The Ordeal of Colonial Virginia**, New York: Norton, 2003.

12. Manisha Sinha, **The Counterrevolution of Slavery: Politics and Ideology in Antebellum South Carolina**, Chapel Hill: University of North Carolina Press, 2000.

13. See, e.g., Emory M. Thomas, **The Confederacy as a Revolutionary Experience**, Englewood Cliffs, New Jersey: Prentice-Hall, 1971, 1; Andre M. Fleche, **The Revolution of 1861: The American Civil War in the Age of Nationalist Conflict**, Chapel Hill: University of North Carolina Press, 2012; Stephanie McCurry, **Confederate Reckoning: Power and Politics in the Civil War South**, Cambridge: Harvard University Press, 2010. On the limitations of 1776 compared to its revolutionary counterparts, see, e.g., Theda Skocpol, **States and Social Revolutions: A Comparative Analysis of France, Russia, and China**, New York: Cambridge University Press, 1979. To the extent that 1861 was truly the logical heir of 1776, it becomes understandable why the so-called Confederacy was defeated militarily and not politically and that the detritus of citizenship garnered by formerly enslaved people was the diseased fruit of a poisonous tree.

14. Interestingly, just as the British monarchy was ousted from North America by republicans as it seemed to be moving toward abolition, a similar fate befell the Brazilian monarchy in 1889: see, e.g., Robert Cottrol, **The Long, Lingering Shadow: Slavery, Race, and Law in the American Hemisphere**, Athens: University of Georgia Press, 2013, 77.

15. See, e.g., Alan Gilbert, **Black Patriots and Loyalists: Fighting for Emancipation in the War for Independence**, Chicago: University of Chicago Press, 2012; Edward Countryman, **Enjoy the Same Liberty: Black Americans and the Revolutionary Era**, Lanham, Maryland: Rowman & Littlefield, 2012; Douglas R. Egerton, **Death or Liberty: African Americans and Revolutionary America**, New York: Oxford University Press, 2009; Seymour Drescher, **Abolition: A History of Slavery and Antislavery**,

New York: Cambridge University Press, 2009; David Brion Davis, **Challenging the Boundaries of Slavery**, Cambridge: Harvard University Press, 2003; Robin Blackburn, **American Crucible: Slavery, Emancipation, and Human Rights**, New York: Verso, 2011; Peter Linebaugh and Marcus Rediker, **The Many-Headed Hydra: Sailors, Slaves, Commoners, and the Hidden History of the Revolutionary Atlantic**, Boston: Beacon, 2000; John Huxtable Elliott, **Spain, Europe, and the Wider World, 1500–1800**, New Haven: Yale University Press, 2009; Jorge Canizares-Esguerra, **How to Write the History of the New World: Histories, Epistemologies, and Identities in the Eighteenth-Century Atlantic**, Stanford: Stanford University Press, 2001.

16. David Walker, **Walker's Appeal**, and Henry Highland Garnet, **Garnet's Address to the Slaves of the United States of America**, Salem, New Hampshire: Ayer, 1969 [in one volume]; W.E.B. Du Bois, **The Suppression of the African Slave Trade to the United States of America, 1638–1870**, New York: Longmans, Green, 1896.

17. Walter Rodney, **How Europe Underdeveloped Africa**, Cape Town, South Africa: Pambazuka, 2012.

18. Gerald Horne, **Blows against the Empire: U.S. Imperialism in Crisis**, New York: International, 2008. See also Martin Jacques, **When China Rules the World: The End of the Western World and the Birth of a New Global Order**, New York: Penguin, 2009; and Arvind Subramanian, **Eclipse: Living in the Shadow of China's Economic Dominance**, Washington, D.C.: Peterson Institute for International Economics, 2011. Experience has taught me that instead of defending the atrocious republican record in dealing with Africans, U.S. patriots instead assail the record of those with whom Africans are compelled to join in order to escape republican atrocities.

19. Thomas James Little, "The Influence of the West Indies upon Slavery in Colonial South Carolina, 1670–1740," M.A. thesis, University of South Carolina, 1989, 52. Interestingly, the plight of Africans in Florida deteriorated drastically after the U.S. takeover in the early 19th century: see, e.g., T.D. Allman, **Finding Florida: The True History of the Sunshine State**, New York: Atlantic Monthly Press, 2013. Cf. Emeka P. Abanime, "The Anti-Negro French Law of 1777," **Journal of Negro History**, 64(Number 1, Winter 1979): 21–29, 21: "Negrophobia was in all probability more pronounced in France than in England during this period." Of course, here one must distinguish the metropolis from the provinces. In a similar vein, see also Christopher Schmidt-Nowara, **Slavery, Freedom, and Abolition in Latin America and the Atlantic**, Albuquerque: University of New Mexico Press, 2011; and William B. Cohen, **The French Encounter with Africans: White Response to Blacks, 1530–1880**, Bloomington: Indiana University Press, 1980. See also Lawrence N. Powell, **The Accidental City: Improvising New Orleans**, Cambridge: Harvard University Press, 2013, 116: "Before the founding of Louisiana, the metropole had even encouraged manumission on its booming sugar island of Saint-Domingue; the Code Noir of 1685, in marked contrast to slave law in British America, went so far as to award freedom to children sired by free men, regardless of race, with slave women, provided that the couple legitimated their relationship through marriage." For example, both Berlin in the World War I era and Washington in the late 20th century were quite willing to be friendly toward so-called Islamic fundamentalism abroad—but not necessarily to the same extent at home. See, e.g., Sean McKeekin, **The Berlin-Baghdad Express: The Ottoman Empire and Germany's Bid for World Power**, Cambridge: Harvard University Press, 2010; and Odd Arne Westad, **The Global Cold War: Third World Interventions and the Making of Our Times**, New York: Cambridge University Press, 2005. See also Robert Dreyfuss, **Devil's Game: How the United States Helped Unleash Fundamentalist Islam**, New York: Metropolitan, 2005.

20. Roger Horowitz, **Negro and White, Unite and Fight! A Social History of Industrial Unionism in Meatpacking, 1930–1990**, Urbana: University of Illinois Press, 1997.
21. Frederick C. Knight, **Working the Diaspora: The Impact of African Labor on the Anglo-American World, 1650–1850**, New York: NYU Press, 2010; Nelson Lichtenstein, **State of the Union: A Century of American Labor**, Princeton: Princeton University Press, 2002; Gerald Horne, **Red Seas: Ferdinand Smith and Radical Black Sailors in the United States and Jamaica**, New York: NYU Press, 2005.
22. Glenn Feldman, ed., **Painting Dixie Red: When, Where, Why, and How the South Became Republican**, Gainesville: University Press of Florida, 2011; Chuck Thompson, **Better Off without 'Em: A Northern Manifesto for Southern Secession**, New York: Simon and Schuster, 2012.

NOTES TO THE INTRODUCTION

1. Steven M. Wise, **Though the Heavens May Fall: The Landmark Trial That Led to the End of Human Slavery**, New York: Da Capo, 2005, xiii, 193.
2. **Virginia Gazette**, 20 August 1772.
3. **New York Journal**, 27 August 1772. See also David A. Copeland, ed., **Debating the Issues in the Colonial Newspapers: Primary Documents on Events of the Period**, Westport, Connecticut: Greenwood, 2000, 279.
4. J. William Harris, **The Hanging of Thomas Jeremiah: A Free Black Man's Encounter with Liberty**, New Haven: Yale University Press, 2009, 71. See also William Max Nelson, "Making Men: Enlightenment Ideas of Racial Engineering," **American Historical Review**, 115(Number 5, December 2010): 1364–1394.
5. See, e.g., Richard Sheridan, "The Jamaican Slave Insurrection Scare of 1776 and the American Revolution," **Journal of Negro History**, 61(Number 3, July 1976): 290–308, 291, 292: "The First Maroon War involved the whites in a fifteen year (1725–1740) struggle against two groups of insurgents. . . . the Maroon leaders were chiefly Coromantee slaves. . . . after long years of losses from ambushes, skirmishes, disease and incompetent leadership, the whites sued for peace. The first treaty of March 1739 was signed between the whites and the Leeward Maroons commanded by Colonel Cudjoe. In 1740 similar terms were agreed to between the whites and Captain Quao, . . . but in 1760 . . . slaves on several plantations in the parish of St. Mary rebelled, broke into a fort and acquired arms and gunpowder. They then marched from plantation to plantation killing the whites and gaining black recruits. . . . the goal of the rebels was 'the entire extirpation of the white inhabitants.'" Thus, "before the rebels were defeated some 60 whites were killed and between 300 and 400 slaves were killed or committed suicide"; then "Coromantee headmen on seventeen estates in St. Mary's parish entered into a conspiracy to rise in armed rebellion sometime in July 1765. . . . one year later the Coromantees struck again, killing nineteen whites in Westmoreland parish. . . . in 1769 a number of slaves were involved in a plot to burn the city of Kingston and kill all its white inhabitants." See also Richard Price, ed., **Maroon Societies: Rebel Slave Communities in the Americas**, Baltimore: Johns Hopkins University Press, 1996; and Kathleen Wilson, "The Performance of Freedom: Maroons and the Colonial Order in Eighteenth-Century Jamaica and the Atlantic Sound," **William and Mary Quarterly**, 66(Number 1, January 2009): 45–86.
6. Claudius Fergus, "'Dread of Insurrection': Abolitionism, Security and Labor in Britain's West Indian Colonies, 1760–1823," **William and Mary Quarterly**, 66(Number 4, October 2009): 757–780, 758. See also Christopher L. Brown, "Empire without Slaves: British Concepts of Emancipation in the Age of the American Revolution," **William and Mary Quarterly**, 56(Number 2, April 1999): 273–308.

7. Christopher Hodson, **The Acadian Diaspora: An Eighteenth-Century History**, New York: Oxford University Press, 2012, 8.

8. Mr. Hargrave, "One of the Counsel for the Negro," "An Argument in the Case of James Somersett a Negro, Lately Determined by the Court of King's Bench . . . ," London: Author, 1772, *Duke University, Durham, North Carolina.*

9. **Virginia Gazette**, 7 May 1772.

10. Benjamin Quarles, **The Negro in the American Revolution**, Chapel Hill: University of North Carolina Press, 1961, 37.

11. Although some of the events in these pages stray beyond 1776, for the most part this book concerns events leading up to this fateful year. See, e.g., Alexander Tsesis, **For Liberty and Equality: The Life and Times of the Declaration of Independence**, New York: Oxford University Press, 2012; and Gwenda Morgan, **The Debate on the American Revolution**, Manchester: Manchester University Press, 2007.

12. On the catastrophe that befell indigenes before and after the 1776 turning point, there is a vast literature. See most recently Brendan C. Lindsay, **Murder State: California's Native Genocide, 1846–1873**, Lincoln: University of Nebraska Press, 2012. See also Michael Freeman, "Puritans and Pequots: The Question of Genocide," **New England Quarterly**, 68(Number 2, 1995): 278–293; Benjamin Madley, "California's Yuki Indians: Defining Genocide in Native American History," **Western Historical Quarterly**, 39(Number 3, 2008): 303–332. It is striking that the violently racist depredations in North America were often popularly driven by the mass of Euro-Americans, utilizing ostensibly democratic procedures—as opposed to state direction. As Bacon's Rebellion—discussed below—suggests, these revolts often targeted state authorities perceived as overly timid. Cf. Jan Gross, **Neighbors: The Destruction of the Jewish Community in Jedwabne, Poland**, Princeton: Princeton University Press, 2001. There have been a number of cases of genocide in past centuries; yet what makes the North American example relatively unique is that the perpetrators of bloody crimes have been hailed—virtually across the ideological spectrum—as being in the vanguard simultaneously of a great leap forward for humanity.

13. The sting of this conflict continues to bite, as evidenced by the recent declaration of Richard Coale Willson, Jr., of the republic, a self-described descendant of Thomas Bennett Willson, "a signatory of the Declaration of Independence." See **The Economist**, 7 January 2012: "The Catholic Calverts founded Maryland and brought in religious freedom, but by 1700 Maryland's legislature, influenced by Anglicans from Virginia, had passed laws forbidding all Catholics from holding office, voting, attending mass or receiving higher education. Rock Hall and other fine Catholic estates in Maryland had priest holes that hid clerics from the sheriff." See also James M. Woods, **A History of the Catholic Church in the American South, 1513–1900**, Gainesville: University Press of Florida, 2011; and Maura Jane Farrelly, **Papist Patriots: The Making of an American Catholic Identity**, New York: Oxford University Press, 2012.

14. See, e.g., Staughton Lynd and David Waldstreicher, "Free Trade, Sovereignty, and Slavery: Toward an Economic Interpretation of American Independence," **William and Mary Quarterly**, 68(Number 4, October 2011): 597–630. See also Woody Holton, **Forced Founders: Indians, Debtors, Slaves, and the Making of the American Revolution in Virginia**, Chapel Hill: University of North Carolina Press, 1999.

15. Vice-Admiral Vernon to His Grace the Duke, 26 April 1741, in **Original Papers Relating to the Expedition to Carthagena**, London: Cooper, 1744, *University of North Carolina, Chapel Hill.*

16. **A Comparison between the British Sugar Colonies and New England as They Relate to the Interest of Great Britain with Some Observations on the State of the Case**

of New England, to Which Is Added a Letter to a Member of Parliament, London: Roberts, 1732, *Huntington Library, San Marino, California.*

17. J. Massie, "General Propositions Relating to Colonies," April 1761, *Huntington Library.*

18. Charles Rappleye, Sons of Providence: The Brown Brothers, the Slave Trade, and the American Revolution, New York: Simon and Schuster, 2006.

19. Rachel Chernos Lin, "The Rhode Island Slave Traders: Butchers, Bakers, and Candlestick Makers," Slavery and Abolition, 23(Number 3, December 2002): 21–38, 31. See also Carleton Beals, Colonial Rhode Island, Camden, New Jersey: Nelson: 1970, 99: "the merchant class, especially the shipowners, were mostly in strong favor [of] independence and a number of them helped organize and direct the militant Sons of Liberty."

20. Lorenzo Greene, "The Antislavery Movement in New England from 1657 to 1781," no date, Box 91, *Lorenzo Greene Papers, Library of Congress.*

21. Report, 18 March 1742, Box I, Folder 5, *Daniel Parish Slavery Transcripts, New-York Historical Society, Manhattan.*

22. John E. Wills, 1688: A Global History, New York: Norton, 2001; Steven C.A. Pincus, 1688: The First Modern Revolution, New York: Norton, 2008; David S. Lovejoy, The Glorious Revolution in America, Middletown, Connecticut: Wesleyan University Press, 1987. See also Julian Go, Patterns of Empire: The British and American Empires, 1688 to the Present, New York: Cambridge University Press, 2011.

23. Eric Eustace Williams, Capitalism and Slavery, Chapel Hill: University of North Carolina Press, 1994; Joseph Inikori, Africans and the Industrial Revolution in England: A Study in International Trade and Economic Development, New York: Cambridge University Press, 2002; Walter Rodney, How Europe Underdeveloped Africa, Cape Town, South Africa: Pambazuka, 2012.

24. Susan Alice Westbury, "Colonial Virginia and the Atlantic Slave Trade," Ph.D. dissertation, University of Illinois–Champaign, 1981, 25, 79.

25. Lorenzo J. Greene, "Mutiny on the Slave Ships," Phylon, 5(Number 4, Fourth Quarter, 1944): 346–354, 346.

26. Lorenzo Greene, "Mutiny on the Slave Ships," 1944, Box 91, *Lorenzo Greene Papers.*

27. Matthew Parker, The Sugar Barons, New York: Walker, 2011.

28. Colin G. Calloway, The Scratch of a Pen: 1763 and the Transformation of North America, New York: Oxford University Press, 2006, 56.

29. William A. Pettigrew, "Free to Enslave: Politics and the Escalation of Britain's Trans-Atlantic Slave Trade, 1688–1714," William and Mary Quarterly, 64(Number 1, January 2007): 3–38, 33.

30. See "Debate on Act of 1750," Box 6, Folder 71, *Daniel Parish Slavery Transcripts.* On the growing number of Africans dragged to Manhattan in the 18th century, see, e.g., "Figures from 1750–1760," vol. 46, *Shelburne Papers, University of Michigan, Ann Arbor.*

31. Cf. Vladimir Shlapentokh and Joshua Woods, Feudal America: Elements of the Middle Ages in Contemporary Society, University Park: Penn State University Press, 2011.

32. Gerald Horne, Negro Comrades of the Crown: African Americans and the British Empire Fight the U.S. before Emancipation, New York: NYU Press, 2012; Gerald Horne, The Deepest South: The United States, Brazil, and the African Slave Trade, New York: NYU Press, 2007.

33. Cf. Joseph Crespino, In Search of Another Country: Mississippi and the Conservative Counterrevolution, Princeton: Princeton University Press, 2007; Dan T. Carter, From George Wallace to Newt Gingrich: Race in the Conservative Counterrevolution, 1963–1994, Baton Rouge: Louisiana State University Press, 1996.

34. Jason T. Sharples, "The Flames of Insurrection: Fearing Slave Conspiracy in Early America, 1670–1780," Ph.D. dissertation, Princeton University, 2010, 24, 312.
35. Report, 26 January 1736, Folder 90, *Daniel Parish Slavery Transcripts*.
36. Report, 30 January 1729, Folder 91, *Daniel Parish Slavery Transcripts*. All spellings in quotations throughout the book are original.
37. **Journals and Letters of Eliza Lucas**, no city: Wormsloe, 1850, *Cleveland Public Library*.
38. **Journal of the House of Representatives of Massachusetts, 1737–1738**, Boston: Massachusetts Historical Society, 1934, 191.
39. Joseph Younger Blanks, Jr., "The Administration of Governor Josiah Martin in North Carolina," M.A. thesis, University of North Carolina, Chapel Hill, 1948.
40. Philip D. Morgan, "The Black Experience and the British Empire, 1680–1810," in Philip D. Morgan and Sean Hawkins, eds., **Black Experience and the Empire**, New York: Oxford University Press, 2004, 86–100, 87, 89.
41. Mark Stoyle, **Soldiers and Strangers: An Ethnic History of the English Civil War**, New Haven: Yale University Press, 2005, 92–92.
42. Minutes of Council in Assembly, South Carolina, 24 January 1748, Box II, Folder 6, *Daniel Parish Slavery Transcripts*.
43. John Preston Moore, **Revolt in Louisiana: The Spanish Occupation, 1766–1770**, Baton Rouge: Louisiana State University Press, 1976, 191.
44. See, e.g., Charles King, "The Scottish Play: Edinburgh's Quest for Independence and the Future of Separatism," **Foreign Affairs**, 91(Number 5, September–October 2012): 113–124.
45. Barbara De Wolfe, ed., **Discoveries of America: Personal Accounts of British Emigrants to North America during the Revolutionary Era**, New York: Cambridge University Press, 1997, 156; Scotus Americanus, **Information Concerning the Province of North Carolina: Addressed to Emigrants from the Highlands and Western Isles of Scotland**, Glasgow: Knox and Elliot, 1773, *University of North Carolina, Chapel Hill*. Cf. Emma Rothschild, **The Inner Life of Empires**, Princeton: Princeton University Press, 2011.
46. List of Land Grants to Scots, 4 November 1767, CGP 10, *William Tryon Papers, North Carolina State Archives, Raleigh*.
47. Arthur Lee to Lt. Governor Colden of New York, 13 February 1776, in Jared Sparks, ed., **The Diplomatic Correspondence of the American Revolution, Volume II**, Boston: Hale and Gray and Bowen, 1829, 8.
48. Richard Archer, **As If an Enemy's Country: The British Occupation of Boston and the Origins of Revolution**, New York: Oxford University Press, 2010, 117. For the Hancock quote, see Nathaniel Philbrick, **Bunker Hill: A City, a Siege, a Revolution**, New York: Viking, 2013, 24.
49. Quoted in Moore, **Revolt in Louisiana**, 45.
50. Lorena S. Walsh, **Motives of Honor, Pleasure, and Profit: Plantation Management in the Colonial Chesapeake, 1607–1763**, Chapel Hill: University of North Carolina Press, 2010, 201, 203, 204.
51. Alejandro de la Fuente, **Havana and the Atlantic in the Sixteenth Century**, Chapel Hill: University of North Carolina Press, 2008, 2, 175, 181.
52. Don Juan Francisco de Guemes y Horcasitas to Don Manuel de Montiano, 2 June 1742, in **Collections of the Georgia Historical Society, Volume VII, Part III, the Spanish Official Account of the Attack on the Colony of Georgia in America, and of Its Defeat on St. Simons Island by General James Oglethorpe**, Savannah, Georgia: Savannah Morning News, 1913, 32–35, *Georgia Historical Society, Savannah*.

53. Philip D. Morgan, **Slave Counterpoint: Black Culture in the Eighteenth-Century Chesapeake and Low Country**, Chapel Hill: University of North Carolina Press, 1998, 11.
54. James Oglethorpe to Trustees, 28 May 1742, in Lucian Lamar Knight, ed., **The Colonial Records of the State of Georgia, Volume 23**, Atlanta: Byrd, 1914, 333, *Western Reserve Historical Society, Cleveland, Ohio.*
55. Report of South Carolina Committee Tasked to Investigate "Causes of the Disappointment of Success in the Late Expedition against Saint Augustine . . . ," 1 July 1741, PRO30/47/14, *National Archives of the United Kingdom, London.*
56. James Oglethorpe, **A New and Accurate Account of the Provinces of South Carolina and Georgia**, London: Worrall, 1733, 50, *Huntington Library.* (Oglethorpe is listed as author in the catalogue but not the text itself.)
57. **The Economist**, 24 November 2012. On this turning point in contemporary Spanish history, see also **Financial Times**, 23 November 2012; and **Wall Street Journal**, 23 November 2012.
58. See, e.g., Margaret Davis Cate, "Fort Frederica and the Battle of Bloody Marsh," **Georgia Historical Quarterly**, 27(Number 2, June 1943): 111–174, 174.
59. Patrick Riordan, "Finding Freedom in Florida: Natives Peoples, African Americans and Colonists, 1670–1816," **Florida Historical Quarterly**, 75(Number 1, Summer 1996): 24–43, 20.
60. See, e.g., "Minutes of Council in Assembly and House of Burgesses," 24 June 1732, Folder 191, *Daniel Parish Slavery Transcripts*: "making more effectual provision against invasions and insurrections"; in the same collection, see also "Minutes of Council in Assembly and House of Burgesses," 18 November 1738, Folder 192: "making provisions against invasions and insurrections"; "Minutes of Council in Assembly and House of Burgesses," 8 June 1757, Folder 194: more on apprehensions about a combined invasion and insurrection. In Folder 195, see "Minutes of House of Burgesses," 3 March 1759: more on same topic.
61. Pankaj Mishra, **From the Ruins of Empire: The Intellectuals Who Remade Asia**, New York: Farrar, Straus and Giroux, 2012, 23.
62. Admiralty to Sir George Pocock, 18 February 1762, in David Syrett, ed., **The Siege and Capture of Havana, 1762**, London: Navy Records Society, 1870, *American Antiquarian Society, Worcester, Massachusetts.*
63. Susan Parker, "African Americans in Florida and the Caribbean, 1763–Today," 1999, Vertical File, *St. Augustine (Florida) Historical Society*: "Among the 3100 evacuees" in 1763, "embarking St. Augustine, Spanish officials counted 420 persons of African ancestry—350 slaves and 80 free blacks and mulattos," most of whom went to Cuba.
64. Daniel L. Schafer, "'Yellow Silk Ferret Tied around Their Wrists': African Americans in British East Florida, 1763–1784," no date, Vertical File, *St. Augustine Historical Society.*
65. James W. Raab, **Spain, Britain, and the American Revolution in Florida, 1763–1783**, Jefferson, North Carolina: McFarland, 2008, 75.
66. Quoted in William I. Ramsey, **The Yamasee War: A Study of Culture, Economy, and Conflict in the Colonial South**, Lincoln: University of Nebraska Press, 2008, 163. Cf. Robert Glenn Parkinson, "Enemies of the People: The Revolutionary War and Race in the New American Nation," Ph.D. dissertation, University of Virginia, 2005.
67. Governor William Gooch to "Popple," 18 May 1736, *Transcriptions of William Gooch Correspondence, Rockefeller Library, Williamsburg, Virginia.*
68. Official in Antigua to Lord Commissioners of Trade and Plantations, 22 January 1751, Folder 88, *Daniel Parish Slavery Transcripts.*

69. "Instructions for Our Right Treaty and Right . . . ," 17 March 1756, *Transcriptions of Francis Fauquier Correspondence, Rockefeller Library.*

70. Jeffrey Amherst to Francis Fauquier, 23 May 1762, *Transcriptions of Francis Fauquier Correspondence*: "a distinction might be made between their offspring and the Descendants of an Englishman, with whom they never were to be accounted equal. This . . . may seem to carry an air of severity to such as are unacquainted with the Nature of Negroes and the pride of a manumitted slave, who looks on himself immediately on his acquiring his freedom to be as good a man as the best of his Neighbours, but especially if he is descended of a white Father or Mother . . . and as most of them are the Bastards of some of the worst of our imported Servants and Convicts." See also Affidavit of James Stokes, 7 August 1776, SP78/300, *National Archives of the United Kingdom, London.*

71. Quoted in Gary B. Nash, **The Unknown American Revolution: The Unruly Birth of Democracy and the Struggle to Create America**, New York: Viking, 2005, 158.

72. **Pennsylvania Gazette**, 27 March 1776, in Peter M. Bergman and Jean McCarroll, compilers, **The Negro in the Continental Congress, Volume I**, New York: Bergman, 1969, 6.

73. Philip J. Schwarz, introduction to Schwarz, ed., **Slavery at the Home of George Washington**, Mount Vernon, Virginia: MVLA, 2001, 1.

74. Lorena S. Walsh, "Slavery and Agriculture at Mount Vernon," in Schwarz, **Slavery at the Home of George Washington**, 47–77, 56.

75. For an example of Adams's handiwork on behalf of slaveholders, see Document, in L.K. Wroth and H.B. Zobel, eds., **Legal Papers of John Adams, Volume II**, Cambridge: Harvard University Press, 1965, 48.

76. Vincent Carretta, **Phillis Wheatley: Biography of a Genius**, Athens: University of Georgia Press, 2011, 103.

77. James Madison to William Bradford, 26 November 1774, in William T. Hutchinson and William M.E. Rachal, eds., **The Papers of James Madison, Volume I, 16 March 1751–December 1779**, Chicago: University of Chicago Press, 1962, 129–130.

78. J. William Harris, **The Hanging of Thomas Jeremiah: A Free Black Man's Encounter with Liberty**, New Haven: Yale University Press, 2009, 3, 4 (quote), 85.

79. Julie Flavell, **When London Was Capital of America**, New Haven: Yale University Press, 2010, 40, 166. See also Catherine Molineux, **Faces of Perfect Ebony: Encountering Atlantic Slavery in Imperial Britain**, Cambridge: Harvard University Press, 2012.

80. Remarks by "Mr. Hartley," 1775, "Parrish Transcripts from Printed Sources and Historical Notes of Daniel Parrish," *Daniel Parish Slavery Transcripts*. In the same collection, see also Letter to Benjamin Franklin, 14 November 1775, "U.S. to 1815 Miscellaneous." This same proposal is made directly: "it would be a satisfaction to receive some respectable or authentic opinion from America upon that subject . . . might give some chance of preventing blood[shed]." Thus, colonies "should endeavour to establish some system by which slavery might in a certain term of years be abolished." For more on this proposal, see Debate in House of Commons, 4 November 1775, in R.C. Simmons and P.D.G. Thomas, eds., **Proceedings and Debates of the British Parliaments Respecting North America, 1754–1783, Volume VI, April 1775 to May 1776**, White Plains, New York: Kraus, 1987, 169–170. Even Edmund Burke, viewed in today's republic as a patron saint of conservatism, not only opposed slavery but in 1765 opposed a plan to seat North American representatives in Parliament since the delegation would include slaveholders: see Drew Maciag, **Edmund Burke**

in America: **The Contested Career of the Father of Modern Conservatism**, Ithaca: Cornell University Press, 2013, 12–13.

81. Gerald Horne, **From the Barrel of a Gun: The United States and the War against Zimbabwe, 1965–1980**, Chapel Hill: University of North Carolina Press, 2001. See also David Armitage, "Secession and Civil War," in Don H. Doyle, ed., **Secession as an International Phenomenon: From America's Civil War to Contemporary Separatist Movements**, Athens: University of Georgia Press, 2010, 37–55, 48–49: "The Declaration of Independence was the first formal proclamation in world history. . . . it was also the first *unilateral declaration* of independence" (emphasis original). See also Carl Watts, **Rhodesia's Unilateral Declaration of Independence: An International History**, New York: Palgrave, 2012.

82. Blas Roca, **The Cuban Revolution: Report to the Eighth National Congress of the Popular Socialist Party of Cuba**, New York: New Century, 1961, 71.

83. Philip S. Foner, **Antonio Maceo: The "Bronze Titan" of Cuba's Struggle for Independence**, New York: Monthly Review Press, 1977.

84. Theodore G. Vincent, **The Legacy of Vicente Guerrero: Mexico's First Black Indian President**, Gainesville: University Press of Florida, 2001.

85. Kenneth W. Mack, **Representing the Race: The Creation of the Civil Rights Lawyer**, Cambridge: Harvard University Press, 2012, 33–34. See also Alice Kaplan, **Dreaming in French: The Paris Years of Jacqueline Bouvier Kennedy, Susan Sontag, and Angela Davis**, Chicago: University of Chicago Press, 2012. See also James Weldon Johnson, **Along This Way: The Autobiography of James Weldon Johnson**, New York: Viking, 1933, 65: The former NAACP leader evaded Jim Crow by speaking Spanish while observing, "in such situations, any kind of a Negro will do; provided he is not one who is an American citizen." See also Babs Gonzales, **I Paid My Dues: Good Times . . . No Bread**, New York: Lancer, 1967: This U.S. Negro—and noted musician—adopted a Spanish-tinged nom de guerre in order to escape the persecutorial obloquy he felt was the birthright of descendants of mainland enslaved Africans. Born Lee Brown in Newark, at times he sported a turban and referred to himself as "Ram Singh" for similar reasons. Though I use the terms "racism" and "racist" in this book to characterize what has befallen Africans on this continent over the centuries, my own view—as the foregoing suggests—is that a more accurate descriptor of their (our) plight is a collective political (and economic) persecution based on a refusal to accept passively the proclamation of a slaveholders' regime, then a Jim Crow regime, then massive inequalities stemming from the two. Thus, my deployment of the terms "racist" and "racism" is intended to invoke the political more than the biological or even the anthropological. If the latter were mostly at issue, there would be little need for these Africans to adopt other "black" identities. See, e.g., Press Release, March 1953, Reel 51, #108, Part 1, Series B, *Claude Barnett Papers, North Carolina State University, Raleigh*: "Negro Folklore is replete with tales of U.S. Negroes who, having gained fluency in a foreign tongue, succeed in dining and residing in accommodations normally closed to them." In the same collection, Press Release, Reel 46, #751, August 1951: "Dr. Suliente Suiman, . . . [a] dark skinned physician" visiting Dixie, "said she did not wear her native dress while visiting the South . . . hoping to be mistaken for a Negro. Although she sat in the front of buses and stayed at white hotels, nothing happened. She decided this was because of her foreign accent." Also in the same collection, see Reel 46, #850, September 1951: "At Miami airport Negroes are not Jim-Crowed as to washrooms nor is there enforcement of the sign 'White Passengers Seat from the Front' on the airport bus . . . for fear of antagonizing West Indian visitors who are also black." See also Colonel Hubert Julian, **Black Eagle as Told to John Bulloch**, London: Jarrolds, 1964. Born in Trinidad in 1909, Julian

found fame and fortune in the U.S. and argued that his "British accent" worked to his advantage in Dixie. During the Jim Crow era, certain U.S. leaders suggested that African diplomats visiting the republic wear a special "button" so they could be distinguished from U.S. Negroes and thus escape the indignities of apartheid: see Gerald Horne, **Mau Mau in Harlem? The United States and the Liberation of Kenya**, New York: Palgrave, 2009, 218. (Obviously, the inference should not be drawn that the dark-skinned bereft of mainland roots managed to escape bias altogether: a relative comparison is being made here with U.S. Negroes and their unique suffering.) Cf. Gerald Horne, **Black and Brown: African Americans and the Mexican Revolution, 1910–1920**, New York: NYU Press, 2005: The U.S. authorities also have been more flexible in their bigotry than some analysts imagine; for example, aligning with the usually degraded African Americans in the southwest and west of the republic against the interests of the indigenous and persons of Mexican origin in certain instances. In some ways, the term "race" is misleading when employed as shorthand to capture the cruel dilemma of Africans within the republic, for—perhaps not accidentally—it encourages some within this oppressed group to view potential allies from Madrid to Moscow as bearing the same "racism" and retrograde attitudes as too many Euro-Americans simply because they are "white."

86. Horne, **Negro Comrades of the Crown**.
87. Winthrop Jordan, **White over Black: American Attitudes toward the Negro, 1550–1812**, Chapel Hill: University of North Carolina Press, 1968.
88. Gerald Horne, **Black and Brown: African Americans and the Mexican Revolution, 1910–1920**, New York: NYU Press, 2005.
89. Gerald Horne, **Race War! White Supremacy and the Japanese Attack on the British Empire**, New York: NYU Press, 2003. See also Gerald Horne, **The White Pacific: U.S. Imperialism and Black Slavery in the South Seas after the Civil War**, Honolulu: University of Hawaii Press, 2007.
90. Gerald Horne, **The End of Empires: African Americans and India**, Philadelphia: Temple University Press, 2008.
91. Gerald Horne, **Black Liberation / Red Scare: Ben Davis and the Communist Party**, Newark: University of Delaware Press, 1994. See also Gerald Horne, **Black Revolutionary: William Patterson and the Globalization of the African American Freedom Struggle**, Urbana: University of Illinois Press, 2013.
92. Michelle Alexander, **The New Jim Crow: Mass Incarceration in the Age of Colorblindness**, New York: New Press, 2010. As the book in hand will seek to demonstrate, today's proclamation that this republic is "color-blind" and the related attempt to obstruct claims for equity by the population of African descent on the basis of this premise is simply another way to obscure the racially chauvinistic roots—and continuing legacy—of slavery and Jim Crow.

NOTES TO CHAPTER 1

1. **A Continuation of the State of New England, Being a Farther Account of the Indian War . . . Together with an Account of the Intended Rebellion of the Negroes in the Barbadoes**, London: Dorman, Newman, 1676, *Huntington Library, San Marino, California.* See also Melanie J. Newton, **The Children of Africa in the Colonies: Free People of Color in Barbados in the Age of Emancipation**, Baton Rouge: Louisiana State University Press, 2008.
2. **Great Newes from the Barbadoes, or A True and Faithful Account of the Grand Conspiracy of the Negroes against the English and Happy Discovery of the Same with the Number of Those That Were Burned Alive, Beheaded, and Otherwise Executed for Their Horrid Crimes . . .** , London: Curtis, 1676, *Huntington Library*

(this work can also be found at Brown University, Providence, Rhode Island): The Africans were set to "have defaced the most flourishing colony the English have in the world. . . . the conspiracy first broke out and was hatched by the Coromantee or Gold Coast Negro . . . about three years since and afterwards cunningly and clandestinely carried and kept secret, even from the knowledge of their own wives. . . . their grand design was to choose them a King. . . . I am induced to believe they intended to Murther all the White People there. . . . this little spot [e]mploying every year above 100 good Merchant Ships to carry off its product."

3. Minutes from the Council of Jamaica, 3 September 1675, in W. Noel Sainsbury, ed., **Calendar of State Papers, Colonial Series, Volume IX, America and West Indies, 1675–1676, Also Addenda, 1574–1674**, London: Eyre and Spottiswoode, 1893, 274: "advices from Barbadoes concerning a late rebellion attempted by the Negroes there and on consideration of the dangers that might accrue to this island by the ill-government of Negroes, ordered that no Negroes concerned in the late rebellion or convicted of any other crime in Barbadoes be permitted to be bought or sold."

4. Sir Jonathan Atkins to Sir Joseph Williamson, 3 October 1675, in Sainsbury, **Calendar of State Papers, Volume IX**, 294.

5. Report, 16 September 1667, in W. Noel Sainsbury, ed., **Calendar of State Papers, Colonial Series, Volume V, America and West Indies, 1661–1668**, London: Longman, 1880, 499.

6. Cf. Norman Etherington, **The Great Treks: The Transformation of Southern Africa, 1815–1854**, New York: Longman, 2001.

7. Report, 1708 [*sic*], in "Transcripts from Printed Sources and Historical Notes . . . ," *Daniel Parish Slavery Transcripts, New-York Historical Society, Manhattan.*

8. Company of Providence Island to Captain Hunt, 19 March 1637, in W. Noel Sainsbury, ed., **Calendar of State Papers, Colonial Series, Volume I, America and West Indies, 1574–1660**, London: Longman, Green, and Roberts, 1860, 57.

9. Laws on Negroes and "Mutiny," in "Trade in Negroes and Slaves by the Royal African Company, 1663–1685," 23 October 1663, Folder 103, *Daniel Parish Slavery Transcripts.* In Folder 104, see "Trade in Negroes and Slaves by the Royal African Company, 1667–1692."

10. Michael J. Jarvis, **In the Eye of All Trade: Bermuda, Bermudians, and the Maritime Atlantic World, 1680–1783**, Chapel Hill: University of North Carolina Press, 2010, 57, 67, 104.

11. William Blathwayt to Thomas Lynch, 20 May 1682, *William Blathwayt Papers, Rockefeller Library, Williamsburg, Virginia.*

12. Larry Gragg, **The Quaker Community on Barbados: Challenging the Culture of the Planter Class**, Columbia: University of Missouri Press, 2009, 31.

13. Minutes of the Council of Jamaica, 15 December 1675, in W. Noel Sainsbury, **Calendar of State Papers, Colonial Series, America and West Indies, 1675–1676, Also Addenda, 1574–1674**, London: Eyre and Spottiswoode, 1893, 315.

14. See, e.g., Anthony Julius, **Trials of the Diaspora: A History of Anti-Semitism in England**, New York: Oxford University Press, 2010.

15. Minutes of the Assembly of Barbadoes, 28–29 September 1675, in Sainsbury, **Calendar of State Papers, 1675–1676**, 288. See also Robert Harry McIntire, **Descendants of Philip McIntire, a Scottish Highlander Who Was Deported by Oliver Cromwell Following the Battle of Dunbar, September 3, 1650, and Settled at Reading, Mass., about 1660**, Baltimore: Gateway, 1982; Robert W. Ramsey, **Studies in Cromwell's Family Circle and Other Papers**, Port Washington, New York: Kennikat, 1971. Oliver Cromwell, **Memoirs of the Protector, Oliver Cromwell, and of His Sons, Richard and Henry**, London: Longman, Hurst, 1820; **Diary of Thomas Burton, Esq., Member**

in the Parliaments of Oliver and Richard Cromwell, from 1656 to 1659 . . . , London: Colburn, 1828. See also **The Story of the Embarkation of Cromwell and His Friends for New England**, Boston: Clap and Son, 1866.

16. Kathleen Wilson, "Rethinking the Colonial State: Family, Gender and Governmentality in 18th Century British Frontiers," **American Historical Review**, 116(Number 5, December 2011): 1294–1322, 1309, 1311.

17. Thomas James Little, "The Influence of the West Indies upon Slavery in Colonial South Carolina, 1670–1738," M.A. thesis, University of South Carolina, 1989, 50.

18. Owen Stanwood, **The Empire Reformed: English America in the Age of the Glorious Revolution**, Philadelphia: University of Pennsylvania Press, 2011, 171. See also Hilary Beckles, **A History of Barbados: From Amerindian Settlement to Nation-State**, New York: Cambridge University Press, 1990.

19. Report from Mark Whiteing, 24 January 1686 and 2 February 1686, in Robin Law, ed., **The English in West Africa, 1685–1688: The Local Correspondence of the Royal African Company of England, 1681–1699, Part 2**, New York: Oxford University Press, 2001, 268, 269.

20. Report from Edward Searle, 12 September 1695, in Robin Law, ed., **The English in West Africa, 1691–1699: The Local Correspondence of the Royal African Company of England, 1681–1699, Part 3**, New York: Oxford University Press, 2006, 541. Cf. Stephen D. Behrendt, A.J.H. Latham, and David Northrup, eds., **The Diary of Antera Duke, an Eighteenth-Century African Slave Trader**, New York: Oxford University Press, 2010.

21. Jason T. Sharples, "The Flames of Insurrection: Fearing Slave Conspiracy in Early America, 1670–1780," Ph.D. dissertation, Princeton University, 2010, 28, 39, 66, 67.

22. Howard A. Fergus, "The Early Laws of Montserrat (1668–1680): The Legal Schema of a Slave Society," **Caribbean Quarterly**, 24(Number 1, March–June 1978): 34–43, 38, 41.

23. Letter from Richard Smith "from Charles Town in Charles County," 10 September 1689, Folder 175, *Daniel Parish Slavery Transcripts.*

24. Minutes of Council in Assembly and Minutes of the House of Burgesses, Folder 179, *Daniel Parish Slavery Transcripts.*

25. Sir William Stapleton to "My Right Honorable Lords," 27 July 1676, Folder 87, *Daniel Parish Slavery Transcripts.*

26. Thomas Gage, **A New Survey of the West Indies**, London: Clark, 1699, 7.

27. Marilyn Delevante and Anthony Alberga, **The Island of One People: An Account of the History of the Jews of Jamaica**, Kingston, Jamaica: Ian Randle, 2008, 10, 52, 55, 65: Though Jews were expelled from England in 1290, English law permitted this group to reside in Jamaica "before they were legally allowed to return to England." Yet in 1655 prominent Jews in Jamaica "helped the English to drive out the Spaniards." On the unrest in England that formed the backdrop for this invasion, see "A Person of Honor," **Cromwell's Bloody Slaughter-House, or His Damnable Designs Laid and Practiced by Him and His Negro's, in Contriving the Murther of His Sacred Majesty King Charles I Discovered**, London: Davis, 1660, *Huntington Library.*

28. Samuel Rawson Gardiner, **Cromwell's Place in History**, London: Longmans, Green, 1897, 14, 92, 100.

29. Orlando Patterson, "Slavery and Social Revolts: A Socio-Historical Analysis of the First Maroon War: Jamaica, 1655–1740," **Social and Economic Studies**, 19(Number 3, September 1970): 289–325, 289. R.C. Dallas, **The History of the Maroons, from Their Origin to the Establishment of Their Chief Tribe at Sierra Leone, Including the Expedition to Cuba for the Purpose of Procuring Spanish Chasseurs . . . , Volume I**, London: Strahan, 1803, 24, 26.

30. Charles Leslie, **A New History of Jamaica, from the Earliest Accounts to the Taking of Porto Bello by Vice-Admiral Vernon,** London: Hodges, 1740, 252.

31. Hender Molesworth to William Blathwayt, 16 February 1685, 25 March 1684, 9 April 1686, 6 August 1686, 9 February 1686, 12 March 1686, 16 June 1687, 4 January 1688, *William Blathwayt Papers.*

32. **An Abridgement of the Laws in Force and Use in Her Majesty's Plantations; (Viz.) of Virginia, Jamaica, Barbadoes, New England, New York, Carolina . . . ,** London: Nicholson, 1704, 145, 147, 239, *University of South Carolina, Columbia.* See also page 239 on Barbadoes in 1699: "every overseer of a family, shall cause all his Negro Houses to be searched once every 14 days for run-away slaves, clubs, wooden swords, and other mischievous weapons."

33. Suggestive of the snares brought by combining colonialism with racism is the fact that more than once the British promised freedom to Africans who fought against the Spanish and French—though "blacks" killing "whites" was not the best advertisement for colonialism or racism. See, e.g., Sidney Kaplan and Emma N. Kaplan, eds., **The Black Presence in the Era of the American Revolution,** Amherst: University of Massachusetts Press, 1989, 73.

34. Gerald Horne, **Cold War in a Hot Zone: The United States Confronts Labor and Independence Struggles in the British West Indies,** Philadelphia: Temple University Press, 2007.

35. Leslie, **New History of Jamaica,** 252–253, 255, 260–261, 286.

36. Little, "Influence of the West Indies," 50, 52. There were six sizeable slave revolts in Jamaica between 1673 and 1694 and two smaller ones shortly thereafter. From 1685 to 1686, this mountainous island experienced a virtual year-long revolt. In July 1685, about 150 Africans rebelled, killing 11 Europeans before heading to the hills. Martial law was proclaimed, but the revolt spread southward when 105 Africans rose in revolt and murdered 15 more Europeans. In 1689, 400 Africans revolted, but half were killed within three weeks of their uprising.

37. **Acts of Assembly Passed in the Island of Jamaica from 1681 to 1737, Inclusive,** London: Basket, 1738, 2, 16, *University of South Carolina.*

38. Wilson, "Rethinking the Colonial State," 1313, 1315.

39. Gary Taylor, **Buying Whiteness: Race, Culture, and Identity from Columbus to Hip-Hop,** New York: Palgrave, 170, 184–185, 263, 330, 332. Strikingly, as the preceding source suggests, John Locke, considered widely as the godfather of the 1776 revolt, was among those who acquiesced in and profited from the enslavement of Africans. See also Phillip Beidler and Gary Taylor, eds., **Writing Race across the Atlantic World,** New York: Palgrave, 2005.

40. **The History of the Bucanier of America . . . , Volume II,** London: Midwinter, 1741, 10.

41. **Acts of Assembly Passed in the Island of Jamaica,** 73, 99.

42. Sharples, "Flames of Insurrection," 74.

43. William Beeston to William Blathwayt, 19 November 1696, *William Blathwayt Papers.*

44. Patterson, "Slavery and Slave Revolts," 290.

45. **The Truest and Largest Account of the Late Earthquake in Jamaica, June the 7th 1692,** London: Parkhurst, 1692, *Huntington Library.* At the same site, see **A Sad and Terrible Relation of Two Dreadful Earthquakes That Happened in England and at Jamaica,** London: Brooksby, 1692; and Leslie, **New History of Jamaica.**

46. Robert Allen, **The Great Importance of Havanna . . . ,** London: Hinxman, 1762.

47. Matthew Restall, "Black Conquistadors: Armed Africans in Early Spanish America," **The Americas,** 57(Number 2, October 2000): 171–205, 172: "Africans were a ubiquitous and pivotal part of Spanish conquest campaigns in the Americas."

48. **Monsier de Pointi's Expedition to Cartagena: Being a Particular Relation . . . of the Taking and Plundering of That City by the French in the Year 1697 . . .**, London: Crouch, 1699, 26, 39, 84, *New-York Historical Society*. (This work can also be found in the Huntington Library.) At the same site, see also **A Geographical and Historical Description of the Principal Objects of the Present War in the West Indies . . .**, London: Gardner, 1741: Addressed, inter alia, are Sir Francis Drake's attack on Cartagena in 1588 and his taking of Porto Bello in 1595, along with the taking of Porto Bello in 1699 by Sir Henry Morgan and the taking of Porto Bello by Admiral Edward Vernon in 1739. See also **A Summarie and True Discourse of Sir Francis Drake's West Indian Voyage Wherein Were Taken the Townes of Saint Jago, Santo Domingo, Cartagena & Saint Augustine**, London: Field, 1589.

49. Daniel H. Usner, Jr., "From African Captivity to American Slavery: The Introduction of Black Laborers to Colonial Louisiana," **Louisiana History**, 20(Number 1, Winter 1979): 25–48, 40.

50. Carl Ekberg et al., **Code Noir: The Colonial Slave Laws of French Mid-America**, Napierville, Illinois: Center for French Colonial Studies, circa 2004, 2, *Missouri Historical Society, St. Louis*.

51. Wilcomb C. Washburn, **Virginia under Charles I and Oliver Cromwell, 1625–1660**, Williamsburg: Virginia 350th Anniversary Celebration Corporation, 1957, 20, 23, *British Library, London*.

52. **Friendly Advice to the Gentlemen-Planters of the East and West Indies in Three Parts**, London: Sowle, 1684, *Huntington Library*.

53. George Keith, **An Exhortation & Caution to Friends Concerning Buying or Keeping of Negroes**, Philadelphia, 1693, *Huntington Library*. See also Richard Newman and James Mueller, eds., **Antislavery and Abolition in Philadelphia: Emancipation and the Long Struggle for Racial Justice in the City of Brotherly Love**, Baton Rouge: Louisiana State University Press, 2011.

54. Wylie Sypher, **Guinea's Captive Kings: British Anti-Slavery Literature of the Eighteenth Century**, Chapel Hill: University of North Carolina Press, 1942, 157–158. See also Daniel Defoe, **An Essay on the South Sea Trade**, London, 1712, *Huntington Library*.

55. Richard Blome, **The Present State of His Majesties Isles and Territories in America . . .**, London: Clark, 1687, 40.

56. Folarin Shyllon, **Black People in Britain, 1555–1833**, London: Oxford University Press, 1977, 17.

57. See, e.g., William Hilton, Commander and Commissioner with Captain Anthony Long . . . , **A Relation of a Discovery Made on the Coast of Florida**, London: Miller, 1664, *Huntington Library*.

58. Samuel Pepys, entry of September 1683, in C.S. Knighton, ed., **Pepys's Later Diaries**, Stroud, United Kingdom: Sutton, 2004, 113, 131–132.

59. Carl R. Gross, "The Negro and Events in Rhode Island, 1696–1968," 1968, *Rhode Island Historical Society, Providence*.

60. Verner W. Crane, **The Southern Frontier, 1670–1732**, Tuscaloosa: University of Alabama Press, 2004 (originally published 1929).

61. Little, "Influence of the West Indies," 74, 79, 83. See also John P. Thomas, "The Barbadians in Early South Carolina," **South Carolina Historical and Genealogical Magazine**, 31(Number 2, April 1930): 75–92. See also "Trade between English Northern Colonies & Sugar Islands, 1689–1760," Folder 109, *Daniel Parish Slavery Transcripts*.

62. Frank Klingberg, **An Appraisal of the Negro in Colonial South Carolina: A Study in Americanization**, Philadelphia: Porcupine, 1975, 102.

63. Letter from Mr. Randolph to the Board, 28 June 1699, in A.S. Salley, ed., **Records in the British Public Record Office Relating to South Carolina, 1698–1700**, Columbia: Historical Commission of South Carolina, 89.
64. James Colleton to Whitehall, 3 March 1687, in **Records in the British Public Records Office Relating to South Carolina, 1685–1690**, Columbia: Historical Commission of South Carolina, n.d., 184, unclear provenance, *University of South Carolina*.
65. Judson J. Conner, **Muskets, Knives and Bloody Marshes: The Fight for Colonial Georgia**, St. Simons Island, Georgia: Saltmarsh, 2001, 7. See also Charles Arnade, **The Siege of St. Augustine in 1702**, Gainesville: University Press of Florida, 1959.
66. Report by Juan Marquez Cabrera, 27 September 1686, in John E. Worth, ed., **The Struggle for the Georgia Coast: An 18th Century Spanish Retrospective on Guala and Mocama**, Tuscaloosa: University of Alabama Press, 2007, 154–156: in this same collection, see also "Reports on Escaping Slave and Yamasee War," 170–171, 146–149.
67. Patrick Riordan, "Finding Freedom in Florida: Native Peoples, African Americans and Colonists, 1670–1816," **Florida Historical Quarterly**, 75(Number 1, Summer 1996): 24–43, 26. See also Jeannette Thurber Connor, ed., **Colonial Records of Spanish Florida, Volume II**, Deland: Florida Historical Society, 1930.
68. Letters from "Dunlop to Sir James Montgomerie," 1686 and 1687, in Charles H. Lesser, ed., **South Carolina Begins: The Records of a Proprietary Colony, 1663–1721**, Columbia: South Carolina Department of Archives and History, 1995, 146.
69. **South Carolina Council Journal**, 10 January 1672, *South Carolina Department of Archives and History, Columbia*.
70. Shirley Carter Hughson, **The Carolina Pirates and Colonial Commerce, 1670–1740**, Baltimore: Johns Hopkins University Press, 1894, 11, 24: The "objectionable statesmen" who migrated to the colony included the "great Earl of Shaftesbury, one of the original Lords Proprietors of Carolina," who "at one time sought to escape a threatened prosecution for his alleged treasonable leanings by fleeing" to Carolina; a "large proportion of the first settlers of many parts of America were banished criminals of the lowest class. . . . there had always been a bitter feeling existing between the colony at Charles Town and the Spaniards at St. Augustine. It was an article of the seventeenth-century Englishman's religious faith to hate a Spaniard as he would the Evil One himself and the Spaniards not only returned the detestation with interest."
71. Pre-1739 report, in B.R. Carroll, ed., **Historical Collections of South Carolina, Embracing Many Rare and Valuable Pamphlets and Other Documents Relating to the History of That State . . . , Volume I**, New York: Harper, 1836, 331.
72. Steven J. Oatis, **A Colonial Complex: South Carolina's Frontiers in the Era of the Yamasee War, 1680–1730**, Lincoln: University of Nebraska Press, 2004, 33–34. See also Governor Nicholson to Council of Trade and Plantations, 20 August 1698, *Walter Johnson Research Notes, Johns Hopkins University, Baltimore*.
73. Stuart Owen Stumpf, "The Merchants of Colonial Charleston, 1680–1756," Ph.D. dissertation, Michigan State University, 1971, 164.
74. Virginia Bever Platt, "The East India Company and the Madagascar Slave Trade," **William and Mary Quarter**, 26(Number 4, October 1969): 548–577.
75. Dallas, **History of the Maroons**, 24, 32.
76. Letter to the Commissioner of Customs, 6 March 1700, Box 1, *Walter Johnson Research Notes*.
77. Nathaniel Blackiston to Board of Trade, London, June 1699, English Microforms, Roll 5, CO5/714–719, 367–367a, *Delaware Historical Society, Wilmington*: reports of extensive pirate activity and much illicit trade.

78. Report, 21 August 1701, in A.S. Salley, ed., **Journal of the Commons House of Assembly of South Carolina for the Session Beginning August 13, 1701, and Ending August 28, 1701,** 1926, *Clemson University, South Carolina.* See, e.g., Reverend W. Blackley, ed., **The Diplomatic Correspondence of the Right Hon. Richard Hill, Envoy Extraordinary from the Court of St. James to the Duke of Savoy in the Reign of Queen Anne from July 1703 to May 1706,** London: Murray, 1845. See also Verner W. Crane, "The Southern Frontier in Queen Anne's War," **American Historical Review,** 44(Number 5, April 1919): 379–395; Herbert E. Bolton, "Spanish Resistance to the Carolina Traders in Western Georgia (1680–1704)," **Georgia Historical Quarterly,** 9(Number 2, June 1925): 115–130.

79. Stanwood, **Empire Reformed,** 171.

80. Report, 4 July 1706, Box 1, *Walter Johnson Research Notes.*

81. Paul Baepler, ed., **White Slaves, African Masters: An Anthology of American Barbary Captivity Narratives,** Chicago: University of Chicago Press, 1999; see also Charles Sumner, **White Slavery in the Barbary States: A Lecture . . . ,** Boston: Ticknor, 1847.

82. Khalid Bekkaoui, ed., **White Women Captives in North Africa: Narratives of Enslavement, 1735–1830,** New York: Palgrave, 2011.

83. Margaret Lillian Mitchell, "Slavery in Colonial Delaware," B.A. thesis, Smith College, 1970, 16.

84. Evan Haefeli, "The Revolt of the Long Swede: Transatlantic Hopes and Fears on the Delaware, 1699," **Pennsylvania Magazine of History and Biography,** 130(Number 2, April 2006): 137–180, 139.

85. Benjamin Quarles, "The Colonial Militia and Negro Manpower," **Mississippi Valley Historical Review,** 14(1959): 643–652.

86. David Cole, "The Origin and Development of the South Carolina Militia, 1670–1719," 1948, *University of South Carolina.*

87. Lorena S. Walsh, **Motives of Honor, Pleasure, and Profit: Plantation Management in the Colonial Chesapeake, 1607–1763,** Chapel Hill: University of North Carolina Press, 2010, 250.

88. Minutes, 30 September 1677, in H.R. McIlwaine, ed., **Minutes of the Council and General Court of Colonial Virginia,** 2nd ed., Richmond: Virginia State Library, 1979.

89. Sharples, "Flames of Insurrection," 62, 140. See also **Strange News from Virginia; Being a Full and True Account of the Life and Death of Nathaniel Bacon,** London: Harris, 1677, *Huntington Library;* "Mss. on Negroes, Slaves, etc. Together with Some Papers on Nathaniel Bacon's Rebellion," Folder 183, *Daniel Parish Slavery Transcripts;* Rebecca Anne Goetz, **The Baptism of Early Virginia: How Christianity Created Race,** Baltimore: Johns Hopkins University Press, 2012, 133: "After the rebellion's conclusion, Anglo-Virginian planters emphasized whiteness and Christianity as the two bonds that held English people together against Indians who threatened from without and enslaved people who threatened from within."

90. James D. Rice, **Tales from a Revolution: Bacon's Rebellion and the Transformation of Early America,** New York: Oxford University Press, 2012.

91. William Shea, **The Virginia Militia in the Seventeenth Century,** Baton Rouge: Louisiana State University Press, 1983, 54, 114.

92. Edmund Morgan, **American Slavery, American Freedom: The Ordeal of Colonial Virginia,** New York: Norton, 1975, 298.

93. "An Act for Preventing Negroes' Insurrection," 8 June 1680, Folder 182, *Daniel Parish Slavery Transcripts.*

94. Legislation, June 1680, in William Waller Henning, ed., **The Statutes at Large; Being a Collection of the Laws of Virginia from the First Session of the Legislature in the Year 1619, Volume II**, New York: Bartow, 1823, 481.
95. Report, 24 October 1687, in H.R. McIlwaine, ed., **Executive Journals of the Council of Colonial Virginia, Volume I (June 11, 1680–June 22, 1699)**, Richmond: Virginia State Library, 1925, 85–87. For another response to slave plotting, see Report, 19 December 1699, in H.R. McIlwaine, ed., **Executive Journals of the Council of Colonial Virginia, Volume II (August 3, 1699–April 27, 1705)**, Richmond: Virginia State Library, 35.
96. Minutes of Council and Assembly, 24 October 1687, Folder 184, *Daniel Parish Slavery Transcripts*.
97. Legislation, 1688 and 30 October 1693, in H.R. McIlwaine, ed., **Journals of the House of Burgesses of Virginia, 1659/1660–1693**, Richmond: Virginia State Library, 1914, 299, 472.
98. Legislation of April 1691, in William Waller Hening, ed., **The Statutes at Large: Being a Collection of All the Laws of Virginia from the First Session of the Legislature in the Year 1619, Volume III**, Richmond, Virginia: Franklin, 1819, 233.
99. T.H. Breen, "A Changing Labor Force and Race Relations in Virginia, 1660–1710," **Journal of Social History**, 7(Number 1, Autumn 1973): 3–25, 18. See also Morgan Godwyn, **The Negros & Indians Advocate Suing for Their Admission into the Church, or A Persuasive to the Instructing and Baptizing of the Negros and Indians in Our Plantations . . .** , London: Morgan Godwyn, 1680, *Huntington Library*.
100. William Byrd, diary entry of 18 April 1710, in Louis B. Wright and Marion Tingling, eds., **The Secret Diary of William Byrd of Westover, 1709–1712**, Richmond, Virginia: Dietz, 1941, 167.
101. Mrs. Flanagan, **Antigua and the Antiguans: A Full Account of the Colony and Its Inhabitants from the Time of the Caribs to the Present Day**, London: Saunders and Ottley, 1844, **Volume I**, 73; and **Volume II**, 79.
102. Michael Ayone to Council of Trade and Plantations, 20 September 1709; and Governor Parke to Council of Trade and Plantations, 14 November 1709, in Cecil Headlam, ed., **Calendar of State Papers, Colonial Series, America and West Indies, June 1708–1709**, London: HM Stationery Office, 1922, 469–471, 519–522.
103. Report on Africans fleeing to the French, 1699; and Walter Douglas to My Lord, 28 September 1711, Folder 93, *Daniel Parish Slavery Transcripts*: In this latter dispatch, the Dutch at St. Eustatius were accused of being "intolerable neighbours by protecting [the English colonists'] Negroes, deserters, from the Regiment and all malefactors who flee there from justice."
104. Report on St. Christopher's, 1 August 1711, Folder 96, *Daniel Parish Slavery Transcripts*.

NOTES TO CHAPTER 2

1. See, e.g., John E. Wills, Jr., **1688: A Global History**, New York: Norton, 2011, 197, 47, 52–53; Michael G. Hall, Lawrence H. Leder, and Michael Kammen, eds., **The Glorious Revolution in America: Documents on the Colonial Crisis of 1689**, Chapel Hill: University of North Carolina Press, 1964. See also Janet Todd, **The Secret Life of Aphra Behn**, New Brunswick: Rutgers University Press, 1997; Angeline Goreau, **Reconstructing Aphra: A Social Biography of Aphra Behn**, New York: Dial, 1980.
2. Elizabeth Donnan, ed., **Documents Illustrative of the Slave Trade to America, Volume II: The Eighteenth Century**, Washington, D.C.: Carnegie, 1931, xlii, 342, 361. See also David Galenson, **Traders, Planters, and Slaves: Market Behavior in Early English America**, New York: Cambridge University Press, 1986.

3. Susan Alice Westbury, "Colonial Virginia and the Atlantic Slave Trade," Ph.D. dissertation, University of Illinois–Champaign, 1981, 24, 29. See also **The Case of the Separate Traders to Africa, with Remarks on the African Company's Memorial**, uncertain provenance, *Virginia Historical Society, Richmond.*

4. **The Case of the Royal African Company of England**, London: Sam Aris, 1730, *Huntington Library, San Marino, California.*

5. William A. Pettigrew, "Free to Enslave: Politics and the Escalation of Britain's Transatlantic Slave Trade, 1688–1714," **William and Mary Quarterly**, 64(Number 1, January 2007): 3–38, 33. See also Edward D. Collins, "Studies in the Colonial Policies of England, 1672–1680: The Plantations, the Royal African Company and the Slave Trade," **Annual Report of the American Historical Association for the Year 1900**, Washington, D.C.: Government Printing Office, 1901, 141–192, *Virginia Historical Society.*

6. Robin L. Einhorn, **American Taxation, American Slavery**, Chicago: University of Chicago Press, 2006, 33, 94.

7. William A. Pettigrew, "Transatlantic Politics and the Africanization of Virginia's Labor Force, 1688–1712," in Douglas Bradburn and John C. Coombs, eds., **Early Modern Virginia: Reconsidering the Old Dominion**, Charlottesville: University of Virginia Press, 2011, 279–299, 280, 281.

8. Reports, 1686–1694, in Leonard Woods Labaree, ed., **Royal Instructions to British Colonial Governors, 1670–1776, Volume II**, New York: D. Appleton-Century, 1935, 665. See also Report, 16 January 1708, in **Journal of the Commissioners for Trade and Plantations from April 1704 to February 1708-1709**, London: HM Stationery Office, 1920, 449: RAC charges that "private traders" are seeking to "defraud the Company."

9. Edward Littleton, **The Groans of the Plantations; or, A True Account of Their Grievous and Extreme Sufferings by the Heavy Impositions upon Sugar and Other Hardships Relating More Particularly to the Island of Barbados**, London: Clark, 1689, *Huntington Library.* See also Petition of Captain Christopher Billop, 1685, "XV Miscellaneous Papers," *Daniel Parish Slavery Transcripts, New-York Historical Society, Manhattan*: Africans purchased on the continent contrary to "Charter granted the Royall Affrican Company" to be "condemned in Admiralty Court."

10. Thomas Lynch to William Blathwayt, 14 August 1683, *William Blathwayt Papers, Rockefeller Library, Williamsburg, Virginia.*

11. Thomas Lynch to William Blathwayt, 21 October 1683; and Thomas Lynch to Benjamin Bathurst, 26 April 1683, *William Blathwayt Papers.*

12. Thomas Lynch to William Blathwayt, 8 April 1684, *William Blathwayt Papers.*

13. W. Bryan Rommel-Ruiz, "Atlantic Revolutions: Slavery and Freedom in Newport, Rhode Island and Halifax, Nova Scotia in the Era of the American Revolution," Ph.D. dissertation, University of Michigan, 1999, 44.

14. **The Falsities of Private Traders to Africa Discover'd and the Mischiefs They Occasion Demonstrated**, 1709, *University of Virginia, Charlottesville.* See also **The Journals of Madam Knight and Rev. Mr. Buckingham from the Original Manuscripts. Written in 1704 & 1710**, New York: Wilder and Campbell, 1825; and "Depositions Relating to Interlopers and Pirate Ships, 1682–1687," Jamaica and Nevis, Folder 106, *Daniel Parish Slavery Transcripts*: "their trading in Negroes against the interests of the Royal African Company of England."

15. Board of Trade to Governors of Colonies, 17 April 1708, "Miscellaneous Papers," *Daniel Parish Slavery Transcripts.*

16. William Wilkinson, **Systema Africanum; or, A Treatise Discovering the Intrigues and Arbitrary Proceedings of the Guiney Company and Also How Prejudicial They**

Are to the American Planters, the Woolen and Other English Manufactures, to the Visible Decay of Trade and Consequently Greatly Impairing the Royal Revenue Which Would Be Infinitely Increased, Provided Merchants and Mariners Were Encouraged, Who Can Discover Several Places Not Yet Known, or Traded unto by the African Company, Together with a True Account of Their Fortifications, London, 1690, *Huntington Library*.

17. Charles Davenant, **Several Arguments Proving That Our Trade to Africa Cannot Be Preserved and Carried on Effectually by Any Other Method than That of a Considerable Joint-Stock with Exclusive Privileges**, 1711, *University of Virginia*. See also **By the King: A Proclamation**, London: John Bill and Christopher Barker, Printers to the King, 1674, *New-York Historical Society, Manhattan*: "traffique with infidel and barbarous nations . . . cannot be carried on without the establishment of forts and factories in places convenient, the maintenance thereof requires so great and constant expense, that it cannot be otherwise defrayed, than by managing the whole leave by a joint stock"; thus, "the whole trade of the coast of Guiny, Buiny and Angola and other parts and places of Africa" mandates "violence and inconstancy of the heathen natives"—hence the need for the RAC. See also RAC Declaration, 1672, Folder 151, *Daniel Parish Slavery Transcripts*: "whereas the Company of Royal Adventurers of England trading into Africa . . . vested in the said company solely [this commerce] . . . how absolutely necessary it was to the interest of His Majesty and his subjects, inhabitants in the American plantations that should have an ample supply of Negroes . . . at a moderate rate."

18. William Pettigrew, "Slaves to the Atlantic World: Politics and the Demise of the Royal African Company, 1688–1713," lecture, College of William and Mary, 19 April 2005, *Virginia Historical Society*. At the same site, see also Walter Minchinton, Celia King, and Peter Waite, eds., **Virginia Slave Trade Statistics, 1698–1775**, Richmond: Virginia State Library, 1984.

19. A Joint Letter from the Most Considerable Proprietors of the Island of Barbadoes, to Colonel Richard Scot, et al., . . . Touching the Petition Which They Lately Transmitted to Be Given in to the Honourable House of Commons for Having the Trade to Africa Carried on by a Company of Sufficient Joint-Stock, Barbadoes, August 1709, *Brown University, Providence, Rhode Island*.

20. Petition, 12 December 1710, in Cecil Headlam, ed., **Calendar of State Papers, Colonial Series, America and West Indies, 1710–June 1711**, London: HM Stationery Office, 1924, 306–308.

21. Barbados Petition, 20 July 1710, in Headlam, **Calendar of State Papers, 1710–June 1711**, 308–309.

22. See reference to 1690 Petition in Richard Beale Davis, ed., **William Fitzhugh and His Chesapeake World, 1676–1701**, Chapel Hill: University of North Carolina Press, 1963, 356.

23. **Reflections upon the Constitution and Management of the Trade to Africa through the Whole Course and Progress Thereof, from the Beginning of the Last Century to This Time** . . . , London: Morphew, 1709, *Brown University*.

24. **The Importance of the African Company's Forts and Settlements Considered. . . . The Importance of Effectually Supporting the Royal African Company of England Impartially Consider'd; Shewing That a Free and Open Trade to Africa and the Support and Preservation of the British Colonies and Plantations in America, Depend upon Maintaining the Forts and Settlements, Rights and Privileges Belonging to That Corporation, against the Encroachments of the French and All Other Foreign Rivals in That Trade** . . . , London: Cooper, 1744, *Huntington Library*.

25. The Case of the Royal African Company of England, London: Sam, Aris, 1730, *Johns Hopkins University, Baltimore.*

26. By the King, a Proclamation to Prohibit His Majesties Subjects to Trade within the Limits Assigned to the Royal African Company of England, Except Those of the Company, 1685, *Huntington Library.*

27. A True State of the Present Difference between the Royal African Company and the Separate Traders . . . , London, 1710, *Huntington Library.*

28. Report, 1724, Box 1, Folder 25, *Daniel Parish Slavery Transcripts.*

29. "A Planter," Some Observations Shewing the Danger of Losing the Trade of the Sugar Colonies, Humbly Offer'd to the Consideration of the Parliament, London, 1714, *University of Virginia.*

30. Petitions, 1697/1698, Box 1, Folder 14, *Daniel Parish Slavery Transcripts.*

31. Queen Anne's Reasons for Her Conduct Both with Respect to the War and Peace and Her Majesty's Characters . . . , London: Roberts, 1715, *Huntington Library.*

32. A Letter from a Merchant at Jamaica to a Member of Parliament Touching the African Trade, to Which Is Added, a Speech Made by a Black of Gardaloupe at the Funeral of a Fellow Negro, London: Baldwin, 1709, *Huntington Library.*

33. Report, 29 July 1708, "Parish Transcripts from Printed Sources and Historical Notes of Daniel Parish," *Daniel Parish Slavery Transcripts.*

34. Governor L.A. Hamilton to Council of Trade and Plantations, 10 October 1712, in Cecil Headlam, ed., Calendar of State Papers, Colonial Series, America and West Indies, July 1712–July 1714, London: HM Stationery Office, 1926, 61–66.

35. The Assiento Contract Consider'd, as Also, the Advantages and Decay of the Trade of Jamaica and the Plantations, with the Causes and Consequences Thereof, in Several Letters to a Member of Parliament, London: Burleigh, 1714, *Huntington Library.* For more on the Asiento, see Materials, 1713, Box 1, Folder 16, *Daniel Parish Slavery Transcripts.* See also The Deplorable State of New England, . . . to Which Is Added an Account of the Shameful Miscarriage of the Late Expedition against Port Royal, London, 1708, *Huntington Library.*

36. The Assiento or Contract for Allowing to the Subjects of Great Britain the Liberty of Importing Negroes into the Spanish America, Sign'd by the Catholick King at Madrid, the Twenty Sixth Day of March 1713 . . . , London: Basket, 1713.

37. A True and Impartial Account of the Rise and Progress of the South Sea Company; Wherein the Assiento Contract Is Particularly Considered: Proving the Great Advantages That Would Have Accrued to England by a Faithful Observance of It on the Part of Spain, . . . Humbly Addressed to Admiral Vernon, by a Gentleman Now Resident in Jamaica, London: Cooper, 1743, *Huntington Library.* At the same site, see also The Trade Granted by the South Sea Company: Considered with Relation to Jamaica; in a Letter to One of the Directors of the South Sea Company; by a Gentleman Who Has Resided Several Years in Jamaica, London: Crouch, 1714; and Convention for Explaining the Articles of the Assiento or Contract for Negroes, between the Most Serene and Potent Prince George, by the Grace of God, King of Great Britain, France and Ireland, Defender of the Faith . . . and the Most Serene and Potent Philip V, the Catholick King of Spain, Concluded at Madrid the 26th of May 1716: this pact was concluded after a "long war . . . for the term of thirty years" beginning in 1713 and was quite detailed. At the same site, see also Daniel Defoe, An Essay on the South Sea Trade, London, 1712. On the difficulties brought by the Asiento, see "South Sea Company & Asiento: Trade in Negroes and Slaves and Grievances against and Trouble with the Spaniards, 1724–1730," Box 1, Folder 24, *Daniel Parish Slavery Transcripts.* Of course, even before the former proclamation of what is referred to as the Asiento, there was trade in Africans between Spanish and

English colonies in the Caribbean: see, e.g., Thomas Lynch to William Blathwayt, 6 October 1683; Thomas Lynch to William Blathwayt, 17 December 1683; and Thomas Lynch to William Blathwayt, 2 May 1683, *William Blathwayt Papers*.

38. Clarence J. Munford, "Slavery in the French Caribbean, 1625–1715: A Marxist Analysis," **Journal of Black Studies**, 17(Number 1, September 1986): 49–69, 49.

39. Minutes of Council in Assembly Relating to the Trade in Negroes and Slaves by the Royal African Company, 1689–1703," Folder 107, *Daniel Parish Slavery Transcripts*. In Folder 108, see Minutes of Council in Assembly, 1690–1725, and Minutes of House of Burgesses, 1686–1721, "relating to trade in Negroes and Slaves by the Royal African Company and the Asiento and South Sea Company." In Folder 111, see Minutes of the Council in Assembly, 1723–1760, and Minutes of House of Burgesses, 1730–1760, "Mss. Relating to the trade in Negroes and Slaves . . . by the Royal African Company and the Asiento & South Sea Company."

40. Thelma Wills Foote, **Black and White Manhattan: The History of Racial Formation in Colonial New York City**, New York: Oxford University Press, 2004, 63.

41. Letter to Lord Commissioners for Trade and Plantations, 8 March 1703, Box 5, Folder 60, *Daniel Parish Slavery Transcripts*: "Praying that . . . Jews in Jamaica may not be taxed more than other inhabitants, . . . that the Jews before the present war with Spain by their industry & interest had procured the Asiento of Negroes to be established at Jamaica which very much promoted the trade between the . . . island & the Spanish West Indies to the great profit of England. . . . it is objected against the Jews that the meaner sort of them buy anything from the Negroes which encourages them to steal from their masters."

42. **The English Hero or Sir Francis Drake Reviv'd by R.B.**, London: Crouch, 1701, *New-York Historical Society*.

43. Report, 3 April 1701, Box 5, Folder 66, *Daniel Parish Slavery Transcripts*.

44. Westbury, "Colonial Virginia and the Atlantic Slave Trade," 145.

45. Minutes of Council in Assembly and House of Burgesses, 19 September 1701, *Daniel Parish Slavery Transcripts*.

46. Minutes of Council in Assembly, 21 March 1709, *Daniel Parish Slavery Transcripts*. In the same collection, in "Miscellaneous Papers," see 1709 reports on this Virginia revolt. For more on this uprising, see Report from Surrey County, 24 March 1709, in William P. Palmer, ed., **Calendar of Virginia State Papers and Other Manuscripts, 1652–1781, Preserved in the Capitol at Richmond**, Richmond, Virginia: Walker, 1875 (repr., New York: Kraus, 1968, 129; subsequent page citations refer to the reprint edition).

47. Report, 21 March 1709, in H.R. McIlwaine, ed., **Executive Journals of the Council of Colonial Virginia, Volume III (May 1, 1705–October 23, 1721)**, Richmond: Virginia State Library, 1928, 573–574.

48. Report, 18 April 1710, in McIlwaine, **Executive Journals of the Council of Colonial Virginia, Volume III**, 234–235.

49. Letter, 24 August 1710, in R.A. Brock, ed., **The Official Letters of Alexander Spotswood, Lieutenant-Governor of the Colony of Virginia, 1710–1722, Volume I**, Richmond: Virginia Historical Society, 1882, 16, *Rockefeller Library*.

50. Minutes of Council in Assembly and House of Burgesses, 1 November 1710, *Daniel Parish Slavery Transcripts*.

51. Governor Alexander Spotswood to Council on Trade and Plantations, 15 October 1712, in Headlam, **Calendar of State Papers, July 1712–July 1714**, 70.

52. Letter from Alexander Spotswood, 15 December 1710, in Brock, **Official Letters of Alexander Spotswood**, 42.

53. Minutes, 26 November 1711, in H.R. McIlwaine, ed., **Legislative Journals of the Council of Colonial Virginia**, Richmond: Virginia State Library, 1979, 521. See also Report, 27 November 1710, in H.R. McIlwaine, ed., **Journals of the House of Burgesses of Virginia, 1702/3–1705, 1705–1706, 1710–1712**, Richmond: Virginia State Library, 1912, 281: "read the third time . . . *an Act for better preventing The Insurrections and Conspiracys of Negros & Other Slaves*" (emphasis original). In the same source, see also xxxv: the Assembly of 1710–1712, "Special Committee ordered to 'examine into and consider the law of this country made for preventing the insurrection of Negroes,'" also "'a bill to prevent the levying of war, taking of arms, keeping of weapons, offensive or defensive, by Negroes, Mulattoes, Indians and other slaves.'"

54. Report, 27 April 1710, in H.R. McIlwaine, ed., **Executive Journals of the Council of Colonial Virginia, Volume III**, 242–243. See also E. Lawrence Lee, **Indian Wars in North Carolina, 1663–1763**, Raleigh: Carolina Charter Tercentenary Commission, 1963. See also "Petition of Richard Wharton . . . for pay for professional services rendered by the Crown in the prosecution of certain Traitors, . . . a Negro slave and an Indian sentenced to death for high treason . . . ," circa December 1710, in Palmer, **Calendar of Virginia State Papers and Other Manuscripts**, 161.

55. Legislation, October 1710, in William Waller Hening, **Statutes at Large: Being a Collection of All the Laws of Virginia from the First Session of the Legislature in the Year 1619, Volume III**, Richmond, Virginia: Franklin, 1819, 537.

56. Reports and proclamations, 21 March 1709 and 21 April 1710, in Headlam, **Calendar of State Papers, 1710–June 1711**, 238.

57. Governor Jennings to Council of Trade and Plantations, 3 July 1710, in Headlam, **Calendar of State Papers, 1710–June 1711**, 83.

58. Lorena S. Walsh, **Motives of Honor, Pleasure, and Profit: Plantation Management in the Colonial Chesapeake, 1607–1763**, Chapel Hill: University of North Carolina Press, 2010, 367.

59. "Most Humble Servants," including Robert Monckton, to "Your Lordships," 17 September 1708, in A.S. Salley, ed., **Records of the British Public Record Office Relating to South Carolina, 1701–1710**, Columbia: Historical Commission of South Carolina, 1947, 205: "we are also often furnished with Negroes from . . . Barbados & Jamaica. . . . we have also commerce with Boston Road Island, Pennsilvania, New York & Virginia."

60. Leonidas Dodson, **Alexander Spotswood: Governor of Colonial Virginia**, Philadelphia: University of Pennsylvania Press, 1932, 46–47.

61. Report, 1723–1726, in H.R. McIlwaine, ed., **Journals of the House of Burgesses of Virginia, 1712–1714, 1715, 1718, 1720–1722, 1723–1726**, Richmond: Virginia State Library, 1912, xlvii–xlviii.

62. See, e.g., **The Allies and the Late Ministry Defended against France and the Present Friends of France in Answer to a Pamphlet, Intituled "The Conduct of the Allies,"** London: Baldwin, 1711, *University of South Carolina, Columbia*. At the same site, see also **Examination of a Book Intituled the Conduct of the Duke of Ormond Anno 1712 in a Letter to a Member of the Secret Committee**, London: More, 1715.

63. **An Account of the British Fleet to Sicily in the Years 1718, 1719 and 1740, under the Command of Sir George Byng, Bart. . . . ,** London: Tonson, 1739, *University of South Carolina*.

64. Council of Trade and Plantations to Lord Bolinbroke, 9 March 1714, in Headlam, **Calendar of State Papers, July 1712–July 1714**, 313–314.

65. Letter from St. Christopher's, 16 September 1710, in Headlam, **Calendar of State Papers, 1710–June 1711**, 305–306.

66. Russell Menard, "The Maryland Slave Population, 1658 to 1730: A Demographic Profile of Blacks in Four Counties," **William and Mary Quarterly**, 32(Number 1, 1975): 29–54, 30, 31. See also "Acts of Assembly . . . 1640 to 1715," Maryland, Folder 175, *Daniel Parish Slavery Transcripts*.

67. Report by William Penn, 23 March 1683, Box 1, *Walter Johnson Research Notes, Johns Hopkins University, Baltimore*.

68. Legislation, 1705, "Miscellaneous Papers," *Daniel Parish Slavery Transcripts*. See also William Renwick Riddell, "Pre-Revolutionary Pennsylvania and the Slave Trade," **Pennsylvania Magazine of History and Biography**, 52(Number 1, 1928): 1–28.

69. Bills, 26 April 1699, 6 August 1700, 7 August 1700, in **Journal of the Legislative Council of the Colony of New York, Began the 9th Day of April 1691; and Ended the 27th Day of September 1743**, Albany, New York: Weed, Parsons, 1861, 132, 147, 148.

70. **The Laws of Her Majesties Colony of New York** . . . , New York; Bradford, 1710, 53, 68, 82, *Huntington Library*.

71. "An Act . . . ," 1703, Folder 150, *Daniel Parish Slavery Transcripts*.

72. Letter to "My Lord," 12 September 1687, Volume 46, *Shelburne Papers, University of Michigan, Ann Arbor*.

73. Letter from Francis Nicholson et al., 15 May 1689, Volume 46, *Shelburne Papers*.

74. Owen Stanwood, **The Empire Reformed: English America in the Age of the Glorious Revolution**, Philadelphia: University of Pennsylvania Press, 2011, 171.

75. John Shea, "The New York Negro Plot of 1741," 1862, *New-York Historical Society*.

76. Brigadier General Hill to Lord Dartmouth, 31 July 1711, in Cecil Headlam, ed., **Calendar of State Papers, Colonial Series, America and West Indies, July 1711–June 1712**, London: HM Stationery Office, 1925, 55–58.

77. James G. Lydon, "New York and the Slave Trade, 1700 to 1774," **William and Mary Quarterly**, 35(Number 2, April 1978): 375–394, 376, 384.

78. Foote, **Black and White Manhattan**, 94, 96, 197.

79. Douglas Edward Leach, **Roots of Conflict: British Armed Forces and Colonial Americans, 1677–1763**, Chapel Hill: University of North Carolina Press, 1986, 26–27. See also **The Laws of Her Majesties Colony of New York . . . Which Began April the 9th . . . 1691 . . .** , New York: Bradford, 1710, *Huntington Library*.

80. Bill, 30 October 1711, in **Journal of the Legislative Council of the Colony of New York**, 324.

81. See, e.g., Captain Jinkins, **Spanish Insolence Corrected by English Bravery; Being an Historical Account of the Many Signal Achievements Obtained by the English over the Spaniards from the Year 1350 to the Present Time**, London: Thomas, 1739, *Huntington Library*.

82. See, e.g., **The Private Journals Kept by Reverend John Buckingham of the Expedition against Canada in the Years 1710 & 1711**, New York: Wilder and Campbell, 1825, 75: "fourteen transports were furnished by Massachusetts, 5 by Connecticut, 2 by New Hampshire, and 3 by Rhode Island."

83. Acts, 15 December 1709 and November/December 1717, Folder 155, *Daniel Parish Slavery Transcripts*.

84. Legislation and Regulations, New York, 1712, "Miscellaneous Papers," *Daniel Parish Slavery Transcripts*. Attempting to keep track of "Negro Slaves" sold by the RAC versus separate traders was a concern not only in the colony of New York: in the same site and container, see also Board of Trade to Governor of Colonies to North American and Caribbean colonies, 25 December 1707 and 17 April 1708.

85. Legislation, New Jersey, 3 January 1710, *Daniel Parish Slavery Transcripts*.

86. Report, circa 1680, in Charles J. Hoadly, ed., **The Public Records of the Colony of Connecticut from May 1678 to June 1689**, Hartford, Connecticut: Case, Lockwood and Brainard, 1859, 298.

87. Daniel Cruson, "Newtown's Slaves: A Case Study in Early Connecticut Rural Black History," Newtown, Connecticut: Newtown Historical Society, 1994, *Connecticut State Library and Archives, Hartford.*

88. Bill, 1 May 1708, in Charles J. Hoadly, ed., **The Public Records of the Colony of Connecticut from October 1706 to February 1717**, Hartford, Connecticut: Case, Lockwood and Brainard, 1870, 53.

89. Connecticut Legislation, 1715, "Miscellaneous Papers," *Daniel Parish Slavery Transcripts.*

90. Denis R. Caron, **A Century in Captivity: The Life and Trial of Prince Mortimer, a Connecticut Slave**, Lebanon: University of New Hampshire Press, 2006, 15.

91. **Providence Journal**, 13 March 2006: this multi-part series was a useful exploration of slavery in the region.

92. **Providence Journal**, 14 March 2006.

93. Letter, November 1687, "Miscellaneous Papers," *Daniel Parish Slave Transcripts.*

94. Petition of Emmanuel Barselia, 12 April 1709, "Miscellaneous Papers," *Daniel Parish Slavery Transcripts.*

95. Thomas Church, **The History of Philip's War, Commonly Called the Great Indian War of 1675 and 1676, Also of the French and Indian Wars at the Eastward of 1689, 1692, 1696 and 1704 . . .** , Exeter, New Hampshire: Williams, 1829.

96. Edgar J. McManus, **Black Bondage in the North**, Syracuse: Syracuse University Press, 1973, 127.

97. Proclamation, 1656, in Nathaniel B. Shurtleff, ed., **Records of the Governor and Company of the Massachusetts Bay in New England, Volume III, 1644–1657**, Boston: White, 1854, 397.

98. Lorenzo J. Greene, "Slave Holding New England and Its Awakening," **Journal of Negro History**, 13(Number 4, October 1920): 492–533, 511.

99. Diary entry, 19 June 1700, in M. Halsey Thomas, ed., **The Diary of Samuel Sewall, 1674–1729, Volume I**, New York: Farrar, Straus and Giroux, 1973, 433.

NOTES TO CHAPTER 3

1. Thelma Wills Foote, **Black and White Manhattan: The History of Racial Formation in Colonial New York City**, New York: Oxford University Press, 2004, 132: the author maintains that eighteen were executed, but see Governor Robert Hunter to Council of Trade and Plantations, 23 June 1712, in Cecil Headlam, ed., **Calendar of State Papers, Colonial Series, America and West Indies, July 1711–June 1712**, London: HM Stationery Office, 1925, 301–306: here it is said that twenty-one were executed. See also "Minutes of Council in Assembly . . . ," New York, 1695–1713, Folder 157, *Daniel Parish Slavery Transcripts, New-York Historical Society, Manhattan.* Moreover, though Africans are given credit for this revolt, as suggested later in this chapter, they may have been—at least partially—of indigenous ancestry.

2. Governor Robert Hunter to the Lords of Trade and Plantations, 23 June 1712, "Miscellaneous Papers," *Daniel Parish Slavery Transcripts.* See also Kenneth Scott, "The Slave Insurrection of 1712," **New-York Historical Society Quarterly** (January 1961), *Missouri Historical Society, St. Louis*: "all told, 39 slaves were indicted for murder or as accessories . . . and of those 23 were convicted and 16 acquitted. . . . the 25 slaves who were convicted were sentenced to death."

3. Governor Robert Hunter to Lords of Trade and Plantations, 23 June 1712.

4. Oscar Williams, **African Americans and Colonial Legislation in the Middle Colonies,** New York: Garland, 1998, 61. See also Timothy Lockley, ed., **Slavery in North America: From the Colonial Period to Emancipation, Volume I: The Colonial Period,** London: Pickering and Chatto, 2009.

5. Graham Russell Hodges, **Root and Branch: African Americans in New York and East Jersey, 1613–1863,** Chapel Hill: University of North Carolina Press, 1999, 72, 77. See also A. Leon Higginbotham, **In the Matter of Color: Race and the American Legal Process: The Colonial Period,** New York: Oxford University Press, 1978.

6. "An Act for the More Effectual . . . Laying a Duty on the Tonnage of Vessels and Slaves," circa 1711, CO412/20, *National Archives of the United Kingdom, London* (hereinafter *NAUK*).

7. "An Act by Which a Duty Is Laid on Negroes . . . ," 1716, CO412/20, *NAUK.*

8. "An Act for Explaining and Rendering More Effectual an Act of the General Assembly of This Colony . . . for Preventing, Suppressing . . . ," 1716, CO412/20, *NAUK.* See also **Acts of Assembly Passed in the Province of New York from 1691 to 1725,** New York: Bradford, 1726, 81.

9. Report, circa 1715, in **Journals of the House of Representatives of Massachusetts, 1715–1717,** Boston: Massachusetts Historical Society, 1919, 48, 52.

10. **An Account of the Endeavours Used by the Society for the Propagation of the Gospel in Foreign Parts to Instruct the Negro Slaves in New York, Together with Two of Bishop Gibson's Letters on That Subject, Being an Extract from Dr. Humphrey's Historical Account of the Incorporated Society for the Propagation of the Gospel in Foreign Parts, from Its Foundation to the Year 1728,** London, 1730, *Johns Hopkins University, Baltimore.*

11. "Slave Uprising of 1712 . . . Religious Education of Negroes in New York City, 1702–1712 & Uprising in 1712," *Society Collection, Historical Society of Pennsylvania, Philadelphia.*

12. Scott, "Slave Insurrection of 1712."

13. "An Act to Encourage the Baptizing of Negro, Indian and Mulatto Slaves," 1706, CO412/20, *NAUK.*

14. "An Act for Preventing the Conspiracy of Slaves . . . ," 1709, *NAUK.*

15. "An Act for Reviving an Continuing an Act . . . ," circa 1715, CO 412/20, *NAUK.*

16. Legislation, New York, 1718, Folder 137, *Daniel Parish Slavery Transcripts.*

17. Minutes of the Common Council of the City of New York, 28 February 1713, *New York City Municipal Archives.*

18. Report, 7 May 1712, in **Journal of the Legislative Council of the Colony of New York Began the 9th Day of April 1691; and Ended the 27th Day of September 1743,** Albany, New York: Weed, Parsons, 1861, 323.

19. Proclamation, New Hampshire, 1714, "Miscellaneous Papers," *Daniel Parish Slavery Transcripts.*

20. Isaac Babin to George Clarke, 30 July 1720, 2 August 1720, and 11 August 1720, in **Letters of Isaac Babin, Esq., Private Secretary of Hon. George Clarke, Secretary of the Province of New York, 1718–1730,** Albany, New York: Munsell, 1872, 33, 36, 39.

21. Minutes of the Common Council of the City of New York, 18 April 1721, *New York City Municipal Archives.*

22. "Number of Negroes Imported from 1701–1726 . . . Taken from the Customs House Books," in Christopher Morgan, ed., **The Documentary History of the State of New York, Volume I,** Albany, New York: Weed, Parsons, 1850, 482.

23. Minutes of the Common Council of the City of New York, 8 August 1727, *New York City Municipal Archives.*

24. Francis Le Jau to Secretary, 30 August 1712 and 22 January 1714, in Frank J. Klingberg, ed., **The Carolina Chronicle of Dr. Francis Le Jau, 1706–1717**, Berkeley: University of California Press, 1956, 123, 136–137.

25. Francis Le Jau to Secretary, 22 January 1714, 136–137. See also Sara E. Johnson, **The Fear of French Negroes: Transcolonial Collaboration in the Revolutionary Americas**, Berkeley: University of California Press, 2012.

26. Quoted in Steven J. Oatis, **A Colonial Complex: South Carolina's Frontiers in the Era of the Yamasee War, 1680–1730**, Lincoln: University of Nebraska Press, 2004, 108.

27. Daniel C. Littlefield, "The Slave Trade to Colonial South Carolina: A Profile," **South Carolina Historical Magazine**, 101(Number 2, April 2000): 110–141, 113.

28. Account of invasion of South Carolina, 1706, Folder 139, *Daniel Parish Slavery Transcripts*.

29. Kenneth R. Jones, "'Full and Particular Account' of the Assault on Charleston in 1706," **South Carolina Historical Magazine**, 83(Number 1, January 1982): 1–11, 6.

30. Quoted in Thomas James Little, "Influence of the West Indies upon Slavery in Colonial South Carolina, 1670–1738," M.A. thesis, University of South Carolina, 1989, 98–99.

31. Report, 24 June 1707, in A.S. Salley, ed., **Journal of the Commons House of Assembly of South Carolina for the Session Beginning June 5, 1707, and Ending July 19, 1707,** Columbia: Historical Commission of South Carolina, 1940, 62, *Clemson University, South Carolina*.

32. Report, 9 December 1706, in A.S. Salley, ed., **Journal of the Commons House of Assembly of South Carolina for the Session Beginning November 20, 1706, and Ending February 8, 1707,** Columbia: Historical Commission of South Carolina, 1939, 3, *Clemson University*.

33. See, e.g., A.S. Salley, ed., **Journal of the Commons House of Assembly of South Carolina for 1703**, Columbia: Historical Commission of South Carolina, 1934, *Clemson University*.

34. Legislation, South Carolina, 1712, "Miscellaneous," *Daniel Parish Slavery Transcripts*.

35. See also **Historical and Political Memoirs Containing Letters Written by Sovereign Princes, State Ministers, Admirals and General Officers . . . from Almost All the Courts in Europe Beginning with 1697 to the End of 1708 . . . Collected by Christian Cole, Esq., Some Time Resident of Venice**, London: Millan, 1735, *University of South Carolina*.

36. Legislation, South Carolina, 1712, "Miscellaneous," *Daniel Parish Slavery Transcripts*.

37. Jason T. Sharples, "Flames of Insurrection: Fearing Slave Conspiracy in Early America, 1670–1780," Ph.D. dissertation, Princeton University, 2010, 145. See also Susan H. Brinn, "Blacks in Colonial North Carolina, 1660–1723," M.A. thesis, University of North Carolina, Chapel Hill, 1978.

38. Letters to Council of Trade, 6 March 1710, 20 March 1710, 24 August 1710, in R.A. Brock, ed., **The Official Letters of Alexander Spotswood, Lieutenant-Governor of the Colony of Virginia, 1710–1722, Volume I**, Richmond: Virginia State Library, 1882, 52, 72, 16.

39. Colonel Spotswood to Lords of Trade, 15 October 1712, in William L. Saunders, ed., **The Colonial Records of North Carolina, Volume I, 1662–1712**, Raleigh: Daniels, 1886, 886.

40. Julia Fretwell Barnwell, "John Barnwell—Carolina Imperialist," M.A. thesis, University of North Carolina, Chapel Hill, 1942, 45, 46.

41. David Lee Johnson, "The Yamasee War," M.A. thesis, University of South Carolina, 1980, 102–103.

42. Legislation, South Carolina, 1712, "Miscellaneous," *Daniel Parish Slavery Transcripts*.

43. Lords Proprietors of Carolina to Council on Trade and Plantations, 27 July 1716, in Cecil Headlam, ed., **Calendar of State Papers, January 1716–July 1717**, London: His Majesty's Stationery Office, 1930, 157.

44. Legislation, 20 July 1715, in **Journal of the Legislative Council of the Colony of New York**, 394.

45. Report, 28 July 1720, in **Journal of the Commissioners for Trade and Plantations from November 1718 to December 1722 . . .**, London: HM Stationery Office, 1925, 189.,

46. Richard P. Sherman, **Robert Johnson: Proprietary and Royal Governor of South Carolina**, Columbia: University of South Carolina Press, 1966, 105.

47. John D. Duncan, "Servitude and Slavery in Colonial South Carolina, 1670–1776," Ph.D. dissertation, Emory University, 1972, 765.

48. Letter to Mr. Boone, 24 June 1720, in Cecil Headlam, ed., **Calendar of State Papers, January 1719 to February 1720**, London: His Majesty's Stationery Office, 1933, 57–58. For a similar account, see Letter to Joseph Boone, 14 June 1720, Folder 2, *Daniel Parish Slavery Transcripts*.

49. Quoted in Duncan, "Servitude and Slavery in Colonial South Carolina," 765.

50. Duncan, "Servitude and Slavery in Colonial South Carolina," 768.

51. Quoted in Sherman, **Robert Johnson**, 105, 108.

52. Governor Burrington to Council on Trade and Plantations, 1 January 1733, in Cecil Headlam, ed., **Calendar of State Papers, 1733**, London: His Majesty's Stationery Office, 1939, 1–2.

53. Dwight Harris, **The History of Negro Servitude in Illinois and of the Slavery Agitation in That State, 1719–1864**, Chicago: McClurg, 1904, 1.

54. Carl Ekberg, "Black Slavery in Illinois, 1720–1765," **Western Illinois Regional Studies**, 12(Number 1, Spring 1989): 5–19, 6, 8.

55. Oatis, **Colonial Complex**, 174, 274.

56. Robert L. Merriwether, **The Expansion of South Carolina, 1729–1765**, Kingsport, Tennessee: Southern, 1940, 8.

57. Reports, 7 April 1725 and 28 May 1725, in A.S. Salley, ed., **Journal of the Commons House of Assembly for South Carolina for the Session Beginning February 23, 1724/1725, and Ending June 1, 1725**, Columbia: Historical Commission of South Carolina, 1945, 73–74, 130, *Clemson University*.

58. **A General Report Concerning the State of His Majesty's Plantations on the Continent of America Made by the Lord's Commissioners of Trade & Plantations**, 8 September 1721, *Huntington Library, San Marino, California*.

59. Draft of a Bill, 16 June 1718, in **Journals of the House of Representatives of Massachusetts, 1718–1720**, Boston: Massachusetts Historical Society, 1921, 25, 242.

60. Legislation, 7 June 1723, 18 September 1723, in **Journals of the House of Representatives of Massachusetts, 1723–1724**, Boston: Massachusetts Historical Society, 1924, 18, 210.

61. **New England Courant**, 17 November 1724, "Miscellaneous," *Daniel Parish Slavery Transcripts*.

62. Report, 12 September 1728, in **Journals of the House of Representatives of Massachusetts, 1727–1729**, Boston: Massachusetts Historical Society, 1927, 322.

63. Reports, 1730–1738, in Leonard Woods Labaree, ed., **Royal Instructions to British Colonial Governors, 1670–1776, Volume II**, New York: D. Appleton-Century, 1935, 678–679.

64. King's Instructions to Governor Jonathan Belcher, 10 December 1731, in **Journals of the House of Representatives of Massachusetts, 1732–1734**, Boston: Massachusetts Historical Society, 1930, 23.

65. Report, 28 November 1725, in A.S. Salley, ed., **Journal of the Commons House of Assembly of South Carolina, November 1, 1725–April 30, 1726**, Columbia: Historical Commission of South Carolina, 1945, 41, *Clemson University*.

66. Legislation, 31 January 1726, in A.S. Salley, ed., **Journal of the Commons House of Assembly of South Carolina, November 15, 1726–March 11, 1726/1727**, Columbia: Historical Commission of South Carolina, 1946, 92, *Clemson University*.

67. Report, 28 October 1707, in A.S. Salley, ed., **Journal of the Commons House of Assembly of South Carolina, October 22, 1707–February 12, 1707/1708**, Columbia: Historical Commission of South Carolina, 1941, 15, *Clemson University*.

68. John Lloyd to "Your Excellency," 23 June 1731, in **South Carolina Council Journal**, *South Carolina Department of Archives and History, Columbia*.

69. Quoted in Daniel H. Usner, Jr., "From African Captivity to American Slavery: The Introduction of Black Laborers to Colonial Louisiana," **Louisiana History**, 20(Number 1, Winter 1979): 25–48, 35, 40, 47–48.

70. Thomas Ingersoll, "Free Blacks in a Slave Society: New Orleans, 1718–1812," **William and Mary Quarterly**, 48(Number 2, April 1991): 173–200, 177.

71. See, e.g., Notes, 1729–1732, "Miscellaneous: U.S. to 1815," *Daniel Parish Slavery Transcripts*.

72. Gilbert C. Din, **Spaniards, Planters, and Slaves: The Spanish Regulation of Slavery in Louisiana, 1763–1803**, College Station: Texas A&M University Press, 1999, 16–17.

73. Thomas N. Ingersoll, **Mammon and Manon in Early New Orleans: The First Slave Society in the Deep South, 1718–1819**, Knoxville: University of Tennessee Press, 1999, 74–75.

74. Traveler to Friend in London, 1 May 1730, in **A Supplement to the Detection of the State and Situation of the Present Sugar Planters of Barbadoes and the Leeward Islands: Shewing . . . That the Surest Way for England to Command the Sugar Market Abroad Is to Contract Rather than Inlarge Her Sugar Colonies in a Letter from an Inhabitant of One of Her Majesty's Leeward Caribbee Islands . . .** , London: Wilford, 1733, *Huntington Library*. On the controversial question as to the various approaches toward the enslaved by various European colonizers, see, e.g., Frank Tannenbaum, **Slave and Citizen: The Negro in the Americas**, New York: Vintage, 1963.

75. R. Johnson to "His Excellency," 3 February 1731, in **South Carolina Council Journal**, *South Carolina Department of Archives and History*.

76. Report from Nathan Coverly, "Master of the Sloop" of New Providence, 10 April 1733, in **South Carolina Council Journal**, *South Carolina Department of Archives and History*.

77. Report, 13 December 1732, in **South Carolina Council Journal**, *South Carolina Department of Archives and History*.

78. Letter from Lieutenant Governor Hugh Drysdale, 1722, Folder 130, *Daniel Parish Slavery Transcripts*. For more on this conspiracy, see Lieutenant Governor Hugh Drysdale to Council on Trade and Plantations, 20 December 1722, in the same location.

79. Legislation, Virginia, 1723, "Miscellaneous," *Daniel Parish Slavery Transcripts*. For more on this legislation, see, e.g., Lieutenant Governor Hugh Drysdale to Council on Trade and Plantations, 29 June 1723, in Cecil Headlam, ed., **Calendar of State Papers, 1722–1723**, London: His Majesty's Stationery Office, 1934, 297: For more on this plot, see, e.g., Virginia Scharf, **The Women Jefferson Loved**, New York: Harper-Collins, 2010, 12.

80. Report, May 1723, in William Hening, ed., **The Statutes at Large: Being a Collection of All the Laws of Virginia from the First Session of the Legislature in the Year 1619, Volume IV**, Richmond, Virginia: Franklin, 1820, 126.

81. William Gooch to Board of Trade, 29 June 1729, *Transcriptions of William Gooch Correspondence, Rockefeller Library, Williamsburg, Virginia.*

82. Anthony S. Parent, Jr., **Foul Means: The Formation of a Slave Society in Virginia, 1660–1740**, Chapel Hill: University of North Carolina Press, 2003, 161.

83. William Gooch to Board of Trade, 12 February 1731, *William Gooch Correspondence.*

84. William Gooch to Bishop of London, 28 May 1731, *William Gooch Correspondence.*

85. William Gooch to Council on Trade and Plantations, 14 September 1730, in Cecil Headlam, ed., **Calendar of State Papers, 1730**, London: His Majesty's Stationery Office, 1937, 277.

86. William Gooch to Bishop of London, 29 June 1729, *William Gooch Correspondence.*

87. Mr. Telednor to Duke of Newcastle, 27 April 1733, in Cecil Headlam, ed., **Calendar of State Papers, 1733**, London: His Majesty's Stationery Office, 1939, 89.

88. Notes, 1723, Box 1, *Walter Johnson Research Notes, Johns Hopkins University, Baltimore.*

89. Stephanie E. Smallwood, **Saltwater Slavery: A Middle Passage from Africa to American Diaspora**, Cambridge: Harvard University Press, 2007, 33–34. See also Duncan, "Servitude and Slavery in Colonial South Carolina," 752.

90. Report, early 1731; Extract of Letter from Captain Moore, 1733; Report by Captain John Major, 1732; Samuel Waldo to Captain Samuel Rhodes, 12 March 1734, all in Elizabeth Donnan, ed., **Documents Illustrative of the Slave Trade to America, Volume III, New England and the Middle Colonies**, Washington, D.C.: Carnegie, 1932, 37, 41, 42, 43–46.

91. Lorenzo Greene, "The Antislavery Movement in New England from 1657 to 1781," no date, Box 91, *Lorenzo Greene Papers, Library of Congress.*

92. William Snelgrave, **A New Account of Some Parts of Guinea and the Slave Trade**, 1734, *University of Virginia, Charlottesville.*

93. Petition from Bristol merchants, 18 February 1726; Objections to Taxes, 17 January 1724; Objections by British merchants, circa 1725, all in **Journal of the Commissioners for Trade and Plantations from January 1722–1723 to December 1728 Preserved in the Public Records Office**, London: HM Stationery Office, 1928, 218, 64–66.

94. Pennsylvania legislation, 1716; Rhode Island legislation, 1732, both in "Miscellaneous Papers," *Daniel Parish Slavery Transcripts.*

95. **An Abstract in the Case of the Royal African Company of England**, London, 1730, *Brown University, Providence, Rhode Island.*

96. **A Supplement to the Case of the Royal African Company of England**, London: Aris, 1730, *Huntington Library.*

97. Reports, 1707–1758, in Labaree, **Royal Instructions to British Colonial Governors, Volume I**, 666–667.

98. Debate, 4 May 1726, in **Journal of the Commissioners for Trade and Plantations**, 254–255.

99. Debate, 1730, in Robert L. Cain, ed., **Records of the Executive Council, 1665–1734**, Raleigh, North Carolina: Division of Archives and History, 1984, 610–611.

100. **The Case of the British Northern Colonies**, 1731, *University of Virginia.*

101. **Observations on the Case of the Northern Colonies**, London: Roberts, 1731, *University of Virginia.*

102. **Some Considerations Humbly Offer'd upon the Bill Now Depending in the House of Lords, Relating to Trade between the Northern Colonies and the Sugar Islands, in a Letter to a Noble Peer**, 1732, *University of Virginia.*

103. **The Present State of the British Sugar Colonies Considered in a Letter from a Gentleman of Barbadoes to His Friend in London**, London, 1731, *University of Virginia.*

104. "Instructions to Orkney," 15 December 1727, *William Gooch Correspondence.*

105. The Case of the Royal African Company on Behalf of Themselves and All Others[,] His Majesty's Subjects Trading to Africa and the British Colonies and Plantations in America, 1720, *University of Virginia.*

106. An Answer to a Calumny with Some Remarks upon an Anonymous Pamphlet, Addressed to His Grace, the Duke of Newcastle, Entitled "Some Observations on the Assiento Trade, as It Has Been Exercised by the South Sea Company . . . Whereby the Damage Which Has, or Is Likely to Accrue Thereby to the *British* Commerce and Planters and Particularly to *Jamaica* Is Also Considered," London: Wilkins, 1728, *Huntington Library.* At the same site, see also Sir H. Macworth's Proposal in Miniature, as It Has Been Put in Practice in New York in America, London: Boreham, 1720; and John Pullen and Governors of Bermudas, Memoirs of the Maritime Affairs of Great Britain, Especially in Relation to Our Concerns in the West Indies . . . South Sea Company, London: Astley, 1732.

107. Remarks, 15–17 February 1732, in Leo Francis Stocks, ed., Proceedings and Debates of the British Parliaments Respecting North America, Volume IV, 1728-1739, Washington, D.C.: Carnegie, 1937, 133.

108. Alexandra Chan, "The Slaves of Colonial New England: Discourses of Colonialism and Identity at the Isaac Royall House, Medford, Massachusetts, 1732–1775," Ph.D. dissertation, Boston University, 2003, 114, 143.

109. Laws of Maryland Enacted at a Session of the Assembly Begun and Held at the City of Annapolis on Thursday the Tenth Day of July . . . 1729, Annapolis, Maryland: Parks, 1729, *Huntington Library.*

110. A Collection of All the Acts of Assembly Now in Force in the Colony of Virginia, Williamsburg, Virginia: Parks, 1733, *Huntington Library.*

NOTES TO CHAPTER 4

1. "Statements Made in the Introduction to the Report of General Oglethorpe's Expedition to St. Augustine," July 1741, in B.R. Carroll, ed., Historical Collections of South Carolina Embracing Many Rare and Valuable Pamphlets and Other Documents Relating to the History of That State . . . , Volume II, New York: Harper, 1836, 356, *Clemson University, South Carolina.* See also Irene A. Wright, "Dispatches of Spanish Officials Bearing on the Free Negro Settlement of Gracia Real de Santa Teresa," Journal of Negro History, 9(Number 2, April 1924): 144–195; and Tolagbe Ogunleye, "The Self-Emancipated Africans of Florida: Pan-African Nationalists in the 'New World,'" Journal of Black Studies, 27(Number 1, September 1996): 24–38. See also Accord between South Carolina and Don Pedro Lambeto, "Spanish Agent," 29 November 1733, Minutes of Council in Assembly, 1731–1735, *Daniel Parish Slavery Transcripts, New-York Historical Society, Manhattan.*

2. Minutes of Council in Assembly, 6 July 1739, Folder 10, *Daniel Parish Slavery Transcripts.* See also David Duncan Wallace, Constitutional History of South Carolina from 1725 to 1775, Abbeyville, South Carolina: Wilson, 1899.

3. Eugene Portlette Southall, "Negroes in Florida Prior to the Civil War," Journal of Negro History, 19(Number 1, January 1934): 77–86, 78.

4. Letter from A. Middleton in South Carolina, 13 June 1728, Folder 2, *Daniel Parish Slavery Transcripts.*

5. Report, 1737, Folder 100, *Daniel Parish Slavery Transcripts.*

6. J. Leitch Wright, "Spanish Reaction to Carolina," North Carolina Historical Review, 41(Number 4, October 1964): 464–476.

7. Report, 1686, in John E. Worth, ed., The Struggle for the Georgia Coast, Tuscaloosa: University of Alabama Press, 2007, 146.

8. Legislation, 1713, in **The Laws of the Province of South Carolina, Volume I**, Charles Town, South Carolina: Timothy, 1736, 285.

9. Julia Fretwell Barnwell, "John Barnwell—Carolina Imperialist," M.A. thesis, University of North Carolina, Chapel Hill, 1942, 100.

10. **A General Report Concerning the State of His Majesty's Plantations on the Continent of America**, 1721, *Huntington Library, San Marino, California.*

11. Discussion in "Council Chamber," 9 September 1725, Folder 148, *Daniel Parish Slavery Transcripts.*

12. Herbert E. Bolton, ed., **Arrendondo's Historical Proof of Spain's Title to Georgia: A Contribution to the History of One of the Spanish Borderlands**, Berkeley: University of California Press, 1925.

13. Statement, circa 1738, in Carroll, **Historical Collections of South Carolina, Volume I**, 331.

14. Thaddeus Mason Harris, **Biographical Memorials of James Oglethorpe, Founder of the Colony of Georgia in North America**, Boston: Author, 1841, 24, *University of South Carolina, Columbia.*

15. Statement by James Oglethorpe, 1732, in Rodney M. Baine, ed., **The Publications of James Edward Oglethorpe**, Athens: University of Georgia Press, 1994, 228. See also **Select Tracts Relating to Colonies**, London: Roberts, 1732, *Huntington Library.*

16. James Oglethorpe, **A New and Accurate Account of the Provinces of South Carolina and Georgia**, London: Worrall, 1733, 15, 50, *Huntington Library.* (Oglethorpe is listed as author in the catalogue but not in the text itself.)

17. **A Sermon Preach'd before the Trustees for Establishing the Colony of Georgia in America and before the Associates of the Late Rev. Dr. Thomas Bray for Converting the Negroes on the British Plantations and for Other Good Purposes . . . February 1730–1731 . . .** , London: March, 1733, *University of Virginia, Charlottesville.*

18. See, e.g., **A New Voyage to Georgia by a Young Gentleman. Giving an Account of His Travels to South Carolina and Part of North Carolina . . .** , London: Wilford, 1737: the writer arrived on the mainland on 10 December 1733 and recounted his perception of the threat said to be presented by indigenes.

19. Darold D. Wax, "'The Great Risque We Run': The Aftermath of Slave Rebellion at Stono, South Carolina, 1739–1745," **Journal of Negro History**, 67(Number 2, Summer 1982): 136–147, 137.

20. Samuel Everleigh to George Morley, 1 May 1735, Folder 132, *Daniel Parish Slavery Transcripts.*

21. Folrain Shyllon, **Black People in Britain, 1555–1833**, London: Oxford University Press, 1977, 93.

22. David E. Van Deventer, **The Emergence of Provincial New Hampshire, 1623–1741**, Baltimore: Johns Hopkins University Press, 1976, 257.

23. William Gooch to Board of Trade, 26 November 1735, *Transcriptions of William Gooch Correspondence, Rockefeller Library, Williamsburg, Virginia.*

24. Report, 6 March 1734, Folder 6, *Daniel Parish Slavery Transcripts.*

25. South Carolina Bill, 1734, "Miscellaneous Papers," *Daniel Parrish Slavery Transcripts.*

26. Betty Wood, "James Edward Oglethorpe, Race and Slavery: A Reassessment," in Phinizy Spalding and Harvey J. Jackson, eds., **Oglethorpe in Perspective: Georgia's Founder after Two Hundred Years**, Tuscaloosa: University of Alabama Press, 1989, 66–79, 70.

27. **Reasons for Establishing the Colony of Georgia with Regard to the Trade of Great Britain**, London: Meadows, 1733.

28. David R. Chesnutt, **South Carolina's Expansion into Colonial Georgia, 1720–1765**, New York: Garland, 1989, 17–18. See also Trevor Reese, ed., **The Most Delightful**

Country of the Universe: Promotional Literature of the Colony of Georgia, 1717–1734, Savannah, Georgia: Beehive, 1972.

29. John Pitts Corry, "Indian Affairs in Georgia, 1732–1756," Ph.D. dissertation, University of Pennsylvania, 1936.

30. Thaddeus Mason Harris, **Biographical Memorials of James Oglethorpe, Founder of the Colony of Georgia in North America**, Boston: Author, 1841, 193–194.

31. Minutes of Council in Assembly and House of Burgesses, 1734–1740, 3 March 1737, Folder 8, *Daniel Parish Slavery Transcripts*.

32. Remarks, 24 April 1734, in **Journal of the Legislative Council of the Colony of New York, Began the 9th Day of April 1691; and Ended the 27th Day of September 1743**, Albany, New York: Weed, Parsons, 1861, 631.

33. **Gentleman's Magazine** (London), 2(September 1732): 970, in Robert McMillan Kennedy, ed., **South Carolina Items in the "Gentleman's Magazine" (London), 1731–1792, Extracted from the File in the University of South Carolina Library**, 1936, *University of South Carolina*. See also S. Max Edelson, **Plantation Enterprise in Colonial South Carolina**, Cambridge: Harvard University Press, 2006.

34. Lieutenant Governor Bennett to Mr. Poppule, 16 February 1718, in Cecil Headlam, ed., **Calendar of State Papers, August 1717–December 1718**, London: His Majesty's Stationery Office, 1930, 186.

35. Council on Trade and Plantations to Duke of Newcastle, 26 February 1735, in **Calendar of State Papers, Colonial Series, America and West Indies, Volume XLI, 1734–1735**, London: HM Stationery Office, 1953, 383.

36. Letter from Antigua, 1719, Folder 99, *Daniel Parish Slavery Transcripts*.

37. Letter from St. Christopher's, 1726, Folder 99, *Daniel Parish Slavery Transcripts*.

38. Jason T. Sharples, "Flames of Insurrection: Fearing Slave Conspiracy in Early America, 1670–1780," Ph.D. dissertation, Princeton University, 2010, 139.

39. Letter from Barbados, 1718, Folder 117, *Daniel Parish Slavery Transcripts*.

40. "Minutes of Council in Assembly Relating to Negroes and Slaves," 8 July 1726, Folder 123, *Daniel Parish Slavery Transcripts*.

41. Governor Hart to Council on Trade and Plantations, 6 January 1726, in Cecil Headlam, **Calendar of State Papers, 1726–1727**, London: His Majesty's Stationery Office, 1936, 1.

42. Thomas Pitt to His Royal Highness, George, Prince of Wales, 16 October 1716, in Cecil Headlam, ed., **Calendar of State Papers, January 1716–July 1717**, London: HM Royal Stationery Office, 1930, 181.

43. Secretary Stanhope to Council on Trade and Plantations, 12 April 1717, in Headlam, **Calendar of State Papers, January 1716–July 1717**, 285.

44. Mr. West to Council on Trade and Plantations, 8 July 1719, in Cecil Headlam, **Calendar of State Papers, January 1719–February 1720**, London: HM Stationery Office, 1933, 152.

45. **A Supplement to the Detection of the State and Situation of the Present Sugar Planters of Barbadoes and the Leeward Islands: Shewing . . . That the Surest Way for England to Command the Sugar Market Abroad Is to Contract Rather than Inlarge Her Sugar Colonies in a Letter from an Inhabitant of One of Her Majesty's Leeward Caribbee Islands . . .**, London: Wilford, 1733, *Huntington Library*.

46. **A Comparison between the British Sugar Colonies and New England as They Relate to the Interest of Great Britain with Some Observations on the State of the Case of New England, to Which Is Added a Letter to a Member of Parliament**, London: Roberts, 1733, *Huntington Library*. At the same site, see also **Observations on the Case of the Northern Colonies**, London: Roberts, 1731: The value of exports to sugar colonies "are upwards of 500,000 . . . a year," while "exportations to New

England–New York and Pensilvania are but 300,000 . . . a year," plus the fisheries of the latter go to Spain, Portugal, and Italy, "while [New England and related colonies] have ousted metropolitan competitors from Newfoundland." Mainland colonists' trade with Hispaniola is "encouraging the settlers in the French islands to increase their settlements by purchasing of Negroes, erecting of mills, . . . which great numbers of the French planters have been enabled to do since the Treaty of Utrecht"; thus, "the French Nation are encouraged to extend and enlarge their trade to the Coast of Africa in which trade they have five ships to one they had ten years ago," and "this trade is a great Discouragement to the British Sugar planters." Hence, these mainland colonies "decrease . . . the wealth and strength" of London by "giving encouragement to the increase of the French Sugar islands"—this "ought immediately to be prohibited." These colonists' rum trade "has destroyed the Trade and Commerce subsisting between the British people and the Indian nations insomuch that there is not one Province on the continent of America who have any trade with the Indian nations." This rum trade was a product of sugar planters from the French Caribbean collaborating with distillers from New England, particularly Rhode Island.

47. **Supplement to the Detection of the State and Situation.**
48. Report, 1737, Folder 100, *Daniel Parish Slavery Transcripts.*
49. **The Dispute between the Northern Colonies and the Sugar Islands Set in a Clear View**, 1732, *University of Virginia.*
50. **An Account of the Endeavours Used by the Society for the Propagation of the Gospel in Foreign Parts to Instruct the Negro Slaves in New York, Together with Two of Bishop Gibson's Letters on That Subject, Being an Extract from Dr. Humphrey's Historical Account of the Incorporated Society for the Propagation of the Gospel in Foreign Parts, from Its Foundation to the Year 1728**, London, 1730, *Johns Hopkins University, Baltimore.*
51. **Some Observations on the Assiento Trade, as It Has Been Exercised by the South Sea Company; Proving the Damage, Which Will Accrue Thereby to the British Commerce and Plantations in America and Particularly to Jamaica; to Which Is Annexed a Sketch of the Advantages to That Island to Great Britain by Its Annual Produce and by Its Situation for Trade or War, Addressed to His Grace, the Duke of Newcastle, One of His Majesty's Principal Secretaries of State, by a Person Who Resided Several Years at Jamaica**, London: Whitridge, 1728, *Huntington Library.*
52. Thomas Pitt to His Royal Highness George, Prince of Wales, 16 October 1716, in Headlam, **Calendar of State Papers, January 1716–July 1717**, 181.
53. Legislation, 1718, in **Acts of Assembly Passed in the Island of Jamaica from 1681 to 1737, Inclusive**, London: Basket, 1738, 163, *University of South Carolina.*
54. Legislation, 1724, in **Acts of Assembly Passed in the Island of Jamaica**, 207.
55. Legislation, 1728, in **Acts of Assembly Passed in the Island of Jamaica**, 229.
56. Legislation, 1730, in **Acts of Assembly Passed in the Island of Jamaica**, 238.
57. Legislation, 1730, in **Acts of Assembly Passed in the Island of Jamaica**, 239.
58. Legislation, 1733, in **Acts of Assembly Passed in the Island of Jamaica**, 267.
59. Address to the Governor's Council & Assembly of Jamaica, 1734, Folder 26, *Daniel Parish Slavery Transcripts.*
60. Remarks, 1734–1738, in Leonard Woods Labaree, ed., **Royal Instructions to British Colonial Governors, 1670–1776, Volume I**, New York: D. Appleton-Century, 1935, 422–423.
61. Letter from Richard Hemings, 5 July 1734, Folder 27, *Daniel Parish Slavery Transcripts.*
62. Charles Leslie, **A New History of Jamaica from the Earliest Accounts to the Taking of Porto Bello by Vice Admiral Vernon**, London: Hodges, 1740, 286.

63. R.C. Dallas, **The History of the Maroons, from Their Origin to the Establishment of Their Chief Tribe at Sierra Leone, Including the Expedition to Cuba for the Purpose of Procuring Spanish Chasseurs . . . , Volume I**, London: Strahan, 1803, 36, 38.

64. Treaty and Commentary, 1739, "Transcripts from Printed Sources . . . ," *Daniel Parish Slavery Transcripts.*

65. Orlando Patterson, "Slavery and Slave Revolts: A Socio-Historical Analysis of the First Maroon War: Jamaica, 1655–1740," **Social and Economic Studies**, 19(Number 3, September 1970): 289–325, 304.

66. Sharples, "Flames of Insurrection," 103.

67. Report on "The Negro Conspiracy of 1729 . . . ," Folder 97, *Daniel Parish Slavery Transcripts.*

68. David Barry Gaspar, "'To Bring Their Offending Slaves to Justice': Compensation and Slave Resistance in Antigua, 1669–1763," **Caribbean Quarterly**, 30(Number 3–4, September–December 1984): 45–59, 46.

69. Report, 17 March 1736, Folder 98, *Daniel Parish Slavery Transcripts.*

70. David Barry Gaspar, "The Antigua Slave Conspiracy of 1736: A Case Study of the Origins of Collective Resistance," **William and Mary Quarterly**, 35(Number 2, April 1978): 308–323, 309, 313, 319.

71. Quoted in Thomas James Little, "Influence of the West Indies upon Slavery in Colonial South Carolina, 1670–1738," M.A. thesis, University of South Carolina, 1989, 126–127. This quotation can also be found in Robert Pringle to Francis Guichard, 5 February 1739, in Walter B. Edgar, ed., **The Letterbook of Robert Pringle, Volume I**, Columbia: University of South Carolina Press, 1972, 68–69.

72. **A Genuine Narrative of the Intended Conspiracy of the Negroes at Antigua: Extracted from an Authentic Copy of a Report Made to the Chief Governor of the Carabee Islands, by the Commissioners or Judges Appointed to Try the Conspirators**, Dublin: Reilly, 1737.

73. Report to Governor Matthew on Conspiracy in Antigua, 30 December 1736, in **Calendar of State Papers, Colonial Series, Volume XLIII, 1937**, London: HM Stationery Office, 1963: thirty-five Africans were executed initially and forty-two banished.

74. **Providence Journal**, 12 March 2006: it is claimed here that eighty-eight Africans were executed as a result of the abortive 1736 revolt.

75. Petition of John Cleland, 2 December 1742, Folder 13, *Daniel Parish Slavery Transcripts.*

76. Affidavit sworn by John Hanson, 23 December 1736, in **Calendar of State Papers, Colonial Series, Volume XLIII**, 11.

77. William Byrd II to Earl of Egmont, 12 July 1736, *William Byrd Letterbooks, University of Virginia.*

78. Benjamin Martyn, **Reasons for Establishing the Colony of Georgia, with Regard to the Trade of Great Britain . . .** , London: Meadows, 1733.

79. Peter Gordon, journal entry, in E. Merlton Coulter, ed., **The Journal of Peter Gordon, 1732–1735**, Athens: University of Georgia Press, 1963, 43, 59.

80. Letter to Trustees, 27 August 1735, in Mills Lane, ed., **General Oglethorpe's Georgia: Colonial Letters, 1733–1743, Volume I**, Savannah, Georgia: Beehive, 1990, 225–227.

81. "Petition" to Trustees, 9 December 1738, in Lane, **General Oglethorpe's Georgia, Volume II**, 371–375.

82. James Oglethorpe to Trustees, 16 January 1739, in Lane, **General Oglethorpe's Georgia, Volume II**, 387–389.

83. Wax, "Great Risque We Run," 137.

84. N.M. Miller Surrey, **The Commerce of Louisiana during the French Regime, 1699–1763**, London: Longmans, Green, 1916, 237.
85. Patrick Riordan, "Finding Freedom in Florida: Native Peoples, African Americans and Colonists, 1670–1816," **Florida Historical Quarterly**, 75(Number 1, Summer 1996): 24–43, 20.
86. **The Miserable Case of the British Sugar Planters; Wherein Contained Some Remarks on the Poverty, Distress and Other Difficulties . . . and Some Comparisons Are Made between the French and the English in Regard to the Sugar Trade . . .**, London: Willock, 1738, *Huntington Library*.
87. Report, 26 February 1733, Minutes of Council in Assembly, 1731–1735, Folder 7, *Daniel Parish Slavery Transcripts*. The same words can be found in **South Carolina Council Journal**, 26 February 1733, *South Carolina Department of Archives and History, Columbia*.
88. **South Carolina Council Journal**, 29 May 1734, *South Carolina Department of Archives and History*.
89. Report, 25 June 1731, Minutes of Council in Assembly, 1731–1735, Folder 6, *Daniel Parish Slavery Transcripts*.
90. See, e.g., William Ryan, **The World of Thomas Jeremiah: Charles Town on the Eve of the American Revolution**, New York: Oxford University Press, 2010.
91. Report, 6 August 1736, Folder 191, *Daniel Parish Slavery Transcripts*.
92. Revolt, 16 September 1736, Folder 191, *Daniel Parish Slavery Transcripts*.
93. William Gooch to the Board of Trade, 18 July 1735, *William Gooch Correspondence*.
94. William Gooch to Secretary of State, Newcastle, 26 May 1735, *William Gooch Correspondence*.
95. Mr. West to Council on Trade and Plantations, 28 November 1735, *William Gooch Correspondence*.
96. William Gooch to Mr. Popple, 18 May 1736, *William Gooch Correspondence*.
97. Peter Wood, **Black Majority: Negroes in Colonial South Carolina from 1670 through the Stono Rebellion**, New York: Norton, 1996.

NOTES TO CHAPTER 5

1. Letter, 5 October 1739, in **Journal of the Commissioners for Trade and Plantations from January 1734–1735 to December 1741 . . .**, London: HM Stationery Office, 1930, 311.
2. Another account asserts that twenty settlers and forty Africans perished as a result of this rebellion: see Report, in Rodney M. Baine, ed., **Publications of James Edward Oglethorpe**, Athens: University of Georgia Press, 1994, 255.
3. "Statements Made in the Introduction to the Report of General Oglethorpe's Expedition to St. Augustine," July 1741, in B.R. Carroll, **Historical Collections of South Carolina Embracing Many Rare and Valuable Pamphlets and Other Documents Relating to the History of That State . . . , Volume II**, New York: Harper, 1836, 358, *Clemson University, South Carolina*.
4. Report of South Carolina Committee Tasked to Investigate "Causes of the Disappointment of Success in the Late Expedition against Saint Augustine . . . ," 1 July 1741, PRO30/47/14, *National Archives of the United Kingdom, London* (hereinafter *NAUK*). See also ". . . Cause of the Disappointment . . . ," in J.H. Easterby, ed., **Journal of the Commons House of Assembly of South Carolina, May 18, 1741–July 10, 1742**, Columbia: Historical Commission of South Carolina, 1951, 83, *Clemson University*. On the reputed attempt to deliver a letter to Oglethorpe, see "Minutes of the House of Burgesses and Council in Assembly, 1743–1745," 13 July 1739, Folder 15, *Daniel Parish Slavery Transcripts, New-York Historical Society, Manhattan*.

5. Andrew C. Nanne, "James Oglethorpe and the Civil-Military Conquest for Authority in Colonial Georgia, 1732–1749," **Georgia Historical Quarterly**, 95(Number 2, Summer 2011): 203–231, 218.

6. "Manuscript on the Negro Insurrection in South Carolina, 1738–1742. Runaways to Spanish Florida," Folder 11, *Daniel Parish Slavery Transcripts*. See also Jefferson Hall, "A Brief Glimpse of the African American Experience in Savannah," 2002, Vertical File, *Georgia Historical Society, Savannah*: "'Tribes imported from Africa were 'the majority in the early period (1716–1744) and one third of the total,'" generally. "Gullah," which is the term ascribed to a people with a distinct culture in that region, is thought to be a corruption of "Angola." Or it might be a corruption of the Hebrew term "golah" or "in exile," a reflection of "an early and prominent Jewish presence in the area." Oglethorpe echoed the idea that Angolans were responsible for the revolt: see "An Account of the Negroe Insurrection in South Carolina," 1740, in Report, in Baine, ed., **Publications of James Edward Oglethorpe**, 252–255.

7. Frank Klingberg, **An Appraisal of the Negro in Colonial South Carolina: A Study in Americanization**, Philadelphia: Porcupine, 1975, 19, 138: apparently there were Portuguese words in the "Gullah" language of the Africans of Carolina.

8. Jason T. Sharples, "Flames of Insurrection: Fearing Slave Conspiracy in Early America, 1670–1780," Ph.D. dissertation, Princeton University, 2010, 160.

9. Remarks, 13 September 1739, in William Stephens, **A Journal of the Proceedings in Georgia Beginning October 20, 1737, Volume II**, London: Meadows, 1742, 128–129, *Georgia Historical Society*.

10. Alan Gallay, **The Formation of a Planter Elite: Jonathan Bryan and the Southern Colonial Frontier**, Athens: University of Georgia Press, 1989.

11. Peter Wood, **Black Majority: Negroes in Colonial South Carolina from 1670 through the Stono Rebellion**, New York: Knopf, 1974. See the account by Oglethorpe: **London Daily Post**, 17 March 1740.

12. Matthew Mulcahy, "'Melancholy and Fatal Calamities': Disaster and Society in Eighteenth-Century South Carolina," in Jack P. Green, Rosemary Brana-Shute, and Randy J. Sparks, eds., **Money, Trade, and Power: The Evolution of South Carolina's Plantation Society**, Columbia: University of South Carolina Press, 2001, 278–298, 280, 281.

13. Excerpt from diary of Captain Hinrichs, circa 1736, in Bernard A. Uhlendorf, ed., **The Siege of Charleston**, Ann Arbor: University of Michigan Press, 1938, 323.

14. Report by Don Manuel de Montiano, 19 August 1739, in **Collections of the Georgia Historical Society, Volume VII, Part I, Letters of Montiano. Siege of St. Augustine**, Savannah, Georgia: Savannah Morning News, 1909, 32, *Georgia Historical Society, Savannah*.

15. Eugene Portlette Southall, "Negroes in Florida Prior to the Civil War," **Journal of Negro History**, 19(Number 1, January 1934): 77–86, 78.

16. Benjamin Robins, **Observations on the Present Convention with Spain**, London: Cooper, 1739, *Georgia Historical Society*.

17. See, e.g., James Ferguson King, "Evolution of the Free Slave Trade Principle in Spanish Colonial Administration," **Hispanic American Historical Review**, February 1942, 35, *Georgia Historical Society*. See also John E. Worth, **The Struggle for the Georgia Coast: An Eighteenth-Century Spanish Retrospective of Guale and Mocama**, Athens: University of Georgia Press, 1995.

18. Billups Phinizy Spalding, "Georgia and South Carolina during the Oglethorpe Period, 1732–1743," Ph.D. dissertation, University of North Carolina, Chapel Hill, 1963, 274.

19. William Bull to "My Lord," 5 October 1739, Folder 11, *Daniel Parish Slavery Transcripts.*

20. **Council Journal, Upper House**, 2 February 1739, *South Carolina Department of Archives and History, Columbia.*

21. Remarks, 8 November 1739, in J.H. Easterby, ed., **Journal of the Commons House of Assembly of South Carolina, September 12, 1739–March 26, 1741**, Columbia: Historical Commission of South Carolina, 1962, 16, *Clemson University.*

22. James Oglethorpe to William Bull, 30 January 1740, in Easterby, **Journal of the Commons House of Assembly of South Carolina, September 12, 1739–March 26, 1741**, 160.

23. Letter, 22 November 1740, *James Glen Papers, University of South Carolina, Columbia.*

24. Remarks by Governor Glen, circa 1742, in Chapman J. Milling, ed., **Colonial South Carolina: Two Contemporary Descriptions by Governor James Glen and Doctor George Milligen Johnson**, Columbia: University of South Carolina Press, 1951, 96.

25. Remarks by Governor Glen, circa early 1740s, in Milling, **Colonial South Carolina**, 135–136. See also Mary F. Carter, "James Glen, Governor of South Carolina: A Study in British Administrative Policies," Ph.D. dissertation, University of California–Los Angeles, 1951.

26. **Council Journal, Upper House,** 19 January 1739, *South Carolina Department of Archives and History.*

27. John Tate Lanning, **The Diplomatic History of Georgia: A Study of the Epoch of Jenkins' Ear**, Chapel Hill: University of North Carolina Press, 1936, 61–62.

28. Patrick Tailfer, Hugh Anderson, and David Douglas, **A True and Historical Narrative of the Colony of Georgia in America**, Charles-town, South Carolina: Timothy, 1741, 32.

29. Lieutenant Governor Thomas Broughton to Duke of Newcastle, 6 February 1737, in **Calendar of State Papers, Colonial Series, Volume XLIII, 1737**, London: HM Stationery Office, 1963, 25–27.

30. William Gooch to Secretary of State, 16 March 1736, *Transcriptions of William Gooch Correspondence, Rockefeller Library, Williamsburg, Virginia.*

31. "Causes of the Disappointment of Success."

32. **Journal of the Upper House of Assembly**, South Carolina, 8 July 1742, CO412/7, *NAUK.*

33. James Oglethorpe to Colonel Stephens, Frederica, 1 February 1740, **Collections of the Georgia Historical Society, Volume III**, Savannah, Georgia, 1873, 105–109, *Huntington Library, San Marino, California.* See also **A Full Reply to Lieut. Cadogan's Spanish Hireling . . . and Lieut. Mackay's Letter, Concerning the Action at Moosa Wherein the Impartial Account of the Late Expedition to St. Augustine Is Clearly Vindicated, by Plain Facts and Evidence,** London: Huggonson, 1743, *University of Virginia, Charlottesville.*

34. **The Spanish Hireling Detected, Being a Refutation of the Several Calumnies and Falsehoods in a Late Pamphlet, Entitled "An Impartial Account of the Late Expedition against St. Augustine under General Oglethorpe," by George Cadogan, Lieutenant in General Oglethorpe's Regiment**, London: Roberts, 1743, *Brown University, Providence, Rhode Island.* A version of this work can also be found at the Huntington Library.

35. John Jay TePaske, **The Governorship of Spanish Florida, 1700–1763**, Durham: Duke University Press, 1964, 241. See also Larry E. Ivers, "The Battle of Fort Mosa," **Georgia Historical Quarterly**, 51(Number 2, March 1967): 135–153.

36. **A Letter from Lieut. Hugh Mackay of General Oglethorpe's Regiment to John Mackay, Esq. in the Shire of Sutherland in Scotland**, London, 1742, *Brown University.*

37. Appeal to the King, 26 July 1740, Folder 11, *Daniel Parish Slavery Transcripts.*

38. Remarks of Kenneth Bayley Cornet, 19 January 1741, Folder 11, *Daniel Parish Slavery Transcripts.*

39. William Bull to "My Lord," 9 May 1739, Folder 11, *Daniel Parish Slavery Transcripts.*

40. Quoted in Robert Anthony Olwell, "Authority and Resistance: Social Order in a Colonial Slave Society, the South Carolina Low Country, 1739–1782," Ph.D. dissertation, Johns Hopkins University, 1991, 386.

41. Remarks of William Bull et al., 23 July 1740, in Easterby, **Journal of the Commons House of Assembly of South Carolina, September 12, 1739–March 26, 1741,** 365.

42. William Bull to "My Lord," 11 February 1739, Folder 11, *Daniel Parish Slavery Transcripts.*

43. Letter, 28 May 1730, Folder 94, *Daniel Parish Slavery Transcripts.*

44. Governor Robert Dinwiddie to Duke of Newcastle, August 1743, *Transcriptions of Correspondence of Governor Robert Dinwiddie, Rockefeller Library, Williamsburg, Virginia.*

45. William Perrin, **The Present State of the British and French Sugar Colonies and Our Own Northern Colonies, Considered Together with Some Remarks on the Decay of Our Trade and the Improvements Made of Late Years by the French in Theirs,** London: Cooper, 1740, *Huntington Library.*

46. Robert Pringle to Francis Guichard, 5 February 1739, in Walter B. Edgar, ed., **The Letterbook of Robert Pringle, Volume I,** Columbia: University of South Carolina Press, 68–69.

47. Robert Pringle to Nathaniel French, 20 August 1739, in Edgar, **Letterbook,** 122.

48. "Causes of the Disappointment of Success."

49. Woody Holton, **Forced Founders: Indians, Debtors, Slaves, and the Making of the American Revolution in Virginia,** Chapel Hill: University of North Carolina Press, 1999, 68. See also William Byrd II to the Earl of Egmont, 12 July 1736, *William Byrd Letterbooks, University of Virginia.*

50. Remarks, June 1740, in Stephens, **Journal of the Proceedings in Georgia,** 402.

51. James Oglethorpe to Andrew Stone, 24 November 1742, **Collections of the Georgia Historical Society, Volume III,** 125–126.

52. Governor Robert Dinwiddie to Board of Trade, 29 April 1740, *Correspondence of Governor Robert Dinwiddie.*

53. Earl of Egmont, journal entry of 22 December 1737, in Robert G. McPherson, ed., **The Journal of the Earl of Egmont: Abstract of the Trustee Proceedings for Establishing the Colony of Georgia, 1732–1738,** Athens: University of Georgia Press, 1962, 325.

54. General Oglethorpe to Trustees, 12 March 1739, in **Collections of the Georgia Historical Society, Volume III,** 70–71.

55. Tailfer, Anderson, and Douglas, **True and Historical Narrative.**

56. Petition to King George II or Parliament, 29 December 1740, in Mills Lane, ed., **General Oglethorpe's Georgia: Colonial Letters, 1733–1743, Volume II,** Savannah, Georgia: Beehive, 1990, 513–524.

57. **An Account Shewing the Progress of the Colony of Georgia in American from Its First Establishment,** London, 1741, *Huntington Library.*

58. Donald W. Wax, "Georgia and the Negro before the American Revolution," **Georgia Historical Quarterly,** 51(Number 1, March 1967): 63–77, 65.

59. John Dobell to Trustees, 18 July 1743, in Lane, **General Oglethorpe's Georgia, Volume II,** Savannah, Georgia: Beehive, 1975, 663–665.

60. James Oglethorpe to Trustees, 29 June 1741, **Collections of the Georgia Historical Society, Volume III,** 117. This document can also be found in Folder 11, *Daniel Parish Slavery Transcripts.*

292 << NOTES TO CHAPTER 5

61. James Oglethorpe to Trustees, 28 May 1742, in **Collections of the Georgia Historical Society, Volume III**, 120–122.
62. "Journal of the Trustees. Minutes of the Trustees. Proceedings of the President and Assistants," 16 January 1740, Folder 171, *Daniel Parish Slavery Transcripts*.
63. Tailfer, Anderson, and Douglas, **True and Historical Narrative**, 45.
64. **Considerations of the American Trade before and since the Establishment of the South-Sea Company**, London: Roberts, 1739, *Huntington Library*. At the same site, see also Daniel Tempelman, **The Secret History of the Late Directors of the South Sea Company**, London: Author, 1735: the author was formerly "clerk in the Secretary's Office of the said company."
65. **Three Letters from the Reverend Mr. G. Whitfield**, Philadelphia: B. Franklin, 1740, *Huntington Library*.
66. Wylie Sypher, **Guinea's Captive Kings: British Anti-Slavery Literature of the XVIIIth Century**, Chapel Hill: University of North Carolina Press, 1942, 60.
67. William H. Williams, **Slavery and Freedom in Delaware, 1639–1865**, Wilmington, Delaware: SR Books, 1996, 73, 74, 75.
68. Remarks by Lieutenant Governor George Thomas, 21 October 1741, in **Minutes of the House of Assembly of the Three Counties upon Delaware at Sessions Held at New Castle in the Years, 1740–1742**, Public Archives Commission of Delaware, 1929, 41, *Delaware Historical Society, Wilmington*: "all the powers of Europe are arming and matters now to be brought to such a great crisis, that it is generally apprehended a war with France is at no great distance . . . [from] the defenceless conditions of these counties."
69. Tailfer, Anderson, and Douglas, **True and Historical Narrative**, 33, 34.
70. Madrid also suffered a setback on the mainland because those who were Jewish tended to flee in all directions when their forces arrived, often to London's lines. See, e.g., Tailfer, Anderson, and Douglas, **True and Historical Narrative**, 30, 84: An early settler was "Abraham De Leon, a Jew, who had been many years a vineron in Portugal and a freeholder in Savannah, cultivated several kinds of grapes in his garden . . . to great perfection. . . . [U]pon the west side of Savannah lie the township lots of the Jews, now deserted, they having all gone to other colonies except three or four." See also David T. Morgan, "Judaism in Eighteenth Century Georgia," **Georgia Historical Quarterly**, 58(Number 1, Spring 1974): 42–54.
71. Tailfer, Anderson, and Douglas, **True and Historical Narrative**, 47.
72. Remarks and Legislation, 9 November 1739, Minutes of the Council in Assembly and House of Burgesses, 1734–1740, Folder 11, *Daniel Parish Slavery Transcripts*: "that every person owning or entitled to any slaves in this province for every ten male slaves above the age of twelve years shall be obliged to find and provide one able white man for the militia, . . . that any person owning or claiming any lands in this province over & above the quantity of 4000 acres and under the quantity of 20,000 acres shall be obliged to find and provide one able white man to serve in the militia for every 2000 acres of land over the said quantity of 4000."
73. Acts of Assembly Relating to Negroes, Servants & Slaves, 1731–1743, Folder 5, *Daniel Parish Slavery Transcripts*.
74. David R. Chestnut, **South Carolina's Expansion into Colonial Georgia, 1720–1765**, New York: Garland, 1989, 35.
75. Robert Pringle to Samuel Saunders, 2 April 1740, in Edgar, **Letterbook**, 174–175.
76. For a broader context, see, e.g., **Memoirs of the Lives and Conduct of Those Illustrious Heroes Prince Eugene of Savoy and John Duke of Marlborough . . .** , London: Rowlands, 1742, *University of South Carolina*; and **The Genuine Speech of the Truly Honourable Admiral Vernon to the Sea Officers at a Council of War, Just before the Attack on Cartagena**, London: Cooper, 1741, *Huntington Library*.

77. Henry R. Viets, **Smollett, the "War of Jenkins's Ear" and an Account of the Expedition to Carthagena, 1743**, Copenhagen, 1940, *Massachusetts Historical Society, Boston*. On Porto-bello, see **Original Papers Relating to the Expedition to Panama**, London: Cooper, 1744, *Brown University*. See also A. Marvell, **Satirical and Panegyrical Instructions to Mr. William Hogarth, Painter, on Admiral Vernon's Taking Porto-Bello with Six Ships of War Only**, London: Goreham, 1740, *Huntington Library*.

78. W. Blakeney to Duke of Newcastle, 31 July 1740, CO5/41, *NAUK*.

79. Speech of George Clarke, His Majesty's Lieutenant Governor and Commander in Chief of the "Province of New York . . . ," September 1740, CO5/41, *NAUK*.

80. W. Blakeney to Duke of Newcastle, 14 December 1740, CO5/41, *NAUK*.

81. William Gooch to Duke of Newcastle, unclear date, CO5/41, *NAUK*.

82. William Gooch to Duke of Newcastle, 7 January 1741, CO5/41, *NAUK*.

83. **A Complete and Historical Description of the Principal Objects of the Present War in the West Indies. Viz. Cartagena, Puerto Bello, La Vera Cruz, the Havana and San Agustin, Shewing Their Situation, Strength, Trade . . .**, London: Gardner, 1741, 14, *New-York Historical Society*.

84. Peter M. Voelz, **Slave and Soldier: The Military Impact of Blacks in Colonial Americas**, New York: Garland, 1993, 78.

85. Report, 10 May 1741, SP36/34, *NAUK*.

86. Lord Cathcart to Duke of Newcastle, 26 June 1740, CO5/41, *NAUK*: "furnishing the levies from North America with provisions when they arrive at the rendezvous at Jamaica, . . . supplying the troops with fresh provisions from North America . . . and for arms for the 500 Negroes proposed to be had from the island of Jamaica if he grace shall judge it proper."

87. Lord Cathcart to Duke of Newcastle, 30 September 1740, CO5/41, *NAUK*: "Letters in London from people in Boston that five thousand men have been levied in the provinces of North America for His Majesty's service. . . . five hundred blacks ordered to be raised in Jamaica."

88. Lanning, **Diplomatic History of Georgia**, 192.

89. Lord Cathcart to Duke of Newcastle, 16 August 1740, CO5/41.

90. Report on "Absent officers" of 8th Regiment "Under the Command" of Lord Cathcart, 11 August 1740, CO5/41, *NAUK*: "refuses to serve," "deserted," "infirm," "very bad state of health."

91. Admiral Vernon to Commodore Lestock, 7 March 1740, in **Original Papers Relating to the Expedition to Carthagena**, London: Cooper, 1744, *University of North Carolina, Chapel Hill* (also available at Brown University).

92. **Original Papers Relating to the Expedition to Carthagena**.

93. James Phelps to Lord Cathcart, 27 July 1740, CO5/41, *NAUK*. On plans to seize Cuba, in the same file, see Lord Cathcart to Duke of Newcastle, 27 August 1740.

94. See, e.g., **Original Letters to an Honest Sailor**, London: Thomas, no date (circa 1742), *Brown University*.

95. Lord Cathcart to Duke of Newcastle, 14 September 1740, CO5/41, *NAUK*: "Fresh provisions" were needed for sailors, which meant sending a "ship to Jamaica to provide. . . . we have six of the field officers of the American regiment on board the transports here." In the same file, see Lord Cathcart to Duke of Newcastle, 27 September 1740: "infectious fever which has been fatal to the fleet. . . . two hundred men only are taken from the Leeward Islands and three hundred men from the companys at Jamaica, but five hundred men are ordered to be taken from the Virgin Islands and the same number of blacks from Jamaica."

96. Report from A. Spotswood, 26 April 1740, CO5/41, *NAUK*.

97. **Authentic Papers Relating to the Expedition against Carthagena: Being the Resolutions of the Councils of War; Both of Sea and Land Officers**, London: Raymond, 1744, *Massachusetts Historical Society*. At the same site, see also Francis Russell Hart, **Spanish Documents Relating to the Scots' Settlement of Darien**, uncertain provenance. The former document can also be found at the University of North Carolina, Chapel Hill.

98. Lord Cathcart to Duke of Newcastle, 3 October 1740, CO5/41, *NAUK*.

99. **Original Papers Relating to the Expedition of Carthagena**; and Sir Charles Knowles, **An Account of the Expedition to Carthagena with Explanatory Notes and Observations**, London: Cooper, 1743, *Massachusetts Historical Society*.

100. Lord Cathcart to Duke of Newcastle, 10 October 1740, CO5/41, *NAUK*.

101. Bruce Campbell MacGunnigle, "Carnage at Cartagena: Captain William Hopkins and His Rhode Island Recruits in the Campaign against Cartagena & Cuba, 1741," Providence, Rhode Island: Society by Webster, 1988, *Brown University*: London deployed about thirty companies in the Caribbean for these battles, including eight from Pennsylvania; five from New York; four each from Massachusetts, North Carolina, and Virginia; three each from Maryland and New Jersey; two each from Rhode Island and Connecticut; and one from New Hampshire. See also Admiral Vernon to His Grace the Duke, 26 April 1741, in **Authentic Papers Relating to the Expedition against Carthagena** . . . , London: Raymond, 1744, *University of North Carolina, Chapel Hill*. For more on the attack on Cuba, see M.S. Anderson, **The War of the Austrian Succession, 1740–1748**, London: Longman, 1995, 18.

102. **A Journal of the Expedition to Carthagena with Notes in Answer to a Little Pamphlet** . . . , London: Robert, 1744, *University of North Carolina, Chapel Hill*. See also **An Account of the Expedition to Carthagena**, uncertain provenance, *Brown University*; and "Expedition to Cartagena in the Year 1741," no date, CO5/41, *NAUK*. See also **Diario de Todo la Ocurrido en la Expugnación de los Fuertes de Boca Chica y . . . la Ciudad**, Cartagena, 1742, *Brown University*: in Cartagena, the redcoats encountered at least two companies of armed Negroes and "Mulattoes" and numerous indigenes on Madrid's side.

103. Albert Harkness, Jr., "Americanism and Jenkins' Ear," **Mississippi Valley Historical Review**, 37(Number 1, June 1950): 61–90, 75, 76, 88, 89. See Lanning, **Diplomatic History of Georgia**, 206: the author argues that in Cartagena, there was a tendency for the African soldiers to "scamper off" to Spanish lines; if true, this underscores London's dilemma in being unable to rely wholly on any segment of the military; this also suggests that Cartagena was little different from St. Augustine, where Africans tended to "scamper off" from Carolina; and, similarly, it suggests that leveling the differences between Madrid and London on Africans—or even providing the redcoats with an advantage—by moving toward abolition was a result.

104. **An Account of the Expedition to Cartagena with Explanatory Notes and Observations** . . . , London: Cooper, 1743, *University of North Carolina, Chapel Hill*.

105. Madrid to Don Juan Francisco de Guemes y Horcasitas, 31 October 1741, in **Collections of the Georgia Historical Society, Volume VII, Part III, The Spanish Official Account of the Attack on the Colony of Georgia in America, and of Its Defeat on St. Simons Island by General James Oglethorpe**, Savannah, Georgia: Savannah Morning News, 1913, 21–24, *Georgia Historical Society*. The "Spanish Official Account" can also be found at Brown University.

106. Instructions for Captain Bruce of HMS Hawk, 9 December 1741, ADM 2/57, X 73. 255.1, *North Carolina State Archives, Raleigh*.

107. Don Juan Francisco de Guemes y Horcasitas to Don Manuel de Montiano, 14 May 1742, in **Collections of the Georgia Historical Society, Volume VII, Part III**, 27–31.

108. From the London Gazette of December 25, 1742. An Account of the Invasion of Georgia, Drawn Out by Lieutenant Patrick Sutherland, of General Oglethorpe's Regiment, Who Lately Arrived in England, and Was Sent Express on That Occasion, but Being Taken by the Spaniards off the Lizard, Was Obliged to Throw the Said Express and His Other Papers Overboard, *Huntington Library*.

109. William Stephens, journal entry of 6 June 1742, in E. Merton Coulter, ed., The Journal of William Stephens, 1741-1743, Athens: University of Georgia Press, 1958, 91.

110. Journal of the Upper House of Assembly, 10 August 1742, CO412/7, *NAUK*.

111. Gentleman's Magazine, December 1742, reprinted from London Gazette, May 1742, in Robert McMillan Kennedy, ed., South Carolina Items in the "Gentleman's Magazine" (London), 1731-1792, Extracted from the File in the University of South Carolina Library, 1936, *University of South Carolina*.

112. Gentleman's Magazine, "Supplement . . . for the year 1742." See also Boston Evening Post, 29 November 1742.

113. Journal of the Upper House of Assembly, 15 July 1742, CO412/7, *NAUK*.

114. Journal of the Upper House of Assembly, 3 August 1742, CO412/7, *NAUK*.

115. Quoted in TePaske, Governorship of Spanish Florida, 147. See also James Oglethorpe to Sir Robert Walpole, 7 December 1741, in Lane, General Oglethorpe's Georgia, Volume II (1975), 602-604.

116. Governor William Gooch to Secretary of State, 28 July 1742, *William Gooch Correspondence*.

117. Journals and Letters of Eliza Lucas (published 1850), *Cleveland Public Library, Ohio*.

118. Quoted in Margaret Davis Cate, "Fort Frederica and the Battle of Bloody Marsh," Georgia Historical Quarterly, 27(Number 2, June 1943): 111-174, 173, 174. On Bloody Marsh, see, e.g., Scrapbook of Otis Ashmore, 1927, *Georgia Historical Society*.

119. Joyce Elizabeth Harman, Trade and Privateering in Spanish Florida, 1732-1763, Tuscaloosa: University of Alabama Press, 2004, 41.

120. Savannah Morning News, 16 February 2008. See An Impartial Account of the Late Expedition against St. Augustine under General Oglethorpe, Occasioned by the Suppression of the Report, Made by a Committee of the General Assembly in South Carolina . . . , London: Huggonson, 1742, *Brown University*: "as the vicinity of St. Augustine can be bad reason for disallowing Negroes in Georgia." Also at Brown, see Edward Kimber, A Relation of a Journal of a Late Expedition to the Gates of St. Augustine on Florida, Conducted by the Hon. General James Oglethorpe . . . , Boston: Goodspeed, 1935, vi: Oglethorpe was the "center of a bitter controversy in England."

121. Julia Floyd Smith, Slavery and Rice Culture in Low Country Georgia, 1750-1860, Knoxville: University of Tennessee Press, 1985, 19.

122. Stephens, journal entries of 8 January 1743 and 5 February 1743, in Coulter, Journal of William Stephens, 1741-1743, 158-159, 168.

123. Betty Wood, "James Edward Oglethorpe, Race and Slavery: A Reassessment," in Phinizy Spalding and Harvey J. Jackson, eds., Oglethorpe in Perspective: Georgia's Founder after Two Hundred Years, Tuscaloosa: University of Alabama Press, 1989, 66-79, 77. See also George Cardigan, The Spanish Hireling Detected: Being a Refutation of the Several Calumnies and Falsehoods in a Late *Pamphlet* Etitul'd An Impartial Account of the Late Expedition against *St. Augustine* under General Oglethorpe, London: Roberts, 1743, *Huntington Library*: the author argues that suppressing subversion from St. Augustine has been successful and that Africans have not been fleeing there of late.

124. TePaske, Governorship of Spanish Florida, 154.

125. Mr. Beaufain to the Earl of Egmont, 6 March 1742, in Lucian Lamar Knight, ed., **The Colonial Records of the State of Georgia, Volume 23**, Atlanta: Byrd, 1914, 530.

126. Joseph Avery to Trustees, 31 January 1742, in Knight, **Colonial Records of the State of Georgia, Volume 23**, 475.

NOTES TO CHAPTER 6

1. See, e.g., Jill Lepore, **New York Burning: Liberty, Slavery, and Conspiracy in Eighteenth-Century Manhattan**, New York: Knopf, 2005.

2. Minutes of Council, New York, CO412/21, 31 August 1741, *National Archives of the United Kingdom, London* (hereinafter *NAUK*).

3. Daniel Horsmanden, **The New York Conspiracy, or a History of the Negro Plot, with the Journal of the Proceedings against the Conspirators at New York in the Years 1741–1742 . . .** , New York: Southwick & Pelsue, 1810, 28, 132, 236, 222, 226, 237, 298, *Cleveland Public Library, Ohio*. See also Minutes of the Common Council of the City of New York, 11 April 1741, *New York City Municipal Archives*: "Order'd that this board request his honour the Lieut. Governor to Issue a Proclamation offering a Reward to any white person, that shall discover any person or persons lately concern'd in setting fire to any dwelling House or Store House in this City."

4. Minutes of Council in Assembly, 24 April 1741, Folder 160, *Daniel Parish Slavery Transcripts, New-York Historical Society, Manhattan*. In the same collection, in Box III, Folder 3, see "Minutes of Council in Assembly," South Carolina, 16 October 1751: Grand jury investigation of "many mean houses who obtain licenses and make it a practice to sell rum [to] spirituous Negroes early in morning and other unreasonable hours to the very great disturbance, . . . great detriment."

5. James Oglethorpe to Trustees, 28 May 1742, in Lucian Lamar Knight, **Colonial Records of the State of Georgia, Volume 23**, Atlanta: Byrd, 1914, 333.

6. Minutes of Council, New York, 15 April 1741, CO412/21, *NAUK*.

7. Minutes of Council, 9 June 1741, CO412/21, *NAUK*.

8. Minutes of Council, 16 July 1741, CO412/21, *NAUK*: This source asserts that eight Africans were convicted.

9. Minutes of Council, 4 August 1741, CO412/21, *NAUK*.

10. Minutes of Council, 14 June 1741, CO412/21, *NAUK*.

11. Letter from Governor Clinton, 13 April 1745, *Lewis Morris Papers, New Jersey Historical Society, Newark*.

12. Governor Clinton to Lewis Morris, 19 August 1745, *Lewis Morris Papers*.

13. W. Bryan Rommel-Ruiz, "Atlantic Revolutions: Slavery and Freedom in Newport, Rhode Island, and Halifax, Nova Scotia, in the Era of the American Revolution," Ph.D. dissertation, University of Michigan, 1999, 195. See also William D. Piersen, **Black Yankees: The Development of Afro-American Subculture in Eighteenth-Century New England**, Amherst: University of Massachusetts Press, 1988.

14. Bill, 18 April 1745, in **Journal of the Legislative Council of the Colony of New York, Began the 8th Day of December 1743; and Ended the 3rd of April 1775**, Albany, New York: Weed, Parsons, 1861, 879.

15. James G. Lydon, "New York and the Slave Trade, 1700 to 1774," **William and Mary Quarterly**, 35(Number 2, April 1978): 375–394.

16. Duke of New Castle, Windsor Castle, to Lewis Morris, 25 September 1730, *Lewis Morris Papers*.

17. **Transcriptions of Early County Records of New Jersey, Gloucester County Series, Slave Documents**, Newark: WPA, Historical Records Survey, 1940, *New Jersey Historical Society*.

18. Comment, in David Mitros, ed., **Slave Records of Morris County, New Jersey: 1756-1841**, Morristown, New Jersey: Morris County Heritage Commission, 2002, 1. See also John S. Lask, "John Woolman: Crusader for Freedom," **Phylon**, 5(Number 1, First Quarter, 1944): 30-40, 32: New Jersey was one of the focal points of the slave trade during Woolman's life—and a focal point of slave insurrection.

19. Proposal, 1744, in Eugene Sheridan, ed., **The Papers of Lewis Morris, Volume III, 1738-1746**, Newark: New Jersey Historical Society, 1993, 344.

20. Thelma Wills Foote, **Black and White Manhattan: The History of Racial Formation in Colonial New York City**, New York: Oxford University Press, 2004, 63, 164, 207.

21. Quoted in Edgar J. McManus, **Black Bondage in the North**, Syracuse: Syracuse University Press, 1973, 136.

22. Governor Clinton to Lewis Morris, 23 July 1741, *Lewis Morris Papers*.

23. John Shea, "The New York Negro Plot of 1741," 1862, *New-York Historical Society*.

24. Samuel McKee, **Labor in Colonial New York, 1664-1776**, New York: Columbia University Press, 1935, 136. See also Billy G. Smith and Richard Wojtowicz, eds., **Blacks Who Stole Themselves: Advertisements for Runaways in the "Pennsylvania Gazette," 1728-1790**, Philadelphia: University of Pennsylvania Press, 1989, 31: 29 June 1749: "Spanish Mulattoe servant man named George . . . may attempt to get on board [a] vessel. . . . privateering [previously]."

25. "Confession of a Negro Belonging to Peter Low," 11 June 1741, Folder 163, *Daniel Parish Slavery Transcripts*.

26. Governor Greene to Governor of Havana, 14 June 1746, in Gertrude Selwyn Kimball, ed., **The Correspondence of the Colonial Governors of Rhode Island, 1723-1775, Volume I**, Boston: Houghton, Mifflin, 1902, 425.

27. Oscar Williams, **African Americans and Colonial Legislation in the Middle Colonies,** New York: Garland, 1998, 67.

28. "Ex Parte Seventeen Indians, Molattos & Negroes," 23 September 1746, in Charles Merrill Hough, ed., **Reports of Cases in the Vice Admiralty of the Province of New York and in the Court of Admiralty of the State of New York, 1715-1788**, New Haven: Yale University Press, 1925, 29-31.

29. Thomas Ingersoll, "Free Blacks in a Slave Society: New Orleans, 1718-1812," **William and Mary Quarterly**, 48(Number 2, April 1991): 173-200, 180.

30. Peter Charles Hoffer, **The Great New York Conspiracy of 1741: Slavery, Crime, and Colonial Law**, Lawrence: University Press of Kansas, 2003, 116.

31. Graham Russell Hodges, **Root and Branch: African Americans in New York and East Jersey, 1613-1863**, Chapel Hill: University of North Carolina Press, 1999, 148.

32. Report by Captain Scott, 26 June 1741, *Lewis Morris Papers*.

33. W. Blakeney to Duke of Newcastle, 8 July 1740, CO5/41, *NAUK*.

34. Report, in **Journals of the House of Representatives of Massachusetts, 1740-1741**, Boston: Massachusetts Historical Society, 1942, 88, 78, 94, 121-122, 182. *Massachusetts Archives, Boston*. See also George H. Moore, **Notes on the History of Slavery in Massachusetts**, New York: Appleton, 1866.

35. 17 August 1741, in **Journals of the House of Representatives of Massachusetts, 1741-1742**, Boston: Massachusetts Historical Society, 1942, 65.

36. 17 June 1742, in **Journals of the House of Representatives of Massachusetts, 1742-1744**, Boston: Massachusetts Historical Society, 1942, 47.

37. J. Belcher to W. Blakeney, 8 September 1740, CO5/41, *NAUK*.

38. **Dr. Houstoun's Memoirs of His Own Life-Time** . . . , London: Lawton Gilliver, 1747, 258, *New-York Historical Society*.

39. J. Belcher to W. Blakeney, 15 September 1740, CO5/41, *NAUK*: The indigenes "are the King's natural born subjects, bred up after the English manner . . . and their having

black hair and tawny faces don't at all disable them from being good soldiers. . . . it will contribute better to the service to have mixt with the English, than to be in a body by themselves. . . . white men should not insult or use them ill."

40. Richard C. Youngken, "African Americans in Newport: An Introduction to the Heritage of African Americans in Newport, Rhode Island, 1700–1765," Providence: Rhode Island Black Heritage Society, no date, *Rhode Island Historical Society, Providence*. See also Robert K. Fitts, **Inventing New England's Slave Paradise: Master/Slave Relations in Eighteenth-Century Narragansett, Rhode Island,** New York: Garland, 1998; and Stephen D. Behrendt, David Eltis, and David Richardson, "The Costs of Coercion: African Agency in the Pre-Modern Atlantic World," **Economic History Review,** 54(Number 3, 2001): 454–476.

41. Sarah Deutsch, "The Elusive Guineamen: Newport Slavers, 1735–1774," **New England Quarterly,** 55(Number 2, June 1982): 229–253, 229.

42. Margaret Shea, "The Story of Colonial Newport," 1962, *Rhode Island Historical Society*.

43. Kevin Gaines and Beth Parkhurst, "African Americans in Newport, 1660–1960," Providence: Rhode Island Black Heritage Society, 1992, *Newport Historical Society*.

44. James R. Markusen, **First Mover Advantages, Blockaded Entry, and the Economics of Uneven Development,** Cambridge, Massachusetts: National Bureau of Economic Research, 1990.

45. Quoted in John Michael Ray, "Newport's Golden Age," **Negro History Bulletin,** 25(Number 3, December 1961): 51–57, 54.

46. Rommel-Ruiz, "Atlantic Revolutions," 166.

47. Lorenzo J. Greene, "Mutiny on the Slave Ships," **Phylon,** 5(Number 4, Fourth Quarter 1944): 346–354, 349.

48. David Richardson, "Shipboard Revolts, African Revolts and the Atlantic Slave Trade," **William and Mary Quarterly,** 58(Number 1, January 2001): 69–92, 69, 77, 89.

49. Quoted in Edward J. Cashin, **Governor Henry Ellis and the Transformation of British North America,** Athens: University of Georgia Press, 1994, 43.

50. Richard E. Bond, "Ebb and Flow: Free Blacks and Urban Slavery in Eighteenth Century New York," Ph.D. dissertation, Johns Hopkins University, 2004, 96. See also John Atkins, **A Voyage to Guinea, Brazil and the West Indies . . . ,** London: Ward and Chandler, 1735.

51. Report, 7 May 1747, in Elizabeth Donnan, ed., **Documents Illustrative of the Slave Trade to America, Volume III, New England and the Middle Colonies,** Washington, D.C.: Carnegie, 1932, 51. See also Stephanie E. Smallwood, "African Guardians, European Slave Ships and the Changing Dynamics of Power in the Early Modern Atlantic," **William and Mary Quarterly,** 64(Number 4, October 2007): 679–716; and **Two Sermons Preached to a Congregation of Black Slaves at the Parish Church of S.P. in the Province of Maryland by an American Pastor,** London: John Oliver, 1749, *Maryland Historical Society, Baltimore*.

52. Michael Jarvis, **In the Eye of All Trade: Bermuda, Bermudians, and the Maritime Atlantic World, 1680–1783,** Chapel Hill: University of North Carolina Press, 2010, 139.

53. Warner Oland Moore, Jr., "Henry Laurens: A Charleston Merchant in the Eighteenth Century, 1747–1771," Ph.D. dissertation, University of Alabama, 1974, 107, 116, 154, 156, 158, 166, 172.

54. Quoted in Rommel-Ruiz, "Atlantic Revolutions," 226.

55. **The Importance of Effectually Supporting the Royal African Company of England Impartially Considered, Shewing That a Free and Open Trade to Africa and the Support and Preservation of the British Colonies and Plantations in America**

Depend upon Maintaining the Forts and Settlements, Rights and Privileges Belonging to That Corporation, against the Encroachments of the French and All Other Foreign Rivals in That Trade, London: Roberts, 1745, *University of Virginia, Charlottesville.*

56. Letter, 1 August 1749, in **Journal of the Commissioners for Trade and Plantations from January 1741–1742 to December 1749 . . .** , London: HM Stationery Office, 1931, 447; "A British Merchant," **The African Trade, the Great Pillar and Support of the British Plantation Trade in America**, London: Robinson, 1745, *Johns Hopkins University.*

57. "A British Merchant," **African Trade**.

58. **The African Trade, the Great Pillar and Support of the British Trade in America . . .** , London: Robinson, 1745, *Boston Public Library, Massachusetts.*

59. William Byrd to "My Lord," 12 July 1736, in Marion Tinling, ed., **The Correspondence of the Three William Byrds of Westover, Virginia, 1684–1776, Volume II,** Charlottesville: University of Virginia Press, 1977, 488.

60. Lawrence H. Gipson, **The British Isles and the American Colonies: The Southern Plantations, 1748–1754,** New York: Knopf, 1967, 78.

61. Alan D. Watson, "Impulse toward Independence: Resistance and Rebellion among North Carolina Slaves, 1750–1775," **Journal of Negro History**, 63(Number 4, October 1978): 317–328, 317.

62. **A Collection of All the Public Acts of Assembly, of the Province of North Carolina: Now in Force and Use,** 1751, 71, *Huntington Library, San Marino, California*: Circa 1741: "if any Number of Negroes or other slaves . . . three, or more, shall, at any time . . . consult, advise or conspire to rebel . . . or make insurrection, or shall plot or conspire the Murther of any person or persons whatsoever . . . shall suffer death."

63. Betty Wood, **Slavery in Colonial Georgia, 1730–1775,** Athens: University of Georgia Press, 1984, 126.

64. See, e.g., Thomas Harrison to Elizabeth Harrison, 31 July 1752, *University of Virginia*: transporting enslaved Africans from Gambia to Virginia.

65. Legislation, 1754, in Robert L. Cain, ed., **Records of the Executive Council, 1735–1754,** Raleigh, North Carolina: Division of Archives and History, 1988, 499, 534: "Whereas acts have been passed in some of the Plantations in America for laying Duties on the Importation and Exportation of Negroes to the great discouragement of Merchants trading thither from the coast of Africa . . . it is our will and pleasure that you do not give your assent to or pass any law imposing Duties upon Negroes imported into our province of North Carolina payable by the Importer or upon any Slaves exported."

66. Remarks of Charles Hicks, 17 February 1743, Folder 12, *Daniel Parish Slavery Transcripts.*

67. Acts of Assembly Relating to Negroes, Servants & Slaves, 1731–1743, 15 June 1743, Folder 5, *Daniel Parish Slavery Transcripts.*

68. **The Advantages of Scotland by an Incorporate Union with England Compar'd with These of a Coalition with the Dutch, or League with France: In Answer to a Pamphlet Call'd, "The Advantages of the Act of Security . . . ," to Which Is Added a Postscript in Answer to the Letter Concerning the Consequence of an Incorporating Union,** Edinburgh, Scotland, 1706, *Yale University, New Haven, Connecticut.* At the same site, see also Thomas Prince, **A Sermon Delivered at the South Church in Boston, N.E. August 14, 1746: Being the Day of General Thanksgiving for the Great Deliverance of the British Nations by the Glorious and Happy Victory Near Culloden, Obtained by His Royal Highness Prince William Duke of Cumberland April 16 Last, Wherein the Greatness of the Publick Danger and Deliverance Is in**

Part Set Forth, to Excite Their Most Grateful Praises to the God of Their Salvation, Boston: Henchman, Kneeland and Green, 1746; and Lord George Murray, **A Particular Account of the Battle of Culloden, April 16, 1746: In a Letter from an Officer of the Highland Army, to His Friend at London . . .** , London: Warner, 1749.

69. **Memoirs of the Rebellion in 1745 and 1746 by the Chevalier de Johnstone, . . . Narrative of the Progress of the Rebellion from the Commencement to the Battle of Culloden, . . . Translated from French . . .** , London: Longman, Hurst, Rees, Orme and Brown, 1822, *University of South Carolina, Columbia.*

70. **Dr. Houstoun's Memoirs of His Own Life-Time**, 344.

71. Henry Wright Newman, **To Maryland from Overseas: A Complete Digest of the Jacobite Loyalists Sold into White Slavery in Maryland and the British and Continental Background of Approximately 1400 Maryland Settlers from 1634 to the Early Federal Period with Source Documentation**, Baltimore: Genealogical, 1985, v.

72. **Dr. Houstoun's Memoirs of His Own Life-Time**, 277: "The Jews make up a very considerable part of the inhabitants and have a larger share of trade than the Christians inn proportion to their number. . . . these were the worst set of rogues that ever I knew, in the whole course of my life; a set of low-life Thieves (as bad as the Negroes themselves, who are all naturally Thieves) the meaner part of whom held a strict correspondence with all thieving Negroes, from whom they received the stolen goods."

73. A.M. Kinghorn, "Robert Burns and Jamaica," **A Review of English Literature**, 8(Number 3, July 1967): 70–80, 77. See also Emma Rothschild, **The Inner Life of Empires: An Eighteenth-Century History**, Princeton: Princeton University Press, 2011.

74. There may be a connection between the growing restiveness of Scots and the growing acceptance of Jews in Carolina, as the province had difficulty in being choosy in the face of a growing threat from Africans, Spaniards, and indigenes alike. See "Miscellaneous Information, Volume II," Beth Elohim 1750, *Jewish Synagogue Church Records, University of South Carolina*: "Offshoot of the old Spanish and Jewish community of London who organized in Charleston under Moses Cohen. . . . services are in accord with Portuguese custom." But cf. Report, in Leo Hershkowitz and Isidore S. Meyer, eds., **The Lee Max Friedman Collection of American Jewish Colonial Correspondence, Letters of the Frank Family (1733–1748)**, Waltham, Massachusetts: American Jewish Historical Society, 1968, 87: "A number of slaves belonging to Jews were implicated in the 'plot'" of 1741 in Manhattan. Arguably a response to real and imagined Scottish dissidence was their being allowed to deepen their engagement with slavery and the slave trade—the latter they arranged and financed in disproportionate numbers: this also propelled a textile-dominated phase of Scottish industrialization—and capitalism—up to about 1830: see, e.g., T.M. Devine, **To the Ends of the Earth: Scotland's Global Diaspora, 1750–2010**, London: Allen Lane, 2011.

75. John Dobell to Trustees, 8 August 1742, in Mills Lane, ed., **General Oglethorpe's Georgia: Colonial Letters, 1733–1743, Volume II**, Savannah, Georgia: Beehive, 1990, 646–647: In Georgia, said one settler, "the Dutch people behaved very well during the alarm or invasion. . . . my own sentiments are that our Dutch-haters are Negro lovers, that our disapprobation of the Dutch proceeds from a hidden insatiable desire of Negroes." Herein one glimpses the constructing of "whiteness" on a basis of anti-blackness. See also Joseph Avery to Harman Verelst, 31 January 1743, in the same volume, 653–658: "there will be little or no clearing or planting land this year, unless it be what is done by the Dutch and Salzburgers. Nor can there any quantity done as there is no hands to do with, black servants are not allowed and white servants not to be got at any rate, their being very few in this part of the colony worth hiring."

76. Article by George Burrington, Esq., January 1745, in Robert McMillan Kennedy, ed., **South Carolina Items in the "Gentleman's Magazine" (London), 1731–1792, Extracted from the File in the University of South Carolina Library**, 1936, *University of South Carolina.*

77. Letter from John Dobell, 11 June 1746, in Lucian Lamar Knight, ed., **The Colonial Records of the State of Georgia, Volume 25**, Atlanta: Byrd, 1915, 72. In the same source, page 347, see also Letter from the President, Assistants and Councilmen to Benjamin Martin, Savannah, 10 January 1748: "whether it would be more for the benefit of the Colony to limit the inhabitants to a certain determinate number of Negroes or that they should be obliged to keep White Men in proportion to the numbers of their Negroes . . . unanimously agreed that the proportion ought to be One White Man to every Five Working Negroes. . . . no Negro Sawyers to be employed in Towns."

78. John Martin Bolzius to John Dobell, 20 May 1748, in Knight, **Colonial Records of the State of Georgia, Volume 25**, 285.

79. Report, 17 July 1742, *Walter Johnson Research Notes, Johns Hopkins University, Baltimore.*

80. Report, 29 November 1745, in **Calendar of Maryland State Papers, Number 1, The Black Books**, Hall of Records Commission, 1943, 74–75, *Georgia Historical Society, Savannah.*

81. Matthew Rowan to Captain William Wilkins, 1 February 1753, *Papers of Governor Matthew Rowan, North Carolina State Archives, Raleigh*. This letter can also be found in Robert J. Cain, ed., **Records of the Executive Council, 1735–1754**, Raleigh: North Carolina State Division of Archives and History, 1988, 297.

82. John Reynolds to Secretary of State, 5 December 1754, WO34/34, *NAUK.*

83. See, e.g., Smith and Wojtowicz, **Blacks Who Stole Themselves**, 24, 31: 20 June 1745, Philadelphia: runaway just arrived from Barbados, "John, . . . born in Dominica and speaks French but very little English." See also Maurice Alfred Crouse, "The Manigault Family of South Carolina, 1685–1783," Ph.D. dissertation, Northwestern University, 1964.

84. Cashin, **Governor Henry Ellis**, 115.

85. Acts of Assembly Relating to Negroes, Servants & Slaves, 1731–1743, 15 January 1742, Folder 5, *Daniel Parish Slavery Transcripts.*

86. James Oglethorpe to "Gentlemen," 28 May 1742, Folder 11, *Daniel Parish Slavery Transcripts.*

87. Minutes of Council in Assembly, 1744–1745, 13 March 1744, Box II, Folder 2, *Daniel Parish Slavery Transcripts.*

88. Minutes of Council in Assembly, 1744–1745, 25 May 1744, Box II, Folder 2, *Daniel Parish Slavery Transcripts.*

89. Minutes of Council in Assembly, 1744–1745, 3 December 1744, Box II, Folder 2, *Daniel Parish Slavery Transcripts.*

90. Minutes of the House of Burgesses, 1745–1747, 29 November 1746, Box II, Folder 4, *Daniel Parish Slavery Transcripts*. See also Edward Anthony Pearson, "From Stono to Vesey: Slavery, Resistance and Ideology in South Carolina, 1739–1822," Ph.D. dissertation, University of Wisconsin, Madison, 1992.

91. Bill, 4 May 1754, in **Council Journal, Upper House**, *South Carolina Department of Archives and History, Columbia*. See also Richard Walsh, ed., **The Writings of Christopher Gadsden, 1746–1805**, Columbia: University of South Carolina Press, 1966.

92. Report, 1 July 1747, *Walter Johnson Research Notes.*

93. Minutes of Council in Assembly, 1745–1748, 22 January 1747, Box II, Folder 5, *Daniel Parish Slavery Transcripts.*

94. See, e.g., John Savage, "'Black Magic' and White Terror: Slave Poisoning and Colonial Society in Early 19th Century Martinique," **Journal of Social History**, 40(Number 3, Spring 2007): 635–662.
95. Watson, "Impulse toward Independence," 320.
96. Legislation, October 1748, in William Waller Henning, ed., **The Statutes at Large; Being a Collection of the Laws of Virginia from the First Session of the Legislature in the Year 1619, Volume VI**, Richmond, Virginia: Franklin, 1819, 104.
97. Quoted in Peter McCandless, **Slavery, Disease, and Suffering in the Southern Low Country**, New York: Cambridge University Press, 2011, 175. See also Judith Ann Carney, **In the Shadow of Slavery: Africa's Botanical Legacy in the Atlantic World**, Berkeley: University of California Press, 2009, 212: Note the use of the "guinea bean" as a poison.
98. William Stephens, entry, 15 August 1744, in E. Merlton Coulter, ed., **The Journal of William Stephens, 1743-1745, Volume II**, Athens: University of Georgia, 1959. See also Minutes of the House of Burgesses and Council in Assembly, 27 February 1753, Box III, Folder 4, *Daniel Parish Slavery Transcripts*.
99. Kinloch Bull, Jr., **The Oligarchs in Colonial and Revolutionary Charleston: Lieutenant Governor William Bull II and His Family**, Columbia: University of South Carolina Press, 1990, 181.
100. But see Report, December 1748, *Walter Johnson Research Notes*: "in the West Indies . . . they are treated very cruelly; therefore no threats make more impression upon a Negro hire, than those of sending him over to the West Indies, in Case he would not reform."
101. Minutes of the House of Burgesses, 17 May 1750, Folder 11, *Daniel Parish Slavery Transcripts*.
102. Peter Kalm, **Peter Kalm's Travel in North America: The English Version of 1770, Volume I**, ed. Adolph Benson, New York: Wilson-Erickson, 1937, 210.
103. Betty Wood, "'Until He Shall Be Dead, Dead, Dead': The Judicial Treatment of Slaves in Eighteenth-Century Georgia," **Georgia Historical Quarterly**, 71(Number 3, Fall 1987): 377–398, 378.
104. Report, 1755, Folder 212, *Daniel Parish Slavery Transcripts*.
105. N.M. Miller Surrey, **The Commerce of Louisiana during the French Regime, 1699-1763**, London: Longmans, Green, 1916, 245.
106. Minutes of Council in Assembly, 1747-1748, 24 January 1748, Box II, Folder 6, *Daniel Parish Slavery Transcripts*.
107. Minutes of Council in Assembly, 1748-1749, 31 January 1749, Box II, Folder 7, *Daniel Parish Slavery Transcripts*.
108. Minutes of Council in Assembly, 1 February 1749, Box II, Folder 7, *Daniel Parish Slavery Transcripts*.
109. Testimony of Kate, 3 February 1749, Box II, Folder 7, *Daniel Parish Slavery Transcripts*.
110. John D. Duncan, "Servitude and Slavery in Colonial South Carolina, 1670–1776," Ph.D. dissertation, Emory University, 1972, 806, 811.
111. Minutes of Council in Assembly, 16 May and 12 December 1749, Box II, Folder 7, *Daniel Parish Slavery Transcripts*.
112. David R. Chesnutt, **South Carolina's Expansion into Colonial Georgia, 1720-1765**, New York: Garland, 1989, 50. See also Kenneth Wiggins Porter, "Negroes on the Southern Frontier, 1670–1763," **Journal of Negro History**, 33(Number 1, January 1948): 53–78.
113. Legislation, October 1748, in William Waller Hening, **The Statutes at Large: Being a Collection of All the Laws of Virginia from the First Session of the Legislature in the Year 1619, Volume VI**, Richmond, Virginia: Franklin, 1819, 112.

114. Letter by "RT," 1749, in H. Roy Merrens, ed., **The Colonial South Carolina Scene: Contemporary Views, 1697-1774**, Columbia: University of South Carolina Press, 1977, 172-174.

115. Wood, **Slavery in Colonial Georgia**, 117.

116. Anthony W. Parker, **Scottish Highlanders in Colonial Georgia: The Recruitment, Emigration and Settlement at Darien, 1735-1748**, Athens: University of Georgia, 1997, 97, 87: "the fear of Spanish intrigue among the slaves to revolt was one of the most persuasive arguments against the introduction of slavery into Georgia." Madrid was "confident" that the enslaved would join their forces when they invaded.

117. Andrew C. Nanne, "James Oglethorpe and the Civil-Military Contest for Authority in Colonial Georgia, 1732-1749," **Georgia Historical Quarterly**, 95(Number 2, Summer 2011): 203-231, 218, 238, 229, 230.

118. Joyce Elizabeth Harman, **Trade and Privateering in Spanish Florida, 1732-1763**, Tuscaloosa: University of Alabama Press, 2004, 52.

119. For a useful overview of the literature on the Enlightenment on the mainland— which too replicates the 18th-century mind-set by managing to give short shrift to enslavement of Africans and dispossession of the indigenous (as does a good deal of the copious amount of books cited)—see Nathalie Caron and Naomi Wulf, "American Enlightenments: Continuity and Renewal," **Journal of American History**, 99(Number 4, March 2013): 1072-1091. See also Jonathan Israel, **Democratic Enlightenment: Philosophy, Revolution and Human Rights, 1750-1790**, New York: Oxford University Press, 2011.

NOTES TO CHAPTER 7

1. See, e.g., **General Orders of 1757: Issued by the Earl of Loudoun and Phineas Lyman in the Campaign against the French**, New York, 1899, *University of South Carolina, Columbia*.

2. For a broader view, see, e.g., Fred Anderson, **Crucible of War: The Seven Years' War and the Fate of Empire in British North America, 1754-1766**, New York: Knopf, 2000. See also Paul W. Mapp, **The Elusive West and the Contest for Empire, 1713-1763**, Chapel Hill: University of North Carolina Press, 2011.

3. Minutes of the House of Burgesses, 1749-1750, 8 May 1750, Box II, Folder 11, *Daniel Parish Slavery Transcripts, New-York Historical Society, Manhattan*. In the same collection, see also Letter from Whitehall, 4 May 1750, Folder 132: "My Lord . . . encouragement given at St. Augustine to slaves deserting . . . propose an agreement for the mutual delivering up all slaves."

4. Robert Dinwiddie and John Esten to the King, 31 October 1752, *Transcriptions of Correspondence of Governor Robert Dinwiddie, Rockefeller Library, Williamsburg, Virginia*.

5. Robert Dinwiddie to Colonel Charles Carter, 18 July 1755, in R.A. Brock, ed., **The Official Records of Robert Dinwiddie, Lieutenant Governor of the Colony of Virginia, 1751-1758 . . . , Volume II**, Richmond: Virginia Historical Society, 1884, 101-103.

6. Minutes of Council in Assembly, 11 November 1754, Box III, Folder 6, *Daniel Parish Slavery Transcripts*.

7. Letter to Governor Dinwiddie, 30 December 1754, Box III, Folder 6, *Daniel Parish Slavery Transcripts*.

8. Governor Robert Dinwiddie to Sir, 18 February 1755, Box III, Folder 6, *Daniel Parish Slavery Transcripts*: "Our dominion is very extensive, our people as remote from each other as any people on this continent & I think the number of our Negroes near the same proportion to whites, as those of your colony & therefore subject to the same disadvantages from an Invader as any other province."

9. Minutes of Council in Assembly, 6 March 1755, Box III, Folder 7, *Daniel Parish Slavery Transcripts*. In the same site and box, see, e.g., "Minutes of the House of Burgesses," 1754–1756; "Minutes of Council-House of Burgesses and the Assembly," 1755–1758; "Minutes of the House of Burgesses," 1758–1759; "Minutes of the House of Burgesses," 1756 and 1760; "Minutes of the Council in Assembly," 1759–1760.

10. Extract from Sermon Preached, 28 October 1756, "U.S. to 1815 Miscellaneous," *Daniel Parish Slavery Transcripts*.

11. "Minutes of Council in Assembly. Minutes of the House of Burgesses," 17 June 1760, Folder 172, *Daniel Parish Slavery Transcripts*.

12. Colin G. Calloway, **The Scratch of a Pen: 1763 and the Transformation of North America**, New York: Oxford University Press, 2006, 59.

13. Robert Dinwiddie to Board of Trade, August 1751, *Correspondence of Governor Robert Dinwiddie*.

14. Quoted in John D. Duncan, "Servitude and Slavery in Colonial South Carolina, 1670–1776," Ph.D. dissertation, Emory University, 1972, 813.

15. Remarks of Samuel Davies, 1757, in Jeffrey Robert Young, ed., **Proslavery and Sectional Thought in Early South Carolina, 1740–1289: An Anthology**, Columbia: University of South Carolina Press, 2006, 121.

16. Gary B. Nash, "Slaves and Slaveowners in Colonial Philadelphia," **William and Mary Quarterly**, 30(Number 2, April 1973): 223–256, 229, 230, 236. See also Anthony Benezet, **Observations on the Inslaving, Importing and Purchasing of Negroes**, Germantown, Pennsylvania: Sower, 1760.

17. Geoffrey Plank, **John Woolman's Path to the Peaceable Kingdom: A Quaker in the British Empire**, Philadelphia: University of Pennsylvania Press, 2012.

18. Catherine Molineux, **Faces of Perfect Ebony: Encountering Atlantic Slavery in Imperial Britain**, Cambridge: Harvard University Press, 2012, 180.

19. Advertisements, 26 August 1762 and 30 December 1762, in Billy G. Smith and Richard Wojtowicz, eds., **Blacks Who Stole Themselves: Advertisements for Runaways in the "Pennsylvania Gazette," 1728–1790**, Philadelphia: University of Pennsylvania Press, 1989, 56–57, 61. See also Robert C. Barnes and Judith M. Pfeiffer, eds., **Laws of the State of Delaware on Slavery, Free Blacks and Mulattoes**, 2002, *Delaware Historical Society, Wilmington*: Note growth in laws imposing ever stiffer penalties on the enslaved who beat or assault their presumed masters. See also Darold Duane Wax, "The Negro Slave Trade in Colonial Pennsylvania," Ph.D. dissertation, University of Washington, 1962.

20. Michael E. Groth, "Black Loyalists and African American Allegiances in the Mid-Hudson Valley," in Joseph S. Tiemann, Eugene R. Fingerhut, and Robert W. Venables, eds., **The Other Loyalists: Ordinary People, Royalism, and the Revolution in the Middle Colonies, 1763–1787**, Albany: SUNY Press, 2009, 81–104, 84. See also **New York (Colony) Census of Slaves, 1755, Part XL [Includes Ulster County, Dutchess County, Westchester County, Long Island . . .]**, *Connecticut Historical Society, Hartford*; and Bernard C. Steiner, **History of Slavery in Connecticut**, New York: Johnson, 1973 (originally published 1893).

21. Richard S. Bond, "Ebb and Flow: Free Blacks and Urban Slavery in Eighteenth Century New York," Ph.D. dissertation, Johns Hopkins University, 2004, 308.

22. James G. Lydon, "New York and the Slave Trade, 1700 to 1774," **William and Mary Quarterly**, 35(Number 2, April 1978): 375–394, 379.

23. Thelma Wills Foote, **Black and White Manhattan: The History of Racial Formation in Colonial New York City**, New York: Oxford University Press, 2004, 69, 76.

24. Matthew Mulcahy, "'Melancholy and Fatal Calamities': Disaster and Society in Eighteenth-Century South Carolina," in Jack P. Green, Rosemary Brana-Shute, and

Randy J. Sparks, eds., **Money, Trade, and Power: The Evolution of South Carolina's Plantation Society**, Columbia: University of South Carolina Press, 2001, 278–298, 289.

25. Robert Weir, **Colonial South Carolina: A History**, Columbia: University of South Carolina Press, 1997, 124.

26. Duncan, "Servitude and Slavery in Colonial South Carolina," 794, 803, 806, 816.

27. Quoted in David Morton Knepper, "The Political Structure of Colonial South Carolina, 1743–1776," Ph.D. dissertation, University of Virginia, 1971, 37, 221.

28. Nicholas Owen, **Journal of a Slave Dealer**, ed. Eveline Martin, London: Routledge, 1930, 68.

29. Quoted in Graham Russell Hodges and Edward Brown, introduction to Hodges and Brown, eds., **"Pretends to Be Free": Runaway Slave Advertisements from Colonial and Revolutionary New York and New Jersey**, New York: Garland, 1994, xiii–xl, xxx.

30. Foote, **Black and White Manhattan**, 198.

31. **The Importance of the African Companys Forts and Settlements Considered, . . . the Importance of Effectually Supporting the Royal African Royal Company of England Impartially Consider'd; Shewing That a Free and Open Trade to Africa and the Support and Preservation of the British Colonies and Plantations in America, Depend upon Maintaining the Forts and Settlements, Rights and Privileges Belonging to That Corporation against the Encroachments of the French and All Other Foreign Rivals in That Trade** . . . , London: Cooper, 1744, *Huntington Library, San Marino, California*.

32. **The Case of the Royal African Company and Their Creditors**, London, 1748, *New-York Historical Society*.

33. **Considerations on the American Trade before and since the Establishment of the South-Sea Company**, London: Roberts, 1739, *Huntington Library*: "whether the Private Trade . . . was not of infinitely more Advantage to the Nation in general, than any Trade that has been carried on by the Company ever since they have had the *Assiento Contract*; which, together with the Act of Parliament mention'd in their Petition, they have made subservient to no other End than distressing and ruining the Private Trade by all manner of Means they could contrive and execute."

34. See, e.g., "Petitions and Debates in the British House of Commons for and against the Monopoly of the Company and Their Trade in Negroes and Slaves for the Plantations in America and Leading Up to the Passing of the Act of 1750 Declaring the Trade to Africa Free and Open," Box 6, Folder 71, *Daniel Parish Slavery Transcripts*. At the same site and box (but in Folder 79), see "Petitions and Debates in Commons for and against the Monopoly . . . Leading Up to Passing of the Act of 1750, Declaring the Trade Free and Open." (Folder 80 has similar content—though note that as of January 2012, when I accessed this collection, it was about to be re-organized.)

35. Remarks, 1752, Folder 124, *Daniel Parish Slavery Transcripts*.

36. **Reasons in Support of the Planters Proposal for Preserving and Extending the Trade to Those Parts of Africa Called the Gold Coast and Whydah against the Powerful Rivalship of Foreign Nations**, circa 1750, *Huntington Library*. At the same site, see also **An Account of the Number of Forts and Castles Necessary to Be Kept Up and Maintained on the Coast of Africa for Preserving and Securing to Great Britain the Trade to Those Parts**, circa 1750s.

37. **Considerations on the Present Dangerous State of the Sugar Colonies**, London, 1749, *Huntington Library*.

38. **The National and Private Advantages of the African Trade Considered; Being an Enquiry, How Far It Concerns the Trading Interest of Great Britain, Effectually to**

Support and Maintain the Forts and Settlements in Africa, Belonging to the Royal
African Company of England, London: Knapton, 1746, *Huntington Library.*
39. Lords of Trade to Lord Loudon and in his absence to Robert Dinwiddie, 17 March
1756, *Correspondence of Governor Robert Dinwiddie*: "Whereas acts have been
passed in some of our plantations in America, for laying duties on the importation
or exportation of Negroes, to the great discouragement of the merchants trading
thither from the coast of Africa . . . it is our will and pleasure that you do not give
your assent to or pass any law imposing duties upon Negroes imported into our
colony of Virginia, payable by the importer, or upon any slaves exported, that have
not been sold in our said colony."
40. Board of Trade to William Gooch, 22 May 1729, *Transcriptions of William Gooch Correspondence, Rockefeller Library, Williamsburg, Virginia*: "the merchants of London,
Bristol & Liverpool trading to Virginia, having petitioned the King against this Act"
to lay duties on slaves: "we are of the Opinion the same ought to be repealed."
41. Report, May 1760, in William Waller Hening, ed., **The Statutes at Large: Being a
Collection of All the Laws of Virginia from the First Session of the Legislature in
the Year 1619, Volume VII**, Richmond, Virginia: WWH, 1820, 363.
42. See, e.g., Stuart Owen Stumpf, "The Merchants of Colonial Charleston, 1680–1756,"
Ph.D. dissertation, Michigan State University, 1971, 181, 189, 242.
43. William Gooch to Board of Trade, circa 10 June 1747, *William Gooch Correspondence.*
44. William Gooch to Board of Trade, 17 February 1747, *William Gooch Correspondence.*
45. **A Description of South Carolina . . .** , London: Dodsley, 1761, *Huntington Library.*
See also Peter Kalm, **Peter Kalm's Travel in North America: The English Version
of 1770, Volume I**, ed. Adolph Benson, New York: Wilson-Erickson, 1937, 206: It is
preferable, it was said in 1750, to have Negro women—as opposed to men—as slaves
since "any children she births belong to master and not master of male slave who
impregnates."
46. See, e.g., Paul Quattlebaum, **The Land Called Chicora: The Carolinas under Spanish
Rule with French Intrusions**, Gainesville: University Press of Florida, 1956.
47. Memorial of Benjamin Martyn to the Right Hon. Earl of Egremont, 14 January 1762,
PRO30/47/14, *National Archives of the United Kingdom, London* (hereinafter *NAUK*).
48. **Considerations on the Advantages of Yielding Up to Spain the Un-Expired Term of
the Assiento Contract for an Equivalent, Shewing That at All Times, the Execution
of It Had Been Injurious to the General Trade of England, but Particularly to That
with Spain and Our Colonies; and More Especially to the Stock-Proprietors of the
South Sea Company, That Had Fatally Experienced the Vesting Their Directors
with Any Power over Their Property, by a Proprietor of the Trading Stock**, London:
Cooper, 1748, *Huntington Library.*
49. See, e.g., **The Definitive Treaty of Peace and Friendship between His Brittanick Majesty, the Most Christian King and the States General of the United Provinces, Concluded at Aix La Chapelle, the 18th Day of October . . . 1748, to Which the Empress
Queen of Hungary, the Kings of Spain and Sardinia, the Duke of Modena and
the Republick of Genoa, Have Acceded**, London: Owen, 1749, *Huntington Library*:
Article XVI: "the Treaty of the Assiento for the Trade of Negroes, signed at Madrid
on the 26th of March 1713 . . . are particularly confirmed by the present Treaty, for
the four years, during which the Enjoyment thereof has been interrupted, since the
commencement of the present war and shall be executed at the same footing, and
under the same conditions, as they have or ought to have been executed before the
said war." At the same site, see also **His Majesty's Most Gracious Speech to Both
Houses of Parliament on Thursday the Twelfth Day of November 1747** (re: war with
France and Spain).

50. See "Figures on Slave Imports to Virginia and South Carolina, 1699–1760," Folder 143, *Daniel Parish Slavery Transcripts*.

51. **A Short Account of the Interest and Conflict of the Jamaica Planters, in an Address to the Merchants, Traders and Liverymen of the City of London**, London: Cooper, 1754, *Huntington Library*.

52. Entry, 21 November 1756, MS 1787, *James Habersham Diary, Georgia Historical Society, Savannah*.

53. **A Letter to a Member of Parliament Concerning the Importance of Our Sugar Colonies to Great Britain, by a Gentleman Who Resided Many Years in the Island of Jamaica**, London: Taylor, 1745, *Huntington Library*.

54. Letter to "My Lord," 2 July 1751, Folder 27, *Daniel Parish Slavery Transcripts*.

55. Claudius Fergus, "'Dread of Insurrection': Abolitionism, Security and Labor in Britain's West Indian Colonies, 1760–1823," **William and Mary Quarterly**, 66(Number 4, October 2009): 757–780, 758.

56. Letter, 28 February 1762, in **Journal of the Commissioners for Trade and Plantations from January 1759 to December 1763**, London: HM Stationery Office, 1935, 295. In the same volume, pages 136, 166, and 182, see detail on the 1760 revolt in Jamaica.

57. Michael J. Jarvis, **In the Eye of All Trade: Bermuda, Bermudians, and the Maritime Atlantic World, 1680–1783**, Chapel Hill: University of North Carolina Press, 2010, 382.

58. Jason T. Sharples, "Flames of Insurrection: Fearing Slave Conspiracy in Early America, 1670–1780," Ph.D. dissertation, Princeton University, 2010, 186.

59. Christopher Alain Cameron, "To Plead Our Own Cause: African Americans in Massachusetts and the Making of the Antislavery Movement, 1630–1835," Ph.D. dissertation, University of North Carolina, Chapel Hill, 2010, 103, 104.

60. Legislation, 20 June 1766, in **Journals of the House of Representatives of Massachusetts, 1766**, Boston: Massachusetts Historical Society, 1973, 110.

61. Legislation, circa 10 December 1767, in **Journals of the House of Representatives of Massachusetts, 1767-1768**, Boston: Massachusetts Historical Society, 1975), 409–410.

62. Bill, 27 October 1767, in **Minutes of the House of Representatives of the Government of the Counties of New Castle, Kent and Sussex upon Delaware at Sessions Held at New Castle in the Years, 1765 . . . 1770**, Wilmington, Delaware: Adams, 1770, 127–128. There were repetitive complaints about fierce verbal assaults by Africans: see, e.g., Act, Virginia, 1730, "for the punishment of Negroes, Indian and Mulatto Slaves for Speaking Defamatory words . . . punished by whipping," *Daniel Parish Slavery Transcripts*.

63. Owen, , **Journal of a Slave Dealer**, 71, 75.

64. Gertrude Selwyn Kimball, introduction to Kimball, ed., **The Correspondence of the Colonial Governors of Rhode Island, 1723-1775**, Volume I, Boston: Houghton Mifflin, 1903, ix–xl, xxxvii.

65. Petition of Benjamin Roberts, 29 May 1749, Box II, Folder 10, *Daniel Parish Slavery Transcripts*: Roberts purchased an African in Antigua and wanted to bring him to South Carolina. In the same collection, in Box III, Folder 7, see Minutes of Council in Assembly, Virginia, Petition to bring ship from Antigua "with a cargo of Negroes." 23 December 1755.

66. **Candid and Impartial Considerations on the Nature of the Sugar Trade; the Comparative Importance of the British and French Islands in the West Indies . . .**, London: Baldwin, 1753, *Huntington Library*.

67. Reports, 1745–1746, in **Journals of the House of Representatives of Massachusetts, 1745-1746**, Boston: Massachusetts Historical Society, 1947, 72–74, 112, 125, 238, 242.

68. Legislation, 1 October 1746, in **Journals of the House of Representatives of Massachusetts, 1746–1747**, Boston: Massachusetts Historical Society, 1948, 187.

69. Report, 19 November 1747, in **Journals of the House of Representatives of Massachusetts, 1747–1748**, Boston: Massachusetts Historical Society, 1949, 212.

70. Memorial, 27 December 1748, and various reports, circa 1748–1749, in **Journals of the House of Representatives of Massachusetts, 1748–1749**, Boston: Massachusetts Historical Society, 1950, 24–25, 56–57, 156, 168–169, 261.

71. William Shirley to William Greene, 3 May 1745, in Charles Henry Lincoln, ed., **Correspondence of William Shirley, Governor of Massachusetts and Military Commander in America, 1731–1760**, New York: Macmillan, 1912, 213–214.

72. William Shirley to Lords of Trade, 1 December 1747, in Lincoln, **Correspondence of William Shirley**, 412–417.

73. Robert Hunter Morris to William Shirley, 29 February 1756, in Lincoln, **Correspondence of William Shirley**, 391.

74. William Shirley to Robert Hunter Morris, 29 February 1756, in Lincoln, **Correspondence of William Shirley**, 405–412.

75. Reports, circa 1754–1755, in **Journals of the House of Representatives of Massachusetts, 1753–1754**, Boston: Massachusetts Historical Society, 1955, 3, 28–54, 62–63, 265–272, 284.

76. Report, 17 February 1756, in **Journals of the House of Representatives of Massachusetts, 1756**, Boston: Massachusetts Historical Society, 1958, 341, 362, 375, 378, 520.

77. Report, 19 November 1754, in **Journals of the House of Representatives of Massachusetts, 1754–1755**, Boston: Massachusetts Historical Society, 1956, 49, 119.

78. Petition, 21 March 1758, in **Journals of the House of Representatives of Massachusetts, 1758**, Boston: Massachusetts Historical Society, 1962, 367–368.

79. Petition, 13 June 1759, in **Journals of the House of Representatives of Massachusetts, 1759–1760**, Boston: Massachusetts Historical Society, 1964, 41.

80. Petition, 4 June 1760, in **Journals of the House of Representatives of Massachusetts, 1760–1761**, Boston: Massachusetts Historical Society, 1965, 24.

81. William Gooch to Secretary of State, 12 February 1747, *William Gooch Correspondence.*

82. George Washington to Francis Fauquier, 5 August 1758, *Francis Fauquier Correspondence Transcriptions, Rockefeller Library.*

83. Douglas Edward Leach, **Roots of Conflict: British Armed Forces and Colonial Americans, 1677–1763**, Chapel Hill: University of North Carolina Press, 1986, 126.

84. General Robert Monckton to My Lord, 9 February 1762, CO166/2, *NAUK.*

85. "Minutes Taken at a Meeting . . . ," March 1757, *Correspondence of Governor Robert Dinwiddie.*

86. Quoted in Duncan, "Servitude and Slavery in Colonial South Carolina," 816.

87. Governor Henry Ellis to General Amherst, 4 April 1760, WO34/34, *NAUK.*

88. William Bull to General Jeffrey Amherst, 5 December 1761, WO34/35, *NAUK.*

89. William Pitt to Governor of Virginia, 23 August 1760, *Francis Fauquier Correspondence.* See also Edict, **Council Journal Upper House,** 4 May 1757, *South Carolina Department of Archives and History, Columbia*: "His Majesty has been informed that in time of war, His subjects in several of His colonies and plantations in America have corresponded with His enemies and supplied them with provisions and warlike stores, [which] . . . greatly prejudiced . . . [the] safety of His dominions"; this commerce was particularly with "subjects of the French King."

90. Lord Jeffrey Amherst to Governor of Virginia, 15 April 1762, *Francis Fauquier Correspondence.*

91. Lord Jeffrey Amherst to Francis Fauquier, 23 May 1762, *Francis Fauquier Correspondence*.
92. Letter to William Pitt, 13 June 1760, CO23/15, *NAUK*.
93. William Shirley to My Lords, 29 March 1760, CO23/15, *NAUK*.
94. General Monckton to My Lord, 31 December 1761, CO166/2, *NAUK*.
95. Report, 17 October 1761, CO166/2, *NAUK*.
96. James Douglas to "Sir," 4 November 1761, CO166/2, *NAUK*.
97. Memorandum, circa 4 February 1762, CO117/1, *NAUK*.
98. Lord Albermarle to "My Lord," 27 May 1762, CO117/1, *NAUK*. In the same file, see, e.g., "Extract from Act Entitled 'An Act for Providing Two Thousand Negroes for the Immediate Service of His Majesty . . . to Pay for All and Every Negro or Negroes Who May Be Killed, Lost or Rendered Useless in the Expedition . . . ,'" no date, circa 1762.
99. Memorandum, no date, PRO30/47/18, *NAUK*.
100. Robert Deshayes to Lords of Treasury, 30 August 1762, T1/419, *NAUK*.
101. Henry Ellis to Earl of Egremont, 3 March 1762, PRO30/47/14, *NAUK*.
102. Henry Ellis to My Lord, 16 January 1762, PRO30/47/14, *NAUK*.
103. **Antigua, an Act Supplementary to an Act Intitled an Act for Regulating the Militia of This Island**, St. John's, Antigua: Offtey, 13 June 1756, *Brown University, Providence, Rhode Island*.
104. Comment, in Stephen Farrell, Melanie Unwin, and James Walvin, eds., **The British Slave Trade: Abolition, Parliament and People: Including the Illustrated Catalogue of the Parliamentary Exhibition in Westminster Hall, 23 May–23 September 2007**, Edinburgh: Edinburgh University Press, 2007, 3.
105. "From the Royal Proclamation on North America, 7 October 1763 . . . by the King," in S.E. Morrison, ed., **Sources and Documents Illustrating the American Revolution, 1764-1788, and the Formation of the Federal Constitution**, Oxford, United Kingdom: Clarendon, 1923, 1–4: This was an attempt to delimit boundaries of mainland colonies so they did not come into conflict with indigenes.
106. See, e.g., Francis Furstenburg, "Atlantic Slavery, Atlantic Freedom: George Washington, Slavery and Transatlantic Abolitionist Networks," **William and Mary Quarterly**, 68(Number 2, April 2011): 247–286.
107. Calloway, **Scratch of a Pen**, 98, 136.
108. William Fleming to Francis Fauquier, 26 July 1763, in George Reese, ed., **The Official Papers of Francis Fauquier, Lieutenant Governor of Virginia, 1758-1768, Volume II, 1761-1763**, Charlottesville: University of Virginia Press, 1981, 997-999.
109. Quoted in Michael A. McDonnell, **The Politics of War: Race, Class, and Conflict in Revolutionary Virginia**, Chapel Hill: University of North Carolina Press, 2007, 22.

NOTES TO CHAPTER 8
1. David Greentree, **A Far-Flung Gamble: Havana 1762**, Oxford, United Kingdom: Osprey, 2010, 4, 10, 99.
2. Nelson Vance Russell, "The Reaction in England and America to the Capture of Havana, 1762," **Hispanic American Historical Review**, 9(Number 3, August 1929): 303–316. On the siege of Havana, see, e.g., **Archibald Robertson, Lieutenant-General Royal Engineers: His Diaries and Sketches in America, 1760–1780**, New York: New York Public Library, 1930, 49–63, *New Jersey Historical Society, Newark*.
3. **An Authentic Journal of the Siege of Havana by an Officer**, London: Jeffreys, 1762, *New-York Historical Society, Manhattan*.
4. Benjamin Quarles, "The Colonial Militia and Negro Manpower," **Mississippi Valley Historical Review**, 14(1959): 643–652, 651.

5. Earl of Albermarle to "Dear Sir," 27 April 1762, *Sir George Pocock Letterbook, Huntington Library, San Marino, California.*

6. See Letter, 27 November 1746, Box II, Folder 5, *Daniel Parish Slavery Transcripts, New-York Historical Society*: The danger of selling slaves to Spanish territories is detailed here.

7. Joseph Sewall, "A Sermon Preached at the Thursday Lecture in Boston, September 16, 1762, before the Great and General Court of the Province of the Massachusetts Bay in New England on the Joyful News of the Reduction of the Havannah," Boston: Draper, 1762, *Yale University, New Haven, Connecticut.*

8. John Niven, **Connecticut Hero: Israel Putnam**, Hartford: American Revolution Bicentennial Commission of Connecticut, 1977, 36. See, e.g., **Benjamin Throop Diary**, 28 November 1762, *Connecticut Historical Society, Hartford*: Throop sorely lamented the death of six of his parishioners in Cuba, while "others" were "sick & not returned." See also Greentree, **Far-Flung Gamble**, 57: New York contributed about 500 troops to the siege of Havana, while Rhode Island contributed about 200. See also Bruce Campbell MacGunnigle, ed., "Red Coats and Yellow Fever: Rhode Island Troops at the Siege of Havana in 1762," **Society of Colonial Wars in the State of Rhode Island**, 1991, *Rhode Island Historical Society, Providence*: Here it is asserted that Rhode Island provided 212 men for the siege, out of a grand total of 2,300 supplied by this province, along with Connecticut, New York, New Jersey, and South Carolina. Of the 212 troops from Rhode Island, 110 died of fever; London suffered altogether 560 killed in battle, with 4,708 deaths from fever.

9. **The Two Putnams, Israel and Rufus in the Havana Expedition of 1762 and the Mississippi River Exploration of 1772–1773 with Some Account of the Company of Military Adventurers**, Hartford: Connecticut Historical Society, 1931, 5, 8–9.

10. Kevin Kenny, **Peaceable Kingdom: The Paxton Boys and the Destruction of William Penn's Holy Experiment**, New York: Oxford University Press, 2009, 231.

11. Entry, 18 July 1764, and David Vanderheyden to Sir William Johnson, 19 October 1763, in Franklin B. Hough, ed., **Diary of the Siege of Detroit in the War with Pontiac, Also a Narrative of the Principal Events of the Siege by Major Robert Rogers**, Albany, New York: Munsell, 1860, 101, 183.

12. See, e.g., Gerald Horne, **Negro Comrades of the Crown: African Americans and the British Empire Fight the U.S. before Emancipation**, New York: NYU Press, 2012.

13. Francis Russell Hart, **The Siege of Havana 1762**, London: Allen and Unwin, 1931, 49, 52, 53, 54.

14. Sonia Keepel, **Three Brothers at Havana, 1762**, Salisbury, United Kingdom: Russell, 1981, 79.

15. Jane L. Landers, "Traditions of African American Freedom and Community in Spanish Colonial Florida," in David R. Colburn and Jane L. Landers, eds., **The African American Heritage of Florida**, Gainesville: University Press of Florida, 1995, 17–41, 25.

16. Jim Piecuch, **Three Peoples, One King: Loyalists, Indians, and Slaves in the Revolutionary South, 1775–1782**, Columbia: University of South Carolina Press, 2008, 42.

17. Report, 14 June 1742, SP89/443, *National Archives of the United Kingdom, London* (hereinafter *NAUK*).

18. **Original Papers Relating to the Island of Cuba**, London: Cooper, 1744, *Brown University, Providence, Rhode Island*: In this volume, see, e.g., "Declaration" by Lieutenant George Lowther, 14 August 1741: "I judge a road might be cut to Guantanamo twenty foot wide in five days by three hundred Negroes"; Letter, 16 January 1742: "about three weeks ago, six Negroes made their Escape from St. Jago de Cuba in [a] canoe. They belonged all to Jamaica. . . . they were employed on the works at St. Jago, all the

while our Army laid on the island of Cuba. Two of them, who are free Negroes and very sensible rational men are very particular in describing the place and fortifications. They affirm that the Governor and principal inhabitants were constantly in the utmost dread, lest our army should march over and land and attack them and so much were they persuaded of this, that the Governor and Grandees would not trust themselves to sleep in the town or forts, but went every night into the woods."

19. **The Defence of Captain Digby Dent to the Complaint Made against Him by Rear Admiral Knowles Concerning His Behaviour in the Expedition Undertaken against Saint Jago de Cuba**, London, 1749, *Brown University*: While in Port Royal, Jamaica, the redcoats received an order on 13 February 1747 "for the attack" on Cuba. See also Letter from Charles Hardy, 14 April 1743, Box 1, Folder 13, *Daniel Parish Slavery Transcripts*: The garrison at St. Augustine has just been bolstered by troops from Havana, as the Spaniards plan to "attempt something on North America, they are fitting out all their capital ships and take in Negroes & Mulattoes as well as white men for seamen." (Note: Depending on the context, "Port Royal" refers to either Jamaica, as here, or South Carolina.)

20. Allan J. Kuethe, **Cuba, 1753–1815: Crown, Military, and Society**, Knoxville: University of Tennessee Press, 1986, 38.

21. "Minutes of Council in Assembly and House of Burgesses," 1752, Folder 160, *Daniel Parish Slavery Transcripts*: See discussion of free Spanish Negroes sold as slaves on the mainland.

22. **Considerations on the Peace, as Far as It Is Relative to the Colonies and the African Trade**, London: Bristow, 1763, *University of Virginia, Charlottesville*.

23. Comment, in David Syrett, ed., **The Siege and Capture of Havana 1762**, London: Navy Records Society, 1970, xiv.

24. Earl of Egremont, Whitehall, to Governor William Henry Lyttleton, January 1762, in Syrett, **Siege and Capture of Havana**, 21–22.

25. Earl of Albermarle to Admiral Pocock, 17 June 1762, in Syrett, **Siege and Capture of Havana**, 194.

26. Keppel to Admiral Pocock, 18 June 1762, in Syrett, **Siege and Capture of Havana**, 195.

27. Keppel to Admiral Pocock, 29 June 1762, in Syrett, **Siege and Capture of Havana**, 208.

28. Douglas to Admiral Pocock, 6 May 1762, in Syrett, **Siege and Capture of Havana**, 107.

29. Patrick Mackellar, Chief Engineer, **A Correct Journal of the Landing of His Majesty's Forces on the Island of Cuba and of the Siege and Surrender of the Havannah, August 13, 1762**, London: Green and Russell, 1762, 9 (I viewed this document at Boston's Massachusetts Historical Society, where it was embedded in yet another document: **The Capture of Havana in 1762 by the Forces of George III**.)

30. Syrett, introduction to **Siege and Capture of Havana**, xviii. See also Memorandum, 1762, CO117/1/1, *NAUK*.

31. Memorandum of Lieutenant General David Dundas, written in 1800, in Syrett, **Siege and Capture of Havana**, 324.

32. Earl of Albermarle to "Dear Sir," June 1762, *Sir George Pocock Letterbook*.

33. Earl of Albermarle to Earl of Egremont, 13 July 1762, Box 7, *Sir George Pocock Papers, Huntington Library*.

34. Earl of Albermarle to Sir, 19 October 1762, CO117/1, *NAUK*.

35. Earl of Albermarle to Admiral Pocock, 27 April 1762, in Syrett, **Siege and Capture of Havana**, 100.

36. Earl of Albermarle to Earl of Egremont, 27 May 1762, in Syrett, **Siege and Capture of Havana**, 107.

37. William Howe to Sir George Pocock, 27 June 1762, Box 7, *Sir George Pocock Papers*.

38. William Howe to Sir George Pocock, 18 June 1762, Box 7, *Sir George Pocock Papers.*

39. Jeffrey Amherst to Sir George Pocock, 20 July 1762, Box 7, *Sir George Pocock Papers.*

40. Sir Francis Bernard to Sir George Pocock, 16 July 1762, Box 7, *Sir George Pocock Papers.*

41. Jeffrey Amherst to Jervis John, 20 July 1762, Box 7, *Sir George Pocock Papers.*

42. Alexander Colville to Sir George Pocock, 6 August 1762, Box 7, *Sir George Pocock Papers.*

43. "Journal of the Siege of Havana," no date, CO117/1, *NAUK.*

44. Report, 2 August 1762, in **The Capture of Havana in 1762 by the Forces of George III**, 1898 (originally published 1762), 36, *Massachusetts Historical Society, Boston.*

45. Robert Monckton to Admiral Pocock, 7 September 1762, Box 7, *Sir George Pocock Papers.*

46. George Rodney to Admiral Pocock, 20 October 1762, Box 7, *Sir George Pocock Papers.*

47. Earl of Albermarle to "My Lord," 21 August 1762, CO117/1, *NAUK.*

48. Earl of Albermarle to "My Lord," August 1762, CO117/1, *NAUK.*

49. Earl of Albermarle to "Sir," 19 October 1762, CO117/1, *NAUK.*

50. Earl of Albermarle to "My Lord," 4 November 1762, CO117/1, *NAUK.*

51. John Robert McNeill, **Atlantic Empires of France and Spain: Louisbourg and Havana, 1700–1763**, Chapel Hill: University of North Carolina Press, 1985, 222.

52. Edict from Earl of Albermarle, 23 October 1762, CO117/1, *NAUK.*

53. Earl of Albermarle to Governor Lyttleton, 16 May 1762, in Syrett, **Siege and Capture of Havana**, 122–123.

54. Gary B. Nash, **The Unknown American Revolution: The Unruly Birth of Democracy and the Struggle to Create America**, New York: Viking, 2005, 151.

55. Memorandum, circa 1766, T1/446, *NAUK.*

56. Gregory E. O'Malley, "Beyond the Middle Passage: Slave Migration from the Caribbean to North America, 1619–1807," **William and Mary Quarterly**, 66(Number 1, January 2009): 125–172, 141, 145, 151, 156.

57. Report, 9 December 1768, CO23/18, *NAUK.*

58. Horne, **Negro Comrades of the Crown.**

59. Thomas Shirley to "My Lord," 12 June 1769, CO23/18, *NAUK.*

60. Thomas Shirley to "Sir," 30 April 1769, CO23/18, *NAUK.*

61. Report, 17 February 1769, CO23/18, *NAUK.*

62. J. Leitch Wright, "British St. Augustine," St. Augustine, Florida: Historic St. Augustine Preservation Board, 1975, *University of South Carolina, Columbia.*

63. **A Description of East Florida with a Journal Kept by John Bartram of Philadelphia, Botanist to His Majesty for the Florida upon a Journey from St. Augustine up the River St. John's as Far as the Lakes**, London: Nicoll, 1769, 211.

64. Whitehall to Governor of Virginia, 16 March 1763, *Francis Fauquier Correspondence Transcriptions, Rockefeller Library, Williamsburg, Virginia.*

65. Letter from the Earl of Hillsborough, 28 November 1770, *Official Letters, Etc., Received by Lord Botecourt While Governor of Virginia, Transcriptions, Rockefeller Library*: "The Spanish Governor of Buenos Ayres hath thought fit to dispossess His Majesty's Subjects to their Settlement at Port Egmont in Falklands Islands; so violent a Proceeding in time of Profound peace, will unless disavowed by the Court of Power and Restitution made, be considered as an open Act of Hostility." See also Letter to Earl of Hillsborough, 3 August 1771, MS 1787, *John Habersham Letterbooks, Georgia Historical Society, Savannah.*

66. "Robinson" of His Majesty's ship to William Bull, 22 December 1770, **South Carolina Council Journal**, *South Carolina Department of Archives and History, Columbia.*

67. Kenneth Coleman, **American Revolution in Georgia, 1763-1789**, Athens: University of Georgia Press, 1958, 265–266.

68. Harold E. Davis, **The Fledgling Province: Social and Cultural Life in Colonial Georgia, 1733-1760**, Chapel Hill: University of North Carolina Press, 1976, 139.

69. Quoted in Gregory D. Massey, **John Laurens and the American Revolution**, Columbia: University of South Carolina Press, 2000, 15.

70. See, e.g., Records of Paul Cross (slave trader, 1770s), *University of South Carolina*.

71. **The Privileges of the Island of Jamaica Vindicated: With an Impartial Narrative of the Late Dispute between the Governor and House of Representatives upon the Case of Mr. Olyphant, a Member of That House**, London: Williams, 1766, 44, 45, *Huntington Library*: "if we are freemen and not slaves, our liberties are as much, our inheritance, as our lands. . . . whereas a slave holds every thing at the pleasure of his master, and has not law, but the will of his tyrant. Can there be a more slavish or famous position, than, that we have no constitution in the Colonies, but what the King is pleased to give us?"

72. John Preston Moore, **Revolt in Louisiana: The Spanish Occupation, 1766-1770**, Baton Rouge: Louisiana State University Press, 157. See also R.E. Chandler, "Ulloa's Account of the 1768 Revolt," **Louisiana History**, 27(Number 4, Autumn 1980): 407–437.

73. Harvey Amani Whitfield, "The American Background of Loyalist Slaves," **Left History**, 14(Number 1, 2009): 58–87, 67.

74. See Georgia to Privy Council, 16 February 1769, PCS1/59/6/2, *NAUK*: Discussion emerges about whether enslaved should be deemed "chattel personal" versus "real estate and descendible to the heir with the lands."

75. "Berbice Revolt," in Junius P. Rodriguez, ed., **Encyclopedia of Slave Resistance and Rebellion, Volume I**, Westport, Connecticut: Greenwood, 2007, 55–56.

76. Thomas N. Ingersoll, **Mammon and Manon in Early New Orleans: The First Slave Society in the Deep South, 1718-1819**, Knoxville: University of Tennessee Press, 1999, 89.

77. **A Short History of Barbados from Its First Discovery and Settlement to the End of the Year 1767**, London: Dodsley, 1768, 110, *University of South Carolina*.

78. Bernard Marshall, "Slave Resistance and White Reaction in the British Windward Islands, 1763-1783," **Caribbean Quarterly**, 28(Number 3, September 1982): 33–46, 33, 34.

79. Rear Admiral Sir G.B. Rodney to Philip Stephens, 6 November 1773, in K.G. Davies, ed., **Documents of the American Revolution, 1770-1783 (Colonial Office Series), Volume VII, Calendar, 1774-30 June 1775**, Dublin: Irish University Press, 1974, 38.

80. Darold D. Wax, "'New Negroes Are Always in Demand': The Slave Trade in Eighteenth-Century Georgia," **Georgia Historical Quarterly**, 68(Number 2, 1984): 193–220, 198, 201, 204, 206, 207, 212.

81. Remarks, 1763 and circa 1767, in Richard J. Hooker, ed., **The Carolina Backcountry on the Eve of the Revolution: The Journal and Other Writings of Charles Woodmason, Anglican Itinerant,** Chapel Hill: University of North Carolina, 1953, xxii, 94.

82. Stanley K. Deaton, "Revolutionary Charleston, 1765-1800," Ph.D. dissertation, University of Florida, 1997, 39, 42.

83. Jonathan Mercantini, **Who Shall Rule at Home? The Evolution of South Carolina Political Culture, 1748-1776**, Columbia: University of South Carolina Press, 2007, 211.

84. Report, 15 November 1765, in Allen D. Candler, ed., **The Colonial Records of the State of Georgia, Volume XIV, Journal of the Commons House of Assembly,** Atlanta: Franklin-Turner, 1907, 292–293.

85. Report, 7 July 1772, in Allen D. Candler, ed., **The Colonial Records of the State of Georgia, Volume XII, Proceedings and Minutes of the Governor and Council, From August 6, 1771 to February 13, 1782,** Atlanta: Franklin-Turner, 1907, 325.

86. Richard Walsh, **Charleston's Sons of Liberty: A Study of the Artisans, 1763–1789,** Columbia: University of South Carolina Press, 1959, 25, 57.

87. Francis Fauquier to Lords of Trade, 17 December 1766, *Francis Fauquier Correspondence*: "Every Gentleman of property, in land and Negroes, have some of their own Negroes bred up in the Trade of blacksmiths and make axes, hoes, ploughshares and such kind of coarse work for the Use of their plantations. I do not know that there is a white smith or maker of Cutlery in the colony."

88. Comment, in William Henry Drayton, **The Letters of Freeman, Etc.: Essays on the Non-Importation Movement in South Carolina,** ed. Robert M. Weir, Columbia: University of South Carolina Press, 1977 (originally published in 1771), xxix.

89. Charles Woodmason, "The Need for Education," in Hooker, **Carolina Backcountry on the Eve of the Revolution,** 121.

90. Legislation, 1765, Robert L. Cain, ed., **Records of the Executive Council, 1755–1775,** Raleigh, North Carolina: Division of Archives and History, 1994, 508. See also **A Continuation of the Impartial Relation of the First Rise and Cause of the Recent Differences, in Publick Affairs, in the Province of North Carolina . . . Second Part,** 1770, *Huntington Library.*

91. Lord Charles Greville Montagu to the Earl of Hillsborough, 19 April 1769; and Charles Garth to Lords Commissioner for Trade and Plantations, circa 1769, in William L. Saunders, ed., **The Colonial Records of North Carolina, Volume VIII, 1769–1771,** Raleigh, North Carolina: Daniels, 1890,

92. Alan D. Watson, "Impulse toward Independence: Resistance and Rebellion among North Carolina Slaves, 1750–1775," **Journal of Negro History,** 63(Number 4, October 1978): 317–328, 324.

93. Legislation, 1765, in Benjamin J. Hillman, ed., **Executive Journals of the Council of Colonial Virginia, Volume VI (June 20, 1754–May 3, 1775),** Richmond: Virginia State Library, 1966, 282. For a similar discussion, see, e.g., Legislation, 17 May 1765, in H.R. McIlwaine, ed., **Legislative Journals of the Council of Colonial Virginia,** Richmond: Virginia State Library, 1979, 1340.

94. Commission of Oyer and Terminer in Chesterfield County, Virginia, issued by Lieutenant Governor Francis Fauquier, 8 June 1764, MS 1939, "Miscellaneous Manuscripts," IX Oversize, M-1561, *Rockefeller Library.*

95. **Extract from an Address in the Virginia Gazette of March 19, 1767 by a Respectable Member of the Community,** *Virginia Historical Society, Richmond.*

96. Report, 1767, in Leonard Woods Labaree, ed., **Royal Instructions to British Colonial Governors, 1670–1776, Volume I,** New York: D. Appleton-Century, 1935, 423.

97. Hugh Rankin, **Criminal Trial Proceedings in the General Court of Colonial Virginia,** Williamsburg, Virginia: Colonial Williamsburg, 1965, 176.

98. Virginia Scharf, **The Women Jefferson Loved,** New York: HarperCollins, 2010, 34.

99. Susan Alice Westbury, "Colonial Virginia and the Atlantic Slave Trade," Ph.D. dissertation, University of Illinois–Champaign, 1981, 79.

100. Quoted in Woody Holton, **Forced Founders: Indians, Debtors, Slaves, and the Making of the American Revolution in Virginia,** Chapel Hill: University of North Carolina Press, 1999, 69.

101. Theodore J. Jervey, **The Slave Trade: Slavery and Color,** Columbia, South Carolina: State Company, 1925, 7–8.

102. Jonathan Mercantini, **Who Shall Rule at Home? The Evolution of South Carolina Political Culture, 1748–1776,** Columbia: University of South Carolina Press, 2007, 14.

103. Richard Archer, **As If an Enemy's Country: The British Occupation of Boston and the Origins of Revolution**, New York: Oxford University Press, 2010, 117 ("Liberty Boys" and "dangerous conspiracy" quotes), 120, 121.

104. Srividhya Swaminathan, **Debating the Slave Trade: Rhetoric of British National Identity, 1759–1815**, Farnham, United Kingdom: Ashgate, 2009, 132.

105. "Committee to Prevent the Importation of Slaves," 7 January 1764, and "A Bill Intitled, *An Act to Prevent the Increase of Slaves within This Province . . .* ," 2 February 1764, in **Journals of the House of Representatives of Massachusetts, 1763–1764**, Boston: Massachusetts Historical Society, 1970, 263–264.

106. See Legislation, October 1774, in Charles J. Hoadly, ed., **The Public Records of the Colony of Connecticut from October 1772 to April 1775, Inclusive**, Hartford, Connecticut: Case, Lockwood and Brainard, 1887, 239.

107. Margaret Lillian Mitchell, "Slavery in Colonial Delaware," B.A. thesis, Smith College, 1970, 51. See also Nash, **Unknown American Revolution**, 151: "the northern colonies, including Massachusetts, Connecticut and Rhode Island banned the slave trade in 1775, as did Virginia and North Carolina. Pennsylvania imposed a duty on imported slaves high enough to dry up the trade."

108. Jay Coughtry, **The Notorious Triangle: Rhode Island and the African Slave Trade, 1700–1807**, Philadelphia: Temple University Press, 1981, xi.

109. "Address of House of Burgesses of Virginia to the King," 1 April 1772, in K.G. Davies, ed., **Documents of the American Revolution, 1770–1783, Volume II,** Shannon: Irish University Press, 1972, 56–57. See also "Address to the House of Burgesses to the King in Opposition to the Slave Trade," 1 April 1772, in Robert L. Scribner and William J. Van Scrivener, eds., **Revolutionary Virginia: The Road to Independence, Volume I: Forming Thunderclouds and the First Convention, 1763–1774: A Documentary Record,** Charlottesville: University Press of Virginia, 1973, 85–87.

110. See, e.g., **An Humble Enquiry into the Nature of the Dependency of the American Colonies upon the Parliament of Great Britain and the Right of Parliament to Lay Taxes on the Said Colonies,** n.d., *Huntington Library.*

111. Report, circa 1731, in Labaree, **Royal Instructions to British Colonial Governors, Volume II,** 973–974: objections to duties levied by "plantation in America . . . on the importation and exportation of Negroes to the great discouragement of the merchants trading thither from the coast of Africa."

112. Report, 10 December 1770, in Labaree, **Royal Instructions to British Colonial Governors, Volume II,** 679: A 15% duty "imposed upon every purchase of slaves imported [or] brought into that colony over and above a duty of ten percent payable by former laws then in force . . . will have the effect to prejudice and obstruct as well the commerce of the kingdom as the cultivation and improvement of the said colony."

113. See Commissioners for Trade and Plantations to His Majesty, 23 November 1770, in Davies, **Documents of the American Revolution, Volume II,** 258–260: objections to December 1769 law imposing new duties on imported Africans. See also Remarks, 16 March 1767, in **Journals of the House of Representatives of Massachusetts, Volume XLIII, Part 2, 1767,** Boston: Massachusetts Historical Society, 1974, 393. See also "Report to the King," 29 July 1768, *Official Letters, Etc., Received by Lord Botecourt While Governor of Virginia*: "A duty of ten per cent on the original purchase is levied on the buyers of slaves imported or brought into this colony, over and above the several duties imposed."

114. Commissioners for Trade and Plantations to the King, 23 November 1770, in K.G. Davies, ed., **Documents of the American Revolution, 1770–1783 (Colonial Office Series), Volume II, Transcripts,** Dublin: Irish University Press, 1985, 123. See also

"Acts of the General Assembly . . . Williamsburg: Rind, 1770," 19–20, *Huntington Library*: continuation of duties on slaves.

115. David S. Lovejoy, **Rhode Island Politics and the American Revolution, 1760–1776**, Providence: Brown University Press, 1958, 40.

116. Paulette Davis, "Aaron Lopez: Patriot or Loyalist?," 1992, *Rhode Island Historical Society*. See also Stanley F. Chyet, **Lopez of Newport: Colonial American Merchant Prince**, Detroit: Wayne State University Press, 1970, 64.

117. Colloquy on Stamp Act, 12 February 1766, in R.C. Simmons and P.D.G. Thomas, eds., **Proceedings and Debates of the British Parliaments Respecting North America, 1765–1768, Volume II**, White Plains, New York: Kraus, 1983, 208.

118. See, e.g., Anthony Benezet, **A Caution and a Warning to Great Britain and Her Colonies, in a Short Representation of the Calamitous State of the Enslaved Negroes in the British Dominions . . .** , Philadelphia: Hall, 1767; Granville Sharp, **Extract from a Representation of the Injustice and Dangerous Tendency of Tolerating Slavery**, Philadelphia: Cruikshank, 1769.

119. See, e.g., Admiral Montagu to Governor of Rhode Island, 8 July 1772; Governor Hutchinson to Samuel Hood, 2 September 1772; Proclamation of King George III, 26 August 1772; **Providence Gazette**, 26 December 1772; Deposition of Aaron Briggs, 14 January 1773; Chief Justice Hormanden to the Earl of Dartmouth, 20 February 1773; Resolution of the House of Burgesses, 12 March 1773; all in **A History of the Destruction of His Brittanic Majesty's Gaspee in Narragansett Bay on the 10th June 1772 . . .** , Providence, Rhode Island: Greene, 1851, *Redwood Library, Newport, Rhode Island*. See also Letter to "My Dear Friend," 4 March 1773, *Henry Marchant Journal & Letterbook, Newport Historical Society, Rhode Island*: re: "the affair of the Gaspee Schooner burnt near Providence."

120. See, e.g., A.S. Hamond, **Logs of the Arethusa and Roebuck**, January 1773, *University of Virginia*: While in Rhode Island, this mariner reported "commerce carried on from hence to the West Indies & coast of Africa is very considerable," and "their flourishing state is chiefly owing to their success in smuggling, which is more carried on here than in the neighboring colonys." See also **Account Book of Caleb Gardner**, *Redwood Library*: Note numerous slave-trade voyages commencing in 1772. At the same site, see also **A Rhode Island Slaver: Trade Book of the Sloop Adventure, 1773–1774**, Providence, Rhode Island: Shepley Library, 1922. Also see Joshua Rotenberg, "Black-Jewish Relations in Eighteenth-Century Newport," **Rhode Island Jewish Historical Notes**, 11(Number 2, November 1992): 117–172, 155.

121. John Millar, "The Gaspee," in **Rhode Island Yearbook 73**, Riverside, Rhode Island: RIY, 1972, 22–25, 22, *Redwood Library*.

122. Ezra Stiles, entries of 13–14 January 1773 and 11–13 June 1773, in Franklin Bowditch Dexter, ed., **The Literary Diary of Ezra Stiles . . .** , New York: Scribner's, 1901.

123. Horatio B. Knox, "The Destruction of the Gaspee," Providence: Department of Education, Rhode Island, 1908, *American Antiquarian Society, Worcester, Massachusetts*.

124. Robert McMillan Kennedy, ed., **South Carolina Items in the "Gentleman's Magazine" (London), 1731–1792, Extracted from the File in the University of South Carolina Library**, 1936, *University of South Carolina*, 45(1775): 20. Revealingly, few are the scholars who have asked why always-restive Quebec did not join the 1776 revolt, when this "vast region" had more reason than most to rebel.

125. William R. Leslie, "The Gaspee Affair: A Study of its Constitutional Significance," **Mississippi Valley Historical Review**, 39(Number 2, September 1952): 233–256, 233.

126. William Bull to Earl of Hillsborough, 30 November 1770, in Davies, **Documents of the American Revolution, Volume II**, 266–280.

127. William Staples, ed., **Documentary History of the Destruction of the Gaspee Compiled for the Providence Journal**, Providence, Rhode Island: Knowles, Vose, Anthony, 1845: See depositions by Negroes seeking to discredit Briggs. See also Ephraim Bowen, **An Account of the Capture and Burning of the British Schooner "Gaspee" Reprinted by John Brown Herreshoff, Great Grandson of the Leader of the Attacking Party**, Bristol, Rhode Island, 1914, *Massachusetts Historical Society.*

128. Charles Rappleye, **Sons of Providence: The Brown Brothers, the Slave Trade, and the American Revolution**, New York: Simon and Schuster, 2006, 171.

129. Michael A. McDonnell, **The Politics of War: Race, Class, and Conflict in Revolutionary Virginia**, Chapel Hill: University of North Carolina Press, 2007, 21.

NOTES TO CHAPTER 9

1. Julie Flavell, **When London Was Capital of America**, New Haven: Yale University Press, 2010, 40, 41, 44, 46, 47, 53, 83, 166.

2. Emma L. Powers, "The Newsworthy 'Somerset Case': Repercussions in Virginia," **Colonial Williamsburg Interpreter**, 23(Number 3, Fall 2002): 1–6, 1.

3. Christopher Alain Cameron, "To Plead Our Own Cause: African Americans in Massachusetts and the Making of the Antislavery Movement, 1630–1835," Ph.D. dissertation, University of North Carolina, 2010, 115.

4. Francis Fauquier to Charles Steuart, 17 June 1763, *Francis Fauquier Correspondence Transcriptions, Rockefeller Library, Williamsburg, Virginia.* See Steven M. Wise, **Though the Heavens May Fall: The Landmark Trial That Led to the End of Human Slavery**, New York: Da Capo, 2005, 4: "Steuart's life dramatically changed when a ship carrying surrendered Spanish sailors . . . made an emergency call in a river near Norfolk and was savagely attacked by the colonists." Steuart helped to rescue them.

5. "Mr. Hargrave, one of the Counsel of the Negro," **An Argument in the Case of James Somersett, a Negro, Lately Determined by the Court of King's Bench: Wherein It Is Attempted to Demonstrate the Present Unlawfulness of Domestic Slavery in England to Which Is Prefixed a State of the Case**, London: Author, 1772, *British Library, London.* See also William R. Ryan, **The World of Thomas Jeremiah: Charles Town on the Eve of the American Revolution**, New York: Oxford University Press, 2010, 29: Interest in South Carolina was no doubt peaked when in 1775, the British pastor of African descent—David Margate—who was "well acquainted with the landmark decision of 'Somerset'" arrived in Charleston.

6. David Waldstreicher, **Runaway America: Benjamin Franklin, Slavery, and the American Revolution**, New York: Hill and Wang, 2004, 199, 201.

7. **By His Excellency the Right Honourable John Earl of Dunmore**, "Proclamation," 1775, *University of Virginia, Charlottesville.*

8. See, e.g., Donald L. Robinson, **Slavery in the Structure of American Politics, 1765–1820**, New York: Norton, 1971; George William Van Cleve, **A Slaveholders' Union: Slavery, Politics, and the Constitution in the Early American Republic**, Chicago: University of Chicago Press, 2010.

9. James Walvin, **An African's Life: The Life and Times of Olaudah Equiano**, London: Cassell, 1998, 50. The decision is also referred to as "Somersett's Case." See also Emory Washburn, "Extinction of Villenage and Slavery in England: With Somerset's Case," a paper read before the Massachusetts Historical Society, Boston: Wilson, 1864, *Huntington Library, San Marino, California*: The existence of villeins led to Wat Tyler's famed revolt that led to the seizure of London, well before the Colombian era. "By a singular coincidence," says the author, "Negro slavery began to obtain a foothold in England about the time of the extinction of that of villeinage," i.e., circa 1553.

10. William R. Ryan, **The World of Thomas Jeremiah: Charles Town on the Eve of the American Revolution**, New York: Oxford University, 2010, 204. See also J. William Harris, **The Hanging of Thomas Jeremiah: A Free Black Man's Encounter with Liberty**, New Haven: Yale University Press, 2009.

11. Powers, "Newsworthy 'Somerset Case,'" 1. See also **A Letter to Philo Africanus upon Slavery . . . with the Sentence of Lord Mansfield in the Case of Somerset and Knowles, 1772 . . .**, London: Newport, *New-York Historical Society, Manhattan.*

12. George Van Cleve, "'Somerset's Case' and its Antecedents in Imperial Perspective," **Law and History Review**, 24(Number 3, Fall 2006): 601–645, 602. See also Carol P. Bauer, "Law, Slavery, and Sommersett's Case in Eighteenth-Century England," Ph.D. dissertation, New York University, 1973.

13. Wise, **Though the Heavens May Fall**, 199, 145 ("honest American" quote).

14. Michael E. Groth, "Black Loyalists and African American Allegiance in the Mid-Hudson Valley," in Joseph S. Tiedmann, Eugene R. Fingerhut, and Robert W. Venables, eds., **The Other Loyalists: Ordinary People, Royalism, and the Revolution in the Middle Colonies, 1763–1787**, Albany: SUNY Press, 2009, 81–104, 82.

15. **Virginia Gazette**, 11 May 1775.

16. **Virginia Gazette**, 13 December 1772.

17. **Virginia Gazette**, 14 October 1773.

18. **Virginia Gazette**, 24 August 1769.

19. **New York Journal**, 3 September 1772, in David A. Copeland, ed., **Debating the Issues in the Colonial Newspapers: Primary Documents on Events of the Period**, Westport, Connecticut: Greenwood, 2000, 278–279.

20. Wise, **Though the Heavens May Fall**, 71, 198. See also **An Address to the Right Honourable Lord Mansfield in Which the Measures of Government Respecting America Are Considered in a New Light with a View to His Lordship's Interposition Therein**, London: Almon, 1775, *British Library.*

21. Samuel Estwick, **Considerations on the Negroe Cause Commonly So Called, Addressed to the Right Honourable Lord Mansfield, Lord Chief Justice of the Court of King's Bench**, London, Dodsley, 1772, *British Library.*

22. Edward Long, **Candid Reflections upon the Judgment Lately Awarded by the King's Bench in Westminster Hall on What Is Commonly Called the Negroe-Cause . . .**, London: Lowndes, 1772, *Boston Public Library, Massachusetts.*

23. **Boston Gazette**, 21 September 1772.

24. Vincent Carretta, **Phillis Wheatley: Biography of a Genius in Bondage**, Athens: University of Georgia Press, 2011, 113, 120, 129. See also Estwick, **Considerations of the Negroe Cause**. Interestingly, London's leading lights—the Countess of Huntingdon and Lord Dartmouth—embraced Wheatley, and the same was true for leading Loyalists, e.g., Thomas Hutchinson, while Thomas Jefferson dismissed her: See, e.g., Folarin Shyllon, **Black People in Britain, 1555–1833**, London: Oxford University Press, 1977, 195. See also Helena Woodard, **African-British Writings in the Eighteenth Century: The Politics of Race and Reason**, Westport, Connecticut: Greenwood, 1999.

25. Long, **Candid Reflections upon the Judgment Lately Awarded**.

26. Catherine Johnson Adams, "'What I Did Is Who I Am': African American Women and Resistance to Slavery in Colonial and Revolutionary New England," Ph.D. dissertation, University of Illinois, 2004, 136.

27. **Virginia Gazette**, 30 June 1774.

28. **Virginia Gazette**, 13 January 1774, in Ulrich B. Phillips, ed., **Plantation and Frontier Documents: 1649–1863: Illustrative of Industrial History in the Colonial and Ante-Bellum South, Volume II**, Cleveland: Clark, 1909, 81–82.

29. Sidney Kaplan and Emma Nogrady Kaplan, **The Black Presence in the Era of the American Revolution**, Amherst: University of Massachusetts Press, 1989, 72.
30. Comment, in Woody Holton, ed., **Black Americans in the Revolutionary Era: A Brief History with Documents**, Boston: Bedford, 2009, 6–7. On this point, see also Christopher Alain Cameron, "To Plead Our Own Cause," 75.
31. Quoted in Kaplan and Kaplan, **Black Presence**, 15. See also **Salem Gazette**, 16 September 1774, *Daniel Parish Slavery Transcripts, New-York Historical Society*: "Petition of the African slaves residing in the province of Massachusetts Bay" to Thomas Gage, "held in a state of slavery within the bowels of a free country."
32. Gary B. Nash, **The Unknown American Revolution: The Unruly Birth of Democracy and the Struggle to Create America**, New York: Viking, 2005, 158.
33. Wise, **Though the Heavens May Fall**, 131, 132.
34. James Madison to William Bradford, fall 1774, in William T. Hutchinson and William M.E. Rachal, eds., **The Papers of James Madison, Volume I, 16 March 1751–16 December 1779**, Chicago: University of Chicago Press, 1962, 253. See also Kaplan and Kaplan, **Black Presence**, 254.
35. William Bradford to James Madison, 4 January 1775, in Hutchinson and Rachal, **Papers of James Madison, Volume I**, 131–132.
36. Peter Bestes, Sambo Freeman, Felix Holbrook, Chester Joie, et al., to "Sir," 20 April 1773, *Boston Public Library*.
37. C.S. Manegold, **Ten Hills Farm: The Forgotten History of Slavery in the North**, Princeton: Princeton University Press, 2010, 209. See also Robert M. Calhoon, Timothy M. Barnes, and Robert S. Davis, **Tory Insurgents: The Loyalist Perception and Other Essays**, Columbia: University of South Carolina Press, 2010.
38. **The Appendix: Or Some Observations on the Expediency of the Petition of the Africans, Living in Boston . . . Lately Presented to the General Assembly of the Province . . . by a Lover of Constitutional Liberty . . .** , Boston: Russell, 1773, *Johns Hopkins University, Baltimore, Maryland*.
39. "Province of the Massachusetts Bay; to His Excellency Thomas Hutchinson . . . 6th day of January 1773; . . . the humble petition of many slaves, living in the town of Boston and other towns in the province . . . ," in **The Appendix**.
40. Foote, **Black and White Manhattan**, 207.
41. Long, **Candid Reflections upon the Judgment Lately Awarded**.
42. Quoted in Shyllon, **Black People in Britain**, 94, 101, 104.
43. Estwick, **Considerations on the Negroe Cause**.
44. J. Rochford to Walpole, 29 June 1773; and Thomas Hutchinson to "My Lord," 23 April 1773, SP89/75, *National Archives of the United Kingdom, London* (hereinafter *NAUK*).
45. **The Dying Negro, a Poem**, London, 1773, *Boston Public Library*.
46. James Swan, **A Dissuasion to Great Britain and the Colonies from the Slave Trade to Africa, Showing the Injustice Thereof**, Boston: Greenleaf, 1773, *Boston Public Library*. A copy of this work can also be found at the Connecticut Historical Society in Hartford. Interestingly, within the first few pages, Swan refers to his Scottish origins three times.
47. Maurice Jackson, **Let This Voice Be Heard: Anthony Benezet, Father of Atlantic Abolitionism**, Philadelphia: University of Pennsylvania Press, 2009, 199.
48. Walvin, **An African's Life**, 101.
49. Nini Rodgers, **Equiano and Anti-Slavery in Eighteenth-Century Belfast**, Belfast, Ireland: Ulster Historical Society, 2000, 2. Cf. John Sainsbury, **Disaffected Patriots: London Supporters of Revolutionary America, 1769–1782**, Montreal: McGill-Queen's University Press, 1987; and Dora Mae Clark, **British Opinion and the American Revolution**, New Haven: Yale University Press, 1930.

50. Vincent Carretta, **Equiano the African: Biography of a Self-Made Man**, Athens: University of Georgia Press, 2005, 194.

51. Letter from Ignatius Sancho, in Paul Edwards and Polly Rewt, ed., **The Letters of Ignatius Sancho**, Edinburgh: Edinburgh University Press, 1994, 115.

52. Maya Jasanoff, **Liberty's Exiles: The Loss of America and the Making of the British Empire**, London: Harper, 2011, 91.

53. **An Answer to a Pamphlet Entitled Taxation No Tyranny Addressed to the Author and to Persons in Power**, London: Almon, 1775, *British Library*.

54. Folarin Shyllon, **James Ramsay: The Unknown Abolitionist**, Edinburgh, United Kingdom: Canongate, 1977.

55. Richard Henry Lee to Arthur Lee, 4 July 1765, in James Curtis Ballagh, ed., **The Letters of Richard Henry Lee, Volume I, 1762-1778**, New York: Macmillan, 1911, 10.

56. Christopher Leslie Brown, "From Slaves to Subjects: Envisioning an Empire without Slavery, 1772–1834," in Philip D. Morgan and Sean Hawkins, eds., **Black Experience and the Empire**, New York: Oxford University Press, 2004, 111–140, 130.

57. Shyllon, **Black People in Britain**, 78. See also Granville Sharp, **The Just Limitation of Slavery in the Laws of God, Compared with the Unbounded Claims of the African Traders and British American Slaveholders**, London: White, 1776, 1; Granville Sharp, **The Law of Retribution; or a Serious Warning to Great Britain and Her Colonies, Founded on Unquestionable Examples of God's Temporal Vengeance against Tyrants, Slaveholders and Oppressors**, London: Richardson, 1776.

58. **Britannia Libera, or a Defence of the Free State of Man in England against the Claim of Any Man There as a Slave Inscribed and Submitted to the Jurisconulti and the Free People of England**, London: Almon, 1772, *Huntington Library*.

59. Srividhya Swaminathan, **Debating the Slave Trade: Rhetoric of British National Identity, 1759–1815**, Farnham, United Kingdom.: Ashgate, 2009, 7. See also Theodore Parsons, "A Forensic Dispute on the Legality of Enslaving the Africans, Held at the Public Commencement in Cambridge, New England, July 21st 1773 by Two Candidates for the Bachelor's Degree," Boston, 1773, *Western Reserve Historical Society, Cleveland, Ohio*.

60. Anthony Benezet to Granville Sharp, 29 March 1773, "U.S. to 1815 Miscellaneous," *Daniel Parish Slavery Transcripts*.

61. Anthony Benezet to Granville Sharp, 1 April 1773, "U.S. to 1815 Miscellaneous," *Daniel Parish Slavery Transcripts*.

62. Legislation, October 1748, in William Waller Henning, ed., **The Statutes at Large; Being a Collection of All the Laws of Virginia . . . , Volume V**, Richmond, Virginia: WWH, 1819, 548.

63. Opinion by Edmund Hoskins, Lincolns Inn, 10 April 1749, in **A Letter to Philo Africanus upon Slavery**, 1788, *Brown University, Providence, Rhode Island*.

64. Comment, in James Walvin, ed., **The Black Presence: A Documentary History of the Negro in England, 1555–1860**, London: Orbach and Chambers, 1971, 12, 21.

65. Carretta, **Phillis Wheatley**, 128–129. Cf. Statute, October 1748, in William Waller Henning, ed., **The Statutes at Large: Being a Collection of the Laws of Virginia from the First Session of the Legislature in the Year 1618, Volume V,** Richmond, Virginia: Franklin, 1819, 548: "that a slave's being in England shall not be a discharge from slavery, without other proof of being manumitted there."

66. **At a Convention of Delegates for the Counties and Corporations in the Colony of Virginia at the Town of Richmond in the County of Henrico**, 25 March 1775, *University of Virginia*: "Resolved unanimously . . . most cordial thanks . . . a tribute justly due to our worthy Governor Lord Dunmore, for his truly noble, wise and spirited conduct on the late expedition against our Indian enemy." See also **Dunmore's**

Proclamation of Emancipation, Charlottesville: University of Virginia, 1941, *Brown University*; and Charles Whittlesey, "A Discourse Relating to the Expedition of Lord Dunmore of Virginia against the Indian Towns upon the Scioto in 1774," delivered before the History and Philosophical Society of Ohio, January 1840, *Huntington Library*.

67. E.O. Randall, "The Dunmore War," **Ohio State Archaeological and Historical Quarterly** 11(October 1902): 4–33, 4–5.

68. Michael Voris, "Lord Dunmore's War," **The Society of Colonial Wars in the State of Ohio** (1972), 1–5, 1, *Rhode Island Historical Society, Providence*. See also Virgil A. Lewis, ed., **The Soldiery of West Virginia in the French and Indian War; Lord Dunmore's War; The Revolution . . .** , Baltimore: Genealogical, 1967.

69. Quoted in Kaplan and Kaplan, **Black Presence**, 73.

70. Earl of Dunmore to Earl of Hillsborough, May 1772, in K.G. Davies, ed., **Documents of the American Revolution, Volume V**, Shannon: Irish University Press, 1972, 94–95.

71. **Journal of Virginia House of Burgesses**, February 1772, *Brown University*. See also **Journals of the House of Representatives of Massachusetts, Volume L, 1773–1774,** Boston: Massachusetts Historical Society, 1981, 25 February 1773: "A Bill to prevent the Importation of Negroes into this Province. Read the second and third time." In retrospect, it is difficult to say if worthy abolitionist sentiment drove such measures or nervousness about bringing to the colonies more potential backers of the Crown or apprehension about the threat to the livelihood of poor Europeans brought by enslaved Africans.

72. Earl of Dunmore to Earl of Dartmouth, 1 May 1775, in K.G. Davies, **Documents of the American Revolution, Volume IX**, Shannon: Irish University Press, 1972, 107–110.

73. Lord Dunmore to Earl of Dartmouth, 1 May 1775, *Transcriptions of Lord Dunmore's Correspondence, Rockefeller Library, Williamsburg, Virginia*.

74. Lord Dunmore to Earl of Dartmouth, 27 June 1775, in K.G. Davies, **Documents of the American Revolution, Volume VII**, Shannon: Irish University Press, 1972, 355.

75. Letter to "Gentlemen," 1 February 1774, in H. Roy Merrens, ed., **The Colonial South Carolina Scene: Contemporary Views, 1697–1774**, Columbia: University of South Carolina Press, 1977, 276–278.

76. **Virginia Gazette**, 31 August 1775.

77. **Virginia Gazette**, 26 October 1775, 28 October 1775, 11 May 1776.

78. Comment, in Holton, **Black Americans in the Revolutionary Era**, 7, 8. See also Woody Holton, **Forced Founders: Indians, Debtors, Slaves, and the Making of the American Revolution in Virginia**, Chapel Hill: University of North Carolina Press, 1999, 220.

79. Dickson Bruce, Jr., **The Origins of African American Literature, 1660–1865**, Charlottesville: University Press of Virginia, 2001, 56, 57.

80. Vincent Carretta, "Venture Smith, One of a Kind," in James Brewer Stewart, ed., **Venture Smith and the Business of Slavery and Freedom**, Amherst: University of Massachusetts Press, 2009, 163–183, 176: "Readers of the accounts of Venture Smith's predecessors Hammon, Gronniosaw, Marrant, George, Liele, King and Equiano are pointedly told that each served in the British military forces before and during the American Revolution"—though Smith "completely erased" his pro-London leanings in his post-U.S. narrative.

81. Ryan, **World of Thomas Jeremiah**, 16. See also Gerald W. Mullin, **Flight and Rebellion: Slave Resistance in Eighteenth-Century Virginia**, London: Oxford University Press, 1972.

82. **Dunmore's Proclamation of Emancipation**.

83. Landon Carter, undated entry, 1775, in Jack P. Greene, ed., **The Diary of Colonel Landon Carter of Sabine Hall, 1752–1778, Volume II**, Richmond: Virginia Historical Society, 1987, 959.

84. Reports, 3–4 June 1775, in William Edwin Hemphill and Wylma Anne Wates, eds., **Extracts from the Journals of the Provincial Congresses of South Carolina, 1775–1776**, Columbia: South Carolina Archives Department, 1960, 36, 37.

85. Quoted in David Morton Knepper, "The Political Structure of Colonial South Carolina, 1743–1776," Ph.D. dissertation, University of Virginia, 1971, 37. See Herbert Treadwell Wade, **A Brief History of the Colonial Wars in America from 1607 to 1775**, New York: Society of Colonial Wars in the State of New York, 1948.

86. Quoted in John D. Duncan, "Servitude and Slavery in Colonial South Carolina," Ph.D. dissertation, Emory University, 1972, 830. See also John Drayton, **Memoirs of the American Revolution as Relating to the State of South Carolina**, New York: Arno, 1969, 231, 258.

87. Robert Anthony Olwell, "Authority and Resistance: Social Order in a Colonial Slave Society, the South Carolina Low Country, 1739–1782," Ph.D. dissertation, Johns Hopkins University, 1991, 387, 388; **South Carolina Gazette**, 29 May 1775.

88. W. Robert Higgins, "The Ambivalence of Freedom: Whites, Blacks, and the Coming of the American Revolution in the South," in W. Robert Higgins, ed., **The Revolutionary War in the South: Power, Conflict, and Leadership**, Durham: Duke University Press, 1979, 43–63, 45.

89. Governor James Wright to Earl of Dartmouth, 25 May 1775, in Davies, **Documents of the American Revolution, Volume VII**, 334.

90. **Virginia Gazette**, 21 September 1775, 26 October 1775.

91. **Virginia Gazette**, 28 April 1775.

92. Benjamin Quarles, "Lord Dunmore as Liberator," **William and Mary Quarterly**, 15(Number 4, October 1958): 494–507, 494, 507. On Africans and Lord Dunmore's edict, see, e.g., **Virginia Gazette**, 2 December 1775.

93. Thad W. Tate, Jr., **The Negro in Eighteenth Century Williamsburg**, Williamsburg, Virginia: Colonial Williamsburg, 1965, 215.

94. Comment, in Graham Russell Hodges, ed., **The Black Loyalist Directory: African Americans in Exile after the American Revolution**, New York: Garland, 1996, xii. See also Andrew Jackson O'Shaughnessy, **The Men Who Lost America: British Leadership, the American Revolution, and the Fate of the Empire**, New Haven: Yale University Press, 2013, 277: Perhaps "up to as many as 100, 000" Africans "joined the British" side.

95. **Dunmore's Proclamation of Emancipation**. Note that the future president may have been thinking of his own Virginia, for surely by 1775 the necessary underpinnings for a settler revolt were in place, as governors were fleeing to British warships offshore, congresses in various provinces had met, loyalty oaths were being administered, and local militia were falling under rebel control. As early as the winter of 1774–1775, the settlers had begun to import gunpowder and arms across the Atlantic. In April 1775 at Lexington and Concord and two months later at Bunker Hill, the settlers had inflicted heavy casualties on the British military. See, e.g., Kevin Phillips, **1775: A Good Year for Revolution**, New York: Viking, 2012. For a glimpse of this settler activism, see T.H. Breen, **American Insurgents, American Patriots: The Revolution of the People**, New York: Hill and Wang, 2010.

96. Virginia Scharf, **The Women Jefferson Loved**, New York: HarperCollins, 2010, 46.

97. Patrick Henry to "Sir," 20 November 1775, *William Augustine Washington Papers, Duke University, Durham, North Carolina*.

98. Lord Dunmore to Earl of Dartmouth, 15 May 1775, *Lord Dunmore's Correspondence.*
99. Precis of Correspondence between Lord Dartmouth and Lord Dunmore, 1775–1776, PRO30/29, 3/5, *NAUK.*
100. Quoted in Ryan, **World of Thomas Jeremiah,** 217.
101. Count de Guines to Count De Vergennes, 4 August 1775, in Clark, **British Opinion and the American Revolution,** 1091.
102. Quoted in Thomas B. Allen, **Tories: Fighting for the King in America's First Civil War,** New York: HarperCollins, 2010, 155.
103. Joanne Pope Melish, **Disowning Slavery: Gradual Emancipation and "Race" in New England, 1780–1860,** Ithaca: Cornell University Press, 1998, 51, 56.
104. "Extract of a Letter from Philadelphia, December 6," 1775, in Margaret Wheeler Willard, ed., **Letters on the American Revolution, 1774–1776,** Boston: Houghton Mifflin, 1923, 233: "Hell itself could not have vomited any things more black than his [Dunmore's] design of emancipating our slaves; and unless he is cut off before he is reinforced, we know not how far the contagion may spread. The flame runs like wild fire through the slaves, who are more than two for one white in the Southern Colonies. The subject of their nocturnal revels, instead of music and dancing, is now turned upon their liberty. I know not whence these troubles may lead us. If our friends in England are not able to oblige the ministry to give way, we are lost; and already gone too far to retract with safety."
105. Ryan, **World of Thomas Jeremiah,** 217n. 51: "A patriot preacher in Maryland would write to London, 'the governor of Virginia, the captains of the men of war and mariners have been tampering with our Negroes, and have nightly meetings with them; all for the glorious purpose of enticing them to cut their masters' throats while they are asleep. Gracious God! That men noble by birth and fortune should descend to such ignoble base servility.'"
106. **History of the War with America, France, Spain and Holland Begun in the Year 1775 and Ended in 1783,** 1787, 119, *New Jersey Historical Society, Newark.*
107. Thomas Hutchinson, entry, 5 October 1775, in Peter Orlando Hutchinson, ed., **The Diary and Letters of His Excellency Thomas Hutchinson, Esq. . . . ,** Boston: Houghton Mifflin, 1884, 233. See also **Copy of Letter Sent to Great Britain by His Excellency Thomas Hutchinson, the Hon. Andrew Oliver and Several Other Persons Born and Educated among Us . . . ,** Boston: Edes and Gill, 1773, *Clemson University, South Carolina.*
108. Stanley K. Deaton, "Revolutionary Charleston, 1765–1800," Ph.D. dissertation, University of Florida, 1997, 104.
109. Robert Olwell, **Masters, Slaves, and Subjects: The Culture of Power in the South Carolina Low Country, 1740–1790,** Ithaca: Cornell University Press, 1998, 246.
110. Frank Klingberg, **An Appraisal of the Negro in Colonial South Carolina: A Study in Americanization,** Philadelphia: Porcupine, 1975, 1.
111. Knepper, "Political Structure of Colonial South Carolina," 36.
112. Quoted in Kinloch Bull, Jr., **The Oligarchs in Colonial and Revolutionary Charleston: Lieutenant Governor William Bull and His Family,** Columbia: University of South Carolina Press, 1991, 217.
113. William Bradford to James Madison, 10 July 1775, in William T. Hutchinson and William M.E. Rachal, eds., **The Papers of James Madison, Volume I, 16 March 1751–16 December 1779,** Chicago: University of Chicago Press, 1962, 156. See also Pauline Maier, **From Resistance to Revolution: Colonial Radicals and the Development of American Opposition to Britain, 1765–1776,** London: Routledge and Kegan Paul, 1973, 283–284: James Simmons in Maryland was similar to Jeremiah but was lucky in that he was only banished from the province—not executed.

114. Statement, 14 November 1774, Box 1, *Robert Carter Papers, Duke University.*

115. Robert Carter to William Taylor, 21 February 1775, Box 1, *Robert Carter Papers.*

116. Robert Carter to "Mr. Wardop," 2 July 1776, Box 1, *Robert Carter Papers.*

117. Governor Josiah Martin to Earl of Dartmouth, 30 June 1775, in Davies, **Documents of the American Revolution, Volume VII,** 302.

118. Quoted in Robert O. De Mond, **The Loyalists in North Carolina during the Revolution,** Hamden, Connecticut: Archon, 1964, 73–74. See also Robert G. Parkinson, book review of **American Insurgents, American Patriots,** by T.H. Breen, **William and Mary Quarterly,** 68(Number 1, January 2011): 160–164.

119. Earl of Dartmouth to Lord Dunmore, 12 July 1775, *Lord Dunmore's Correspondence.*

120. Quoted in Edmund Alexander Bator, **South Carolina 1775: A Crucible Year,** Franklin, Tennessee: American History Imprints, 2009, 12.

121. Vernon O. Stumpf, **Josiah Martin: The Last Royal Governor of North Carolina,** Durham: Carolina Academic Press, 1986, 126, 118.

122. Jeffrey J. Crow, "Slave Rebelliousness and Social Conflict in North Carolina, 1775 to 1802," **William and Mary Quarterly,** 37(January 1980): 79–102, 83, 85. See also Governor Tonyn to Lord Dartmouth, 24 August 1775, MC-63, PRO CO5/555, *St. Augustine Historical Society, Florida*: Negro pilots purloin vessel with gunpowder.

123. Janet Schaw, **Journal of a Lady of Quality; Being the Narrative of a Journey from Scotland to the West Indies, North Carolina and Portugal in the Years 1774 to 1776,** ed. Evangeline Walker Andrew and Charles McLean Andrews, New Haven: Yale University Press, 1939, 199, 200, 201.

124. Lorenzo Johnston Greene, **The Negro in Colonial New England, 1620–1776,** New York: Columbia University Press, 1942, 162, 164.

125. Legal Decision, 29 October 1773, CR 044 928 15, Granville County, Criminal Actions Concerning Slaves & Free Persons of Color, *North Carolina State Archives, Raleigh.*

126. Nash, **Unknown American Revolution,** 155.

127. Quoted in Sidney Kaplan, "The 'Domestic Insurrections' of the Declaration of Independence," **Journal of Negro History,** 61(Number 3, July 1976): 243–255, 251.

128. Joseph Hewes to James Iredell, 8 July 1775, in Don Higginbotham, ed., **The Papers of James Iredell, Volume I, 1767–1777,** Raleigh, North Carolina: Division of Archives and History, 1976, 131: London "had in contemplation a scheme to set our slaves free and arm them against us."

129. "A Declaration of the People of the Colony and Dominion of Virginia . . . ," 14 December 1775, in David John Mays, ed., **The Letters and Papers of Edmund Pendleton, 1734–1803, Volume I,** Charlottesville: University Press of Virginia, 1967, 138.

130. Edict, January 1776, in Robert L. Scribner and Brent Tarter, eds., **Revolutionary Virginia: The Road to Independence, Volume IV: The Committee of Safety and the Balance of Forces, 1775: A Documentary Record,** Charlottesville: University Press of Virginia, 1978, 465.

131. **The Proceedings of the Convention of Delegates Held at the Town of Richmond in the Colony of Virginia, on Friday the 1st of December 1775 and Afterwards by Adjournment in the City of Williamsburg,** Williamsburg, Virginia: Purdie, 1776, *Huntington Library.*

132. Benjamin Franklin to Jonathan Shipley, 7 July 1775, in Paul Smith, ed., **Letters of Delegates to Congress, 1774–1789: August 1774–August 1775,** Washington, D.C.: Library of Congress, 1976, 606–607.

133. See Petition, 1775; Report, 1775; Report 1775; Proceedings of Third Virginia Convention, 19 July 1775; and Report from John Tazewell, 1775, in Robert L. Scribner, ed., **Revolutionary Virginia: The Road to Independence, Volume III: The Breaking**

Storm and the Third Convention, 1775: A Documentary Record, Charlottesville: University Press of Virginia, 1977, 140–141, 144, 310, 319, 323.

134. Entry, 15 July 1776, Diary of Miguel Antonio Eduardo, in William James Morgan, ed., Naval Documents of the American Revolution, Volume V, Washington, D.C.: Government Printing Office, 1970, 1346. In the same volume, page 1346, see also Entry, Diary of Miguel Antonio Eduardo, 15 July 1776: "Ethiopians disembarked, . . . undertook a grand sack of the few houses that had been abandoned by their owners that same morning."

135. Remarks, 15 June 1776, in John Pendleton Kennedy, ed., Journals of the House of Burgesses of Virginia, 1773–1776, Including the Records of the Committee of Correspondence, Richmond: Virginia State Library, 1905, 245.

136. Dunmore's Proclamation of Emancipation.

137. Report by Richard Henry Lee, circa 1775, in Scribner and Tarter, Revolutionary Virginia, 419.

138. History of the War with America, France, Spain and Holland, 130. Perhaps these Scots were like those French speakers in Quebec who quarreled with London yet refused to join the rebels because of a perception that the latter were not sufficiently sensitive to their interests. Cf. "Extract of a Letter from Philadelphia, December 6," 231–233: This anti-London writer claimed that "the Scotch and Irish people are hand in hand with us and very spirited."

139. Lord Dunmore to Earl of Dartmouth, 5 October 1775, Lord Dunmore's Correspondence.

140. Quoted in Nash, Unknown American Revolution, 159.

141. Debates, 1775–1776, in R.C. Simmons and P.D.G. Thomas, eds., Proceedings and Debates of the British Parliaments Respecting North America, 1754–1783, Volume VI, April 1775 to May 1776, White Plains, New York: Kraus, 1987, 169–170, 571, 97, 565, 332. See also John Wesley, Thoughts upon Slavery, London: Hawes, 1774: This is a sharp critique of Africans dragged to "America," with Virginia among the provinces singled out.

142. Debates, 22 March 1775, in R.C. Simmons and P.D.G. Thomas, eds., Proceedings and Debates of the British Parliaments, Volume V, June 1774–March 1775, White Plains, New York: Kraus, 1986, 607. Cf. Barbara Clark Smith, The Freedoms We Lost: Consent and Resistance in Revolutionary America, New York: New Press, 2010.

143. Statement by James Iredell, June 1776, in Higginbotham, Papers of James Iredell, 409.

144. Robert Carter to "Sir," 30 December 1775, Box 1, Robert Carter Papers.

145. Extracts from the Proceedings of the American Continental Congress, Held at Philadelphia, on the Tenth Day of May 1775, Containing an Address to the People of Ireland, an Address to the Assembly of Jamaica, a Letter to the Lord Mayor of London . . . , Providence, Rhode Island: John Carter, 1775, Huntington Library.

146. Entry in John Adams's Diary, 24 September 1775, in Paul Smith, ed., Letters of Delegates to Congress, 1774–1789: September–December 1775, Washington, D.C.: Library of Congress, 1976, 50–51.

147. Geoffrey Mohlman, "Lincolnville: An Anthropological History of Black St. Augustine," B.A. thesis, New College, University of South Florida, 1991, 24, 27.

NOTES TO CHAPTER 10

1. Frances Moorman Walker, "Lord Dunmore in Virginia," M.S. thesis, University of Virginia, 1933, 123, 124.

2. Jason T. Sharples, "Flames of Insurrection: Fearing Slave Conspiracy in Early America, 1670–1780," Ph.D. dissertation, Princeton University, 2010, 318.

3. Remarks by Duke of Manchester, 10 May 1776, in R.C. Simmons and P.D.G. Thomas, eds., **Proceedings and Debates of the British Parliaments, Respecting North America, 1754-1783, Volume VI, April 1775 to May 1776**, White Plains, New York: Kraus International, 1987, 565.

4. Troy Bickham, **Making Headlines: The American Revolution as Seen through the British Press**, DeKalb: Northern Illinois University Press, 2009, 211.

5. Comment by Josiah Quincy, circa 1775, in Daniel R. Coquilette and Neil Longley York, eds., **Portrait of a Patriot: The Major Political and Legal Papers of Josiah Quincy Junior, Volume IV**, Boston: Colonial Society of Massachusetts, 2009, 37. See also Granville Sharp, **The Law of Retribution, or a Serious Warning to Great Britain and Her Colonies, Founded on Unquestionable Examples of God's Temporal Vengeance against Tyrants, Slave-Holders and Oppressors**, London: Richardson, 1776.

6. Quoted in David Waldstreicher, **Runaway America: Benjamin Franklin, Slavery, and the American Revolution**, New York: Hill and Wang, 2004, 211.

7. Sidney Kaplan, "The 'Domestic Insurrections' of the Declaration of Independence," **Journal of Negro History**, 61(Number 3, July 1976): 243–255, 247. See also Watson W. Jennison, **Cultivating Race: The Expansion of Slavery in Georgia, 1750-1860**, Lexington: University Press of Kentucky, 2012.

8. **The Proceedings of the Convention of Delegates Held at the Town of Richmond in the Colony of Virginia on Friday the 1st of December 1775**, Williamsburg, Virginia, embedded in **At a Convention of Delegates for the Counties and Corporations in the Colony of Virginia at the Town of Richmond in the County of Henrico**, *University of Virginia, Charlottesville.*

9. Governor Thomas Gage to Lord Dartmouth, 15 May 1775, in William Bell Clark, ed., **Naval Documents of the American Revolution, Volume I,** Washington, D.C.: Government Printing Office, 1964, 338.

10. Minutes, 2 January 1776, in **The Proceedings of the Convention of Delegates Held at the Town of Richmond in the Colony of Virginia, on Friday the 1st of December 1775 and Afterwards by Adjournment in the City of Williamsburg**, Williamsburg, Virginia: Purdie, 1776, *Huntington Library, San Marino, California.*

11. Lord Dunmore to Lord George Germain, 30 March 1776, in William Bell Clark, ed., **Naval Documents of the American Revolution, Volume IV**, Washington, D.C.: Government Printing Office, 1969, 585.

12. Major General Henry Clinton to Major General William Howe, 20 April 1776, in Clark, **Naval Documents of the American Revolution, Volume IV**, 1182.

13. Minutes, 17 January 1776, in **Proceedings of the Convention of Delegates**, *University of Virginia.*

14. Extract of letter from Philadelphia, 21 June 1776, in William James Morgan, ed., **Naval Documents of the American Revolution, Volume V**, Washington, D.C.: Government Printing Office, 1970, 670. For more on the devastating impact of smallpox on African troops, see, e.g., 1775–1776 Entries, *A.S. Hamond Diaries, University of Virginia.*

15. **Virginia Gazette**, 8 March 1776.

16. **Virginia Gazette**, 2 August 1775.

17. Edmund Pendleton to Thomas Jefferson, 24 May 1776, in Morgan, **Naval Documents of the American Revolution, Volume V**, 240.

18. **Virginia Gazette**, 15 June 1776.

19. Lord Dunmore to Lord George Germain, 30 March 1776, in Clark, **Naval Documents of the American Revolution, Volume IV**, 585.

20. Entries 10 June 1776 and 6 August 1776, *A.S. Hamond Diaries.*

21. Entry, August 1776, *A.S. Hamond Diaries.*

22. Woody Holton, "'Rebel against Rebel': Enslaved Virginians and the Coming of the American Revolution," **Virginia Magazine of History and Biography,** 105(Number 2, Spring 1997): 157–192, 161, 163.

23. Fritz Hirschfeld, **George Washington and Slavery: A Documentary Portrayal,** Columbia: University of Missouri Press, 1997, 146–147.

24. Vincent Carretta, **Phillis Wheatley: Biography of a Genius in Bondage,** Athens: University of Georgia Press, 2011, 154.

25. George Washington to John Laurens, 30 March 1779, in Edward G. Lenel, ed., **The Glorious Struggle: George Washington's Revolutionary Letters,** New York: HarperCollins, 2007, 175. Though anti-London sentiment was quite strong in Quebec, Washington was leery of collaborating with his ally in Paris in winning over this vast land. See, e.g., in the same volume, George Washington to Nathaniel Greene, 1 September 1778, 164; and George Washington to Henry Laurens, 14 November 1778, 166–168.

26. Ellen Gibson Wilson, **The Loyal Blacks,** New York: Putnam's, 1976, 21, 25, 28.

27. Duncan McLeod, **Slavery, Race and the American Revolution,** New York: Cambridge University Press, 1974, 7.

28. David Brion Davis, "Was Thomas Jefferson an Authentic Enemy of Slavery?," Inaugural Lecture at Oxford, 18 February 1970, *British Library, London.* Cf. Paul Finkelman, "Thomas Jefferson and Antislavery: The Myth Goes on," **Virginia Magazine of History and Biography,** 102(Number 2, April 1994): 193–228.

29. Thomas Jefferson, "Notes of Proceedings in Congress," July 1776, in Paul Smith, ed., **Letters of Delegates to Congress, 1774–1789: January 1–May 15, 1776,** Washington, D.C.: Library of Congress, 1978, 359. See, e.g., Legislation, circa 1774, in John Russell Bartlett, ed., **Records of the Colony of Rhode Island and Providence Plantations in New England,** Providence: Greene, 1862, 251; see also Jay Coughtry, **The Notorious Triangle: Rhode Island and the African Slave Trade, 1700–1807,** Philadelphia: Temple University Press, 1981, xi: "the Rhode Island slave trade and the American slave trade are virtually synonymous." On the enormous pre-1776 commerce between Massachusetts and the Caribbean, including slave sales, sales gone bad, petitions for freedom, etc., see "Massachusetts Folders, 196–212," *Daniel Parish Slavery Transcripts, New-York Historical Society, Manhattan;* See also Virginia Scharf, **The Women Jefferson Loved,** New York: HarperCollins, 2010, 121: In the original draft of the Declaration, Jefferson castigated the Crown for "exciting those very people [enslaved] to rise in arms among us, . . . murdering the people on whom he also obtruded them."

30. Quoted in Kenneth Morgan, **Slavery and Servitude in North America, 1607–1800,** Edinburgh: Edinburgh University Press, 2000, 102.

31. Quoted in Bickham, **Making Headlines,** 212.

32. John Penn to John Adams, 17 April 1776, in Smith, **Letters of Delegates to Congress,** 596.

33. John Adams to John Penn, 28 April 1776, in Smith, **Letters of Delegates to Congress,** 596–597.

34. Unidentified writer to John Adams, 9 June 1775, Mss. 2 AD, 1836a1, *Virginia Historical Society, Richmond.*

35. "'The People' to Josiah Martin," 16 July 1775, in Clark, **Naval Documents of the American Revolution, Volume I,** 898: "base encouragement of slaves eloped from their masters, feeding and employing them and his atrocious and horrid declaration that he would excite them to an Insurrection, . . . indignation and resentment."

36. Quoted in Carretta, **Phillis Wheatley,** 70.

37. Minutes of the Committee of Safety, Wilmington, North Carolina, 21 January 1775, in Clark, **Naval Documents of the American Revolution, Volume I,** 68.

38. "Proceedings of the Safety Committee at New Bern . . . ," 2 August 1775, in William L. Saunders, **The Colonial Records of North Carolina, Volume X, 1775–1776,** Raleigh, North Carolina: Daniels, 1890, 138a.

39. Governor Martin to "Sir," 24 June 1774, in Saunders, **Colonial Records of North Carolina, Volume X,** 128.

40. Minutes of the "Congress," 11 April 1776, in Saunders, **Colonial Records of North Carolina, Volume X,** 509–513. See also "The Halifax Resolves, April 12, 1776," in Phillip Margulies, **A Primary Source History of the Colony of North Carolina: Primary Sources of the Thirteen Colonies and the Lost Colony,** New York: Rosen, 2006, 54–55.

41. John Simpson, Chairman of Safety Committee in Pitt County, to Colonel Richard Cogdell, 15 July 1775, in Saunders, **Colonial Records of North Carolina, Volume X,** 94–95.

42. Letter from John Simpson, 15 July 1775, *Richard Cogdell Papers, North Carolina State Archives, Raleigh.*

43. "Minutes of the Committee of New Bern," 7 August 1775, in Clark, **Naval Documents of the American Revolution, Volume I,** 1091.

44. Richard B. Sheridan, "The Jamaican Insurrection Scare of 1776 and the American Revolution," **Journal of Negro History,** 61(Number 3, July 1976): 290–308, 307. See also Jeffrey J. Crow, "'Equal Justice': Afro-American Perceptions of the Revolution in North Carolina, 1775–1802," March 1988, *University of North Carolina, Chapel Hill.* See also Kenneth Coleman, **The American Revolution in Georgia, 1763–1789,** Athens: University of Georgia Press, 1958.

45. Minutes of Congress at Chasten, 26 March 1776, in William Edwin Hemphill and Wylma Anne Wates, eds., **Extracts from the Journals of the Provincial Congresses of South Carolina, 1775–1776,** Columbia: South Carolina Archives Department, 1960, 257.

46. Gabriel Manigault to Mrs. Manigault, 5 September 1775, *Manigault Family Papers, University of South Carolina, Columbia.*

47. Colonel Lachlan McIntosh to George Washington, 23 February to 3 August 1776, in Clark, **Naval Documents of the American Revolution, Volume IV,** 246–247.

48. Report, 1776, "Parish Transcripts . . . and Historical Notes . . . ," *Daniel Parish Slavery Transcripts.*

49. Benjamin L. Carp, **Rebels Rising: Cities and the American Revolution,** New York: Oxford University Press, 2007, 167. See also Eva Poythress, "Revolution by Committee: An Administrative History of the Extralegal Committees in South Carolina, 1774–1776," Ph.D. dissertation, University of North Carolina, 1975, 261, 262, 267, 278.

50. See, e.g., Levinus Clarkson to David Van Horne, 2 January 1775, in Clark, **Naval Documents of the American Revolution, Volume I,** 49.

51. Resolution, 6 April 1776, in Morgan, **Naval Documents of the American Revolution, Volume V,** 683.

52. Interestingly, officers of the Vice-Admiralty Court and customs' officers in particular in Rhode Island—where smuggling was particularly well developed—tended to be loyalists and were informed by rebels that such a position had to change, or they should find a different nation in which to reside. See, e.g., **The Diary of Thomas Vernon, a Loyalist Banished from Newport by the Rhode Island General Assembly in 1776, with Notes by Sidney S. Rider . . . ,** Providence, Rhode Island: SSR, 1881.

53. William Pollard to "Messrs. B & Bowers," 1 February 1774, in H. Roy Merrens, ed., **The Colonial South Carolina Scene: Contemporary Views, 1697–1774,** Columbia: University of South Carolina Press, 1977, 276–278.

54. Samuel Johnson, **Taxation No Tyranny: An Answer to the Resolutions and Address of the American Congress**, London: Cadell, 1775, *British Library.*

55. Sheldon S. Cohen, **British Supporters of the American Revolution, 1775-1783**, Rochester, New York: Boydell, 2004, 17.

56. **The Pamphlet Entitled "Taxation No Tyranny," Candidly Considered and Its Arguments, and Pernicious Doctrines, Exposed and Refuted**, London: Davis, circa 1775, *British Library.*

57. "A Member of Parliament," **A Short Address to the Government, the Merchants, Manufacturers and the Colonies in America and the Sugar Islands on the Present State of Affairs**, London: Robinson, 1775, *Huntington Library.*

58. Gerald Horne, **The Deepest South: The United States, Brazil, and the African Slave Trade**, New York: NYU Press, 2007.

59. Coughtry, **Notorious Triangle**, 174, 175.

60. John Gordon Freymann, **The Sorrel Family in Saint-Domingue (Haiti), 1763-1813**, Avon, Connecticut: JGF, 2000, 7.

61. Woody Holton, **Forced Founders: Indians, Debtors, Slaves, and the Making of the American Revolution in Virginia**, Chapel Hill: University of North Carolina Press, 1999, 220.

62. John Richard Alden, **John Stuart and the Southern Colonial Frontier: A Study of Indian Relations, War, Trade, and Land Problems in the Southern Wilderness, 1754-1775**, New York: Gordian, 1966, 171, 233. See also T. Bailey Myers, **The Tories or Loyalists in America, Being Slight Historical Tracings from the Footprints of Sir John Johnson and His Contemporaries in the Revolution**, Albany, New York: Munsell, 1882; Kenneth Walter Cameron, ed., **The Church of England in Pre-Revolutionary Connecticut: New Documents and Letters Concerning the Loyalist Clergy and the Plight of Their Surviving Church**, Hartford, Connecticut: Transcendental, 1976.

63. John Stuart to Earl of Dartmouth, 21 July 1775, in Saunders, **Colonial Records of North Carolina, Volume X**, 117-119.

64. J. Leitch Wright, **British St. Augustine**, St. Augustine, Florida: Historic St. Augustine Preservation Board, 1975.

65. Robert McMillan Kennedy, ed., **South Carolina Items in the "Gentleman's Magazine" (London), 1731-1792, Extracted from the File in the University of South Carolina Library**, 1936, *University of South Carolina*, 1775, 247-250: "Account of the Proceedings of the American colonists. . . . Nor can we forbear mentioning the jealousies which have been excited in the colonies by the extension of the limits of the province of Quebec, which the Roman Catholic religion has received such ample supports." See also Jane Quinn, **Minorcans in Florida: Their History and Heritage**, St. Augustine, Florida: Mission, 1975, 85.

66. Robert Anthony Olwell, "Authority and Resistance: Social Order in a Colonial Slave Society, the South Carolina Low Country, 1739-1782," Ph.D. dissertation, Johns Hopkins University, 1991, 389.

67. Committee of Norfolk to Peyton Randolph, 21 July 1775, in Clark, **Naval Documents of the American Revolution, Volume I**, 947.

68. Proceedings of the Georgia Council of Safety, 5 July 1776, in **Collections of the Georgia Historical Society, Volume V, Part I**, Savannah, Georgia: Savannah Morning News, 1901, *Georgia Historical Society, Savannah.*

69. Vice Admiral Clark Gayton to Philip Stephens, 2 July 1776, in Morgan, **Naval Documents of the American Revolution, Volume V**, 887.

70. Sir Basil Keith to Lord George Germain, 27 March 1776, in Clark, **Naval Documents of the American Revolution, Volume IV**, 544-546.

71. Vice Admiral Clark Gayton to Philip Stephens, 5 August 1776, in William James Morgan, ed., **Naval Documents of the American Revolution, Volume VI**, Washington, D.C.: Government Printing Office, 1972, 74–75.

72. **Pennsylvania Journal**, 2 October 1776. See also Report, 20 September 1775, "Parish Transcripts . . . and Historical Notes . . . ," *Daniel Parish Slavery Transcripts*: A vessel arrives from Hispaniola with the news of "an insurrection of the Negroes in Jamaica," with "between sixty and seventy white people . . . killed." See also the revealing letter about Jamaica at this time: Letter from Mrs. Manby, 6 August 1776, *Duke University, Durham, North Carolina.*

73. Report, 30 March 1775, in **Journal of the Commissioners for Trade and Plantations from January 1768 to December 1775 . . .** , London: His Majesty's Stationery Office, 1937, 415: At that point there were an estimated 220,000 Africans and less than 16,000 Europeans on the island.

74. Solomon Lutnick, **The American Revolution and the British Press, 1775–1783**, Columbia: University of Missouri Press, 1967, 146. See also Andrew Symmer to "My Lord," 12 November 1775, CO23/20, *National Archives of the United Kingdom, London* (hereinafter NAUK): From the Turks Islands, it was reported, "sundry Negroes having made their escape from these islands, to the adjacent French & Spanish settlements on the neighboring island of St. Domingo, I was extremely alarmed at the probability of the fatal consequences which would attend this young settlement if a stop was not put to the asylum which these slaves received at St. Domingo. . . . governors of Jamaica and New Providence have never been able to prevail with the French and Spanish Governors to restore such runaway slaves as have escaped to St. Domingo and Cuba."

75. Thomas Shirley to "My Lords," 29 July 1775, T1/513, NAUK: Those who are "supplying Negroes on the Government account" in Dominica acknowledge "that their contract will run out . . . and the Negroes furnished under it must be then given up," which will mean "very great distress" given "the impossibility that soldiers can do their duty in these islands without having some assistance in the most laborious parts," which was "so well known." See also John French to "Sir," 1 August 1775, T1/514, NAUK: "the Negroes now employed in supplying the Garrison" in Dominica with "wood and water are to be taken away the tenth of this month"; this would mean "many hardships" for the "troops."

76. Report, 29 January 1776, SP78/298, NAUK: "Negroes escaping to the French islands in the neighborhood," thus the "proposition" of "setting a cartel for the exchange of run-away Negroes & Deserters for the mutual advantage of both nations." See also Clarence J. Mumford and Michael Zeuske, "Black Slavery, Class Struggle, Fear and Revolution in St. Domingue and Cuba, 1785–1795," **Journal of Negro History**, 73(First Quarter, Fall 1988): 12–32.

77. Thelma Wills Foote, **Black and White Manhattan: The History of Racial Formation in Colonial New York City**, New York: Oxford University Press, 2004, 17–18, 221, 286. See also Epaphroditus Peck, "The Loyalists of Connecticut," Tercentenary Commission of the State of Connecticut, Committee on Historical Publications, 1934, *Rhode Island Historical Society, Providence*: "In New York, the supporters of the King were in a clear majority, if not in number, at least in wealth. . . . the loyalists of Connecticut suffered many hardships." At the same site, see **A List of Tories Who Took Part with Great Britain in the Revolutionary War, and Were Attained of High Treason Commonly Called the Blacklist**, New York, 1865.

78. Cassandra Pybus, "Jefferson's Faulty Math: The Question of Slave Defections in the American Revolution," **William and Mary Quarterly**, 62(Number 2, April 2005): 243–264. See also Mary Louise Clifford, **From Slavery to Freedom: Black Loyalists**

after the American Revolution, Jefferson, North Carolina: McFarland, 1999; and A.W. Savary, ed., **David Fanning's Narrative of His Exploits and Adventures as a Loyalist of North Carolina in the American Revolution, Supplying Important Omissions in the Copy Published in the United States**, Toronto: Canadian Magazine, 1908.

79. Cf. Andreas Lixl, "Introduction: Carolinian Immigrants: Memories of Pride, Grief, and Liberty," in Lixl, ed., **Memories of Carolinian Immigrants: Autobiographies, Diaries, and Letters from Colonial Times to the Present**, Lanham, Maryland: University Press of America, xix–xxxiv, xx.

80. See, e.g., "Knight v. Wedderburn," 1778, in David Dabydeen, John Gilmore, and Cecily Jones, eds., **The Oxford Companion to Black British History**, New York: Oxford University Press, 2007, 244–246.

81. Quoted in Foote, **Black and White Manhattan**, 213, 215.

82. Gerald Horne, **Negro Comrades of the Crown: African Americans and the British Empire Fight the U.S. before Emancipation**, New York: NYU Press, 2012.

83. Dennis R. Caron, **A Century in Captivity: The Life and Trial of Prince Mortimer, A Connecticut Slave**, Lebanon: University of New Hampshire Press, 2006, 22. See also Barbara A. Barnes, "Venture Smith's Family," Wesleyan University, 1996, *Connecticut State Library and Archives, Hartford*: "it may well be that Venture," a well-known African in New England, "strongly disapproved of [his son] Cuff's enlistment in the Continental Army and his long period of services to it."

84. Quoted in Michael E. Groth, "Black Loyalists and African American Allegiances in the Mid-Hudson Valley," in Joseph S. Tiedmann, Eugene R. Fingerhut, and Robert W. Venables, eds., **The Other Loyalists: Ordinary People, Royalism, and the Revolution in the Middle Colonies, 1763–1787**, Albany: SUNY Press, 2009, 81–104, 83.

85. Steven M. Wise, **Though the Heavens May Fall: The Landmark Trial That Led to the End of Human Slavery**, New York: Da Capo, 2005, 201.

86. Foote, **Black and White Manhattan**, 213.

87. Comments, 1794–1796, on failure to compensate slaveholders, Peter M. Bergman and Jean McCarroll, eds., **The Negro in the Congressional Record, 1789–1801, Volume II**, New York: Bergman, 1969, 78–105, 137–138.

88. Maya Jasanoff, **Liberty's Exiles: The Loss of America and the Remaking of the British Empire**, London: Harper, 2011, 49. See also Catherine S. Crary, ed., **The Price of Loyalty: Tory Writings from the Revolutionary Era**, New York: McGraw Hill, 1973; and James W. St.G. Walker, **The Black Loyalists: The Search for a Promised Land in Nova Scotia and Sierra Leone, 1783–1870**, New York: Holmes and Meier, 1976.

89. John Bakeless, **Turncoats, Traitors, and Heroes**, Philadelphia: Lippincott, 1959, 268, 100. See also John T. Hassam, "The Confiscated Estates of Boston Loyalists," Cambridge, Massachusetts: Wilson, 1895, *Rhode Island Historical Society*.

90. Bobby Gilmer and Michael E. Scroggins, **African American Loyalists in the Southern Campaign of the American Revolution**, Blacksburg, South Carolina: Scotia-Hibernia, 2005, vi.

91. Report, March 1779, in **Journals of the Continental Congress, 1774–1789, Volume XIII**, Washington, D.C.: Government Printing Office, 1909, 386. See also David K. Wilson, **The Southern Strategy: Britain's Conquest of South Carolina and Georgia, 1775–1780**, Columbia: University of South Carolina Press, 2005.

92. Report by Chevalier de Fleury, 16 November 1779, in **B.F. Stevens' Facsimiles of Manuscripts in European Archives Relating to America, 1773–1783 . . . , Volume XVII**, London: BFS, 1893, 1616.

93. Quoted in Carretta, **Phillis Wheatley**, 127.

94. **Financial Times**, 29 July 2011.

95. **Financial Times**, 22 July 2011.
96. See, e.g., Karen E. Fields and Barbara J. Fields, **Racecraft: The Soul of Inequality in American Life**, New York: Verso, 2012.
97. Don E. Fehrenbacher, **The Slaveholding Republic: An Account of the United States Government's Relation to Slavery**, New York: Oxford University Press, 2001.
98. Rayford Logan, **The Betrayal of the Negro, from Rutherford B. Hayes to Woodrow Wilson**, New York: Da Capo, 1997; Richard Kluger, **Simple Justice: The History of "Brown v. Board of Education" and Black America's Struggle for Equality**, New York: Knopf, 1976.
99. See, e.g., John W. Cell, **The Highest Stage of White Supremacy: The Origins of Segregation in South Africa and the American South**, New York: Cambridge University Press, 1982. As the preceding pages suggest, I believe that the U.S. is better understood in comparison to other settler regimes—especially in Africa—as opposed to peers in western Europe. See, for example, Gerald Horne, **Mau Mau in Harlem? The United States and the Liberation of Kenya**, New York: Palgrave, 2009. See also Karim Murji and John Solomos, eds., **Racialization: Studies in Theory and Practice**, New York: Oxford University Press, 2005; Imani Perry, **More Beautiful and More Terrible: The Embrace and Transcendence of Racial Inequality in the United States**, New York: NYU Press, 2011.
100. See, e.g., Heather Cox Richardson, **West from Appomattox: The Reconstruction of America after the Civil War**, New Haven: Yale University Press, 2007; Elizabeth D. Leonard, **Men of Color to Arms! Black Soldiers, Indian Wars, and the Quest for Equality**, New York: Norton, 2010. Even today, African comrades in North America have yet to fully ponder that the understandably celebrated Civil War carried the seeds of the resultant third-class citizenship for the formerly enslaved. This was not only because of the republic beginning to normalize relations with abolitionist London in the aftermath of this titanic conflict, thereby lessening pressure on Washington, but also because of the setback the Civil War inflicted on Negro allies,, e.g., once feistily independent Native American sovereigns. Brendan C. Lindsay, **Murder State: California's Native American Genocide, 1846–1873**, Lincoln: University of Nebraska Press, 2012, 170, 177: "The Civil War years only intensified the neglect of the Indigenous peoples of southern California. . . . because of the location of the Gold Rush and the collapse of many miners' dreams of quick riches, northern California's Native population faced a genocidal assault perhaps unrivaled in North America in terms of its ferocity, bloodiness, and loss of human life." See also Scott W. Berg, **38 Nooses: Lincoln, Little Crow, and the Beginning of the Frontier's End**, New York: Pantheon, 2012. Like others too numerous to note, these comrades most likely have underestimated severely the pressure needed to correct design flaws of what could well be considered history's first modern apartheid state. Given the outsized role that enslavement of Africans and the slave trade played on the west bank of the Atlantic—compared to Pretoria—the comparison of the two nations may do a disservice to South Africa.
101. Margaret Whitman Blair, **Liberty or Death: The Surprising Story of Runaway Slaves Who Sided with the British during the American Revolution**, Washington, D.C.: National Geographic, 2010, *British Library*.
102. Quoted in Daniel J. Tichenor, **Dividing Lines: The Politics of Immigration Control in America**, Princeton: Princeton University Press, 2002, 53. See also Clara Rodriguez, **Changing Race: Latinos, the Census, and the History of Ethnicity in the United States**, New York: NYU Press, 2000, 67–69.
103. William J. Duiker, **Ho Chi Minh**, New York: Hyperion, 2000; Bernard B. Fall, ed., **Ho Chi Minh on Revolution: Selected Writings, 1920–1966**, New York: New American Library, 1968.

104. V.I. Lenin, **Lenin on the United States: Selected Writings**, New York: International, 1970. Like many Marxists, Lenin may have overestimated the positive impact on the global balance of forces when the leading power that was London was defeated—and underestimated the negative impact that the republic would come to exert globally.

105. See, e.g., Stuart Macintyre and Anna Clark, **The History Wars**, Carlton, Australia: Melbourne University Press, 2004. On similarities between the U.S. and Australia, see, e.g., Gerald Horne, **The White Pacific: U.S. Imperialism and Black Slavery in the South Seas after the Civil War**, Honolulu: University of Hawaii Press, 2007.

106. Allen Wells, **Tropical Zion: General Trujillo, FDR, and the Jews of Sosua**, Durham: Duke University Press, 2009. Trujillo, like his northern neighbor, "favored immigrants without African ancestry." See Brenda Gayle Plummer, **In Search of Power: African Americans in the Era of Decolonization, 1956–1974**, New York: Cambridge University Press, 2013, 147.

107. Frank Moya Pons, **The Dominican Republic: A National History**, Princeton, New Jersey: Markus Wiener, 2010, 368; Edwidge Danticat, **The Farming of Bones: A Novel**, New York: Soho, 1998. See also Juan Manuel Garcia, **La Matanza de los Haitianos**, Santo Domingo: Alfa and Omega, 1983.

108. John Cell, **The Highest Stage of White Supremacy: The Origins of Segregation in South Africa and the American South**, New York: Cambridge University Press, 1982; George Fredrickson, **White Supremacy: A Comparative Study in American and South African History**, New York: Oxford University Press, 1982.

109. In 1992, I accumulated 305,000 votes in a failed third-party race for the U.S. Senate in California: See, e.g., **Los Angeles Times**, 5 November 1992.

110. Ryan Lizza, "The Party Next Time," **New Yorker**, 88(Number 36, 19 November 2012): 50–57; **New York Times**, 13 December 2012. The shrinkage of the conservative sector of the U.S. electorate also creates the possibility for yet another guiding slogan, similarly lacking poetry and catchiness, i.e., "Peoples of color unite and fight against white supremacy in league with a powerful foreign patron." This slogan inferentially raises another point: few contemporary observers have noticed that the vibrant anti-abortion movement in today's republic has been driven in no small measure by a concern that stretches back to the 18th century on this continent: from whence would "whites" come if white supremacy is to be maintained? A similar motivation has driven sectors of the anti-immigrant movement, which—effectively—is an anti-Latino- and anti-Asian-immigrant movement. Both movements have been a locomotive of conservatism. See, e.g., Patrick J. Buchanan, **The Death of the West: How Dying Populations and Immigrant Invasions Imperil Our Country and Civilization**, New York: Dunne, 2002; and Ben J. Wattenberg, **The Birth Dearth**, New York: Pharos, 1987.

111. Thomas Frank, **What's the Matter with Kansas? How Conservatives Won the Heart of America**, New York: Metropolitan, 2004; Joan Walsh, **What's the Matter with White People? Why We Long for a Golden Age That Never Was**, New York: Wiley, 2012.

112. Ira Katznelson, **When Affirmative Action Was White: An Untold History of Racial Inequality in Twentieth-Century America**, New York: Norton, 2005; Mary Poole, **The Segregated Origins of Social Security: African Americans and the Welfare State**, Chapel Hill: University of North Carolina Press, 2006; Alexander Saxton, **The Rise and Fall of the White Republic: Class Politics in Nineteenth-Century America**, New York: Verso, 1990; Angie Debo, **And Still the Waters Run: The Betrayal of the Five Civilized Tribes**, Norman: University of Oklahoma Press, 1984; Jean M. O'Brien, **Dispossession by Degrees: Indian Land and Identity in Natick, Massachusetts, 1650–1790**, New York: Cambridge University Press, 1997.

113. Not atypically, William Prentis arrived in early 18th-century Virginia from England as an indentured servant but rapidly climbed the class ladder as a slaveholder residing on land formerly under the dominion of indigenes. His son, Joseph, became part of the colonial elite—and a prominent rebel against London's rule. And the grandson, John, became a prominent slave trader, disrupting forcibly numerous African families and selling these bonded laborers to distant frontiers, where they participated—involuntarily—in building the productive forces of what was to become a leading superpower: see Kari J. Winter, **The American Dreams of John B. Prentis, Slave Trader,** Athens: University of Georgia Press, 2011. As the title smartly suggests, in many ways the Prentis family exemplifies the "American Dream."

114. See, e.g., John C. Kuzenski, Charles S. Bullock III, and Ronald Keith Gaddie, eds., **David Duke and the Politics of Race in the South,** Nashville: Vanderbilt University Press, 1995; Douglas D. Rose, ed., **The Emergence of David Duke and the Politics of Race,** Chapel Hill: University of North Carolina Press, 1992.

New York City: cabbies in, xiii; slave population, 57, 61, 165, 215; slave trading, 53, 165. *See also* Manhattan
New York Historical Society, vii, xiii
New York–New Jersey region, 167
Newcastle, Thomas Pelham-Holles, 1st Duke of, 80, 127–129, 131
Newfoundland, 137, 190
Newport, Antigua, 103
Newport, Rhode Island, 6, 35, 46, 144, 201, 203–204
Norfolk County, Virginia, 79
North America. *See* British North America
North Carolina: American Revolution, 239–240; British troops, demand for, 153; New Bern, 240; objections to taxes on slaves, 199; poisonings in, 156; rumors, 228; slave insurrections, fear of, 229, 239; slave population, 149; slave resistance, 221, 239–240; Spanish privateers, 132
Norton, John, 231

Oglethorpe, James: Angolans, 289n6; assassination plot against, 93–94; Catholics, 13; expected invasions, 120–121; Fort Mose ("Moosa"), attack on, 116; Georgia, abandonment of, 134; Georgia as African-free, 105; "mutinous temper" in Savannah, Georgia, 154–155; Royal African Company (RAC), 91, 134; rum, warnings about, 137; St. Augustine, Florida, 114, 115, 127; Spanish delegation from Florida, 110–111; Spanish Florida, 91; Spanish relations with slaves, 13–14, 123, 133
O'Reilly, Alejandro, 10
Otis, James, 201
Owens, Nicholas, 145

Palatines, 74
Panama, 55
Patterson, Orlando, 29
Paul, David, 247–248
Pendarvis, John, 178
Penn, William, 57
Pennsylvania: exports to, value of, 285n46; indigenous people, 185; Philadelphia, 153, 164, 176, 225; Quakers, 74; servants, 57; Seven Years' War (1756-1763), 176–177; slave importation, 82; slave population, 165, 194; slave resistance, 57, 240; taxes on slave importation, 65; trade with Cuba, 17

Pepys, Samuel, 35
Philadelphia, 153, 164, 176, 225
Philipse, Frederick, 53
Pinckney, Charles, 8, 164
Pitt, William, 179
Pocock, George, 186, 190
Port Royal, South Carolina, 12, 33, 77–78, 114
Porto-bello (Portobelo, Panama), 127, 140, 185
Portuguese slave traders, 48, 49, 50
Powell, James Edward, 160
Prentis, John, 334n113
Prentis, Joseph, 334n113
Prentis, William, 334n113
Princess Anne County, Virginia, 79
Pringle, Robert, 102, 119, 126, 145–146
Protestants, 3, 195
Providence, Rhode Island, 6
Providence Island, 31
Puerto Rico, 162
Purry, Charles, 156–157

Quakers, 74, 164, 177, 201
Quarles, Benjamin, 2
Quebec: British invasion, 59; France ousted from, 161, 163–164, 174–175, 182; slave migrations from New York, xii, 58, 66
Quincy, Josiah, 223, 234

RAC. *See* Royal African Company (RAC)
"race" (the term), 262n85
racial privilege in British North America, 11
racial ratio: Barbados, 41–42; British North America, 36, 54, 220; Caribbean region, 8, 41–42, 54, 96–97; Connecticut, 61; Jamaica, 51; Virginia, 225–226
"racism" (the term), 248, 262n85
racism in United States, 248
"racist" (the term), 262n85
Radcliffe, John, 37
Ramsay, James, 217
Reconstruction, 248
Redwood, Abraham, 103, 109
Republican Party, 251
Rhode Island: Bristol, 6; Bristol County, 214; *Gaspee* Affair, 203–208; Newport, 6, 35, 46, 144, 201, 203–204; Providence, 6; rum trade, 285n46; slave importation, 82; slave population, 61, 143–144, 194; slave trading, 4–5, 5–6, 15, 35, 46, 143–144, 201–202, 203–205, 207

ABOUT THE AUTHOR

Gerald Horne, Moores Professor of History & African American Studies at the University of Houston, has published over thirty books,
including *Negro Comrades of the Crown.*